Political Correctness and Higher Education

How many times have you heard the phrase: 'It's all political correctness gone mad!'? Are colleges and universities really awash with trivial concerns about the use of language, or are they actually trying to address serious concerns relating to discrimination, equal opportunities, and the nature of knowledge in the curriculum?

In looking at the roots of the term 'political correctness' the book contrasts British and American perspectives, and demonstrates how the term has complicated the traditional boundaries between the political left and right. The book also captures the reflections of prominent academics and educationalists on both sides of the Atlantic, who have worked in environments where the term has impinged on aspects of their work over the past twenty-five years.

This book is intended to be of interest to a number of readers: academics working in colleges and universities; teacher educators and student teachers working on programmes of initial teacher education; and students studying undergraduate programmes in comparative politics and/or sociology and cultural studies.

If you think that 'political correctness' simply amounts to what jokes you are allowed to tell in British and American classrooms, hopefully this book will challenge you to think again.

John Lea is a Principal Lecturer in Education at Canterbury Christ Church University, UK, where he is the programme director for the Post Graduate Certificate in Learning and Teaching (HE). He is a sociologist by background and also teaches on the university's American Studies degree programme.

Political Correctness and Higher Education

British and American Perspectives

John Lea

Foreword by
Jonathan Zimmerman

Routledge
Taylor & Francis Group

NEW YORK AND LONDON

First published 2009
by Routledge
270 Madison Ave, New York, NY 10016

Simultaneously published in the UK
by Routledge
2 Park Square, Milton Park, Abingdon, Oxon OX14 4RN

Routledge is an imprint of the Taylor & Francis Group, an informa business

Typeset in Minion by
Keystroke, 28 High Street, Tettenhall, Wolverhampton
Printed and bound in the United States of America on acid-free paper by
Walsworth Publishing Company, Marceline, MO

Cover image: Pedro Berruguete (Ca. 1495), 'Saint Dominic Presides over
an Auto da Fe', Museo Nacional del Prado, Madrid.

Library of Congress Cataloging-in-Publication Data
Lea, John.
   Political correctness and higher education : British and American
   perspectives / John Lea.
        p. cm.
      Includes bibliographical references and index.
   1. Education, Higher – Political aspects – Great Britain.   2. Education,
   Higher – Political aspects – United States.   3. Academic freedom –
   Great Britain.   4. Academic freedom – United States.   5. Political
   correctness – Great Britain.   6. Political correctness – United States.
   I. Title.
   LC178.G7L43 2008
   378.73 – dc22   2008014941

ISBN10: 0–415–96258–7 (hbk)
ISBN10: 0–415–96259–5 (pbk)
ISBN10: 0–203–88862–6 (ebk)

ISBN13: 978–0–415–96258–2 (hbk)
ISBN13: 978–0–415–96259–9 (pbk)
ISBN13: 978–0–203–88862–9 (ebk)

Contents

Foreword

In Philip Roth's 2000 novel, *The Human Stain*, American classics professor Coleman Silk is drummed out of his college for using the term 'spook'. The word has a long and nasty history as an anti-black epithet, of course. However Silk used it in a non-racial context, asking his class if several absent students were spooks – that is, ghosts – or real. And as the reader knows – but Silk's antagonists do not – he is black himself. Born to African-American parents, Silk 'passes' as a white person until the bitter end.

And the end *is* bitter, for all of us. At the most basic level, *The Human Stain* is a tragic reminder of the many ways in which race continues to confuse, enrage, and divide American society. But it is also a more specific indictment of the American university, especially of the language that administrators, professors, and students use to talk *about* race.

In other words, it's about being politically correct. And it's about you, if you work or study at a university.

Are you PC? Of course not. As John Lea makes clear in this remarkable little book, political correctness is a label that's always applied to the other guy. Like body odor or accented speech, we notice it in our peers but not in ourselves.

And it's not just an American phenomenon. In the US, of course, we like to think that we invented the sun, moon, and stars alongside the frisbee, the hamburger, and the electric guitar. In the early 1980s, we probably did coin the term 'politically correct' to denounce certain left-wing behaviors and attitudes. But a similar trend was already underway in the UK, where media outlets led a high-profile campaign against the 'Loony Left'. By the 1990s, it had transmuted into an all-out assault upon something called 'PC'. In the UK as well as in the US, it seemed, political correctness was a problem.

What *was* the problem, exactly? It depends on who you ask, of course, and where. But most complaints about PC have focused upon language – that is, upon the way that our words have changed. Sometime in the 1980s, the story goes, left-leaning American and British professors made racial minorities into 'people of color', the handicapped into the 'differently abled', and older students into 'non-traditional learners'. The rest of us – both inside and outside the university – followed behind.

And along the way, to continue this bleak winter's tale, we lost our capacity to reason and judge. The new idioms symbolize a kind of intellectual group-think, a herd mentality that discourages dissent, discussion, and debate. To critics in the US, who stand mostly on the political right, PC allowed sanctimonious liberals and radicals to impose their favorite hobby horses – especially affirmative action and multiculturalism – upon the unwilling and the unwary. In the UK, where anti-PC jeremiads often come from the left, critics complained that PC's insistent focus on language – 'mere words' – diverted attention from more pressing structural and economic inequalities. The net result was a kind of Alice-in-Wonderland chamber of horrors, we are told, where nothing means what it says – and nobody says what they mean.

If all this sounds a bit overblown, it probably should. Critics of PC 'dominance' and 'conformity' have somehow found their own language for attacking it, which suggests that PC might not be so dominant after all. Especially in the US, meanwhile, they also exaggerate the power and influence of the university itself. Consider affirmative action, which holds that certain races and ethnicities – or, less often, certain social classes – should receive special consideration in university admissions. The idea is so deeply inscribed at American universities – in our language, in our conversations, and of course in our admission policies – that it might fairly be labeled 'PC'. But not in American society, writ large, where affirmative action is one of the most hotly contested political questions of all. In this sense, PC's reach far exceeds its grasp. If anything, the entire phenomenon underscores the irrelevance of the university to contemporary society.

And that should worry anyone who teaches or studies there, no matter where they might sit on the political spectrum. The more that we tailor our words and thoughts to meet the imagined demands of our institutions, the less we have to say to people who live outside them. In the UK, PC is disseminated by an intimidating array of quasi-state agencies with bland bureaucratic names, like the Learning and Skills Council and the Adult Learning Inspectorate. But in the US, we do it to ourselves! Compared to their British brethren, American universities enjoy an extraordinary degree of independence and autonomy. Just as Tocqueville predicted, however, this very freedom can foster its own brand of conformity. I can list dozens of key figures in government, the media, and business who have inveighed against affirmative action. But I can't name a single prominent American university leader who has done so. That can't be good news for the university or even for affirmative action, which could only benefit from the deep scrutiny of a true scholarly dialogue.

In the end, that's the real danger of political correctness: it further isolates the university, all in the guise of making it more 'relevant' and 'student-friendly'. And it brings us back to *The Human Stain*, where Coleman Silk's attackers surely believed that they were defending the college's black students (sorry: people of color!) from his alleged slur. But they were wrong. The truly spooky thing about PC is that it removes entire words and subjects from debate, including the term 'political correctness' itself. Perhaps John Lea's fine book can provide a small remedy, sparking exactly the type of discussion that all of us need.

Jonathan Zimmerman
New York University

Preface

The more I became interested in political correctness the less I found myself looking for the truth behind the hundreds of stories about so-called 'PC behaviour', and the more I became interested in what the term itself invokes. This book is about the latter rather than the former.

Given the huge imbalance between what has been written about political correctness in the US compared with Britain it is difficult to conduct a simple comparative study. For this reason the first section of the book, on the US, is an attempt to reflect on some of the broad themes which have emerged from this huge literature base, and the second section, on Britain, is a more speculative account, which attempts to draw on some of the more implicit implications of cultural debate on that side of the Atlantic. Part of the aim behind this book was to try to give British readers a clear sense of what all the fuss has been about in the US, and because of this many American readers, perhaps already very familiar with that scene, might prefer to begin reading the book from Chapter 8 onwards, which focuses on British perspectives. In the book itself the word 'American' should be read as a reference to the US, not the continent.

The specific context for the book is *higher education*. The term, however, does not translate easily between the two national contexts. Whereas in the US it might be readily taken to be a reference to education beyond school, in Britain the term tends to refer exclusively to university education. For this reason I have chosen to use the term post-16 education when writing specifically about the British national context.

I am extremely grateful to all the people who took part in the interviews which feature in the book: John Searle, Robin Lakoff, Genaro Padilla, Philip Day, John McWhorter, Jonathan Zimmerman, Allen McFarlane, Todd Gitlin, Kathryn Ecclestone, James Tooley, Dennis Hayes, Frank Furedi, Tony Booth, Irfaan Arif, Ruth Silver, and Angela Milln.

The interviews and the surrounding discussion were invaluable in helping me to understand some of the subtleties and nuances in debates that surround such a controversial term. And particular thanks go to Jonathan Zimmerman, who kindly agreed to write the foreword to the book, and to Tony Booth whose advice on the interpretation of transcript data was an enormous help. I am also extremely grateful to Ashleigh Stewart who painstakingly transcribed all the interviews, and to Nicky Galer who helped compile the references.

John Lea
February 2008

Acknowledgements

I am extremely grateful for permission to quote from the following:

Monty Python's Life of Brian: Python (Monty) Pictures Ltd., Bar Chambers, 40 North Bar within Beverley, East Yorkshire, HU17 8DW, UK;

South Park: Comedy Central, 1633 Broadway, New York, NY 10019, USA;

Curb Your Enthusiasm: Home Box Office Inc., 2500 Broadway, Suite 400, Santa Monica, CA 90404, USA.

Some of the ideas in Chapter 9 are based on those first presented in: John Lea (2004) 'Getting your lines right: scripted communication in post-compulsory education', in D. Hayes (ed.) *The RoutledgeFalmer Guide to Key Debates in Education*, London: RoutledgeFalmer.

1
PC world
Political correctness and the modern zeitgeist

STAN (AS LORETTA): 'It's every man's right to have babies if he wants them.'
REG: 'But you can't have babies.'
STAN (AS LORETTA): 'Don't you oppress me!'

> (from *Monty Python's Life of Brian*, scene 7, 1979;
> reprinted with permission from Python (Monty) Pictures Ltd)

JUDGE TO CARTMAN: 'I am making an example of you, to send a message out to people everywhere: that if you want to hurt another human being, you'd better make damn sure they're the same color as you are!'

> (from *South Park* season 4 (1) *Cartman's Silly Hate Crime*, 2000; reprinted with permission)

WHEELCHAIR USER (AFTER ENTERING A PUBLIC RESTROOM): 'There's one stall for me and you're in it!'
LARRY DAVID: 'You know, if you were here I would have given you first dibs. But honestly I haven't seen a handicapped person in the bathroom maybe ever. So I thought I could perhaps take my chances.'
WHEELCHAIR USER: 'A handicapped person? That's nice. Oh, that's nice. It's called disabled.'
LARRY DAVID: 'Disabled? Well, that doesn't sound so hot.'

> (from *Curb Your Enthusiasm*, season 5 (2),
> *The Bowtie*, 2005; reprinted with permission)

Overview

The term 'political correctness' (PC) has become part of the vocabulary of contemporary life both in Britain and, more especially, in the US. It seems to capture an essential quality of the modern zeitgeist and incidents have often become *causes célèbres*. It has also been able to accommodate both negative and positive connotations. On the one hand, people have been able to demonstrate their progressive outlook by reference to it, but equally, and increasingly, people have been able to use it to distance themselves from what they see as the ludicrous and the demeaning. Rarely has a week gone by in the past twenty years when the term was not used to describe an unwarranted intrusion into the status quo of everyday professional life. In all of this, what is perhaps a little surprising is that the term, although part of a huge academic industry in the US, is rarely the subject of serious scholarly scrutiny in Britain. First and foremost, therefore, this book is an attempt to produce an Anglo-American cross-cultural analysis of the term.

The book will compare and contrast the history of the use of the term 'political correctness' in the US, where it has been widely discussed in the intellectual media, and in Britain, where the term has been mostly used in the popular media. The specific context in which the discussion will be applied is post-16 education (for Britain) or higher education (for the US), defined simply as educational institutions whose student body is beyond the statutory school leaving age (essentially colleges and universities). An undercurrent running throughout will be the extent to which political correctness has contributed either to the reprofessionalization or the deprofessionalization of teachers within this sector. The sub-headings used throughout this introduction will signpost some of the more specific dimensions that will be explored.

Playing the PC game

It is not difficult to demonstrate that the term political correctness has invaded almost every area of the cultural landscape of Britain and the US. On the occasions when the term itself is not used it is obvious where there is an intention that it should be invoked. Furthermore it could be argued that the term has gained such wide currency particularly in the popular media that it can often be used without any need for explanation. In the most extreme cases the term appears to have been granted general permission to be used whenever someone is looking for a shorthand term to distance themselves from decisions they find unpalatable, and very often this is accompanied by the phrase 'That's political correctness gone mad!'

There is little doubt that stories and debates which surround the term are hotly contested, and only a cursory glance would indicate that, more often than not, the *gloves are off* and the ensuing fight is almost always a dirty one. From the accusation in the mid-1980s that UK local government councils in London had banned black coffee, black bin (trash) liners, and the nursery rhyme *Baa, Baa Black Sheep*, all for being racist, to the ridicule heaped on US colleges in the early 1990s for having established demeaning anti-harassment codes of conduct, including in one case a 'dating etiquette', it is clear that the PC terrain is a minefield (Curran *et al.* 2005; D'Souza 1992). Dogged by counter-accusations of exaggeration and fabrication it is perhaps not surprising that it is difficult to get to the bottom of all this, and seek the truth. It is important to signpost that this book is not intended to be read as a whodunit, that is as an attempt to uncover what is the truth behind specific incidents which have been labelled PC. Rather, it is much more literally *about* political correctness: what the term itself invokes, and the contexts in which one is most likely to hear the term. In this sense the book does not ask where are the facts in PC stories, but asks why are the stories told in the way they are.

One of the most striking features of political correctness is just how quickly the term *is* invoked. For example, consider how many people living in Britain or the US in the early twenty-first century would be able instantly to connect the term with the extracts from popular media reproduced at the head of this chapter. In 1991 the *New York* magazine asked its readers 'Are you politically correct?' (Taylor 1991, reproduced in Beckwith and Bauman 1993). Fifteen years later the UK-based *The Mail on Sunday* newspaper produced the headline 'We are biased admit the stars of BBC News', where a veteran BBC executive is reported as saying: 'There was widespread acknowledgement that we may have gone too far in the direction of political correctness. Unfortunately much of it is so deeply embedded in the BBC's culture that it is very hard to change it' (*The Mail on Sunday*, 22 October 2006).

It is not a question of us all somehow having become PC in the intervening years, but more that as this perception has grown the more this seems to have prompted others to become avowedly non-PC. In this respect PC seems to encapsulate much of what James Davison Hunter implied in his use of the term 'culture wars', that the US is fundamentally divided on key questions of right and wrong (Hunter 1991). PC might not have the same kind of moral underpinning as the 'orthodox' and 'progressive' mindsets he articulates, but it is clear that a real division exists on matters which have become associated with the term. One way to demonstrate this is through a simple question and answer game.

Please answer yes or no to the following questions:
1 Would you be concerned if you saw someone vociferously dismissing the validity of the *Qu'ran* on a TV show?
2 If you hear someone use the word 'handicapped' when referring to another person would you rather he or she had chosen an alternative word that you felt was more appropriate?
3 If you read a newspaper article where a journalist or author was beseeching single/lone parents not to be so dependent on welfare payments, would your first reaction be to question whether he or she fully understands the social circumstances of many families?

If you answered *yes* to all three questions, congratulations you win the game, and are officially 'PC'. If you answered *no* to all three, commiserations you lose the game, and are officially 'non-PC'. If your answers were a combination of *yes* and *no*, *maybe*, or *not sure*, then you are officially a 'waiverer on matters of PC'. Finally, if you object to me congratulating the winners, then you might be either 'super PC', or 'super non-PC', depending on how you read the virtues of winning such games.

The main focus for this book will be post-16 or higher education, and the game could be adapted for an audience of professionals in that sector, as in the second box.

> Consider the following scenarios:
> 1 You work in a college and a colleague who is moderating some of your students' work suggests that although your first marker's feedback to students is accurate it could perhaps be a little more positive. Would you largely ignore this comment?
> 2 You work in a university and one day you receive an email from an Ethics Committee stating that, from now on, anyone who wishes to use surveys, questionnaires, and interviews with students in order to elicit information about their 'student experience', must first submit a proposal to the Committee to assess whether students could be harmed in the process. Would your first reaction to this email be rather scornful?
> 3 You are in a college committee meeting where a colleague suggests, in the interests of enhancing learner achievement, that wherever the word 'fail' currently appears on a student's work, or transcript of work, it should be replaced with the term 'needs development'. Would you wish that you could leave the room at this point?

The only difference this time is that the *yes* votes get the 'non-PC' label. Political correctness may elude a simple definition, but I doubt that there are many people who would not know that in answering these questions they were giving their views on it. However, the more difficult question to answer is what connects all the various strands of thought. One of the key purposes of this book is to try to explore and explain these connections.

The parameters of PC

> Fired for consistently showing up late at work, a former school district employee sues his former employers, arguing that he is a victim of what his lawyer calls 'chronic lateness syndrome'.
>
> (Sykes 1992: 3)

Of all the thousands of examples of so-called PC behaviour, there seems to be something all-encompassing about this one. It seems to capture the essence of what many people see as increasingly problematic in contemporary society, and contains what appear to be three key ingredients in a PC scenario. First, it is funny to the point of being ridiculous. Second, it appears to absolve someone of a responsibility that they once had for their own behaviour. And third, it produces a label for a form of behaviour which until now had not crossed anyone's mind as needing a label. Or, as in many cases, it produces a new euphemistic label with the intention that it should become a substitute for a more commonly accepted label. Thus, in the extreme, 'a fat corpse is a differently sized non-living person' (Hughes 1993: 20).

Many of these euphemisms are exploited for maximum comic effect in guides to PC in the US and in Britain (e.g. Beard and Cerf 1994; Garner 1994; Leo 1994; Midgley and Midgley 2005). My intention throughout this book is not to list the euphemisms, but rather to explore the broader political context in which this labelling has occurred, or, to put it simply, to ask what are the political beliefs which lurk behind these labels, both those which are produced with sincerity and those which are clearly produced with a large measure of insincerity?

An early example of this, indeed one from before the term became popular, was the invitation to think carefully about the use of words like 'man' and 'he' and to consider whether more appropriate words could be used where women were intended to be included in the usage (Spender 1980; Sarah and Spender 1980). In feminist circles this very quickly began a broader debate about whether 'wo-men' was an appropriate word at all, and that perhaps 'wimin' or 'wimyn' might be a better (PC) alternative, and in more popular circles whether British 'dustbin men' should be referred to as 'refuse collectors' and 'manholes' should become 'inspection covers'. In the US feminists began to question such terms as 'seminal text' and 'seminar', with one suggestion that the latter might become 'ovular', and 'ad feminem' arguments could sit alongside 'ad hominem' arguments (quoted in D'Souza 1992: 212). Indeed, to counter the contention that the discipline of history was largely one of documenting events which had affected men, this was counterposed with the suggestion that there should be more 'her-stories' (Morgan 1970).

It is not always clear whether the intention in such debate is that we should *literally* adopt these changes in language, or whether they intend simply to direct us to look at how language reflects power structures, or indeed, in postmodern circles, to demonstrate how to be more playful with language. Neither is it always clear whether the producer of these new words has ridicule as his/her aim. In this context, I have no reason to doubt the sincerity behind referring to animals as 'non-human persons' (Singer 1975), but equally I do have suspicions about some people's sincerity when referring to girls as 'young female persons'.

A detailed discussion of many of the implications behind language usage will be conducted in Chapter 4; suffice to say here that these debates have all the hallmarks of being a 'moving target'. First, in the sense that if the purpose behind the suggested change to language is largely 'awareness raising' (or in many feminist circles 'consciousness raising') then it could be argued that once this work is done the actual words themselves matter very little. And, second, to reflect the postmodern times, that it is now not so much a question of substituting one word with a more appropriate one, or indeed banning words because they are seen as offensive, but accepting that once the bond is broken between a word and the reality that it is intended to represent, any word is able to take on new and potentially multiple meanings. To take an extreme example, and one which will be discussed in detail later, it is no longer necessary to consider whether the word 'nigger' should be banned, because once it has been subject to a 'linguistic turn', and is freed from only having one meaning, multiple meanings thereby become possible. Indeed, it might even become a term of endearment. This argument might be taken one step further with the suggestion that far from banning offensive words, it would be much more politically astute to have people take back the language of oppression and thereby emasculate the original oppressor. Having said that, the emotionally charged nature of racial slurs, particularly in the US, will be a central feature of Chapter 4.

The question of euphemistic language is complicated by the fact that it is often not clear whether the euphemism has simply been created for the purpose of politeness, or whether it should be used exclusively, and subsequently policed, such that users of the more traditional terms could be reprimanded in some way. Clearly this raises the question of the *correctness* as much as the politics, and a major concern through the following chapters will be to try to highlight what exactly is *political* and *correct* about PC. A further significant development in the US has been to connect the policing of language with an unwarranted undermining of the First Amendment, and the right to free speech. In some cases this has resulted in PCers being castigated as somehow un-American. This theme will be explored throughout the book.

Although the term is most commonly associated with the use of euphemistic language, only a cursory glance at relevant literature, particularly in the US, would indicate that this is only one dimension. There are two other dimensions which are, arguably, more important, particularly in terms of their impact on higher education. The first of these is the steady rise in forms of 'multicultural' curricula, and the ways that these have challenged traditional notions about the content and purpose of education. In the case of content this has been most commonly associated with challenges to the traditional 'canon' of wisdom reflected by certain authors and texts; and in the case of the purpose of education, whether the emphasis in higher education should always be on the academic aspects of learning, or that this should be more balanced with the affective and self-developmental aspects of learning. These issues will be discussed in some detail in Chapter 5.

The other dimension concerns access to higher education, and the ways in which admission and participation are managed and monitored. In the US this is commonly associated with the term 'affirmative action', and although this term is rarely used in Britain, it is clear that allied terms like 'positive' or 'reverse' discrimination often act as the appropriate British equivalents. Furthermore, although in the US the term affirmative action is most often found in literature which discusses the ways that black, or African-American, participation in higher education might be expanded, the debates in Britain about how to increase the participation rates of, so-called, 'non-traditional learners' (which itself might be taken as a euphemism for 'working class') are not dissimilar. That said, it is clear that the question of whether universities and colleges in the US should use, or indeed have used, quotas for racial groups in their admissions procedures is a much more politically charged question than any similar questions that have been asked in Britain. This question of the advocacy of quotas will be discussed in some detail in Chapter 6, and the companion arguments in Britain can be found in Chapter 10.

The politics of PC

A significant thread running through all the following chapters is a careful consideration of what exactly the word *political* means in the term PC, and what are the politics of those who would use the term. As will soon become clear, one of the most intriguing questions to have emerged from debates concerning political correctness is: 'Who's to blame?' Put simply, is PC an orchestrated campaign from the political right designed to discredit everyone and everything which challenges the canons of right-thinking people, including affirmative action, minority rights, relativism in knowledge, and, in general, theories connected in some way with Marxism? Or is it the product of those on the political left who see themselves as guardians of the path which will lead us all to a future society which is both just and humane and centred on a *real* equality between people, as opposed to the political rhetoric which currently masks fundamental social inequalities?

A significant aim of this book is to seek to carefully unravel the various strands of PC-related thought from across the spectrum of political ideology, as well as to analyse the wider complex interplay between not just political forces on the left and right but also more general social and intellectual forces, most notably the rise of a postmodern sensibility throughout, particularly, the humanities and social sciences, and the concurrent demise of general social theory. Far from trivializing intellectual and public educational debate, as opponents of PC have often argued, these contexts can be used to highlight that there are extremely important issues at stake. Chief amongst these are: a thoroughgoing social constructivism running throughout intellectual disciplines (Choi and Murphy 1992); a rise in forms of postmodernism centred on anti-foundational thinking (Fish 1994); and a steady accommodation of psychoanalytically informed clinical ideas in cultural analysis and 'identity politics' (Frosh 1991; Giddens 1992). Given this broader context, this book will also address whether the traditional left–right political spectrum is an adequate conceptual tool for discussing contemporary political debate.

The self-policing PC college

There is a sense in which, at least in professional life, 'we are all PC now'. Most professionals, including teachers, social workers, doctors and nurses, will be used to the term, and might be reminded from time to time by colleagues that what they just did or said 'wasn't very PC'. This might be a whispered comment in a meeting, and one which might prompt the thought that the person doing the whispering was being ironic. However, in response, it's best if one does not make too much of an issue of it, just in case other colleagues in the room can't see, or don't want to see, the joke. Furthermore, although one might not hear the actual term it is perhaps instructive to remind ourselves that, often, the execution of power is at its strongest when we do not immediately register its existence. That is, political correctness is now so much part of the taken-for-granted of public sector professional life that one instinctively knows what should be said here, and not there, what needs to be done to satisfy this requirement without compromising that, and so on. And, as in all such cases, it is a brave person who decides deliberately to rock the status quo, particularly if one is untenured, as is often the case in the US, or on a short-term, or fractional, contract, as is often the case in Britain.

This might also be taken as evidence of how successful the campaign against political correctness has been. Not that it has stopped people continuing to embrace the causes most often associated with term – the use of enlightened language; the promotion of multicultural forms of curriculum; and forms of affirmative action – but in making the term itself a wholly derogatory one it has made everyone feel that they should avoid it, and distance their behaviour from its connotations. In this context, consider for a moment the proposal to refer to someone as 'differently able' in a college prospectus or catalogue, and how this might, at one and the same time, court some support, disdain, or even bewilderment amongst a group of post-16 educators. Furthermore, imagine a college that decides to rethink the way in which it will collect its student cohort monitoring data. One suggestion might be that students, rather than being asked to tick a box indicating whether they are male or female, could be given a blank space to self-report their gendered status or sexual orientation. Imagine further a discussion in the senior management team of the college, where one group opposes this on the grounds that the college should only record what regulatory bodies require (i.e. male or female), and another group who opposes it on the grounds that it may be construed as an intrusion into the private affairs of its student body. However, imagine a further group who accept both of these points, but want to use the opportunity to widen the monitoring of minority students, to include sexual identity, the first step towards which will need to be the identification of the categories under which students might wish to be classified. Finally, imagine a fourth group in the room, who smell the scent of political correctness and who fear the ridicule that will be heaped onto the institution by the local press!

PC in the British and in the US contexts

The final and equally important theme of this book is to compare and contrast the ways in which the term has come to be understood in Britain and in the US. It is not a traditional comparative study that seeks to look at how the same 'object' has fared in two different national contexts, but one which looks at whether the different cultural contexts have produced distinct versions of the same 'object', or perhaps better how the 'object' itself has been manufactured by those cultural contexts. The 'object' here, of course, is PC and the question is thus whether it means the same thing in the US that it does in Britain, and furthermore whether PC should be listed alongside McDonald's, Starbucks, and iPods as one more example of a significant export from the US? Or, as I will argue in the final chapters, are the roots of PC, in reality, much deeper in Britain? The more substantial point I wish to make in this context is that PC in Britain is probably much closer to the original meaning of the term than the one that was popularized in the late 1980s and early 1990s in the US. The precise contours of the original meaning will be discussed at the end of this chapter. The term as popularized in the US in the late 1980s and early 1990s will be discussed in Chapter 2, and the relationship between both and their significance for UK PC debates will be a central theme running throughout chapters 8 to 11. Overall, the book has two clear sections: a historically based first section which centres on how the term 'PC' has fared in the US from the early 1980s onwards, and a more comparative second section which centres on raising the analytical profile of PC in a UK context.

One of the most significant points that I hope will emerge from chapters 8 to 11 is that because teachers and academics in Britain are subject to much more stringent regulation from central state sources compared with the US, this has had a marked effect on the way that PC debates have been conducted on the British side of the Atlantic. As a preface to this it is important to understand that the public policy framework within which UK post-16 education takes place is much more regulatory and more tightly controlled by the state and its quangos – technically defined as quasi autonomous non-governmental organizations – that is, agencies that are run independently of the state but report directly to the state.

It is debatable whether some of the following agencies are *technically* quangos. However, my point here is not a technical one, but to consider, through their effects, some of the consequences of this regulatory framework for UK post-16 education, and the significance of this in the context of PC.

The important quangos are Lifelong Learning UK (LLUK) which oversees the professional standards for teachers in mainly the further education sector, and which sits alongside the inspection arm, the Office of Standards in Education (Ofsted); and in higher education the equivalent arms are the Higher Education Academy (HEA) and the Quality Assurance Agency for Higher Education (QAA). Although clearly separate, higher education also has a quality assurance regime for research known as the Research Assessment Exercise (RAE). On top of this, central state funding to both sectors is tightly regulated, for further education by the Learning and Skills Council (LSC) along with its 47 regional offices and by the Higher Education Funding Councils, with one for each of the four nations in the UK. This framework has been the subject of much academic debate and discussion in the UK (Kogan and Hanney 2000; Lucas 2004). The point in this book will be to consider how this has impacted on the ways in which teachers and academics in the UK have accommodated to the quangos, or arms of the state, and the extent to which they 'toe the party line' accordingly. As I hope to demonstrate shortly the idea of 'toeing the party line' is an important strand in the aetiology of the term PC.

The aetiology of PC

The term political correctness has a long history and its meaning has changed several times. Also, particularly in the contemporary context, it has begun to be used in a number of different ways, and it has thereby developed multi-dimensional qualities. Indeed, given that it appears to have been granted a free reign to encroach almost willy-nilly on all aspects of the cultural landscape, we probably should be as much concerned with how this has come about, as with trying to track down any precise meanings. The final parts of this introductory chapter will outline key themes in the term's aetiology, and raise awareness of the need to read definitions with a view to uncovering their more covert political meanings.

Several authors have attempted to trace the first use of the term 'political correctness' (Levy 1991; Perry 1992; Ellis 1992, 2002). What is clear in these discussions is the way in which it has changed its meaning over time, indeed to such an extent that it might even be said to have reversed its meaning in the process. It is often said that it emanated originally in left-wing communist circles to refer to comrades found guilty of doing what was *politically* correct, but because it was being done slavishly, in an unthinking way, they might be castigated for it. Straightaway we can see that this might be contrasted with a more literal usage, which is that if one is 'politically correct' then one's thinking must be in line with the Party ideology:

> Stalin's real enemy was the non-communist left, social democrats, progressives, and liberals. In this he only had to follow Marx and Lenin.

Non-communist leftists were not only 'insubordinate,' and 'rebellious,' they, and they alone . . . could slow and perhaps defeat the 'inevitable revolution.' By improving the workers' lot, they counteracted the 'immiseration of the proletariat'.

(Drucker 1994: 59)

In this reading we can see that these reactionaries and enemies are simply those who do not understand History, they have not read 'the materialist conception of history' correctly, and in consequence they have come to an incorrect political assessment of the situation, that is of how to bring about a truly communist future. However, it is equally possible that one might follow the Party line without really understanding it or, perhaps worse, simply by paying lip service to it. When one considers that an extended stay in some remote part of Siberia was a very real possibility for any comrade during much of the period of Stalin's leadership of the Soviet Union (1928–1953) it is easy to understand that one might quickly have to consider what the 'politically correct' position was, regardless of whether one understood it, or even believed it.

This second interpretation is much closer to the variation of its usage in Western left-wing circles, when the term was used in mocking, ironic, and essentially light-hearted ways, to indicate that it is common to *know* what is the right thing to do, but one does not always do it, or, put simply, 'to err is to be human'. In this context, those on the political left might castigate themselves or others where words and deeds don't correspond: 'to comment ironically on their . . . inability to live up to their ideals, their acknowledgement of the complexity of human beings, and the limits of any cherished beliefs' (Feldstein 1997: 6). But an important historical shift seems have occurred in the 1980s when the term increasingly came to be used by the political right, particularly in the US, to refer to those who were seen to be challenging the fundamental tenets of the American Dream – individual rights, freedom of speech, equality of opportunity, and, for some at least, the idea of Universal Truths (Bennett 1984; Cheney 1992).

This interpretation of meaning very quickly came to be further associated with a form of Orwellian doublespeak, which overtly espoused the cause of liberty but covertly represented a totalitarian tyranny. Although it could be argued that the term has always had derogatory overtones these clearly became central in this use of the term.

This is a Kafkaesque world in which, more often that not, you do not know the rules until you have violated them. And woe betide the violators, for the wrath of the offended 'victims' will descend upon them – aided and abetted by an army of committees and administrators.

(Fox-Genovese 1995: 10)

Here, a liberal notion of justice has been replaced by a more radical, egalitarian, and un-American one, and it was being policed by a new army of cadres, who wittingly or unwittingly were undermining the professional integrity of their colleagues. And thus, in the space of fifty years, we clearly see a return to a Stalinist world, albeit this time a metaphorical one, where the Party line is everything. As we will see later, this is a significant emphasis in meaning because it invokes a Cold War, McCarthyite rhetoric, with a distinct sense of there being an un-American 'enemy within', and one against which we should all be on guard.

It is from this context that the term began to be used to label (and castigate) a political opponent rather than be applied to a political ally, or indeed oneself. It is for this reason that the term is used, more often than not, as a derogatory epithet – to label what one is opposed to rather than label what one espouses. And, of course, the more successful this derogatory association becomes the more one might want to distance oneself from the term even if one supports the causes to which the label has been applied. In much the same way that Wilson (1987) began to question the use of the term 'the underclass', seeing it as having been hijacked by the political right, perhaps, by the mid-1990s, much the same could be said about the term PC. Couched in this way, it becomes increasingly important always to engage in a political reading of literature on political correctness.

Deconstructing definitions

Political Correctness refers to matters of inclusive speech, advocacy of nonracist, nonageist, nonsexist terminology, an insistence on affirmative action policies, avoidance of Eurocentrism as reflected in a 'traditional' canon of literature, acceptance of multiculturalism as a valued feature of American society and dismantling hierarchy as controlled by a white male power structure.

(Hoover and Howard 1995: 964)

This sentence neatly summarizes the causes with which PC is most commonly associated. Rather than seeing PC as a definition, this seems to work better by seeing it as a demarcation of territory and offers some clues to the nature of its rocky terrain. However, it is not clear from the sentence whether any of the causes are either good or bad or what is actually political or correct about being in favour or against them. This is not intended as a criticism of the authors, but is just a way of highlighting the importance of understanding what actually is implied by the words *political* and *correct* in the term PC. In this section I will use some common definitions of PC, taken mainly from academic literature in the US. My general point is a relatively straightforward one: the term is never neutral in its usage. Not only does it refer to many aspects of thought and behaviour (as reflected in the above quotation), but also below the surface of all its uses lurks deeper ideological commitments. With this in mind I offer here not so much a list of alternative definitions, but some deconstructions of meaning. This will serve as the preface to a fuller discussion of the broader political and ideological contexts in the chapters that follow. An excellent example of this ideological undercurrent can be gleaned from the following:

> Political correctness turns out to be a subunit of the larger transformation of society reflected in the ascendancy of psychological over political terminology. What began as an attempt to politicise psychology (and psychologise politics) has led to the swallowing of each by the other and the emergence of synthesis: therapeutic politics.
>
> (Sykes 1992: 164)

In this thesis PC is associated with the much broader social trend, which has turned movements for civil rights and state entitlements into a culture of dependency and victimhood (Samuelson 1995). Read literally, it would appear that any number of people from both the traditional left and right of the political spectrum could find a significant intellectual purchase here, that is that political struggle has been turned into a branch of a burgeoning therapy industry. This clearly has a long tradition in Marxist literature, dating back to Marx's own criticisms of Hegelian philosophy, that it sought to reorient individuals to their social contexts, through acts of the mind, rather than seeking to transform that context, the true political act.

However, as soon as one introduces the notion of dependency we find ourselves being able to move very quickly from a Marxist stance to a more libertarian plea for individuals to be seen to be taking responsibility for their own actions, and that poverty and deprivation have more to do with one's *own* cultural identity (Murray and Hernstein 1994). And this is in strict opposition to the view that disadvantage is caused by one's *structural* positioning in a society rooted in endemic income, wealth, and political inequality, a view much more popular on the political left (Wilson 1990). In this reading, although the notion of 'therapeutic politics' might resonant with many on the political left, its roots, in the US at least, might be said to be much more clearly found on the political right, with the intention that it should be used to discredit egalitarian policies aimed at redistributive justice.

This dilemma in having to read carefully the political ideology behind an attack on PC can also be seen in British-based literature on PC:

> Through the prism of the culture of abuse, people have been rediscovered as sad and damaged individuals in need of professional guidance. From this emerges the diminished subject; ineffective individuals and collectivities with low expectations. Increasingly we feel more comfortable with seeing people as victims of their circumstances rather than as authors of their lives.
>
> (Furedi 1997: 147)

Since victims are supported not because they are right but because they are vulnerable, critically questioning them is seen as attacking them, and those who do so are vilified as oppressors. In the world of PC, victims can say anything or ask anything, not because they are right or deserve it, but because they are safe from public scrutiny or objection.

(Browne 2006: 13)

At one level both authors can be viewed as writing within the paradigm of 'a nation of victims' and the quotations could easily appear as logical extensions of the same argument. But, at another, although they may have very similar views about PC, we need to ask whether both authors actually share the same political ideology and fundamental beliefs about human nature.

Ironies and contradictions in utopian thinking

Although there is much evidence that people on the right seek to use PC as a means to discredit left-wing ideas, the term clearly has its critics on the left also. In Britain, Furedi may be considered to be a case in point, and in the US this view can be found in the works of several authors (e.g. Gitlin 1995; Scatamburlo 1998). For Furedi the question has become whether left and right are conceptually able to do justice to more fundamental beliefs about humanity (Furedi 2005a), but for Gitlin and Scatamburlo it seems to be a simpler question about PC being a misguided form of left-wing thinking. Put simply, it is not left wing enough! This issue will be discussed in more detail in the next chapter. For others on the left however, it is more a question of irony:

Politically Correct is an idea that emerges from the well meaning attempt in social movements to bring the unsatisfactory present into line with the utopian future . . . Politically correct behaviour, including invisible language and ideas as well as observable action, is that which adheres to a movement's morality and hastens its goals . . . the ideology of political correctness emerges in all sorts of movements, applying to behaviour, social institutions, and systems of thought and value.

(Dimen 1984, quoted in Richer and Weir 1995: 57)

The phrase 'well meaning' is instructive here, for it alerts us to the awareness that, as in all social movements which promote change, it is possible for worthy ends to be associated with unworthy means, made manifest as ironies or contradictions, or simply unintended consequences. Thus, in a variation on the adage that one should be careful not to throw the baby out with the bath water, it is perfectly possible to maintain a vision of a 'New Jerusalem' or 'Promised Land', and see PC behaviour simply as the misguided means to a better society. In this reading of PC we need to be careful to distinguish between those whose aim is solely to discredit the means, and those who do this because their real (perhaps disguised) aim is to discredit the end – an egalitarian, socialist society, as opposed to a free enterprise, capitalist one.

The essence of political correctness is not the specific beliefs and ideologies disliked by conservatives. It is rather, the way in which (conservatives allege) liberals and radicals hold and act on their beliefs: namely, narrowly, dogmatically, unfairly, intolerantly, self-righteously, and oppressively . . . I define political correctness as an ideological narrowing, intolerance, and silencing of dissent, commonly attributed to the left by the right.

(Cummings 2001:10)

This definition highlights two important facets of PC debate. First, although the politics behind certain causes may be troubling to a whole range of commentators, an equally important element is the way in which those causes are pursued. Here, the emphasis is put on the correctness rather than the politics. However, in deconstructing this notion we need to be careful to consider whether the correctness is really as troubling as the politics, that is are some people very keen to emphasize the correctness in order simply to smear the politics? And second, to what extent might it be possible to argue that many on the left know that the right tend to do this, and, therefore, so as not to give further ammunition to the right, they always seek to underplay forms of correctness? More generally, such definitions begin to alert us to the fact that whenever any political creed finds it difficult to tolerate any form of dissent in pursuing its causes there could be a case for an accusation of political correctness. This theme will be explored in detail in the British section of the book (Chapters 8 to 11).

The PC straw men

The myth of political correctness has made every radical idea, no matter how trivial or harmless, seem like the coming of an apocalypse for higher education, complete with four new horse people – Speech Codes, Multiculturalism, Sexual Correctness, and Affirmative Action.

(Wilson 1996: 2)

A theme amongst some left-wing theorists is that PC really is a myth. It is not a question that some progressive equal opportunities strategies in some universities and colleges have been misguided, and right-wing critics have seized on this, but that organizations on the right have been engaged in an orchestrated campaign to manufacture a notion of PC, which they have then systematically imposed at every opportunity. Thus the metaphorical horse people are polemical straw men, manufactured from *real* political causes in order to discredit them. Wilson can thus be identified with the left but not those on the left who oppose PC, but those on the left who oppose those on the right for using the term PC to discredit the left! It is clear from the context in which the following is taken that a horse person of PC has ridden into town:

Test scores and grade point averages are mere measurements of achievement, which are necessary to register how much intellectual progress is
being made. They provide a common index for those who seek to improve
themselves, regardless of race, sex, or background. High standards do not
discriminate against anyone except those who fail to meet them. Such
discrimination is entirely just and ought not to be blamed for our
individual differences.

(D'Souza 1992: 250)

Here, we need to engage in the most careful and potentially most conspiratorial
political reading. Is this the position of someone who believes that the status quo
actually delivers, or this someone seeking to defend a *vested* interest; someone
who recognizes that PC causes (such as affirmative action) would end up
undermining a status quo where certain people are privileged and replacing
them with other groups? In the conspiratorial reading the status quo does not
represent a form of social justice, but simply the vested interest of those who
benefit most from it, ideologically supported by general myths (e.g. that society
is meritocratic), and PC myths (e.g. that an intellectual *au courant* is out to
undermine educational standards).

This leaves us considering whether PC is really little more than a smear term,
simply an attempt to discredit undesirable political causes and, at worse, not
from the point of view of what they envision, but the means employed to take
us nearer to this vision. Although this argument clearly makes sense from the
point of view of the right-wing critic, it holds little for those on the left who share
an egalitarian vision, but are still anti-PC. This argument will be central to the
next chapter.

'Politically Correct' was never a unifying political principle, and even as a
slogan, it was rarely used to describe oneself or one's group, except in
mocking self-deprecation. In seizing upon the term as the watchword of
some new leftist movement, conservative alarmists and their liberal allies
have rather spectacularly missed the joke. Political correctness is a spectre
of the past the left itself has disavowed.

(Scanlon 1995: 9)

In this article Scanlon seeks not only to undermine the credibility of many
conservative scare stories about PC, but also to articulate the democratic
credentials of the literary theorists who were being accused of being PC at that
time (this point will be discussed in detail in Chapter 5). However, for authors
such as D'Souza and Bloom (see next chapter) these democratic credentials are
simply veiled attempts to defend a general trend towards 'dumbing down' in all
aspects of education. In this reading of PC, either one is a progressive promoter
of a wide range of textual sources on the educational curriculum, or one is a
conservative defender of a traditional curriculum centred on Arnold's 'the best
that has been known or thought'.

Mind your language!

Whether it is because of the undesirable nature of certain political causes, or the unacceptable zeal or pious way in which these causes are pursued, a common theme in discussions of PC is to associate those political causes with forms of totalitarianism. Sometimes a connection is made with American McCarthyism, and sometimes with Soviet Stalinism, but in all cases the message is a clear one: watch out because dissent will not be tolerated, and will be acted on by using 'the favourite tool of the Thought Police: sensitivity training, which is a euphemism for directly applied thought control – a kind of modern-day nonsurgical lobotomy' (Bruce 2001: 27). But how much should we read this as an attack on these means, or as Bruce's own means to defend a particular political ideology?: 'It's time that we admit the failure of socialism and embrace the benefits of capitalism and competition' (Bruce 2001: 241).

The most common definitions of PC focus on the need to be sensitive about language. For those who have promoted PC causes this is often connected to a broader philosophy about the relationship between words and the reality that they 'represent' (see Chapter 4 for a detailed discussion of this), and thereby the power of words to frame the ways in which we understand the world around us. For those who have been anti-PC this has provided a rich arena in which to engage in relentless ridicule.

> We do not fail, we underachieve. We are not junkies, but substance abusers; not handicapped, but differently-abled. And we are mealy-mouthed unto death: a corpse, the New England Journal of Medicine urged in 1988, should be referred to as a 'nonliving person.' By extension, a fat corpse is a differently sized nonliving person.
>
> (Hughes 1993: 20)

Here PC is castigated not for its tyranny but its triviality – changing words does not change the world. As Hughes goes on to say in the next paragraph, changing the word 'nigger' to something else is not what changes people's attitudes to racism. Put so bluntly and, in the context of his whole argument, so eloquently, it is difficult to disagree. But, once again, we need to ask whether this should so easily seduce us, and the first step is to demand that we address the political ideology from which such authors write.

For many this monitoring of language has become a source of great humour and, as already mentioned, it has spawned several good books and cartoons. However, scratch below the surface and one often finds that there is more than a hint of the scurrilous at work here. For example, in the week that I write this I find that the Royal Society for the Protection of Birds (RSPB) in Britain has banned the use of the word 'cock' from its website. It turns out this is simply because the software filter that the organization uses automatically puts asterisks where it finds offensive words. And thus, although at one level it can be read as yet another example of 'political correctness gone mad', at another it is simply an administrative problem caused by the purchase of a commercial software package. Of course, this leaves open the question as to why the designers of these software packages feel the need to engage in such censorship, but I doubt the answer to that would be anywhere near as good as newspaper headline stories which imply that the RSPB no longer have *****. Or as one newspaper put it: 'Cock bad, tit good, says RSPB' (http://www.metro.co.uk/weird/article.html?in_article_id=51672&in_page_id=2 accessed 7June 2007).

In the context of higher education, the 1990s saw the proliferation of 'speech codes' on many American campuses, and similar attempts to mirror this in some colleges and universities in the UK. This issue will be discussed in some detail in Chapter 4, but suffice it to say here that one needs to read very carefully the cases made both for and against such policing of language. It is one thing to say that a word has been banned outright, and another to suggest that staff and students become sensitive to the ways in which language can stifle or promote learning; and to recognize that words can have many associations, but that alerting people to this is not thereby an attempt to 'lobotomize' thought. However, in effect, there may be little difference between Big Brother and his more affectionate Nanny, but it is always possible to read intentions and effects differently. For example: 'It is helpful to use positive images of disabled people in case studies etc., in order to illustrate that disability is incidental to the activity being undertaken.' This sentence is taken from a UK university's equal opportunities guidance document. The question it raises is surely now an obvious one: How much is this really Big Brother (or his Sister), or his or her Nanny (or Grandmother, or Grandfather) at work, but, more importantly, what would lurk behind anyone's need to ridicule or undermine it?

Raising the postmodern stakes

In the light of these political readings of PC it would not be surprising to see many on the left abandoning the use of the term altogether. However, some authors have clearly seen that there is really much more at stake:

> What pc is about . . . is who will control social life. Will the traditional centers of power be allowed to hide behind the facade of neutrality, or will political discussion expand in such a way that options are not restricted by hierarchy, class antagonisms, racial or sexual discrimination, or other forms of repression? The question is, will democracy finally arrive, or will the current cycle of ineffective reforms continue?
>
> (Choi and Murphy 1992: xii)

Here we see the authors unwilling to grant credence to the view that PC is either about control or tyranny, or trivialization. It is in fact diametrically opposed to the first two, and *very* serious. Forget the ironies and contradictions, which when highlighted by left or right will only give credence to these charges. These authors seem determined to keep the PC debate on higher philosophical ground. To them, at heart, PC is about democracy and, fundamentally, about epistemology. Whenever the left or the right denigrate PC as the tyranny of Party lines, and the trivialization of everyday life, the view here is that we should raise the postmodern stakes and ask the protagonists what is their theory of know-ledge, and, furthermore, ask who actually benefits from current conceptions of representative government, meritocracy, and canonical sources of truth?

Of course, for some, this postmodern assault on truth strikes at the heart of the matter. For to give up on truth and absolute authority will put us on the most slippery of slopes, down to mediocrity and ludicrous forms of radical relativism, where, for example, a child's painting can be mentioned in the same breath as the *Mona Lisa*:

> Intellectual authority came to be replaced by intellectual relativism as a guiding principle of the curriculum. Because colleges and universities believed they no longer could or should assert the primacy of one fact or one book over another, all knowledge came to be seen as relative in importance, relative to consumer or faculty interest.
>
> (Bennett 1984: 20)

And, in a further theme which will run throughout the book, there is much that many on the left and right can agree on here, fundamentally that there are Enlightenment principles at stake, concerning reason, truth, and the autonomy of the individual.

Individual freedom

The importance of the individual in PC debates is double-edged. On one side a battle has raged largely in the Humanities departments of many universities about the 'death of the subject' and the ways in which literary theory has questioned whether any notion of an autonomous individual has much intellectual meaning, while on the other side there is a more overtly political battle about whether human agency can have much meaning in societies rooted in vast inequalities of income and wealth. As in the old Marxist adage, there is little point in being free to dine at the Ritz restaurant in London if one does not have the means to do so. This latter component has been carefully orchestrated by those who oppose PC in the US, by associating those who promote forms of redistributive justice with being anti-American: 'The campaign against political correctness has been so successful because it has portrayed the attempt to uphold the rights of disadvantaged groups as the infringement of individual rights' (Brennan, in Feldstein 1997: x).

The question of individual rights is also often connected with the further right to free speech, and, particularly in the US, this has been an extremely powerful weapon against those who promote PC causes. The point is a simple one: if the First Amendment ('government shall pass no law that inhibits the freedom of speech') is a fundamental principle then anyone who would dare to interfere with it can be easily castigated as un-American. PC has been tarred with this brush on many occasions, and the irony that it is in universities where there have been the most reported restrictions on free speech has not been lost. However, some authors have sought to rise to this challenge:

> racist slurs do not serve any First Amendment purposes: they contribute little to self-realization, to dialogue on important matters of public policy, or to the discovery of truth. Rather, they impair the growth of those who use them by encouraging rigid thinking and impeding moral develop-ment, they close off dialogue by insulting others, and they amount to a slap in the face rather than the statement or criticism of a proposition.
>
> (Shiell 1998: 45)

Once again we need to ask what actually is being defended when one speaks in favour of a principled position on the First Amendment, when one argues for measured restrictions. Is the former simply giving credence to the manipulation of political arenas by the rich and powerful, and the latter simply giving equal credence to the perpetuation of 'a culture of dependency', where self-appointed welfare tsars make judgements about the harmful effects of some people's speech and behaviour on others? This theme is discussed in some details in the following two chapters.

Conclusion

This chapter has served to introduce many of the causes and themes that are associated with the term PC. Chief amongst the causes are: the power of language to bring about political change; the importance of widening the content and purposes of higher education; and the case for widening access to higher education through forms of affirmative action. The chapter has also hinted at the fact that these causes have been granted a firm intellectual founda-tion through the increasing acceptance in academe of forms of postmodern and poststructural thinking, and that traditional forms of knowledge and edu-cational standards are not objective, and thereby represent unacceptable vested interests. In opposition to this many others have found themselves wishing to defend more traditional notions, and have variously charged PC with having promoted new forms of cultural tyranny, the dumbing down of educational standards, and having created a victim's charter for those who have benefited from PC educational strategies.

The chapter has also served to indicate that although the term PC has become part of the language of everyday professional life it eludes precise definition, and because of this it has been able to grant itself permission to be used in a number of ways and, most insidiously, to indicate that a particular intellectual or political position is somehow unworthy, disreputable, unwarranted, or even sinister.

Furthermore, in professional circles, it seems to be able to suggest that there is an unwritten code of behaviour that one must learn, but because it is not exactly clear what it is, and what might happen if one contravenes it, it is able to produce a large amount of conservative self-policing.

However, the main intention behind this chapter was to raise awareness of the need to be sensitive to the fact that beneath the various uses of the term PC there are many competing political ideas and beliefs. Indeed, on the surface, the same view of PC might mask opposing political ideologies. Furthermore, the term might often be used as a form of smear in order to associate certain political causes unfavourably with the tyrannical and the totalitarian. Even amongst those who generally support some of the causes it is possible to detect a range of concerns about the term: from those who support the causes but would rather not be associated with the term, to those who freely recognize that undesirable consequences can follow from virtuous causes. For all these reasons it is important to be always engaged in a political reading of PC definitions and to deconstruct the meanings.

In what follow there are two main sections which are broadly split between a consideration of the way that PC has fared in the US, followed by a similar consideration for Britain. As might be expected, there is clearly a tone in some British literature that 'what has happened in the US simply couldn't happen in Britain'; that there is something about cultural life in the US which makes it ripe for PC, and something about cultural life in Britain which prevents it. This might be starkly exemplified by the case in the US of Stella Liebeck, who successfully sued McDonald's when, in 1992, she was scalded by a cup of their coffee, which she had spilt on herself. When Sam Bogle (and others) tried to do the same in Britain ten years later it was dismissed by the judge along the lines that there is a normal expectation that coffee be served hot and one should take due care because of that fact (http://www.hmcourts-service.gov.uk/judgmentsfiles/j1118/Bogle_v_McDonalds.htm).

Also, and as was indicated at the beginning of this chapter, it is important to remember that the term PC has a huge intellectual literature base in the US, which is made much more striking when compared with the relatively small amount that has been written in equivalent journals and books in Britain.

A key feature of the second section will be to argue that PC debate in Britain seems to be much more in keeping with some of the more traditional notions of PC – that is the politics and correctness involved in establishing orthodoxies. Indeed, one possible explanation of why the literature base on PC is so great in the US is because much of that literature is an attempt to redefine, or perhaps better, to reorient the term in order that it be marshalled to defend a particular kind of higher education and form of wider social solidarity. In this context the emphasis lay in ensuring that the term be associated with very particular political and social causes. The next chapter contains a detailed reading of some key American texts that signalled the nature of this reorientation.

2
Loose canons and straw men of the Apocalypse
The conservative campaign against PC in the US

Introduction

The term political correctness (PC) became part of the everyday discourse of educational debate in the late 1980s and early 1990s, particularly in the United States. Slowly it came to be associated with ideas emanating from the cultural left in the US, including restrictions on speech, the promotion of multicultural educational curricula, and the support of affirmative action in the recruitment of students to colleges and universities. These ideas will be fully explored in later chapters, but before this can be meaningfully undertaken it is important to understand the background to these developments. It was conservative thinkers who seem to have been the most vocal in identifying the key parameters within which the debates would be subsequently framed. The main sources were a number of polemics, and some key academic books. In this chapter I will undertake a close reading of three significant polemics: Bennett (1984), Searle (1990), and Cheney (1992); and three best-selling books by Bloom (1987), D'Souza (1992), and Sykes (1992). The main purpose here is to examine critically the arguments which helped identify the contours of the subsequent debates about PC in US colleges and universities in the 1990s.

A killer B

In the first of the polemics Bennett reports on the findings of a group of educationalists on the state of the humanities in higher education in the mid-1980s. Recognizing that it is difficult to define such a broad and heterogeneous area of study, Bennett reminds us of Matthew Arnold: 'I would describe the humanities as the best that has been said, thought, written, and otherwise expressed about the human experience' (Bennett 1984: 3).

It is not unusual for conservative thinkers to refer to Arnold, largely because he gives intellectual credibility to what is often referred to as 'high culture'. But, straightaway, we can see in the use of the word 'best' why many radical thinkers quickly became alarmed. Why is only the 'best' to be considered worthy of inclusion in the humanities; and who will decide what constitutes the 'best'? These questions are as obvious to the mind of the radical, as they are contemptible to the mind of the conservative. Surely, literary criticism has established the rules for judgements on what is great and what is not; and of what lasting value is there in celebrating mediocrity? Is it not the case that the study of the history of civilization is, for the most part at least, the study of what is 'best' in any particular epoch?

Bennett moves on to state the essential characteristics required of a good teacher – mastery of the material and engagement: 'they [good teachers] are moved and are seen to be moved by the power of the works and are able to convey that power to their students' (Bennett 1984: 6). He then moves on to the good curriculum: balance between breadth and depth, the study of original texts, continuous exposure to the humanities throughout college life, a strong faculty, and conviction about the centrality of the humanities (Bennett 1984: 8). Naturally, those teaching subjects other than the humanities might argue that this places too high a value on the humanities, but, in general, there is surely little to seriously object to in these comments. Indeed, even when he moves on to state what exactly the curriculum should broadly comprise it is hardly controversial: students should have an understanding of their own civilization; an understanding of the most significant ideas and debates in the history of philosophy; demonstrable proficiency in a foreign language. He even recommends that students should have some familiarity with at least one non-Western culture or civilization (Bennett 1984: 9). However, in amongst his original list is the significant comment that a curriculum requires: 'a careful reading of several masterworks of English, American, and European literature' (Bennett 1984: 9). He points out that such a list could never be exhaustive; that it should reflect what people actually feel is important literature; and that books are not the only source of significant knowledge.

However, from this point on we can begin to see why Bennett has become a bogeyman for the cultural left, for he is about to strike at the heart of what was fast becoming *de rigueur* in many of the humanities departments throughout the US:

> The study group was alarmed by the tendency of some humanities professors to present their subjects in a tendentious, ideological manner. Sometimes the humanities are used as if they were the handmaiden of ideology, subordinated to particular prejudices and valued or rejected on the basis of their relation to a certain social stance.
>
> At the other extreme, the humanities are declared to have no inherent meaning because all meaning is subjective and relative to one's own perspective. There is no longer agreement on the value of historical facts, empirical evidence, or even rationality itself.
>
> (Bennett 1984: 16)

Clearly, as someone who is bemoaning this tendency, some of these comments are couched in a derogatory tone. But, the point is clear, that the humanities have been hijacked, both by an ideological politicization: all knowledge has vested interest; and by an epistemological politicization: all truths are merely individual perspectives. Bennett concedes that these positions may have some merit, but they are generally not popular with students, and they undermine 'a legacy our students deserve to know' (Bennett 1984: 17).

This undermining has been achieved through two hijackings: 'intellectual authority came to be replaced by intellectual relativism' (Bennett 1984: 20) and 'the desired ends of education changed from knowledge to "inquiry", from content to "skills"' (Bennett 1984: 20). Clearly, if one supports the hijacking, it is obvious why this needed to happen: if it is no longer possible to establish the grounds upon which something is considered to be 'best', other than as an ideological commitment, then it is no longer possible to justify the grounds upon which the content of a curriculum is founded on any other grounds either.

> The willingness of too many colleges to act as if all learning were relative is a self-inflicted wound that has impaired our ability to defend our subjects as necessary for learning or important for life.
>
> (Bennett 1984: 20)

It is unfortunate that this key statement offers not so much an argument as a commitment, and every bit an ideological commitment as the ones he is bemoaning amongst fellow humanitarians. For, isn't the ability to deconstruct truth claims and develop critical skills just as much a valuable educational endeavour as being engagingly taught the contents of a carefully constructed set of masterworks, notwithstanding the other essential ingredients referred to above? It is not at all clear that this defence of a legacy is anything other than an ideological commitment, albeit one shared by a large number of people. But here we see the emergence of an important anti-PC tenet, that PC is a concerted attempt to undermine the accepted rules of literary criticism and reasoned debate.

The storm in the university

Searle's polemic takes a different form, it being a review of three, then recently published academic books. Searle is clear throughout as to his target: 'The spread of "poststructuralist" literary theory is perhaps the best known example of a silly but noncatastrophic phenomenon' (Searle 1990: 34). Moving on, once again, to quote Matthew Arnold, he calmly suggests that a sensible reaction to the 'great books' controversy might simply be to: 'open the doors to admit the work of talented writers who are not white, or not male, or not European' (Searle 1990: 34).

This enables him to cast the radicals as beyond common sense. He finds it easy to collect relevant quotations, particularly from one professor of comparative literature:

Few doubt that behind the Bennett–Bloom program is a desire to close not the American mind, but the American University, to all but a narrow and highly uniform elite with no commitment to either multiculturalism or educational democracy.. . . The B's act as they do not because they are unaware of the cultural and demographic diversification underway in this country; they are utterly aware.

(Pratt, in Searle 1990: 34–35)

Searle reacts dismissively to both sets of suggestions:

So you cannot reform education by admitting new members to the club, by opening up the canon, the whole idea of 'the canon' has to be abolished. It has to be abolished in favour of something that is 'multicultural' and 'non-hierarchical'.

(Searle 1990: 25)

At this point Searle moves on to discuss in much more detail two interrelated key reservations: first, that the knowledge of the humanities is increasingly being used to bring about social transformation, or that it has become instrumental in its aims, and, second, that all the emphasis is placed within the humanities, leaving most other subjects, particularly the sciences, untouched by the radical agenda.

The first reservation contains an important element in many PC debates: the sense that the right understands the term 'political' to refer to the ways in which knowledge is used for political ends, to be contrasted with the left, who were increasingly promoting the view that all knowledge is, inherently, political, that is, it is political in its construction and not just in its use. The word construction is double-edged here for it is also a route into the other key reservation of Searle, that the sciences seem to be able to produce knowledge that is untainted by politics. This is primarily because scientific knowledge is discovered rather than made, and that the role of theory is very different. In the sciences theory is produced as a result of empirical observation of natural reality, whereas, increasingly, in the humanities theory was being identified as the spectacles through which one views reality: theory is brought to reality, rather than vice versa. It is in this sense that one can speak of knowledge as 'constructed' rather than as being revealed or discovered.

Searle has two bogeymen of the left clearly in his sights at this point: Giroux and Rorty. He quotes Giroux in order to castigate the left for unnecessarily politicizing knowledge:

the liberal arts should be defended in the interests of creating critical rather than 'good' citizens. The notion of the liberal arts has to be reconstituted around a knowledge–power relationship in which the question of the curriculum is seen as a form of cultural and political production grounded in a radical conception of citizenship and public wisdom.

(Giroux, in Searle 1990: 36)

Searle's point is clear, that the intrinsic value of liberal education is being sacrificed in the interest of producing political radicals. However, in making this point he perhaps misses the more fundamental point usually made by radical scholars, that if all knowledge, by its very nature, is political, then being critical is not just about promoting social transformation, but also about developing the skills of deconstructing knowledge. Searle's argument is thus only single-edged, for he debates the validity of the social transformation thesis, but simply dismisses the deconstruction tradition as being 'silly'. That said, he does defend a 'correspondence theory of truth' by arguing, logically, that discussion as to whether language is meaningful 'presupposes that there is an independently existing reality to which expressions in those utterances can refer' (Searle 1990: 40). But this is presented more in the form of a proposition in favour of correspondence rather than against other theories which do not rely on external referent, and whose validity might be judged by a whole host of other criteria, such as logical consistency, generalizabilty, or even beauty.

Although he has previously questioned why all the radicals seem to congregate in the humanities these days (not even the Social Sciences, often only the English department!), he proceeds via his discussion of the work of Kimball to question the alliance of this new radical tradition with developments in the philosophy of science:

> They [The American Council of Learned Societies] also confidently quote 'relativity and quantum mechanics' as supporting their new conception of the humanities. One wishes they had told us in some detail how the study of, say, inertial frames in relativity theory or the collapse of the wave function in quantum mechanics support their peculiar conception of the humanities.
>
> (Searle 1990: 39)

The support does appear to be fairly straightforward however. For if language can be conceived without the need for an external referent, that is if language does not represent reality, then a literary text *can* be compared with a scientific text, and both can become subject to discourse-based textual analysis. And many members of the New Physics community seemed to be well aware of this when considering the theory of the movements of subatomic particles because the language through which they described the particles actually constructed the reality of those 'objects'. At this point Searle would be able to claim that this only proves that the theory must have an external referent, for we are referring to the particles as 'objects', but the point of the New Physics was surely to indicate that particles only take on the characteristics of being objects by being *conceived* as such (see Zukav 1980). We can begin to see here another emerging strand of many subsequent PC debates, that is the extent to which it would come to be associated, at least in part, with those who were perceived as having lost confidence in their ability to *discover* the truth, and thereby make valid judgements, having no access to criteria which is beyond the contingency of their own constructions.

Moving on to the work of Oakeshott, Searle focuses on the author's conception of the nature of learning and its culture: 'A culture for Oakeshott is not a set of beliefs or perceptions or attitudes – and certainly not a body of knowledge or a "canon" – but a variety of distinct "languages" of understanding, including self-understanding' (Searle 1990: 40). This clearly speaks to the view that learning should not be considered *of* something, but rather should be conceived as a way of speaking *about* something, or perhaps better, concerns how one comes to be involved in a conversation. Somewhat ironically, Searle manages to align Oakeshott with a rather conservative position, in conceiving learning to be about how one learns the language of a discipline's discourse: 'a kind of acceptance of the rules of the various discourses' (Searle 1990: 41). But his more damning criticism is how Oakeshott, like others, seems to tacitly accept that the knowledge of the humanities *is* knowledge, ignoring the fact that scientific knowledge is very different: 'The natural sciences do not fit his model because, for the most part, the world of the natural sciences is not a world of meanings; it is a world of things' (Searle 1990: 41).

This element of PC is as much an epistemological one as a political one, because it divides those who see method as a way to objectively discover an independently existing reality and those who see it as the means by which 'reality' is manufactured from human language, concepts, and theories, that is any truth is made not found (Rorty 1989). Here Searle divides knowledge of the first type from knowledge of the second type, in order to protect the natural sciences from disputes in the human sciences. This is much easier to achieve if the former are conceived as being about 'things'. It is much more difficult once the focus is shifted away from the 'object' of study to the human processes involved in studying anything. Adopting the latter view was fast becoming a PC position at the time that Searle was writing.

Searle concludes with a simple, measured set of recommendations for becoming a well-educated person: knowledge of one's own culture, knowledge of important philosophical and literary texts, knowledge of the natural sciences (as he conceives them of course), some knowledge of political economy, knowledge of at least one foreign language, knowledge of analytical philosophy, and finally the ability to write and speak clearly. He finishes by indicating that these are very much prerequisites, the attributes that are most likely to make one want to continue with one's education. Furthermore, like Bennett before, he is not averse to students learning critically, and he actively encourages 'works from other cultural traditions . . . to be studied as well' (Searle 1990: 42). And he does not see a canon functioning in its literal sense:

> In my experience there never was, in fact, a canon; there was rather a certain set of tentative judgements about what had importance and

quality. Such judgements are always subject to revision, and, in fact, they were constantly being revised.

(Searle 1990: 37)

Thus we have here some simple recommendations for a general liberal education, including a very loose canon; a call to ignore poststructural silliness in humanities departments; a defence of the natural sciences from this silliness, and a statement concerning their achievements through the use of forms of methodological realism. Put this way it is hard to see what a lot of PC fuss was about at that time. But all these positions were increasingly under attack, and the term PC was fast becoming a convenient label to attach to those who were opposing these conclusions.

Telling the truth

Cheney's report was produced under the auspices of the conservative body the National Endowment for the Humanities (Cheney 1992). Continuing in the same vein as the previous two authors she begins the report with reference to the politicization of the humanities and its damaging effects, quoting the then president of Yale University:

> The most serious problems of freedom of expression in our society today exists on our campuses.. . . The assumption seems to be that the purpose of education is to induce correct opinion rather than to search for wisdom and liberate the mind.
>
> (Schmidt, in Cheney 1992: 5)

Here we see that knowledge is not just being politicized, but it is also being controlled, in order to establish a new orthodoxy; that is, a form of 'correctness' is emerging. She sees this as being extremely worrying, largely because of its tyrannical nature. Straightaway we see why she has called the report 'Telling the Truth'. It is double-edged because somebody needs to speak out against this tyranny, that is, somebody needs to tell the truth about what is happening, but also, to return to one of the important themes of the previous two authors, we are being told that a crucial element – indeed, an important cornerstone – of the new orthodoxy is that there is no truth anymore. Thus we have an old theme, reiterated, and a new theme emerging: 'suppressing thought that is ideologically inconvenient simply does not work. In the long run, neither individuals nor societies flourish when truth becomes the servant of politics' (Cheney 1992: 8).

Postmodern theorists are often criticized for the apparent paradox at the heart of their thinking: if all truth is relative, isn't this an absolute statement? However, Cheney's position at this point is equally paradoxical, for on the one hand she castigates the new radicals for their freedom of thought (e.g. 'Is Alice still in Phallus Land?'), but on the other hand warns of the restrictions on freedom of speech (e.g. 'inappropriately directed laughter'). Of course, her examples are carefully chosen, for it is the academics who have the freedom of thought, it is the students who have the restrictions on their speech. Perhaps not surprisingly she was criticized at the time for the manner of her argument throughout the text (Lazare 1997).

She dismisses the ideas of Stanley Fish, who, at the time, was defending restrictions on speech on the grounds that, in reality, free speech only protects the rich and powerful: 'the first amendment is the first refuge of scoundrels' (Fish 1994), and proceeds to give examples of double standards. Essentially this amounts to saying that when some groups speak out against others they are celebrated for doing so, but when others do so they are castigated. Of course, she does not go on to say that this is, precisely, part of Fish's point, that, because there isn't 'a level playing field' in terms of access to resources and power, it is right that those who speak from privileged positions should be treated differently from those who don't. This issue of the level playing field will become an important issue in the subsequent debates concerning affirmative action, and we can see here a clear statement by Cheney that she has little time for it.

Furthermore, she abhors the overt politicizing of the classroom by using several examples of college professors who have an avowedly political mission in their teaching, and who use their teaching 'to further various "progressive" political agendas' (Ellesworth, in Cheney 1992: 12). This argument is premised on the belief that one can always clearly distinguish what is political from what is not, and this was another important element in many PC debates at that time. For example, she castigates those who indoctrinate their students into the view that capitalism can be an exploitative economic system, but fails to mention any examples of professors who might be engaged in exactly the same form of indoctrination when they don't mention any negative consequences of capitalistic behaviour. As was fast becoming clear, it is those who challenge the status quo who are most likely to be labelled, in derogatory tones, PC. This itself could be considered to be a significant political ploy because it makes it appear that those who support the status quo are not at all political.

Cheney saves her most vehement attacks for the feminist professors who were using the classroom to promote various feminist causes, usually at the expense of the students in the class. Quoting examples of professors who utterly reject any views that oppose the orthodoxy they are trying to establish, she dismisses this pedagogy as unengaging, narrowly focused, and intimidating for all those who are made subject to it: 'it is all too easy to bring new theories into the classroom as dogma since they often deny the possibility of objectivity – the very principle that a genuine exploration of ideas requires' (Cheney 1992: 23).

Two important pillars of PC debates can be found here: first, that a dogmatic approach, later to be increasingly seen as tyrannical, is being adopted by those who espouse radical political views and that this is being used as a form of indoctrination and, second, that an increasing number of radical scholars are giving up on the view that there is such a thing as 'objective truth'. Of course, the two points are clearly connected, for if the latter position is adopted, all classroom knowledge, is, in effect, ideological and thus political. This clearly cements previous points made by both Bennett (1984) and Searle (1990) as already discussed above.

Cheney was quick to see the connection between this unnecessary politicization and the attack on educational standards. In what was fast becoming an important feature of multicultural and affirmative action debates, Cheney questions how it is possible to justify the kind of non-judgemental world which was becoming increasingly visible in certain educational circles:

> Educators . . . should not be concerned with A's and honors and other signs of excellence or even with the hard work and accomplishments that outstanding grades and high honors have traditionally recognized; instead the goal should be political change, such as the creation of a society in which people do not compete with one another and everyone feels good about him- or herself.
>
> (Cheney 1992: 25)

Quoting Rita Kramer and Randall Kennedy she argues that this undermines any attempt to maintain a notion of excellence, and it can be conceived as racist and/or sexist. The first argument is relatively straightforward, for if we cannot make judgements about what is best, how is it possible to conceive of greatness, indeed, human progress? In a variation on an argument we have already encountered, that some literature is clearly better than other, we slide down an extremely slippery slope if we encourage our children to see all human endeavour as equally valid. The second argument is more complicated and rests on the attack on the view, popularized by the work of Gilligan (1982), that females, and, by associated argument, blacks, speak with a 'different voice' and, thus, that it is not possible to judge, objectively, criteria through which we might value a speaker's words. As Kennedy noted, this seems to rest on a dubious assumption that to be black is to be, essentially, different from someone who is white. If this is not overtly racist, then it certainly borders on it.

These arguments were to feature in many subsequent PC debates, and often surfaced in discussions of the importance of self-esteem and self-development particularly for young pupils, for example that teachers should seek to value all contributions made by children, and be as non-judgemental as possible. This was an important argument within multicultural education, and would become much derided in PC debates. Another example is the hiring of personnel, particularly when trying to broaden the basis upon which candidates are selected for various positions, it is important to reflect the fact that people speak with 'different voices' when being interviewed. More importantly we should seek to ensure that the personnel of a college reflect these different voices in its overall composition. This is a short step from the accusation that we have created politically motivated recruitment criteria and quotas, and affirmative action debates are still littered with this accusation.

This leaves the question as to whether the desire to want to hear 'distant voices' is actually a racist (or sexist) position. If, as is common in postmodern thinking, a voice is conceived as historically and contextually conditioned, then, although it is important to hear it, it is not indicative of the essential qualities of its speaker. And, furthermore, utilizing an argument from Fish earlier, the need to hear the distant voices is surely justifiable purely on the grounds that they are distant, distant from privileged positions of power. It is surely on these grounds that one would be promoting their position, not that it would perpetuate essential differences between social groups.

Cheney concludes her polemic with a restatement of the need to return to the traditional rationale for academic freedom: 'that it makes possible the disinterested pursuit of knowledge' (Cheney 1992: 29). In an argument, which is itself highly political, she persists in the view that what is invalid in the new radicalism on US university campuses is the *dogmatic* way in which *political* causes are pursued. Unfortunately, like Bennett and Searle before, she is much better at stating her own position as opposed to arguing against her opponents. Subsequently we are left with a choice: continue with the 'modern' conception of truth, that disinterested knowledge is not only possible, but, also, that it contributes to human progress; or accept the postmodern conception, that all knowledge is historically contingent, and that progress is simply a belief in the desirability of certain human projects. We are not actually given any stronger intellectual arguments as to why the latter is a flawed position, only that when it comes to university teaching this position tends to be adopted dogmatically.

In a theme which features significantly in Bloom (discussed below) Cheney finishes with a further damaging paradox in multicultural educational thinking, that in promoting forms of non-judgemental education we often end up tolerating things that we shouldn't: 'Everything one tolerates that one shouldn't inevitability returns' (Patai in Cheney 1992: 46). This point also acts as a convenient rhetorical device, because it enables her to conclude that the fundamental problem in US university education in the early 1990s was that it had lost confidence in, literally, speaking the truth.

Horsemen or straw men of the Apocalypse?

Many of the themes that were becoming essential ingredients in PC debates were cemented in a number of key academic books. Many of these were published in the first half of the 1990s and will be discussed in the next chapter. Alongside these several edited volumes provided an opportunity for polemical positions to be contrasted (Berman 1992; Beckwith and Bauman 1993; Horowitz and Collier 1994; Friedman and Narveson 1995; Richer and Weir 1995). This was followed by books which began to look forward and anticipated cultural debate beyond political correctness (Newfield and Strickland 1995; Levitt *et al.* 1999; Cummings 2001). For some this latter period was considered a second wave of PC debate where the emphasis was perceived as having moved away from concerns over speech and more to forms of multicultural education, and the importance of 'identity' politics, and 'standpoint' knowledge in colleges and universities. The rest of this chapter will focus on a close reading of three important foundational texts for almost all of the subsequent debates contained in these above-mentioned texts: Bloom (1987), D'Souza (1992), and Sykes (1992).

Opening or closing minds?

Bloom's book was an intellectual polemic in defence of the university as an academy, centred on the pursuit of truth, but throughout the twentieth century it had slowly capitulated to a multicultural and reconstructivist social agenda, which sought to use the academy to help engineer a more tolerant and diverse citizenry. Less intellectual in its composition, but comprehensive in its coverage, is D'Souza's survey of policy and practice at a number of leading American universities in the early 1990s. D'Souza charges these institutions with a flagrant mismanagement of the university's mission to pursue, in open and intellectual ways, the truth, by pandering to the demands of radical minority interests and allowing high standards and the principle of equal opportunity based on individual merit to be undermined. Sykes's book uses broader themes in social theory, particularly the medicalization of social pathology, to mount a polemic against cultures of dependency and victimhood, which he saw as its inevitable outcome. In the process he bemoans how we have allowed education to become a branch of the burgeoning therapy industry.

Although all three books have overlapping themes, taken separately it might be argued that Bloom is most immediately concerned with a critique of *multicultural* forms of education, D'Souza with the disastrous effects of a politicized curriculum and admissions policies based on forms of *affirmative action*, and Sykes with the replacement of individual responsibility by group entitlements and the status of *victimhood*. In this respect each author was an important midwife to the birth of Wilson's horsemen of the Apocalypse, mentioned previously, namely: multiculturalism (Bloom); speech codes and sexual correctness (Sykes); and affirmative action (D'Souza) (Wilson 1996).

Bloom pulls no punches in his attack on what he sees as passing for education in America's colleges and universities: 'Practically all that young Americans have today is an insubstantial awareness that there are many cultures, accompanied by a saccharine moral drawn from this awareness: We should all get along. Why fight?' (Bloom 1987: 35). Bloom contends throughout the book that the intellectual foundation for forms of multicultural education is little more than this 'saccharine moral'. He contrasts this with the more worthy and substantial pursuit of the truth through the use of Reason, which had been the original intellectual foundation for the Western university, before the hijacking by social engineering projects took hold. Although Bloom skilfully denigrates the multi-cultural agenda, it is clearly debatable the extent to which multiculturalism's real intellectual base is simply a form of moralising. As we have already seen, it might be argued that its more substantial foundation is a form of postmodernity, that truth claims are just that, claims built on contingent and historically conditioned modes of discourse and understanding, which when deconstructed amount to little more than the vested interests of their proponents.

Clearly Bloom is aware of this more solid foundation and mounts attacks on it throughout the book, although they feature very little in the key sections, where the easier target is fired at: 'The relativity of truth is not a theoretical insight but a moral postulate, the condition of a free society, or so they see it' (Bloom 1987: 25). In terms of curriculum ideologies, Bloom is clearly defending the classical humanist position from the progressivist and reconstructivist positions. He argues that education should not be seen in instrumental terms, neither serving the needs of nurturing an individual's self-confidence and development, nor pandering to any fleeting social agenda, be it for the purposes of social integration or forms of vocationalism. His defence is clear:

> In order to know such an amorphous being as man, Rousseau himself and his particular history are, in his view, more important than Socrates' quest for man in general or man in himself. The difference is made apparent by comparing the image of Socrates talking to two young men about the best regime, with the image of Rousseau, lying on his back on a raft floating on a gentle undulating lake, sensing his existence.
>
> (Bloom 1987: 179)

But to what extent could it be argued that Bloom is rather too keen to *assert* the authority of the Greek Academy rather than to engage in critical dialogue with modern-day deconstructivists? Indeed, as a method, the Elenchus would appear to have much in common with the deconstructivist desire to bring authoritative knowledge down from its constructed pedestals.

> She [the psyche] cannot profit from the knowledge offered to her until the Elenchus is applied and the man is refuted and brought to shame, thus purifying him from opinions that hinder learning and causing him to think he knows only what he knows and no more.
>
> (Plato, quoted in Abbs 1994: 18)

In this context it is one thing to argue that minority groups should not be allowed to use the academy as a way to raise their self-esteem and self-affirmation, quite another to argue that experience has no place in the university curriculum. Here, it would be incorrect to assume that just because courses in women's studies, black studies, and so on have as their starting point the experience of those groups it does not follow that those experiences should not be made subject to the most critical of deconstructions (hooks 1996).

Finally, it is unclear why bemoaning the mediocrity which he sees all around him in the university is integral to a defence of elitism:

> Words that were meant to describe and encourage Beethoven and Goethe are now applied to every school child. It is in the nature of democracy to deny no one access to good things. If those things are really not accessible to all, then the tendency is to deny the fact – simply to proclaim, for example, that what is not art is art. There is in American society a mad rush to distinguish oneself, and, as soon as something has been accepted as distinguishing, to package it in such a way that everyone can feel included. Creativity and personality were intended to be terms of distinction.
>
> (Bloom 1987: 183)

These arguments go a long way in helping to decry the university's change of mission, but they do little to justify why the university should not be able to educate more people. The argument here seems to rest on the fact that changes in the curriculum have simply made it easier for people to succeed in the university. This is not the same as arguing that more people couldn't benefit from a university education, however conceived.

The title of Bloom's book – *The Closing of the American Mind* – is important because it alludes to the way that education has become its opposite. 'Openness used to be the virtue that permitted us to seek the good by using reason. It now means accepting everything and denying reason's power' (Bloom 1987: 38), although others have pointed out that Bloom's own argument is itself rather closed (Plante and Eatwell 1992). For Bloom, at best we now have two kinds of education competing for our attention, at worst we have something passing for education which does not deserve the title:

> there are two kinds of openness, the openness of indifference – promoted with the twin purposes of humbling our intellectual pride and letting us be whatever we want to be, just as long as we don't want to be knowers – and the openness that invites us to the quest for knowledge and certitude, for which history and the various cultures provide a brilliant array of examples for examination.
>
> (Bloom 1987: 41)

In the same way that D'Souza will later argue that liberal education has become illiberal, Bloom argues that the openness implied by this new found democracy in knowledge is actually a closing of the mind to the serious matter of pursing the Truth. We have already seen the extent to which definitional discussions of PC often revolve around this Orwellian oppositional logic – freedom as tyranny, and so on – and both authors use this logic in the titles of their books. 'In short, instead of liberal education, what American students are getting is its diametrical opposite, an education in closed-mindedness and intolerance, which is to say, illiberal education' (D'Souza 1992: 229). Bloom argues that this closed-mindedness is the result of replacing one definition of virtue with another where: 'All that has really happened is that reason has been knocked off its perch, is less influential and more vulnerable as it joins the crowd of less worthy claims to the attention and support of civil society' (Bloom 1987: 208).

D'Souza, however, is more interested in highlighting the tyrannical way in which this new, so-called democratic education is upheld by its followers, that is, it is democratic in name, but not in nature, where 'debates are best conducted not by rational and civil exchange of ideas, but by accusation, intimidation, and official prosecution' (D'Souza 1992: 229). Here we see an important anti-PC theme, already referred to in the work of Cheney (1992), that PC is anti-freedom because of the slavish mentality it encourages amongst it supporters, and that once the political line is established it is acceptable to castigate those who do not follow the line. D'Souza, on his travels around US colleges, is able to find college professors who are able to support this position: 'ideological dogmatism is the norm, not the exception, in the "studies" programs, especially Women's Studies. Intimidation of nonfeminists in the classroom is routine' (Thomas Short, quoted in D'Souza 1992: 247).

Bloom is more subtle in his attack on this new form of slavery, arguing that democratic man has simply become a democratic *personality*, that is the man who has open access to exercise his critical faculties on everything around him has been replaced by the man who has been taught (*sic*) to accept that he must be tolerant of every idea that he comes across (Bloom 1987: 27). This is paradoxical because if D'Souza is correct then many colleges and universities are singularly unable to tolerate opinions not in keeping with a culture of PC. Although paradoxical it is not a significant difference in the texts of Bloom and D'Souza, for both accept the key Bloom point that a form of intellectual laziness has taken over the academy:

> It is truth itself which the *au courant* critics spurn, or more precisely, by reducing all truth to the level of opinion they spurn the legitimacy of any distinctions between truth and error. Yet what is the goal of liberal education if not the pursuit of truth?
>
> (D'Souza 1992: 179)

And they both agree on one of D'Souza's key points, that a distinguishing characteristic of this *au courant* is the intimidating atmosphere that surrounds it:

> It became almost impossible to question the radical orthodoxy without risking vilification, classroom disruption. Loss of confidence and respect for teaching, and the hostility of colleagues . . . Nothing could be said with impunity. Such an atmosphere made detached, dispassionate study impossible.
>
> (Bloom 1987: 355)

This brings us back to the adage referred to in the introductory chapter, that one should be careful not to throw the baby out with the bath water. Dirty bath water can be replaced, that is, an atmosphere of intimidation should be resisted. However, the deconstructivist baby remains to be countered. And this baby demands to be considered on intellectual grounds, because it is not that truth and error are now interchangeable, but that the traditional epistemological grounds for distinguishing between truth and opinion are being questioned. Indeed D'Souza names one of the key foes here, Stanley Fish, but is happy to dismiss him as more of a political radical: 'relativism paves the way for a toppling of the old rules, and the establishment of new ones based on political strength' (D'Souza 1992: 175). There would be no reason for Fish to disagree with this assessment, but the intellectual weight behind this comment is much more than 'he who shouts loudest wins' because this is a consequence of his case, not the foundation for it. The epistemological foundation for Fish's politics is that poststructural theory is every bit as robust as any 'light of reason' theory and, in this respect, both theories deserve to be debated on these merits rather than the extent to which they have been used to support 'the minority victim's revolution' (D'Souza 1992: 175), and the case for the 'equality in the republic of cultures' (Bloom 1987: 39).

Ultimately Bloom is concerned to protect the autonomy of the academy from various forms of social engineering. At one level they may only be very fleeting, and 'gone tomorrow', but at another more profound level they will, at some point, compromise the nature of the knowledge which is generated and disseminated in universities: 'Commitment was understood to be profounder than science, passion than reason, history than nature, the young than the old' (Bloom 1987: 314). And through the backdoor of this transformation will come the unfortunate consequence that a university will be seen as much about raising self-esteem as the search for truth. And, furthermore, that black studies, women's studies, etc., do nothing but disunite the common purpose that should be behind all intellectual endeavours. Ultimately for Bloom the task is straightforward: the 'light of reason' must be allowed to shine in the misguided mist of cultural relativism.

Liberal or illiberal education?

D'Souza takes the argument a step further, claiming that not only is the university no place to engage in life-affirming social projects, but in the process it is highly likely that it will become a centre for myths concerning individuals and social groups. This is little short of 'social therapy', not intellectual endeavour:

> There are many valid arguments against subscribing to the salutary 'noble lie,' but one is decisive. Even if it were deemed necessary for blacks to adopt a mythic view of their past, elaborating such a myth should not be

the task of the university. It is rather politicians and theologians who may be expected to comfort and inspire the people in this way. The university cannot engage in such an understanding without repudiating its fundamental purpose: the disinterested pursuit of truth. The University is not responsible for the preservation of political and psychic order. Often its mission is to disturb the peace, or arouse the conscience. No one who supports the university can live with noble lies, however benignly intended.

(D'Souza 1992: 120)

For D'Souza it is inevitable that such steps will undermine standards in the university. Not only will the criteria for what is acceptable on the university curriculum now be politically rather than intellectually based, but also the criteria for determining who is worthy of a university place will now have to be politically based. To use the colloquial term, this is 'dumbing-down big style', and, in Bloom's terms, can only result in the study of 'man' rather than 'Man'. It will inevitably result in the study of cultures, not Culture, particulars not Universals, and therefore will completely undermine the principles of epistemic knowledge established by Plato in *The Republic*. For D'Souza the practical consequences are dire:

Many minority students can now explain why they had such a hard time with Milton and Publius and Heisenberg. These men reflected white aesthetics, white philosophy, white science. Obviously minority students would fare much better if the university assigned black or Latino or Third World thought.

(D'Souza 1992: 244)

D'Souza's critique of 'studies' programmes is linked to his other main concern about the way in which the principle of equality of opportunity has been undermined:

Proportional representation for ethnic groups directly violates the democratic principle of equal opportunity for individuals, and the underlying concept of group justice is hostile both to individual equality and to excellence.

(D'Souza 1992: 55)

There are two important issues here. First, a fair system (of individual merit) is being replaced by an unfair system (of proportional representation). And, second, centring the representation on minority groups who have been discriminated against in the past will inevitably produce a range of unintended consequences. In practice we will have moved to a position where if a local community or a state (or, indeed, a whole country) has a percentage of variously defined social groupings, it is deemed to be just when the proportion of college places (or indeed in the wider context, jobs) are filled in exact correspondence.

D'Souza claims that this notion is widespread through higher education in the US and takes many guises. For example:

> Under Hyman's leadership, Berkeley began to depreciate the importance of merit criteria for admissions, in the belief that such criteria simply reflected and reproduced the effects of discrimination. In an effort to equalise racial representation on campus, Berkeley would continue to use merit criteria, but only to measure differences in academic preparation *within* groups.
>
> (D'Souza 1992: 27)

In philosophical terms this redefines equality as referring to outcomes rather than opportunities, and this is what D'Souza objects to, arguing that it is unfair on individual students to be competing for college places only with others in their social group. This might well result in a student from one social group achieving a place at a university, while another, who may have scored higher on the same test, is rejected, simply because s/he was a member of a different social group, with a higher average test score. There appear to be many other undesirable consequences at work here. For example social groups could be identified not purely from their statistical representation in the population, but through a political discussion concerning their worthiness to be considered as victims of past discriminations. Thus black students could be high on the list to be included, but children from one-parent families might not. It is clear that D'Souza is unhappy about the politics involved in these discussions, which can only result in social groups vying for victim status (a theme which is central to Sykes's polemic discussed below). Ultimately: 'high standards do not discriminate against anyone except those who fail to meet them' (D'Souza 1992: 250).

For D'Souza, a notion of social justice has replaced one based on individual merit, which is poorer in principle and ill-conceived in practice: 'Prior to entrance to university there is only one way to determine academic excellence and that is on the grounds of academic preparation' (D'Souza 1992: 54). The consequences are, again, dire:

> Separatist black and Hispanic groups become a haven for the anxieties that spring from sharp differences in academic preparation among various social groups. Indeed separatism can serve as a form of group therapy, in which affirmative action beneficiaries persuade themselves that their difficulties on campus are predominantly, if not exclusively, the consequence of rampant bigotry.
>
> (D'Souza 1992: 51)

The problem with this line of argument is that it can easily distract us from considering similar problems when one adopts an equality of opportunity principle. That is, it is not a case of a clear principle being undermined by an ill-conceived one, because the former has many undesirable consequences as well.

Not least of which is the extent to which the resources at one's disposal in order to take advantage of educational opportunities are unevenly distributed, and thus it will never be clear whether a place at university was won on individual merit, and how much this was effectively 'sponsored' in various ways. This sponsorship might include the large variation between monies available to local school districts, private coaching for test preparation, parental savings accounts for their offspring's chosen university course, and of course the 'cultural capital' invested by parents themselves in their offspring's general education. It is surely for these reasons that many commentators speak of the need for a 'level playing field', before we can even begin to consider dismantling affirmative action policies. That is to say, it is as much the 'savage inequalities' (Kozol 1992) of today as reparations for the past which has produced the need for affirmative action. D'Souza's counter to this is to recognize that there are such inequalities in the US, and it is right that they should be addressed. But the case should be made on the merits of individual cases, and not on one's membership of a particular social group: 'One can only raise the statistical average of a group by improving the achievement of the individuals within it' (D'Souza 1992: 189).

The most damning criticisms of the university by both Bloom and D'Souza are reserved for curriculum matters:

> There is an enormous difference between saying, as teachers once did, 'You must learn to see the world as Homer and Shakespeare did,' and saying, as teachers now do, 'Homer and Shakespeare had some of the same concerns as you and can enrich your vision of the world.' In the former approach students are challenged to discover new experiences and reassess the old; in the latter, they are free to use the books in any way they please.
>
> (Bloom 1987: 374)

> Certainly arguments can be made to include or exclude a theory or a book in a science or literature course, but such arguments must be made in terms of scholarly merit, which is the only currency in which the academy is qualified to trade.
>
> (D'Souza 1992: 85)

There are pedagogical questions here as well as canonical ones. And both have been important in PC debates concerning multiculturalism. These will be discussed in some detail in Chapter 5, but we can see here that both authors are troubled by how the cognitive component in pedagogy has slowly given way to a more affective one (Bloom), and how decisions on curriculum content have been unnecessarily politicized (D'Souza). The problem in both cases is clear. It is not that their arguments are not sound, but they want to rest them on criteria which are not political, and thereby they want the accusation of PC to rest solely on the shoulders of those who want change, and not on those, like themselves, who wish to uphold tradition. It is one thing to appeal to the idea that: 'Programs based upon judicious use of great texts provide the royal road to students' hearts. Their gratitude at learning of Achilles or the categorical imperative is boundless' (Bloom 1987: 344). Quite another to claim that this is not an appeal at all, but a simple fact. The statement may be true but surely it could equally be said that students might be eternally grateful for what they learnt about Malcolm X or Derrida.

If the life of Malcolm X is simply being used to encourage black students to identify with him it is clear that Bloom has a case. However, to use his life as the basis for a discussion about how individuals form their identities and whether these are discovered or constructed, is surely to *analyse* identity, not affirm it. Similarly, if the work of Derrida causes students to reread authoritative texts with a view to their readerly or writerly qualities, to what is absent as well as present in a text, and how much the author is 'spoken' rather than being the speaker, these are surely academic questions, and highly appropriate in encouraging a critical engagement with canonical works, particularly if there is a danger that they themselves might be celebrated rather than analysed. Similarly, although physics students may come to reject much of the sociology and philosophy of science, both disciplines are surely worthy of some merit in encouraging students to interrogate their own conceptions of scientific knowledge.

D'Souza is measured in his conclusions, and it is clear from the following that he is really much more concerned with *how* things are taught rather than who or what is granted canonical status: 'Colleges would promote better understanding among students, and future respect among cultures, if they taught both western and non-western philosophy, history, and literature in a more balanced and truthful manner' (D'Souza 1992: 93).

Ultimately, for both Bloom and D'Souza the key problem is the way that universities have begun pandering to various social engineering projects:

> Historians were asked to rewrite the history of the world, and of the United States in particular, to show that nations were always conspiratorial systems of domination and exploitation. Psychologists were being pestered to prove the psychological damage done by inequality and the existence of nuclear weapons, and to show that American statesmen were paranoid about the Soviet Union. Political scientists were urged to interpret the North Vietnamese as nationalist and to remove the stigma of totalitarianism from the Soviet Union.
>
> (Bloom 1987: 354–355)

From this perspective it is imperative that universities maintain autonomy in all matters of their work, because how can 'the disinterested pursuit of truth' proceed if facts need to fit political, social, and economic agendas? It simply should not be the job of a university to ensure that any of these agendas are met. There are other ways and institutions through which this can be done, and in this regard a PC university is not a university. The problem with this argument should now be clear: many theorists working in universities today simply do not hold to a traditional view of truth. This is a PC matter because it has politicized epistemological questions. And, logically, this should not mean that these PC academics also share a belief in the need for *affirming* university knowledge. Also, it is not clear that the kind of Greek academy envisaged by Plato has ever really been a key defining characteristic of the whole history of any Western university, and thus Bloom's argument is really more aspirational than an appeal to return to something that has been lost through forms of political correctness.

The victim's charter?

Sykes's book looks beyond higher education in order to discover the roots of a much wider social movement (Sykes 1992). For him what is being witnessed in education is symptomatic of broader social trends. Indeed, D'Souza paves the way: 'Diversity, tolerance, multiculturalism, pluralism – these phrases are perennially on the lips of the university administrators. They are the principles and slogans of the victim's revolution' (D'Souza 1992: 17). Sykes's book is more about social theory than the demise of academic excellence, and he attempts to lay bare the background to the cultural changes that have brought about this demise. For Sykes the cultural malaise is all around us, typified in the belief that: 'Increasingly, Americans act as if they had received a lifelong indemnification from misfortune and a contractual release from personal responsibility' (Sykes 1992: 15).

The 'lawyer's charter', as it is often portrayed in the popular media because of the way it enables lawyers to hold to account every organization in the US for their, so-called, negligent behaviour towards their clients, customers, or employees, is roundly condemned by Sykes with the use of telling examples: 'In Framington, Massachusetts, a young man steals a car from a parking lot and is killed while driving it. His family then sues the proprietor of the parking lot for failing to take steps to prevent such thefts' (Sykes 1992: 3).

However, Sykes does not just want to document the absurd consequences of the victim's revolution, his main aim is to uncover its social causes. To do this he turns first to the work of Nisbet and Rieff, and later to the work of Lasch (Sykes 1992). The thesis is relatively straightforward: the twentieth century saw the gradual demise of inner-directed man, the Protestant beloved of Weberian sociology, who was driven by the need to prove his or her worthiness to enter the gates of Heaven, and who consequently carried a huge burden of guilt should this worthiness be questioned. The demise of this man is a theme of much twentieth-century literature, typified by Kafka's K, lost in an alien and alienating world, and in more psychoanalytic work by the theme of narcissism: 'Not the free individual, but the lost individual; not independence but isolation; not self-discovery but self-obsession; not to conquer but to be conquered; these are the major states of mind in contemporary literature' (Nisbet quoted in Sykes 1992: 30).

The symptom manifests itself as a deep-felt sense of anxiety: where there was once purpose there is now alienation, where there was once surety there is now fear, where there was once security there is now drift.

> Somehow, as man became more and more highly individualized, he became less human, less attached to a sense of place or purpose that had been, it seemed in retrospect, an essential part of the human condition. Instead of being freed from the oppressive bonds of the past, he often found himself alone in a world without mooring, norms, sense of direction, or purpose.
>
> (Sykes 1992: 49)

It is in this context that inner-directed man begins to seek refuge from this turmoil, not from his own resolve but by conformity to new forms of social regulation. This is exactly the intellectual space that Sykes needs in order to outline the nature of the cultural transformation that has taken place. It is as if 'modern' man simply does not have the inner resolve to deal with his own anxiety and looks instead in 'other' directions for comfort. For Sykes this is exactly the moment when personal responsibility exits the social stage, and a completely new play begins, where:

> Fears become phobias, concerns become complexes, and anxieties become compulsions. Smoking can be transmuted into 'Tobacco Use Disorder,' shyness into 'Social phobia,' and lousy grades into 'Academic Achievement Disorder'.
>
> (Sykes 1992: 39)

It is as if twentieth-century America could be summarized as a period in which an army of social institutions emerged in order to deal with the anxieties caused by modernity. Furthermore, that these services became commodities, where thirty minutes of therapy could be bought as the first step towards the cure for social phobia. And where the 'normal' frustrations and challenges of everyday life became medicalized 'symptoms' of social 'diseases', requiring an army of qualified practitioners to treat: 'Once the language of disease and addiction could be applied to behaviour rather than merely to biological disorders, almost any aspect of human life could be redefined in medical terms' (Sykes 1992: 136).

This theme, explored by Szasz twenty years earlier, and popularized in Kesey's novel, *One Flew Over the Cuckoo's Nest*, is placed into a contemporary PC context by Sykes (Szasz 1972; Kesey 1968). Whereas Szasz had argued that 'mental illness' was merely a metaphor, albeit an extremely useful one for psychiatry, and was being used as a means of social control, and where those who were a social nuisance to society were reclassified as ill, Sykes utilizes the idea to castigate a more general therapeutic industry: 'Since existential doubt was now a sickness, the role of the priest could be assumed by the psychotherapist' (Sykes 1992: 88).

However the earlier work of Szasz is instructive for two reasons. First, Szasz recognized the extent to which 'mental illness' could be an extremely useful label to have, for, in certain circumstances, it could act as the means to absolve oneself of personal responsibility for one's actions. This is a central feature of the McMurphy character in *One Flew Over the Cuckoo's Nest*, where he feigns mental illness because he perceives life in the mental institution to be far easier than life in jail. This paradox in absolving oneself of personal responsibility is clearly present in Sykes's work. However, it is not clear the extent to which it perhaps contradicts part of his central thesis, for if other-directed man lacks the resolve to deal with his own anxieties, is not the deliberate, rational decision to exploit a victimizing label evidence that he is not so much a victim as a free agent?

Furthermore, if the blanket term 'mental illness' is a social construct, and simply a convenient blanket term through which one might label the 'undesir-able', what is there to stop a more thoroughgoing 'social construction of reality', where terms like 'intelligence' and 'academic standards' are made subject to the same theorizing? In this reading much of the interactionist sociology of the 1960s might be viewed as an important forerunner to what Bloom and D'Souza came to see as the politicization of education. For authors such as Becker and Keddie it would have been inconceivable that one would not recognize how all educational concepts are socially constructed (Becker 1952; Keddie 1974). Thus we have Sykes engaged in the politicization of terms at the same time as Bloom and D'Souza are seeking to depoliticize terms.

Sykes's main concern is with the way in which American citizens are only so in name because in reality they have become 'clients' of a burgeoning therapy industry. And this has produced the most invidious consequence: by not seeing themselves as having to take responsibility for the paths of their lives, they have increasingly come to see themselves not just as victims, but also as entitled, by right, to some assurance that they will be furnished with 'life, love, and the pursuit of happiness'. Here, the notion of 'a right' has been transformed from its 'negative' formulation, that there should be no impediment to individuals pursuing their own interests, into its 'positive' formulation, that there should be social policy to ensure that everyone has the means to pursue equally their interests. In terms of political ideology this has had the effect of moving away from a liberal approach to freedom towards a more avowedly egalitarian approach (Berlin 1958). It is here where we can see the most obvious connection between Sykes's work and the earlier work of Bloom and D'Souza, that is, how equality of opportunity and competition on the basis of individual merit has become equality of outcome and social justice for all for social groups. And not only was this fast becoming an important pillar in PC debates, but it also indicates how much traditional political ideologies were never far from the surface.

In a variation on the theme that the ends don't justify the means, and how PC causes have often ended up with undesirable consequences, Sykes is quick to indicate that the left are divided on the question of what exactly entitlement entitles one to: 'We must not let the fact that we are the victims of injustice lull us into abrogating respect for our own lives' (King, quoted in Sykes 1992: 68). However, for Sykes the ensuing social policy did just that:

> The insistence that minorities be given all the benefits they would have had, had they not been the victims of racism drove the civil rights movement to shift its focus from equality of *opportunity* to equality of *result*s. This translated into policies of redress in which race alone was regarded as an entitlement.
>
> (Sykes 1992: 198)

Indeed, Sykes has support for this view from within the black community: 'This racism is based on sympathy that says that because of your race, we will give you excuses for not preparing yourself and not being as good as you can be' (Thomas, quoted in Sykes 1992: 201). Either this is the unintended consequence of pursuing egalitarian social policies or it is embedded in the social policies themselves. Either way, the result has simply exacerbated the sense that, as victim, one is entitled to redress. And, as we have already seen in the work of D'Souza, this is an entitlement based on membership of a *social group* who have been identified as suffering from oppression in the past, and nothing to do with an *individual*'s social circumstances in the present. D'Souza is scathing and dismissive: 'The old racists sought to prove inferiority through ridiculous methods such as craniology; the new racists in the dean's office take inferiority for granted' (D'Souza 1992: 241).

In this thesis victim status is itself victimizing, at best it simply perpetuates a state of dependence – on the institutions that uphold their victim status – and, at worst it actively contributes to individuals seeing themselves as victims and not agents in the first place. The political ideology underneath these sentiments is not entirely clear, because there will be those on the left who will see a system of entitlements as simply an accommodation to a fundamentally unequal and unfair society, but equally there will be those on the right who will see it as an impediment to an emerging system of more open opportunities. More broadly it might be opposed because individual liberty is the core defining principle of American society, and a large welfare state is anathema to that principle. Furthermore, as Sykes makes clear towards the end of the book, it is important that this imbalance in the social order be put right:

> The best model for *caritas* is the functioning family, which blends instruction, affection, and reproof. Just as the family is the crucible of character, it is also the indispensable institution for transmitting values. Only in the family do we see that freedom and responsibility are not necessarily exclusive or contradictory. Society can offer support and assistance to the family in its mission; it can never take its place.
>
> (Sykes 1992: 251)

In this reading PC is problematic because it upsets the role of the traditional American family. Regardless of whether it has any resonance with the ways in which millions of Americans actually live their lives, the appeal is a powerful one. What is much more controversial is whether this will, in reality, simply ease the tax burden of those who already enjoy considerable educational opportunities, and dismantle the platform by which those who are the offspring of dysfunctional and economically unsuccessful families might seek more opportunities. Sykes's conclusion is thus a very conservative one with an appeal to a traditional right-wing message that we would do better to roll back the state, and with it all the social policy that supports the therapeutic culture and the victim status of its recipients. And this confirms the need to read carefully the political ideology which supports arguments against forms of political correctness.

Conclusion

Bloom, D'Souza, and Sykes are damning in their criticisms of the ways in which higher education changed considerably for the worst in the latter part of the twentieth century. For Bloom multiculturalism has substituted reasoned debate for life-affirming identity politics. For D'Souza a politicized curriculum and ill-conceived notions of social justice have substituted for academic excellence based on individual merit. And for Sykes a series of entitlements and victim status have substituted for personal responsibility, and produced the rally call: 'I am not responsible; it's not my fault' (Sykes 1992: 11). In broad terms, the grandest substitution has been of 'Man', and the study of what is Universal, for 'man' and the study of what is particular. And when victim status is added into the equation the combination is lethal. Not only does the lofty become low, but the emancipatory potential of education becomes its opposite:

> The term liberal derives from the term liberalism, which refers to the free person, as distinguished from the slave. It is in liberal education, properly devised and understood that minorities and indeed all students will find the means for their true and permanent emancipation.
>
> (D'Souza 1992: 23)

In PC debates we see this strand of liberal education and 'cultural literacy' (Hirsch 1988) critiqued and defended. The authors in this chapter have all sought to defend it. Many of the authors who will appear in subsequent chapters have sought to critique it. What is interesting in debates about PC is how conservative authors helped to shape the view that those who opposed this traditional liberal argument were its opposite, that is, 'illiberal'. In this way the authors were able to considerably shape the contours of PC debate. Fundamentally, the question became one of challenging those who would oppose truth, openness, and fairness. Put this way it is hardly surprising that it was more likely that one would become proud of being anti-PC rather than pro-PC. However, in rising to the challenges set by these authors several key PC questions emerged: Upon what grounds is 'greatness' determined? Upon what foundation is truth founded? Why is support for the status quo not considered to be political? Upon what basis is an educational test deemed to be objective? And how can competition be equal in an unequal society?

3

Look right and left before proceeding
The political contours of PC debate in the US

Introduction

In the previous chapter key themes in the rise of political correctness in the US in the late 1980s and early 1990s were identified. A consistent message of many conservative texts was to show how the educational status quo – built on the disinterested pursuit of truth, the dissemination of canonical texts, and access to higher education through individual merit – had been disrupted by forms of political correctness. The key purpose behind this chapter is to look at the extent to which this mounting campaign against PC was *manufactured* by right-leaning intellectuals and commentators, and thus to ask whether PC was simply a convenient derogatory label to discredit broader left-wing political ideas. Furthermore, if PC causes *are truly* representative of the left, how universal is the support for it on the left itself? Put simply, is PC a straw man manufactured by the right, or has it always been a brainchild of the left? Throughout the chapter the broader question of the usefulness of the categories right and left will also be considered, as well as to ask what light can be shed on this question by a consideration of PC.

Political radicals and epistemological conservatives

From the rise of communitarianism in the US (Etzioni 2000) and the allied notion of the Third Way in British politics (Giddens 1998), to the question of whether the US is best described as being morally divided rather than politically divided (Hunter 1991), and whether British political debate has undermined people's interest in politics in general (Furedi 2005a), it is clear that the traditional divide between right and left has been under challenge for some considerable time. A major contention of this book is that just below the surface of all debates about PC are deeper questions about political ideologies, and these ideologies are broadly still those of the right and the left. That said it is clear that PC debates are extremely helpful in identifying the ways in which the terms right and left have changed, or perhaps better, new emphases have emerged. These emphases might best be described as epistemological rather than strictly political, and they will be raised in this chapter and returned to throughout the rest of the book.

There is a simple answer to the question of whether the terms right and left still have much resonance in political discussions, and that is that they are still used frequently in order to contrast political positions. They are also used frequently by protagonists in debates about PC, as should become clear throughout this chapter. In those debates, although it is not always overtly clear, right-wing commentators usually support most if not all of the following: a general support for the merits of a capitalist economic system, and the validity of a representative system of democratic government, and where free enterprise, the profit motive, consumer sovereignty, and individual responsibility are important cornerstones. These cornerstones are usually given some ideological bolstering by the promotion of ideas such as individuals know best how to spend their own money, that social inequality is an important motivator, and that this, in some way, reflects a state of nature. Although the role of the state would generally be underplayed, it would always be portrayed variously as: independent arbitrator; defender of basic democratic rights; and overseer of the rule of law, through which everyone is guaranteed equal treatment. The texts by Friedman and Friedman and Hayek are seminal in this respect (Friedman and Friedman 1980; Hayek 1944).

Those on the left usually promote the view that a capitalist economy, if left to its own devices, would always privilege economic power over political power, and that those who have wealth will always be able to privilege themselves and their offspring when it comes to educational opportunities and life chances. These views would normally be supported by reference to the unacceptable use and exploitation of human and natural resources in the pursuit of profit, and to how all institutions of the state are prone to be compromised by the self-interest of those representing capitalist interests. These views usually lead to the conclusion that the arbitrary social inequality and sense of injustice that this system inevitably generates requires that we design forms of redistributive justice, and make the necessary interventions to produce 'a level playing field' in access to educational opportunities and life chances. This is often bolstered by a belief in notions of equality which emphasize equality of outcome rather than simply equality of opportunity. Clearly, many of these ideas can be found in Marxist and Socialist literature (e.g. Tawney 1931; Miliband 1969), although it is not always clear in PC debates whether the implications of this are fully understood.

These contrasting ideological positions are themselves often supported by bedrock ideas about human nature. Whereas the right tend to use the metaphor of the jungle – emphasizing the inevitability of inequality and competition for resources – the left, in contrast, questions the inevitability of both, suggesting that forms of social justice are the hallmarks of civilization. The right's appeal to justice usually comes in the form of respect for the rule of law, and the fact that, on the one hand, competition is rooted in meritocratic principles, and, on the other, that individual liberty is a more important principle than state-administered forms of social justice. Finally, whereas the left's emphasis on equality of outcome usually ends up as an argument in favour of forms of egalitarianism and an equal distribution of societal resources, the right, in defining equality in terms of equality of opportunity, would emphasize the fairness of an equal competition for societal resources.

There are two further clusters of ideas, at whose hearts are problematic cores, at least for the purposes of maintaining a clear ideological dichotomy between left and right. The first relates to the ways in which the left and right use notions of the truth. Whereas the right are usually quick to make references to 'Nature', 'Reason', 'positivistic rules of method', 'objectivity', and, generally, the disinterested pursuit of truth, the left are similarly quick to point out that human nature can invariably be demonstrated to be socially constructed, and that references to 'objectivity' and 'disinterested' more often than not are simply strategies to hide vested interests, and to bolster an *ideological* position by giving it an air of abstract authority, which either it does not deserve or simply doesn't exist. This contrast between left and right however is complicated by the fact that many on the left do share a belief (*sic*) in The Truth and hold an epistemological position not dissimilar to many on the right. In this context many PC debates highlight how radical politics and conservative epistemologies are at the heart of why the contrast between left and right appears increasingly unhelpful as a fundamental ideological dichotomy.

Furthermore, whereas many on the right would support the idea that Western societies represent a pinnacle of civilized living – that they somehow embody all that Reason has to offer – many on the left are scathing of this ideological gloss which has been brushed over an imperialistic cultural edifice. However, that said, it is clear that at least some on the left do share much that has come to be associated with Enlightenment thinking, and, in general, share the belief that Western societies continue to contribute positively to the idea of human progress. In what might be argued to be the most controversial area of political thought, this would include subscribing to notions of the 'end of history', where on the right there is often adherence to the ideas of Fukuyama (1992), and the claim that Western liberal democracies are superior to all other social formations throughout history, and on the left, we often find the analogous view that the 'rainbow alliance' of groups disadvantaged by the capitalist mode of production do represent a universal call to the formation of a truly Socialist State, and the beginning of a truly *human* history (which in strict Marxist terms is also an end to history – that is, one based on economic class antagonism).

This Socialist end of history needs to be contrasted with those on the left who have jettisoned any notions of meta-narrative, and who now entertain the idea that all political debate is inevitably fractured; that all universal principles are, in reality, forms of rhetoric; and that any references to 'universals' are nothing more than appeals. In this strand of thinking Marxism maintains its appeal by reference to 'all that is solid melts into air', rather than to the historic mission of the proletariat to do what history requires of them. For some this will sound dangerously close to pessimistic forms of postmodernism, and is rejected by those on the left who wish to hold on to the idea that within Marx's theory of historical materialism there is a realist epistemology which will enable us to see the reality behind the capitalist appearance, and maintain our belief that there *is* more to political debate than mere rhetoric. Couched in these terms it is clear that there will be many on the left and right who may differ on the *content* of political ideology, but who will agree on method, and on the validity of Enlightenment principles.

In what follows I have taken works by many of the leading figures in PC debates in the US over the past twenty years. Before proceeding to discuss liberal left texts the first two sections look at the first round of conservative texts. For the purposes of clarity in exposition I have separated those authors whose main concern is with the politics of PC from those whose main concern is the correctness of PC.

The political curriculum

As we have already seen, a recurrent theme in PC literature is the castigation of those who are perceived as unnecessarily politicizing education (Cheney 1992). This encroachment takes many forms: college administrators who seek to recruit staff and students on grounds which are not strictly meritocratic; teachers who avowedly support political positions in the classroom; curricular material chosen because of its sensitivity to political causes. And, most fundamentally of all, there is a mocking contempt for those who have given up on the 'disinterested pursuit of truth'. All these themes are present in the work of Atlas (1990), Kimball (1990), and Anderson (1992).

> Many [of these] changes, such as the demand that the curriculum be recast to accommodate racial, sexual, or ethnic quotas, are overtly political. Other changes, such as the attack on the ideal of disinterested scholarship or the rise of deconstruction and its potency, also rest partly on political presuppositions, although often in ways that are not immediately apparent.
>
> (Kimball 1990: 34)

Anderson is clear that overt political bias is almost endemic within American universities. Quoting studies on the political allegiances of academic staff in the humanities and social sciences he is adamant that something must be afoot: 'There is nothing in the natural order of things that would dictate such a small representation of republicans and conservatives in [some] intellectual fields' (Anderson 1992: 145). One of Anderson's recommendations to rectify political bias is to ask that the governing bodies of universities take more care to appoint on the grounds of intellectual acumen: 'Milton Friedman an overseer of Harvard, Jacques Barzun a trustee of Stanford, Allan Bloom a trustee of Dartmouth, Thomas Sowell, a trustee of Yale, William Bennett a regent of the University of California. No timid, uncertain voices here' (Anderson 1992: 201) – but perhaps rather conservative?

Bennett's work is alluded to by Atlas, Kimball, and Anderson, and expressed as a concern for the ways in which 'all that is good' is currently being interpreted in curriculum circles:

> Textbooks are being revised to reflect the new dogmas of inclusion. Revisionist interpretations of history that seek to rectify a perceived imbalance in the treatment of minorities by dwelling on their achievements have been widely adopted. The politics of ethnic representation are as common a feature of American public education now as the pledge of allegiance and compulsory gym.
>
> (Atlas 1990: 14)

> this self-righteous emphasis on 'diversity,' 'relevance,' and 'sensitivity' provides a graphic example of the way in which the teaching of the humanities in our colleges and universities has been appropriated by special interests and corrupted by politics.
>
> (Kimball 1990:3)

We can also see in both of these cases echoes of Bloom's concerns that multi-cultural agendas are changing not just the content of the curriculum, but its nature as well, promoting a concern for well-being and self-esteem above disinterested scholarship. One potential solution to this problem is promoted by Graff (1992). He suggests that the careful dissemination and discussion of controversial political matters should mean that 'both sides of each coin' would always be considered, leaving it up to individual students to pursue their own lines of argument in defence of particular political positions. Indeed, it could be argued that curriculum models which emphasize process over content, and skills over knowledge, are slowly being given a more central place in the higher education curriculum. And, thereby, the ability to critically assess and to sustain an argument is taken to be the axis around which the higher education curriculum should revolve, as opposed to a more traditional notion based on the possession of particular educational knowledge and content.

Although this proposition merits serious consideration it clearly fails to address what other authors consider to be the root problem, that the ability to argue, or engage in rhetoric, cannot, and should not, be a substitute for the disinterested pursuit of truth. In this line of reasoning what is wrong with education (more often than not education in the humanities and the social sciences) is that too many academics today not only lack confidence in their knowledge, but also actively support the view that there is little difference between truth and falsehood, right and wrong.

the traditional ideal of disinterested scholarship is bluntly dismissed as a cover for class or ethnic privilege and western culture is itself pilloried as a bastion of unacknowledged sexist and imperialistic attitudes. Given this intellectual climate, it is hardly surprising that criticism should degenerate into a species of cynicism for which nothing is properly understood until it is exposed as corrupt, duplicitous, or hypocritical.

(Kimball 1990: 76)

Here again the bogeyman is 'deconstruction' – the literary textual method – and it is perhaps not too much of an exaggeration to suggest that PC often acts merely as a context in which to denigrate and poke fun at this intellectual tradition: 'Do you suppose Professor Fish would be offended if we agree with his nutty theses and pointed out that what he wrote confirms that his words have no literal meaning and no intrinsic merit?' (Anderson 1992: 150). Atlas is a little more considered in his approach and recognizes the usefulness of developing critical skills, and even using deconstruction in teaching, but his conclusion is much more conservative: 'without a common culture, a culture that possesses certain shared assumptions, there will soon be no America to imagine, no common myth around which to organize our aspirations' (Atlas 1990: 131).

This conclusion is reached by many authors, perhaps not quite as starkly, but nonetheless it is very common, and it suggests that, somehow, those who support PC causes are 'un-American'. Here, PC is itself a euphemism, which implies that one would prefer to denigrate one's nationhood rather than celebrate it. Here, PC signals a Mannheimian split between ideologues and utopians (Mannheim 1936), between those who defend the status quo and those who want it radically transformed; between Western civilization and the rest; truth seekers and relativists; etc. In a related fashion the term PC can also act as a euphemism for a lack of faith in the rationality and sovereignty of the 'individual'. For the right he is the autonomous, rational, calculating man, for the left she is the hapless victim of situated, contingent, historical forces. Here we see, on the one hand, the individual as the personification of the Enlightenment, able, through calm but rigorous reasoning, to position himself on the top of Mount Olympus and see the world for what it really is, to be contrasted with the postmodern individual who is situated by time, space, and language and lacking the tools to represent a reality existing independently of her interpretation. Furthermore, we have the individual as the agent of his actions, the author of his words, and in charge of his life-chance trajectory, to be contrasted with the individual who is hopelessly compromised and victimized by the social, economic, and historical circumstances over which she has little or no real control.

The significance of these contrasts can be seen most starkly in higher education in the politicization of the very notion of the individual. From general debates about what it means to succeed through one's own efforts, through to literary debates about whether authors are actually author-ities, we have seen PC act as a conduit for those who would, and would not, use the word. This was starkly highlighted in the *cause célèbre* case of the college memo, which pointed out that the word 'individual' should be given a 'red flag' status, as if to imply that users of the word were demonstrating an insensitivity to the circumstances of minorities on campus, and thereby undermining progressive causes (D'Souza 1992: 10). However, it is one thing to promote an Enlightenment view of the 'disinterested pursuit of the truth' by autonomous, rational, individuals, quite another to claim that it is somehow inherently connected to a belief in the desirability of American capitalism and representative government:

> With their criticism of the 'logocentric' and 'phallocratic' Western tradition, their insistence that language always refers only to itself, and their suspicion of logic and rationality, they exhibit a species of scepticism that is essentially nihilistic and deeply at odds with the ideal of a liberal arts education – ideals, it must be added, that also underlie the democratic institutions and social life of the West.
>
> (Kimball 1990: xii)

A consistent theme in anti-PC literature is how a radicalized group of 'impostors in the temple' have unacceptably politicized the higher education curriculum (Anderson 1992). However, this may simply have the effect of drawing attention away from the political foundations of their own arguments. What PC debates reveal here is how support for traditions in higher education and the status quo in general are not political acts, but criticisms of them are. Ultimately, this support rests on a fundamental belief that key features of the American way of life are somehow 'natural', and because of this they must be more valid than those which emphasize social construction and political rhetoric.

The correct curriculum

The debate about what exactly the word political means in the term PC is multi-layered, but there are many authors who are concerned about the *correctness*, that is, the *means* by which this assault on Western democracy is carried through – not through argument and discussion, but through intimidation. This is ironic in the extreme, because the scepticism towards 'truth' which one often sees in radical thinkers does not appear to apply when it comes to moral self-righteousness. This approach to PC is adopted most notably by Sowell (1993), Bernstein (1994), and Leo (1994).

Bernstein is forthright in his critique, and is quick to connect PC with The Terror of the French Revolution; the sense that when you *know absolutely* that you are right, any means are thereby justified by those ends, and this is precisely what produces a *Dictatorship of Virtue* (Bernstein 1994). Given the early reference to The Terror it might be assumed that Bernstein's critique will be uncompromising. However, he emphasizes that the dictatorship is likely to be temporary and, unlike Marx's 'Dictatorship of the Proletariat', it will not lead inexorably to a fully fledged maturation, but eventually return to the hard fought-for pre-revolutionary traditions. The current phase of PC is, therefore, just that, an unfortunate phase, a *dérapage*, a slide into dogmaticism. In education this slide is typified by the uncritical acceptance of the dogma of multiculturalism, a dogma worthy of a religious sect, along with some damning language for non-believers thrown in for good measure.

In one of numerous associations with the ideas of George Orwell, Bernstein is guided by Orwell's pronouncement that: 'The object of power is power . . . One does not establish a dictatorship in order to safeguard a revolution: one makes the revolution in order to safeguard the dictatorship' (Orwell, quoted in Bernstein 1994: 343). In this regard *correctness* is the machinery that one uses in order to maintain power, which ultimately comes to a head when everything in the political orthodoxy becomes beyond question, in fact any questioning of it is punished. What is chilling in this message is not that intolerance has been adopted by those within left-wing political parties, for it is not uncommon for the right to associate such tactics with, for example, Mao's cultural revolution, Castro's Cuba, or a Trotskyite world revolutionary movement, but that it should be associated with schools, colleges, and universities, in their virtuous pursuit of a multicultural agenda. And that it should need policing by an army of revolutionary cadres who are firmly ensconced in the administrative, faculty, and senior management structures of all educational establishments:

> They will cover us over with a thick glue of piousness, which, in turn, will smother argument. They will undermine the quest for objective truth with a riot of subjectivities. They will turn almost anything that they do not like into one of the new cardinal sins – racism, sexism, sexual harassment, homophobia – and they will try to punish those who commit those sins. They will confuse knowledge and an appreciation of other cultures with cultural chauvinism, the super patriotism of the small group. They will turn reading into an exercise in ethnic boosterism and the cultivation of 'self-esteem'.
>
> (Bernstein 1994: 345)

This multicultural theme of 'raising esteem' has already been discussed in the context of Bloom's work, and will be returned to in Chapter 5 on multi-culturalism itself. The pertinent point here is not so much whether this should be part of the curriculum, but the unacceptable means by which it is administrated – through a self-righteous understanding that it is unquestionably the right thing to do, and indeed, that it would be 'insensitive' to question it. In this context PC has come to be associated with forms of indoctrination and brainwashing, where not only is it deemed to be intuitively obvious what should be taught but one is cast as an enemy if one doesn't see it. Leo, like many others, has been able to poke enormous fun at the burgeoning sensitivity culture, particularly at the means by which those who are 'insensitive' might become more enlightened, or properly adjusted. White males are deemed to be particularly culpable in this regard and must learn to own their privilege as a prerequisite for change: 'the attempt to bewilder and disorient young whites with the startling news that they are oppressors, followed a concerted attempt to render them guilty enough to seek approved re-education by an anointed diversity consultant' (Leo 1994: 288).

Here the word *correctness* in PC quickly becomes endowed with a host of undesirable connotations – from ensuring that people act and think in certain ways, through to adjusting their thinking if they don't. Educational establishments are thereby charged with having produced their own correctional facilities to mirror those more traditionally associated with penal reform institutions. But, once again we find ourselves having to ask whether the overt concern for 'dirty bath water' is actually masking a covert desire to dispose of a political 'baby'? For example, throughout Sowell's detailed discussion of all that is wrong with American education he constantly emphasizes how forms of indoctrination have replaced real education, but doesn't give anywhere near the attention to a defence of American political institutions that one might imagine would be required if we are to accept the premise he outlines in his preface:

> The particular subject matter of these ideological courses and programs may range from race to the environment or foreign policy, but the general approach is the same, not only in its fundamental anti-intellectualism, but also in its underlying hostility to American society and western civilization, and the tenaciousness or even dishonesty with which it attempts to indoctrinate.
>
> (Sowell 1993: x)

Sowell's examples of the latter are telling, based on testimonies from numerous people working throughout education, but these appear to suffice as the defence for the efficacy of the American way of life. Echoing the work of Sykes (1992), Sowell castigates psycho-therapeutic 'education', and the fact that students are much more likely to preface a statement with the words 'I feel', rather than 'I think' or 'I conclude' (Sowell 1993: 5), and proceeds to discuss the ways in which these forms of multiculturalism are policed rather than taught: 'Being "politically correct" is *not* simply a matter of holding certain opinions on various social or educational issues. Political correctness is *imposing those opinions on others* by harassment or punishment for expressing different views' (Sowell 1993: 201). But throughout the book one struggles to find examples of how exactly 'real' education might be brought to bear on re-establishing a more traditional educational orthodoxy. Indeed, perhaps we should just accept that this is not an orthodoxy at all, but a common-sense, factual education, and needs little justification.

The left strikes back

In the late 1980s and the early 1990s almost all the books on PC came from conservative thinkers. However, increasingly, authors from the liberal left began to publish their responses. These responses were not uniform: some authors defended many of the PC causes (e.g. Choi and Murphy 1992), some sought to expose the anti-PC campaign as mythical (e.g. Wilson 1996; Feldstein 1997), some accepted much of the right-wing critique but restated a more traditional left-wing political agenda (e.g. Gitlin 1995; Scatamburlo 1998), while others broadly accepted and embraced the right-wing critique (e.g. Bruce 2001), and still others sought to maintain a distance between themselves and a traditional left–right dichotomy, most notably Fish (1994) and Cummings (2001). In response other conservative thinkers began to respond to the left with more broadly based and profound critiques than those seen in the original round of conservative writing (e.g. Ellis 1997; Schwartz 2003). Whereas many of the earlier conservative texts concentrated on education as their context, most of the texts just mentioned were more far-reaching in their approach. However, throughout these texts the connection with education is easy to make.

The myth of political correctness

In the work of Wilson and Feldstein we see attempts to expose political correctness as a myth, that it has no real substantial existence. In these texts PC exists only at the level of political propaganda, or as a *neosignifier*, one without any real referent. In this line of reasoning PC is either depicted as half-truth, hyperbole, or outright fabrication, aimed explicitly at ridiculing and under-mining attempts to address examples of inequality of opportunity in the US (Wilson 1996). Or, it is portrayed as an example of *paranoid projection* on behalf of a McCarthyite political and religious clique, accused of, unconsciously, aiming their unwanted desires at their political opponents in the hope of making the symbolic mud stick: 'It is crucial that left-wing cultural critics do not accept the "politically correct" label that neoconservatives have fabricated to stigmatize them. To do so is to accept the act of projection associated with this demeaning classification' (Feldstein 1997: 183–184).

Wilson and Feldstein charge the right in the US with orchestrating a political campaign to undermine the intellectual credentials of those who are perceived as undermining key tenets in the American way of life, such as truth, democracy and meritocracy. Both authors argue that left wing challenges to these social pillars, rather than being countered on intellectual grounds, have simply been undermined by more overtly political means. Thus, moral panics have been deliberately engineered, falsely demonstrating how universities have been 'taken over', and simply *labelling* the left's actions as tyrannical and totalitarian, and as unpatriotic: 'To judge from the news, most people thought the "pc police" posed a greater threat to free speech than neo-Nazi vandals' (Wilson 1996: 31). For both authors the 'PC police' are straw men, aimed at discrediting the left rather than arguing against it. These ideas are important because they address the question of why the right in the US would want to re-establish the use of a term that had almost completely fallen out of common usage.

Feldstein suggests that it is rooted in the desire to counter what was perceived in right-wing circles as a cultural coup enacted by the left within higher education (particularly the humanities) in the US in the 1980s. That is, the humanities departments of most higher education establishments in the US had become havens for left-wing thinking, to the detriment of the right (Feldstein 1996). If this is true it implies that the right acknowledged the power of cultural knowledge as opposed to overtly political and religious knowledge, and that it did indeed need to be countered. It is not difficult to find evidence to support this position. Particularly in the writings of Cheney, Searle, D'Souza, and Bernstein we see this cultural coup being alluded to in a number of ways. It is also not too difficult to see this as a campaign, and not just a series of independently authored texts. Most of the conservative books and articles written in the late 1980s and early 1990s repeat the same stories, use the same terms, and were largely funded by bodies known to have right-wing leanings (Wilson1996; Feldstein 1997).

> As is the case with any mythology, certain stories about political correct-ness have achieved the status of a canon and are recited religiously in almost every piece of writing on the subject. When it comes to pc horror stories, conservatives are more devoted to recycling than the most com-mitted environmentalist.
>
> (Wilson 1996: 21)

But what exactly was under threat such that it needed such an orchestrated campaign? It is difficult to answer this question in a detached way. Either the right were seeking to defend their own vested interests and privileges or simply mobilizing a more general defence of customary features of American life, such as freedom of speech, equality of opportunity, equality before the law, and free market entrepreneurship. Either way the right are perceived here as being frightened by an intellectual assault which they felt unable to confront on strictly intellectual terms, thus necessitating a more political, and, perhaps, moral crusade.

If this analysis is correct it has to be asked what is potentially so frightening about certain left-wing causes? It is not too difficult to list the right's 'usual suspects': anything connected with Marxism, the feminist movement, certain strands within the Civil Rights movement, the gay community, and to some extent the environment movement. Each in their own way could easily be cast as enemies of free speech, equality of opportunity, equality before the law, and the desirability of unfettered free market entrepreneurship. And therefore it is perhaps no surprise at all that they would be robustly challenged. Both Feldstein and Wilson however claim that the challenge is fundamentally unfair largely because it resorts far too quickly to forms of fear and smear in order to discredit. But it also raises a deeper and more thorny question as to whether the right here are simply defending the privileges of powerful groups, or whether they are really questioning the ability of radical politics to bring about the kinds of reforms which would enhance the opportunities of marginalized social groups.

The most successful strategy in undermining the credibility of radical political ideas was not just to associate it with a derogatory interpretation of PC, but that the term itself implies a form of politics which practices the opposite of what it preaches. Utilizing the imagery and language of Orwell's Thought Police, where, for example, War can become Peace, the accusation is that, in the name of openness, debate is actually being closed down. And, in one of the most interesting twists of language, the term 'McCarthyism', once associated with the right in American politics, is now claimed to be a hallmark of the left, along with all the allied accusations of witch-hunts and paranoia. Three scenarios now present themselves: the cultural left *have* produced strategies which will open up opportunities in the US – the right know this and feel that they can only counter it by smear; the cultural left does contain a Stalinist/McCarthyite political core – the right's political campaign is therefore soundly based; the cultural left have produced ideas and strategies which contain contradictions, ironies, and unintended consequences – the right's campaign is merely highlighting these as examples of sloppy thinking. Evidence presented throughout this book would indicate that all three scenarios have credibility. Feldstein and Wilson, however, concentrate their attention on the first of these.

For Feldstein the explanation for the right's campaign against PC is largely unconscious. It is rooted in their own paranoia, and is thus a projection of that paranoia onto a new 'object' or container. The theory of *projective identification* contains two components. First, that paranoid *projections* represent the actions of an individual (or group) unable to contain within themselves their own anxieties, necessitating that these are projected elsewhere. Second, the *identification* refers to the process whereby the individuals or groups who are the objects of the projections come to identify, in some way, with the projection, that is they accept that they are the container for the unwanted projections, and begin to own them (Young 1994). On the latter Wilson agrees: 'The success of conservatives at spreading the myth of political correctness can be attributed largely to the willingness of liberals to believe them' (Wilson 1996: 15).

Those unwilling to accept Feldstein's use of psychoanalytic terms might still be able to see this operating at a more conscious level. Indeed, given that some of the PC stories that have circulated in the media since the early 1990s have become such *causes célèbres* it is difficult to resist the observation that behind all this smoke there must be some fire. For example there was the accusation that the University of Pennsylvania reprimanded a student for using the term 'water buffalo', that Stanford University capitulated to mob rule in abandoning its

Western Civilization course, and that the University of Michigan operated a quota system in its admissions procedures. Regardless of whether there was any substance to any of these accusations, they all produced an enormous amount of smoke, indeed enough for some liberals to question whether all that was done in the interests of equality was any such thing. The background to each of these stories will feature in the following three chapters respectively. For others what this does is simply highlight that unintended consequences can always follow from sound principles, or in simple terms, sound ends are often associated with unsound means. For Feldstein, however, it is clear what is happening: 'The game is afoot, and its aim is to discredit cultural pluralists as PC dogmatists, while arch conservatives slyly project their own dialectical agenda of correct and incorrect behaviour onto the university environment' (Feldstein 1997: 103).

This is a subtle argument which suggests that in making the left appear to be the enemy within, the right, wracked, in reality, with their own insecurities about their political beliefs, are able to portray themselves as representing an unquestionable normality: 'the oppositional teacher who tries to expose the political interest of the status quo is often perceived by students as the one who "imposes" politics or is "ideological", whereas conservatives and liberals are presumably just teaching their subjects' (Graff and Jay in Feldstein 1997: 209). Furthermore: 'the real danger in the struggle to be correct does not arise from those trying to read change, but the ideologies of the right who have far less doubt about their correctness than any of the intellectual approaches accused of PC' (Cope and Kalantzis 1997: 326).

Both Feldstein and Wilson are instructive in highlighting how much of the anti-PC literature of the late 1980s and early 1990s was *orchestrated*, and contained deliberate attempts to tar opponents rather than argue on intellectual terms. Whether or not it was largely unconscious it certainly had the effect of placing many proponents of progressive equal opportunities policies and strategies on the back foot. However, in seeking to come to the defence of many of those strategies they may they have unwittingly lent support to behaviours which have subsequently been questioned: 'there is a tendency among those who react to it on the Left to ignore the fact that it is sometimes accurate and justifiable. PC is a real problem even if Bill Bennett and Lynne Cheney say it's a menace' (Graff and Jay in Feldstein 1997: 207). And, finally, we should remember that although authors like Bloom and D'Souza do point the finger at the intimidatory tactics of university administrators, much of their analysis concerns the validity of the actual knowledge that is generated and disseminated in universities, rather than how it is managed and policed.

A polarized left?

Bruce, the ex-president of the LA chapter of the National Organization for Women (NOW), maintains that PC is not a right-wing myth but is actually an orchestrated *left*-wing conspiracy (Bruce 2001). Her book is an 'insider's' attempt to expose the tactics of those on the political left who use PC to police a zealous pathway to their own political ends. Here, PC is not the unintended consequences of progressive equal opportunities strategies, because, at heart, it *is* an assault on individual freedom. It is not unwitting, but very witting, and, when uncovered, it demonstrates that there is a form of narrow-minded Stalinism at the heart of the left in the US.

Bruce, therefore, accepts that much of the right-wing attack on PC in the late 1980s and 1990s was soundly based, particularly the accusation that the left had become tyrannical. She also shares many of Sykes's concerns about 'victimology', and how this can only result in the opposite of what is intended:

> The sense of perpetual victim hood precludes even the concept that the members of a victimized minority could actually rise above their assigned position in society and meet that society on their own terms. To do that would mean taking personal responsibility for the conditions of their own lives; instead, today's 'progressives' have designed an argument that leads not to the encouragement of personal change and growth but to entitlement, group rights, and the eradication of the individual, all in the name of progress.
>
> (Bruce 2001: 10)

But, as we saw in Chapter 1, Bruce's 'insider's view' is from the perspective of a spy rather than a comrade. For her political ideology is clearly one which rests on the assumption that a free market approach to the pursuit of happiness is much more likely to be successful when compared with any notions of redistributive justice.

On the surface it might appear that Bruce's exposé has much in common with other left-wing critics of PC. For example in the work of Gitlin and Scatamburlo we see a similar attack on the undesirability of 'group rights' (Gitlin 1995; Scatamburlo 1997). But here the foundation of the argument is that these strategies are not actually left wing. The left have certainly lost their way but this should not mean that we must now embrace a more conservative political ideology, but rather the left should restate a more traditional radical ideology. Put simply, it is not that PC is too left wing, it is not left wing enough. Both authors are concerned that a once unified coalition of radical thought, centred on a 'common goal' of a future Socialist social order, has been torn asunder by infighting amongst the various disadvantaged social groups, who seem more concerned to attack each other than what used to be perceived as the common enemy:

> Why are so many people attached to their marginality and why is so much of their intellectual labor spent developing theories to justify it? Why insist

on difference with such rigidity, rancor, and blindness, to the exclusion of
the possibility of common knowledge and common dreams?

(Gitlin 1995: 32)

Scatamburlo senses that the problem has more of an epistemological foundation:

> the signs of culture are severed from the conditions of their production.
> Rather than being conceived of as part of an ideological field circum-
> scribed by capitalist social relations, signs are conceived of as historically
> indeterminate, free-floating chains of signifiers . . . we are left with an
> empty politics, a series of metaphorical gestures which, in the end, have
> little impact on actual existing relations of power and privilege, either
> inside or outside of the academy.
>
> (Scatamburlo 1998: 174–175)

In paradoxical fashion both authors appear to share many of the right's concerns
about PC. First, the way in which the US has produced a 'victim's charter' for
various social groups to fight over, and, second, a belief in a form of 'hyper-
reality' where anything and everything is able to have multiple meanings. This
is troubling in radical political theory particularly if it is rooted in Marxism, for,
in the first instance, we lose our sense that exploitation and disadvantage have
common roots and, in the second, political action aimed at producing a more
humane social order gets lost in an amorphous and endless round of reinter-
pretations of meaning, and of a kind for which Marx originally castigated the
'Young Hegelians'. Thus, although the diagnoses for the left and right are
similar, the aetiologies and prognoses are entirely different. As Gitlin points out,
this is not without some considerable irony:

> Between Left and Right there has taken place a curious reversal. Through-
> out the nineteenth and twentieth centuries, the Left believed in a common
> condition, the Right in fundamental differences among classes, nations,
> races. The Left wanted collective acts of renewal; the Right endorsed
> primordial ties of tradition and community against all disruptions.
>
> (Gitlin 1995: 84)

Ultimately, for Gitlin, the left have lost their 'common dream'. Disillusioned
perhaps by events in the Soviet block in the late 1980s, and combined with an
invigorated postmodern sensibility, many on the left have put their intellectual
energy elsewhere. It is difficult to argue that, *per se*, this created the space for a
politics of entitlement to embed itself, but either way this is a lethal political
cocktail for anyone with a more traditional Marxist sensibility to swallow. And,
as Gitlin eloquently argues, the 'culture wars' in the US are really just the logical
extension of the Cold War, with internal rather than external enemies. Or maybe
the Cold War always was an internal cultural war between capitalist and socialist

ideologies within the US. In this context the right have had much to celebrate in the past twenty years, where a new 'common dream' has been able to embed itself, rooted in the victory of liberal democracies over Soviet-style dictatorships, and a sense that Americans are united by being 'American' rather than black, white, working class, or whatever.

By this analysis it is clear that the left are in crisis, and PC is just a hopeless example of shooting oneself in the foot:

> What we have . . . is an ill-fitting sum of groups overly concerned with protecting and purifying what they imagine to be their identities. Yet the conscience they still tug is on the conscience of the Left. The energies they drain are the energies of the Left. What we are witnessing in the culture wars is not the triumph of the Left but its decline.
>
> (Gitlin 1995: 33)

In similar vein Scatamburlo argues that it simply isn't enough to attack the right for manufacturing PC, because there is weight to many of the right's arguments, but in the process she is careful to maintain her *political* distance:

> Kimball's account of the 'cult of theory' among leftists is rather difficult to deny, as are D'Souza's charges of a burgeoning relativism. Conservatives abhor these developments because they view them as 'radical' threats to the established order: yet, I would suggest that progressives be concerned with these developments because they are *not radical enough.*
>
> (Scatamburlo 1998: 159)

It is not radical enough because these 'progressives' concern themselves too much with the affirmation of identity, and the power of words, as against the power of direct social action:

> while it is necessary to recognise the importance of language, it is equally important to acknowledge the limits of a politics that concerns itself with aesthetic changes to language and terminology. Such efforts do not pose serious challenges to hegemonic assumptions, material conditions, and structural arrangements; rather they are intended to avoid offending individuals in particular contexts according to liberal notions of polite- ness, sensitivity and intolerance.
>
> (Scatamburlo 1998: 102)

Here we see a typical response to PC, that is, a castigation of its misplaced sensitivity to language, but it is combined with a more traditional left-wing politics which rallies against those (so-called) political actions that leave the basic structures of power and inequality untouched. As we shall see in Chapter 5 these views are often encountered in critiques of multicultural education. However, as we shall also see, it is not clear at all that this must necessarily constitute a form of woolly liberalism, for it can often contain a deeply subversive component. In this, more postmodern, version of multiculturalism, the tolerance of difference quickly turns to a critique of ethnic identity. In this argument 'identities' are fictions – necessary perhaps – but, particularly in higher education, they are there to be subverted rather than celebrated. This may not be the kind of political action that would ideally suit radicals like Scatamburlo, but it would be difficult to maintain the view that it was a form of woolly liberalism.

Ultimately, like Gitlin before, Scatamburlo wishes to distance the politics of PC from a more truthful radical politics, and part of her conclusion is worth quoting at length:

> Contemporary post-al theory suffers from some major theoretical and political ailments. First of all, in privileging the discursive and the textual, it has often failed to address concrete material conditions and, in doing so, has forfeited the possibility of making meaningful interventions in the interests of social change. Secondly, in negating the feasibility of making 'truth' claims, they lack the 'requisite sociology on which to build a new ethical foundation' for a project directed toward possibility (McClaren 1994: 197). In their relativist extremes, they have actually crippled the very concept of the political by dissolving it into a bubbling vat of indeterminacy. Moreover, the corrosive scepticism found in much postmodernism/poststructuralism has exacerbated the pervasive sense of despair and hopelessness by rendering visions of social transformation as hopelessly obsolete.
>
> (Scatamburlo 1998: 196)

Given that postmodern writing does often preach a politics of despair and hopeless forms of nihilism, and which, thereby, seriously questions the viability of calling people to unite around 'fictive' causes, there is a substantive core to Scatamburlo's argument. However, her appeal 'to build a new ethical founda-tion' for a socialist future is as un-Marxist as the utopians he castigated over one hundred and fifty years ago. In this respect, perhaps one of the unacknowledged lasting legacies of postmodern thinking on the left will be the way that it forced Marxists to give up on the idea that 'history is on their side' and return to more traditional arguments rooted in morality and rhetoric.

A sceptical left?

Throughout the past twenty years the key PC bogeyman of the right has been Stanley Fish. Portrayed as a 'Godfather of PC', his attacks on the foundations of most of the right's arguments have been a constant irritant to their sensibilities. However, his attacks might equally apply to many on the left, for their target is not the content of a political ideology, but the structure of arguments mounted in its defence. In this regard Fish does not represent the left or the right, but simply applies forms of poststructural theory to political ideologies, and specifically those which mask their appeal for support with bogus claims about having discovered universal principles or truths, and thereby implying that their ideology is in fact no such thing. Thus: 'Someone who says to you, "This is *our* common ground," is really saying "This is *my* common ground, the substratum of assumptions and values that produces *my* judgements, and it should be yours, too"' (Fish 1994: 35).

For Fish both left and right are often dogged by a determination to hang on to these forms of 'foundational' thinking; thinking which is actually beyond thought itself. That these 'foundational' arguments might end up as supports for entirely different visions of socio-economic and political realities is of little consequence when the argument is couched in epistemological terms. It is as if:

> reasons come from nowhere, that they reflect the structure of the universe or at least of the human brain; but in fact reasons always come from somewhere, and the somewhere they come from is precisely the realm to which they are (rhetorically) opposed, the realm of the particular (angled, partisan, biased) assumptions and agendas.
>
> (Fish 1994: 135)

Thus, although in supporting many of the causes that came to be associated with PC, Fish is not partisan in his arguments. For example by supporting some curbs on freedom of speech (see next chapter for a more detailed discussion of this), particularly in the climate of the right-wing campaign against PC in the late 1980s and early 1990s, it is easy to see Fish as a left-wing thinker. However, in a reversal of the claim made earlier that political radicals can often be epistemological conservatives, it is perfectly possible for political conservatives to be epistemological radicals. And, as hinted at before, we should probably be looking here if we want to question the validity of the traditional left–right dichotomy, and not at the ideologies themselves.

It would also be easy to claim that the line of argument pursued by Fish, and his supporters, must inevitably end up in a form of hopeless scepticism and pessimism about political debate. This is perfectly possible, but it is not inevitable because it does not preclude one holding on to one's traditional political allegiances. It is simply an argument about the basis of those allegiances. Put simply, the strength of a political argument lies in its ability to convince someone that it is worthy of support, not in how it masks this in some appeal to forces beyond this. In a variation on Sartre's 'bad faith', it could be argued that there is an enormous amount of political bad faith on both the left and the right, or: 'a huge disparity between the claim of Reason to be independent of ideology and the pedigree of any of the reasons you might think to give' (Fish 1994: 17).

A concerted attempt to support left-wing causes but avoid the pitfalls of foundational thinking is contained in the work of Choi and Murphy (1992). While fully embracing a postmodern sensibility they are equally keen to maintain an optimistic political commitment to the causes most commonly

associated with PC, most notably forms of multicultural curricula and affirmative action. As we saw in Chapter 1 their commitment rests on the conviction
that: 'What PC is about . . . is who will control social life' (Choi and Murphy
1992: xii), and the necessity to constantly challenge the traditional power
structures, that is, those hierarchies who claim to be working in everyone's
interests, but who really serve only their own. In a variation on the popular
theme that 'American democracy is the best that money can buy' the challenge
here is to question whether American citizens really do have access to, and
influence in, the key decision-making chambers. However, because the bulk of
their polemic concentrates on dismantling the 'foundationalist' claims of the
right, they do not proceed to give any concrete examples of strategies which
might actually promote the kinds of democratic reforms they envisage.

> What the cultural Right has successfully done is to link their political
> agenda to traditionally accepted epistemological themes. After all, most
> citizens would support disinterested research, the unbiased pursuit of
> truth, or the protection of standards of morality. These ideas are thought
> by most persons to be the cornerstones of justice and order.
>
> (Choi and Murphy 1992: 50)

As we have already seen the right made great strides at this time in aligning PCers
with being un-American. Here we see the 'foundation' for this argument in the
idea that the US must be democratic, because the Founding Fathers had
discovered some Universal principles, rather than manufactured them. (In this
respect the Founding Fathers are more like 'Foundational Fathers'.) However,
in a concerted attempt not to end up in a nihilistic cul-de-sac Choi and Murphy
work hard to maintain the view that in being anti-foundational this does not
mean that one must give up on traditional political causes:

> Contrary to conservatives, PCers work to promote an awareness of how
> universals are socially manufactured. Recognizing that common know-
> ledge is produced, rather than simply discovered, is central to democracy.
> Instead of being restricted by facts that are considered to be scientific or
> objective, debate can proceed in practically any direction. Discussion, in
> other words, does not have to be sacrificed to safeguard order. In this sense
> PC seems to be more compatible with democracy than conservatism,
> because PCers do not identify a specific type of knowledge as undoubtedly
> valid and the centrepiece of civility. Hence, PCers invite the challenges to
> knowledge that are necessary for the unfettered debate to take place.
>
> (Choi and Murphy 1992: 151)

In a clever anti-Platonic manner, the authors rescue democratic ideals from the
clutches of the right, who, by appealing to Universals, thereby demonstrate that
they have no real commitment to the value of democratic argument and debate
at all. For, in essence, what is there to debate? There can only ever be an appeal

by (Philosopher) Rulers to the unerring rightness of Universal claims to justice, freedom, rights, etc. Thus rescued, democratic debate and discussion can now proceed to work towards the kinds of social reforms which would *really* address the inequalities, disadvantage, and repression that those on the left traditionally rally against. That this might well be the last thing that truly democratic debate would bring about is clearly a moot point at this juncture. And, of course, the kinds of social reforms which Choi and Murphy would welcome would surely involve the very challenges to corporate America that have prompted many of the left to speak of revolution rather than reform.

Ends, means, and unintended consequences

It is probably unfair on Choi and Murphy to ask that they outline some clear political strategies because the real purpose behind their book is to challenge the 'foundationalist' thinking of the right, and thereby protect the causes which are most commonly associated with PC. However, it is clear that some authors on the left *have* been worried by the ways that PC causes have been pursued. In what might be referred to as the 'theory of unintended consequences' it is clear that one might espouse many of the causes associated with PC, but equally recognize that ends and means have no necessarily harmonious connection. In accepting the point that unacceptable correctness can often get in the way of righteous politics, or worse that the latter might simply produce undesirable consequences, it is clear that the left do have a case to answer, not just to the right, but within the left itself: 'The point is to rescue progressive causes from a kind of closure and distortion that culminate in their advocates' shooting themselves in the foot and trumping the transformation of society' (Cummings 2001: 11).

Putting aside the broader 'common dream' of an egalitarian society, and the democratization of all institutions of power, and returning to the narrower walls of higher education, it is not at all clear whether all those accused of being PC are in fact pursuing the *same* causes. For example, if one is seeking to provide more opportunities for black youth to advance through higher education, this is not necessarily the same as advancing the causes of an Afro-centrist curriculum. It may well be that many students would excel in an Afro-centrist environment, but this might equally prompt others to argue that the true measure of success is when the same black youth actually excel in a traditional curriculum (D'Souza 1992). This example has a double-edged political dimension, because it is perfectly possible for different people on the left to espouse each of these positions, but equally the latter position might also be espoused by someone from the right. Again, we should not be too quick to use this to undermine the traditional left–right dichotomy because whereas the diagnosis might be the same, that is, black youth are not excelling in the traditional curriculum and we want this changed, the traditional left-wing solution to act 'affirmatively' (Ryan 1972), might be counterposed with a right-wing solution which centres on more directly challenging the validity of 'counter-school cultures' (Willis 1977), or the 'cult of anti-intellectualism' amongst black youth (McWhorter 2001). Furthermore, even in accepting the validity of the latter argument, this is just as likely to lead on the left to a form of 'critical pedagogy' (Aronowitz and Giroux 1988), as it is on the right to espousing the virtues of canonical authors (Bloom 1987). The precise contours of these debates will be discussed in Chapter 5.

Unsurprisingly perhaps, these debates prompted many black authors in the US to try to steer coherent paths through them, which both acknowledge their fractious nature while seeking to maintain some sense of common cause. Some of the most provocative were Carter (1991), Gates (1993), hooks (1996), and Gates and West (1996). These authors outline the contours of seemingly contradictory and, at times, intractable debate, while maintaining a distinct sense that advancing the position of black people in American society is a common goal. From defending 'I got in law school because I am black. So what?' (Carter 1991: 17), through 'demand[ing] of every person with whom I chanced to interact that they earn the right to learn my name' (Gates in Gates and West 1996: 32), to the deeply ironic fact that at the very moment black folk find their voice it becomes deconstructed by the postmodernists (hooks 1996). Many of these issues will be considered in more detail in Chapter 5. The important point in the context of this chapter is to consider whether these issues undermine the traditional left–right dichotomy.

On one level arguments concerning the advancement of blacks in the US clearly do undermine the left–right dichotomy, in the sense that 'race' is considered to be *the* axis of conflict. In this line of reasoning it is political ideology which emerges from an understanding of race, rather than vice versa. This was clearly witnessed in the controversies surrounding the publication of Wilson's book on *The Declining Significance of Race* (1978). However, keeping the horse before the cart is often not that easy, nor necessarily desirable. For example, Carter provides a rich insight into the experience of being black in an elite university as an 'affirmative action baby', but his conclusion, that we must hold on to traditional notions of 'excellence', is undeniably a traditional conservative position (Carter 1991). Carter's book provides excellent evidence of how a correct political line is difficult to draw, not only because of the way that opposing political ideologies can impinge on debate, but also because the debates themselves often contain ironic postmodern implications (hooks 1996). For Carter this was most notably in him having to spend most of his adult life dealing with the accusation that he had not achieved his lot in life on merit. However, the terse retort 'so what?', indicates that although, at one level regrettable, this is not, *per se*, a substantial critique of affirmative action, because, as he argues, it is not how you get into law school that really counts, it's what you do when you get there, and we'll simply never know what many blacks might have been able to achieve with or without affirmative action (Carter 1991).

In all this there might be a serious danger of mistakenly elevating 'group politics' above 'class politics'. This is a dangerous political strategy, not only because of the backlashes (white guilt, black enclaves in higher education, etc.), but also because it might easily result in federal funds being diverted from the 'truly disadvantaged' (Wilson 1987). If it is not already clear that PC is a highly charged term it is here where it can be most obviously demonstrated. Because even to suggest that we might consider seeing class as the most important axis of conflict one is apt to find oneself labelled a 'racist' – for this is clearly not the PC position that one should take on racial matters. This is perhaps the most dangerous of unintended consequences because in advancing a political position one should surely consider *first* the coherence of the position, not its correctness in terms of already agreed principles, or whether somebody has a pre-ordained authority to speak on such matters.

The return of the repressed

Throughout the 1990s the left in the US were actively responding to the right's attack on PC. In some cases the right were accused of manufacturing a straw man, in others parts of the attack were accepted, and, as we have just seen, in other cases it resulted in a complicated series of arguments about political ends, means, and dealing with unintended consequences. If Wilson and Feldstein are correct in their assessment that most of the right's attack was an orchestrated, and funded, political campaign, it would not be surprising that this should, like most campaigns, come to a rather abrupt end. There would appear to be some evidence for this, not just because many of the books and pamphlets of the late 1980s and early 1990s were published by the same sources, but also because by the mid-1990s it was mainly the left who were publishing polemics on PC. That said, two significant contributions from conservative authors were published in the late 1990s and early 2000s (Ellis 1997; Schwartz 2003), and both authors look at what they consider to be the fundamental root of the problem: PC has dangerously unbalanced some fundamental aspects of the human condition.

For Schwartz, PC represents a 'revolt of the primitive'. It is a psychically driven attempt to restore a form of primordial well-being in the face of a restrictive and oppressive present reality (Schwartz 2003). For Ellis, the result is similar, an attempt to create a form of common humanity, but through a form of regressive utopianism (Ellis 1997). For both, PC represents a kind of child-like attempt to recreate a sense of oneness from an uncomfortable world: 'There is more than a broadbrush similarity between today's political correctness and . . . recurring fantasies of the primitive innocence to be found outside a corrupt Western society' (Ellis 1997: 18).

Given that PC is often associated by the right with Marxist thinking, it is perhaps somewhat surprising that this kind of romanticism, roundly condemned by Marx in his own writing as 'utopian socialism', should resurface and be reattached so easily. That aside, both theses cast the PCer as a form of deviant, one who messes, either with a Natural (Schwartz 2003) or a Rational (Ellis 1997) order, and due, in both cases, to his or her own inadequacies:

> Intellectuals who are alienated from their own society and who in their disgust with its imperfections imagine a primitive society full of sweetness and light. . . . The outsider denigrates the dominant culture not because of his disgust with its imperfections but because he does not feel part of it. Resentment is the reason for his adulation of primitive cultures.
>
> (Ellis 1997: 20)

This position appears to recreate the classic Mannheimian opposition between the ideologue and the utopian (Mannheim 1936). For Ellis, the utopian can only see societal imperfections, and thereby wishes to sweep everything away: 'They [alienated intellectuals] must . . . attribute all blame to society and none to humanity' (Ellis 1997: 28). In a desperate attempt to save humanity from fallen social forms the utopian intellectual seeks sanctuary in primitive, unsullied cultures. Of course this thereby raises the question of the extent to which this would make Ellis simply an ideologue.

Schwartz's psychoanalytic exploration of the roots of political correctness is overtly depth psychology. It explores what underlies the outward appearance of human behaviour to reveal the inner psychic drivers. Again, forms of dissatisfaction occupy centre stage. However, this time the root (depth) cause of the problem is a disturbance in the healthy working of the family structure, where the role of the father in orienting the child towards 'reality' has been overtaken by the role of the mother as the container for primordial feelings of 'oneness' and narcissism. That is, a desire not to be shaped by the needs of an external reality, where one is an object, but to continue to live in a world where nothing is external to one's own subjective experience: 'it [PC] has come to be the way that our ideas of ourselves are shaped in the absence of a direct engagement with reality' (Schwartz 2003: 115).

PC is thus primitive and regressive in its outlook. It is a longing for a type of social order, which seeks to replicate a kind of 'womb-like' state. Using different intellectual traditions, both authors arrive at a similar diagnosis. For Ellis PC is an anti-Enlightenment philosophy, for Schwartz it attempts to replace the Freudian reality principle with the pleasure principle. In both cases PCers are deficient in their thinking, unable to see the world, reality, for what it really is. 'Reality' is not a playground, where one fantasies about moulding the world as one would like to see it, nor is it an extension of one's own thoughts, but it is that which must be confronted and come to terms with. 'Reality' has an objective existence, and it is part of growing up that one comes to recognize this. Clearly, this line of reasoning also opens up the possibility that this primitivism might lead one to adopt a postmodern epistemology, and thus, herein, also lies a 'depth' explanation and critique of this sensibility.

As we will see through the rest of this book both authors strike at the heart of much of what lies deep beneath the surface of most debates about PC. And in somewhat paradoxical fashion the work of Marx is integral to understanding and unravelling the various strands. On the one hand his critique of capitalism and subsequent emergence of Communism contains a hermeneutic key to uncover the reality of surface appearances, but, on the other, he also offers the possibility that 'all that is solid will melt into air'. This *is* paradoxical, for he holds onto an Enlightenment notion of unlocking truths about human progress, but also offers the possibility that everything might be endlessly remoulded. Either way both notions are troubling to conservative thinkers. First, his understanding of capitalism as exploitative and contradictory is not a political position that the right can feel at all comfortable with, for it suggests that real human progress is yet to be made. For Ellis, of course, this is not really progress at all, but a return to a more primitive form of communism, the like of which Marx himself roundly criticized. Second, the thought that reality might be endlessly remoulded and reconstituted suggests that there are no universal truths, only what is historically contingent. For Schwartz this is what fundamentally disturbs the human psyche, despite, of course, the intellectual protestations of authors like Weeks and Butler on the constructed nature of sexuality and gender (Weeks 1985; Butler 1990). The right do not tend to exploit the extent to which these strands of thinking in Marxist thought are actually contradictory and, in PC debates, the ways in which the latter have become quickly allied with forms of postmodern thinking.

Ultimately, what Ellis and Schwartz produce are critiques which confirm that there is Reason, and there is Nature, and each deserves its capital letter. Ultimately, to be PC is to demand that both words have their capital letters removed. This is why Stanley Fish is the godfather of PC because he demands that all such abstract nouns be defrocked in this way. And herein lies the biggest challenge to the maintenance of a traditional left–right dichotomy. For the right it is reasonably clear that Reason and Nature do deserve their traditional status. For the left it is unclear. Those who have embraced a postmodern sensibility are happy to see 'particular' natures and reasons or, in more sociological circles, a series of 'social constructions'. However those who are more traditional and 'modern' in their outlook might want to retain nouns with capital letters, but use them to defend very different visions of the human condition and the good life.

Conclusion

Scratch below the surface of any debate about PC and you will find a deeper debate about political ideology. Furthermore, almost all these debates follow the contours of the traditional left–right dichotomy as outlined at the beginning of this chapter. If this is so, the thornier question to ask is why the term PC is invoked when the contours of the original debates are much clearer. For authors like Feldstein the answer is relatively straightforward. The right knew they were losing an intellectual battle for ideas in higher education in the 1980s, and PC became the perfect smear to undermine the credibility of many left-wing ideas which were in ascendance. That this campaign hit hard is evidenced by concerns on the left itself about the direction that many of the debates associated with PC were taking. For some this may only have been because of the paradoxes and unintended consequences, but there certainly *were* concerns about the correct-ness, if not the politics.

For others on the left the problem was more deep-rooted. The right were wrong to claim that PC was too political, because, in reality, it was not political enough. Or perhaps better it had replaced a concern for changing the material circumstances of people's lives in favour of breeding a sensitivity towards the different circumstances in which people live their lives. And, in the process, it had replaced the traditional Socialist axis of universal conflict rooted in class inequality with a plethora of single issue and disparate social group concerns revolving around identity affirmation. This itself reignited a series of debates about whether social class conflict deserves its status as the most fundamental axis of conflict, or whether other axes deserve equal, or top, billing. This debate is an old one and can be traced back to Weber's concerns about Marx's over-emphasis on economic class over social class, and the ways in which 'modes of social closure' might have many *status* axes. It was refuelled in the early 1970s in feminist circles with the publication of Firestone's *Dialectic of Sex* (1970) and the consequent charge that Marxists can be sexists quickly spilled over into claims that they can also be racists, or even species-ists. In PC debates it quickly became clear that this was also a concern about who has the authority to speak about what, and whether there is any such thing as detached, disinterested scholarship. These issues will be returned to in Chapter 5.

This last point highlights the real reason why PC is troubling for the left. Although there is some evidence that the right *have* touched a raw nerve around correctness, the more troubling problem is that the left are divided epistemo-logically rather than politically. Of course, to many postmodernists this *is* a political question, that is all knowledge is thoroughly and irrevocably political in nature. However, in more traditional terms one might say that many on the left have embraced a 'linguistic turn' (Hall 1994). This is not as might first appear a new-found sensitivity in the use of language, particularly in the pres-ence of the 'vulnerable', but a more profound concern for the way that language frames our perception of reality. In this line of argument language doesn't re-present reality, because our words are not in 'correspondence' with reality. They are rather the means by which we choose to present reality. This is the real power of words, and the problem is not that they might harm us, but that we might not understand the truly existential nature of their existence. This issue will be discussed in more detail in the next chapter.

In this epistemological context the most troubling aspect of PC is the way that it doesn't undermine the traditional left–right dichotomy, but complicates it.

What PC debates do is unite those on the left and the right who believe in the fundamental principle of the Enlightenment, that through the application of Reason, and a realist epistemology, one might understand the nature of the world, and use that understanding to better the conditions in which people live their lives. That they might come to very different conclusions about how best to enhance the human condition remains a fundamental issue, but this is now joined by a fundamental question concerning the 'foundational' nature of their thinking. For this reason Stanley Fish does merit the title 'Godfather of PC' because, along with authors such as Choi and Murphy, he understood the real significance of replacing Principle with principles, and the subsequent demand that one always engage in transparent political debate, rather than seeking to hide it within an argument beyond itself. Although this does not address the correctness question it certainly explains what the word political means in PC. And for this reason it is perhaps no surprise that conservative authors like Ellis and Schwartz should follow quickly on the shirt tails of radicals such as Gitlin and Scatamburlo in condemning PC for being, at heart, an anti-Enlightenment project. In this context both the left and right have, in equal measure, much to lose in this high stakes critique.

In re-establishing the importance of Reason (Ellis) and Nature (Schwartz) both authors strike at the heart of what troubles many on the right about PC. Have we really given up on the mission of the university to engage in the disinterested pursuit of truth? And have we really come to a point where we can no longer speak of 'normal' and 'healthy' human relationships? Are we truly living in a world where 'anything goes' and, if we are, is it any wonder that nations like the US are facing a fundamental identity crisis? The rhetoric may be different for the right when compared with the left but authors like Gitlin and Scatamburlo are just as dismayed about the nihilistic consequences of abandoning a more enlightened/Enlightenment political outlook. Much of that enlightened political outlook on the left can be traced back to Marx, and many of the roots of PC probably do lie in his work (see Chapter 8), and the right are therefore correct to associate Marxists with PC. However, the right do so for the wrong reason, for in constantly associating Marxism with much more recent trends in poststructural literary theory they completely lose sight of the fact that, when compared with authors like Fish, Marx is as 'enlightened' and 'foundational' as they come.

In summary, the late 1980s and early 1990s saw a concerted attempt by many right-wing authors and commentators to resurrect the term PC to denigrate left-wing political opponents. A lot of the time it was used to label certain people and ideas as threats to the American way of life, and as proponents of a totalitarian alternative. In more intellectual terms PC was associated with those who had granted themselves an unwarranted power to police the use of language in higher education, in the interests of protecting the sensitivities of the vulnerable. Also it became associated with those who opposed canonical truth and with those who promoted forms of cultural and intellectual relativism (and was often labelled as either silly or lazy thinking). Finally, it was used to question the validity of arguments in favour of affirmative action in university admissions and the new ways that knowledge in the curriculum was increasingly being validated and tested. Each of these strands will be the subject of more detailed discussion in the following three chapters.

4

Water buffaloes in Pennsylvania
Closing free speech

Eden Jacobowitz is a student at the University of Pennsylvania. His
studies were interrupted by a noisy crowd of students, many black and
female. He yelled out of his window, 'Shut up, you water buffalo.' He is
now charged with racial harassment under the University's Code of
Conduct. The school offered to dismiss the charge if he would apologize,
attend a racial sensitivity seminar, agree to dormitory probation, and
accept a temporary mark on his record which would brand him as
guilty. He was told the term 'water buffalo' could be interpreted as racist
because a water buffalo is a dark primitive animal that lives in Africa.
That is questionable semantics, dubious zoology, and incorrect
geography. Water buffalo live in Asia, not in Africa. This from the
University of Pennsylvania. Mr. Jacobowitz is fighting back. The rest of
us, however, are still in trouble. The language police are at work on the
campuses of our better schools. The word cops are marching under the
banner of political correctness. The culture of victimization is hunting
for quarry. American English is in danger of losing its muscle and
energy. That's what these bozos are doing to us.

(John Chancellor *NBC Nightly News*
13 May 1993, quoted in Kors and Silverglate 1998: 28)

Introduction

When a student refers to a noisy group of fellow students as 'water buffalo' it
might reasonably be assumed that it would give rise to some discussion and
perhaps even a little bewilderment. When the noisy group of students were black
females it might also be assumed that it would arouse some argument and debate.
The fact that the student who uttered the words should be subject to a prolonged
investigation and, indeed, suspended might well produce some surprise and even
perhaps beggar belief. This is the tone of the critique undertaken by Kors and
Silverglate concerning this affair and it has entered the dictionary of PC as an
example of the absurdity that is said to be at its heart (Kors and Silverglate 1998).

Such cases hang on the extent to which it is possible to be harmed by the
words of others. Or, the extent to which certain words or phrases might be

construed as 'hate speech' or 'fighting talk' and to be taken, in the US at least, as legitimate exceptions to the First Amendment: 'Congress shall make no law respecting an establishment of religion, or prohibiting the free exercise thereof; or abridging the freedom of speech, or of the press; or the right of the people peaceably to assemble, and to petition the government for a redress of grievances.' If the First Amendment is taken literally it should not be possible to curtail, let alone outlaw, the right of any individual to say anything they please, in any context, so long as it emanates from within the geographical boundaries of the US. Indeed, anyone's right to do this would be vigorously defended in law. A notorious example was the case mounted by Larry Flint who successfully defended his right to refer to Jerry Falwell, of the Moral Majority, as someone who has slept with his mother. Although there was no evidence of this, and Flint offered no evidence of this, his right to say it was defended and he won the case. Although, to all intents and purposes, this was a show trial it did indicate the extent to which the First Amendment is something of a cherished national belief.

In this chapter I will be looking at the relationship between freedom of speech and the First Amendment, and the extent to which this relationship has been altered by the controversies generated by PC. American literature on this subject is wide ranging and polarized, including passionate defences of freedom of speech, and calls to reconsider the implications (e.g. Matsuda *et al.* 1993; Fish 1994; Shiell 1998; Downs 2005; Thomas 2005). Whilst agreeing that Kors and Silverglate's defence of freedom of speech is substantial, I will argue that there *are* important grounds for questioning whether the First Amendment should be used as a fundamental principle, and that it is possible to argue a sound case for restricting some speech in higher education – on the grounds that it has no place in the 'marketplace of ideas'. These arguments will be embedded in a broader debate about the relationship between words and actions, and the role of language in culture. I conclude by suggesting that if we need a principle it might be wiser to look back to a Kantian categorical imperative for guidance.

The First Amendment as the refuge of the scoundrel?

Although the First Amendment is often treated as sacred, and as one of the defining characteristics of the US, we should not forget that US history is littered with examples of where it has been amended, or perhaps better, precedents for exceptions have been generated. Indeed, Kors and Silverglate are concise in their summary of the exceptions:

> The [Supreme] Court has established four primary exceptions to free speech: (1) Speech posing a 'clear and present danger' of 'imminent violence or lawlessness'; (2) disclosures threatening 'national security'; (3) 'obscenity'; and (4) so called 'fighting words' that would provoke a 'reasonable person' to an imminent, violent response.
>
> (Kors and Silverglate 1998: 36)

A good example, for the purpose of exploration, is the Supreme Court case of 1971 concerning the offence caused by a T-shirt, which announced 'Fuck the Draft' (*Cohen* v. *California* 403 US 15, 1971). The Court found that the shirt was not erotic, and thus could not be seen as obscene, and, furthermore, it was not aimed at a person and was, thus, not 'fighting talk' (see Kors and Silverglate 1998: 44 for a more detailed discussion of the case). It might be argued that the shirt constituted a 'clear and present danger' of imminent lawlessness. However, presumably, the fact that a man wearing it in the street would be unlikely to leave a trail of such behaviour behind him would have made this difficult to prove. Finally, the fact that national security might have been breached due to the incitement to challenge the military establishment of the US, would, equally, have been difficult to prove. The Court upheld his right to wear it.

Cases such as these indicate that courts of law will vigorously defend freedom of speech, but success or failure is difficult to predict before the event. This is what prompted Fish to argue that the *principle* of freedom of speech actually hangs on how the adversaries in court mount their cases and this is mostly little more than one-upmanship in rhetorical manoeuvring (Fish 1994). Indeed, this is precisely why authors such as Fish (1994), and Marcuse (1965) before him, have sought to argue that it is a dangerous political strategy to promote the principle of freedom of speech, precisely because it is a notion without substantive content and thus likely to be defined and defended, in practice, by those who have the wherewithal to do so.

Although Kors and Silverglate are quick to associate Marcuse with Orwellian doublespeak, it is clear that the argument mounted by Marcuse in *Repressive Toleration* (Wolff *et al.* 1965) demands serious attention, for it posits that the 'freedom' to express ideas cannot exist in a vacuum, but must be framed from within the historical context in which one lives. Clearly drawing on Marx and Engels's original conception of 'capitalist hegemony' and the fact that the ruling ideas are always the ideas of the ruling class (Marx and Engels 1846), Marcuse challenges us to question who would benefit from a *principled* defence of the First Amendment. Indeed, as Marxists often point out, it is often by engendering some framed dissent that the bourgeoisie are able to maintain the illusion of freedom. As Fish points out in quoting 'Yes, the law of France is impartial; it forbids the rich as well as the poor from sleeping under bridges' (Fish 1994), there are occasions when it is easy to see capitalist law for what it, perhaps, *really* is.

The questions posed by Marcuse and Fish about who benefits from the First Amendment have a simple answer: the powerful and the scoundrel. But, is this a price worth paying? Could it not be argued that in accepting a principle of freedom of speech, while knowing that it is prone to be used and abused, we might still be better off, for to lose it would allow all sorts of restrictions on what could or could not be done and said, much of which might be promulgated precisely by the powerful and the scoundrel, and thus their free reign would be that much greater?

This is surely why so many commentators in the US support the First Amendment as an honest and robust means to *prevent*, rather than promote, the abuse of power. For, fundamentally, it aims (if not always successfully) to defend each individual's right to live his or her life as he or she chooses, and to believe what he or she chooses. Indeed this is precisely the context in which Kors and Silverglate mount their substantial attack on the use of speech codes in American colleges and universities: that regardless of the intention of speech codes, they inevitably constitute an incursion into the right of an individual to hold his or her own beliefs. Furthermore, of all the institutions in the US where one might expect this principle to be upheld, it should surely be the university.

Harassment in higher education

Speech codes proliferated in American colleges and universities throughout the 1990s. Although many have subsequently been modified and withdrawn, it is clear that the very idea of the need for such a document is indicative of a significant cultural change. Some amount to little more than a mission state-ment to indicate that the institution in question wishes to uphold and promote 'a culture of tolerance and diversity'. Others, however, are lengthy documents, which outline what can and cannot be said, where it can and cannot be said, and what the consequences are for miscreants. Naturally anti-PCers have been quick to demean and ridicule these developments:

> At Tufts, the administration proclaimed three separate 'zones' on campus – public areas, where speech could not be regulated; class rooms, dining halls, and libraries, where 'derogatory and demeaning' speech could be punished; and dormitories, where offensive remarks would be held to violate students' 'right to privacy'. Protesting Tufts students dubbed the university a 'concentration campus' and used tape and chalk to demarcate the three zones which they marked, 'Free Speech Zone', 'Limited Speech Zone' and 'Twilight Zone'.
>
> (D'Souza 1992: 146)

In perhaps the most notorious example, particularly for PC ridicule, an etiquette was established at Antioch College intended to apply before the initiation of sexual contact with another person within the boundaries of the college campus: 'Consent is defined as the act of willingly and verbally agreeing to engage in specific sexual conduct' (http://www.antioch-college.edu/Campus/sopp/index.html; accessed 30 November 2006). The following are some of the clarifying points that have drawn a lot of wider attention:

- Consent is required each and every time there is sexual activity.
- All parties must have a clear and accurate understanding of the sexual activity.
- Each new level of sexual activity requires consent.

- Consent is required regardless of the parties' relationship, prior sexual history, or current activity (e.g. grinding on the dance floor is not consent for further sexual activity).
- Body movements and non-verbal responses such as moans are not consent.
- A person can not give consent while sleeping.

(http://www.antioch-college.edu/Campus/sopp/index.html;
accessed 30 November 2006)

This Sexual Offense Prevention Policy (SOPP) has a long history at Antioch (1991 onwards), and it is clear from this history that the policy is well inten-tioned, regardless of the humour it has generated. Indeed, I'm sure that most of the people who have found humour in the policy wording would be equally scornful of the behaviour it is primarily intended to prevent, that is, sexual harassment and rape. The real issue therefore is whether such policies work, and also whether they are responsible for, on the one hand, unhelpfully expanding the domain of 'harrassing' behaviour, and, on the other, further expanding the sense that we are all persistently prone to being cast as the victims of other people's unwanted behaviours.

There is little substantial evidence of the term PC being invoked when it is clear that an intimidatory sexual environment is being discussed. Furthermore there is no obvious evidence that any university or college in the US (or the UK) would not take seriously any male or female complaint of this nature, whether from a member of staff or a student. The question therefore is whether prescriptive policies such as the one at Antioch have wittingly or unwittingly blurred an important boundary between words and behaviour, as well as helping to cast all individuals in the role of victim rather than agent. And it is precisely in these contexts where the term PC is most used, and usually to indicate that the implications are unacceptable.

With the benefit of hindsight it is unlikely that the controversies surrounding these policies can be convincingly resolved. In part this is because, conceptually, it is difficult to agree on what exactly is 'sexual harassment' – all the way from legal definitions of rape to forms of 'prolonged staring' and 'lookism'. And, furthermore, it has proved to be extremely difficult to decide convincingly whether inappropriate words and/or thoughts are, conceptually, equal when it comes to inflicting harm on another human being. A further dimension also became apparent when the long-term value of strategies aimed at 'protecting' women from intimidatory male behaviour began to be questioned in feminist circles, for fear that they are not, ultimately, liberatory. This issue was brought to the fore most pointedly by the publication of *The Morning After* (Roiphe 1993), and the ensuing debate about adopting a more liberal understanding of the relationship between victim and agent. Put simply, we all make mistakes, and in the long term there is much more to be gained by seeing males and females as equals in the, sometimes, high-risk stakes of sexual encounters.

To which might be added that it is precisely in stepping into the unknown that human sexual behaviour is able to satisfy and capture an essential quality of human desire.

However, there is an imminent danger in being seduced by this line of argument for fear that one might be accused of underestimating the true nature of a hostile environment, that is an environment where someone feels so uncomfortable that s/he comes to question his/her safety. And it is surely in this context that one should view the underlying premise of the speech and/or conduct code, that it is founded on the belief that such a hostile environment has no place within an institution of education (indeed, perhaps anywhere). And this is precisely the premise upon which many authors mount a defence of the need for some sort of 'code' (Wilson 1996; Shiell 1998): 'Study after study has shown that hate speech can cause fear in the gut, difficulty in breathing, nightmares, post-traumatic stress disorder, hypertension, even psychosis and suicide' (Matsuda, quoted in Shiell 1998: 2). In this context certain speech, 'hate speech', is taken not to be speech in the ordinary sense, as 'mere words', but as something which constitutes a form of intimidation, and which can 'wound' (Matsuda *et al.* 1993); and, as such, we should treat this intimidation no differently from administered physical violence. Although anti-PCers such as D'Souza are quick to call on the Victorian champion of free speech, J. S. Mill, in order to undermine this argument, D'Souza himself does entertain the view that there is some logic in referring to some speech as, metaphorically, a 'bullet': 'To me racial epithets are not speech. They are bullets. They can be outlawed in the same way that bank robbery can be outlawed' (Alenikoff, quoted in D'Souza 1992: 152).

Sticks, stones, and words

The previous quotation raises two, fundamentally important points. First, speech uttered by those in privileged social positions should not be treated in the same way as speech uttered by those in disadvantaged positions, that is, derogatory epithets aimed at minority groups carry a weight of oppression which simply cannot be equated with those aimed at privileged groups. For example, for a white person to refer to a black person as a 'nigger' simply cannot be compared with a black person referring to a white person as a 'honky'. Furthermore, and perhaps more importantly in terms of philosophical principle, words and phrases which are intended to be 'victimizing' should not be treated any differently from actions which are intended to have the same effect. This principle, most commonly associated with the philosopher J. L. Austin, has its foundation in the view that words and actions are not separate orders of reality. Thus, if in law it is established that person-to-person physical violence is liable to prosecution, there is no reason, in principle, that such a law should not be extended to include words and phrases which have the same intimidatory effect. Of course, it is one thing to establish a philosophical principle, it is quite another to establish an effective, workable, law.

The question of the circumstances in which one might be harmed by the actions of others was at the heart of J. S. Mill's defence of liberty in his essay on the subject (Mill 1869). In many respects it was an essay of its time because Mill wanted to protect individuals from what he saw as the invidious incursions of the Victorian state into private affairs. It would appear that the essay has become popular once more with neo-conservatives who have similar worries. But, as Lakoff pointedly remarks, it is odd that neo-conservatives in the US should become champions of free speech and the First Amendment, when they spent much of the twentieth century happy to curb what they saw as the excess and abuses of liberty in American society:

> Historically, the First Amendment was a thorn in the conservative side: it offered protection to nonmajoritarian views, lost causes, and the disenfranchised – not to mention, of course, Communists and worse. From the sedition Act of the Adams administration to continual attempts to pass constitutional amendment banning flag-desecration, conservatives have always tried to impose sanctions on free expression, while liberals have tried to keep 'the marketplace of ideas' open to all traders.
>
> (Lakoff 2000: 100)

It is clear to Lakoff's liberal mind that these neo-conservatives have a vested interest to protect their investment in a status quo that has served them well, and which could be irrevocably disturbed by a long list of left-wing causes (i.e. those identified in the previous chapters). As has already been argued, a careful political reading of PC debate is always required. In this case Mill's liberal position – that no one has a monopoly on truth – should be contrasted with the neo-conservative position – that minority causes are seeking to impose their will on the majority, or, perhaps better, the American way of life. A surface reading could lead one to believe that both political ideologies have come together to unite against a common foe – a radical left-wing alliance who would destroy the principle of freedom of speech and run amok through America's democratic institutions. This would not be so much a misreading as a partial reading for there probably *is* much for both the liberal and the neo-conservative to lose in these debates, but for *different* reasons.

The question at stake revolves around the extent to which the US has *already* established a social order through which all social groups might see themselves reflected, or how near or far we are from this mission. In a slightly more conspiratorial reading of the neo-conservative position we might also ask whether, in reality, they are defending a vested interest, for to argue for the *principle* of equality before the law might easily be interpreted as rhetoric to hide the extent to which this is palpably not the case (see the French law case, quoted by Fish, above). However, the question is complicated by the introduction of the radical position that sees truth as a form of vested interest. This argument, as we have already seen, is commonly associated in contemporary times with Stanley Fish, and it seriously complicates the 'marketplace of ideas' for, unlike in Mill's case where much argument establishes the foundation for the truth, the postmodern twist would contend that a marketplace of ideas is only ever just that, a *marketplace*, and as in any 'real' marketplace some have louder voices, more money, more influence, and, ultimately, more power. Obviously, this is the context in which Fish contended that 'there's no such thing as free speech and it's a good thing too', because all that one does by arguing this position is disguise the vested interests that are being pursued in what *appears* to be a free market (Fish 1994).

Radical opinion on freedom of speech is clearly divided. Not only are postmodern and modern radicals split on whether more speech simply creates more perspectives or whether it brings us closer to the truth, but also there are those who contend that there is more to be gained by defending the First Amendment than by attacking it. A key figure here is Gates, who was quick to recognize what he saw as the undesirable and possible unintended consequences of restrictions on freedom of speech (Gates 1993): that by restricting speech in the name of defending the disadvantaged and powerless the result will inevitably cast them as victims, in constant need of protection, exactly as Sykes outlines. As we have seen before, the left and right appear to be united in this context also, against the 'culture of dependency'. However, the background ideology of Sykes is clearly much more aligned with a 'cultural' theory of the underclass. Gates's position however is clearly one which is much easier to align with a more 'socio-structural' model where: 'even if hate did disappear, aggregative patterns of segregation and segmentation in housing and employment would not disappear' (Gates 1993: 49).

So where does this leave the case for 'hate speech' and the need to legislate against it? It is clearly opposed by those who would contend that we are, ultimately, all equally protected, and liberated, by the First Amendment. Furthermore, following Mill, words should always, wherever possible, be treated as 'words' (i.e. they are not actions and, furthermore, one cannot be 'harmed' by them). By extension, and on the grounds of 'the infallibility argument', the truth is more likely to emerge from lots of speech rather than restrictions on it (Mill 1869). That said, anyone who has been on the receiving end of vitriolic diatribes and epithets knows that there are occasions when it feels no different from a punch in the face. Indeed, as already argued, if there is legislation against the latter then why not the former? Furthermore, if one accepts that certain forms of social inequality are now deemed unacceptable, then surely speech which alludes to their *acceptability* should be as outlawed as the practices which previously sustained the inequality. In this context, surely the word 'nigger' is no such thing; it is not simply a word, but the summation of an attitude about the acceptance of certain forms of social apartheid.

Finally, if we add the Fish and Marcuse line that the First Amendment in practice is not a principle, but simply a series of rhetorical manoeuvrings designed to defend certain positions and vested interests, it would appear that we do have strong grounds for some legislation designed to outlaw certain forms of speech. However, being able to cast such legislation so that it is meaningful, practical, and without undesirable consequences seems to be an entirely different matter. And the most obvious lesson here seems to be that where 'codes' are deemed necessary they should act as guidance in promoting forms of civility rather than be punitive and couched in the language of legal sanction.

The right to be offensive?

It is for these reasons that 'hate speech' legislation and 'speech codes' – where they were deemed a necessity – were usually very carefully drawn, emphasizing the need to identify a clear and obvious individual victim. Thus, 'fuck the draft' was not worthy of being taken as 'hate speech' because it was not meaningful to cast 'the draft' as a victim. This much may be clear, but if we take a look at examples where hate speech has been invoked we can see that the most significant feature is not the victimized individual, but the identification of social groups. Bruce makes the point clearly and markedly:

> a man can murder his wife, whom he hates at the moment (perhaps he's always hated her), and that's not a hate crime. An office worker who has been fired hates his colleagues for betraying him and comes back to the office and kills them all with a sawed-off shotgun, but that's not a hate crime. How is it that we have accepted the idea that hate adds to the severity of a crime when it is identified as homophobic or racist but not when it is personal?
>
> (Bruce 2001: 48)

It might be argued that these examples actually miss the point. The reason why the first two cases would not be seen as hate crime is that the hate must come a very poor second to what is likely to be the charge in both cases (i.e. murder). However, placards proclaiming 'Death to Gays and Blacks', although perhaps intended to incite acts of murder, in themselves only constitute the act of hate, and not the act of murder. In this case, those holding the placards are (potentially) guilty of the hate crime, those committing acts of murder because the placards incited them are (potentially) guilty of murder.

However, given the context in which Bruce is writing it is clear that her real point is that hate crime is more likely to be invoked when the hate is directed at a social group rather than at an individual, and, more importantly, when the social group has been identified as a minority in need of protection. Here is an example of where 'sticks and stones may break my bones but words will never harm me' is reinterpreted to mean that certain social groups may be harmed by words more than others. This is an extremely difficult minefield to negotiate, because every component part of the argument is potentially explosive. It is premised on the view, first, that power inequalities demand a form of retributive justice; put simply, powerless groups need some form of protection from the powerful. Second, that inciteful words have an essential quality of harm, such that those who inflict them need punishment. And finally, and perhaps most damning in the context of PC debates, that the law should speak on behalf of the powerless, and determine, a priori, without reference to the intentions of the speaker, or to the reactions of the recipient, that a crime has taken place. To take a simple example, if a university decides that calling another student 'fat' is offensive, it matters not what the two parties involved in the offence actually think about what has taken place. But, and crucially in terms of hate speech, 'fat' could only become offensive in the first place if those who are obese (or rotund, or whatever other euphemism is chosen) have been previously identified as a powerless minority in need of protection from those who are 'thin' (or within a weight range deemed 'normal').

Again, right and left might unite on the unacceptable PC quality which these examples display, but the crucial political questions then become: To what extent are the combatants standing on a level playing field? And how far would a form of protectionism inevitably lead to a form of dependency? As we have already seen, there is still much to divide the left and right in their answers to these two questions. The thorniest question of all here is how far would one go in seeking to alleviate the stigma of a label, or accept that this is simply part of life, and one should 'get over it'. People on the left too may have their concerns about 'cultures of dependency', but in all such cases aren't they still much more likely to consider themselves their 'brother's keeper', and thereby baulk at those on the right who consider that the best metaphor for life is the one about 'the jungle'?

The problem with the n-word

The most controversial context for discussing appropriate interventions in the use of language surrounds the word 'nigger' or 'the n-word'. There is little doubt in the US that this word, beyond all others, is so uniquely charged by its combination of intellectual and emotional meaning that it is difficult to consider it as a *mere* word. Indeed, it seems to be able to contain the thoughts and emotions of generations through its very utterance. It is not surprising therefore that many have come to the conclusion that it is best avoided altogether. Even if the intention of the speaker is clear, what is not clear is how those hearing it will react. Indeed, it might be *so* charged that, upon hearing it, many people might not ever be sure what their reaction will be.

That said, it is a word through which the notion of 'hate speech' can be given its ultimate test. Given its unique ability to capture and summarize the most derogatory and demeaning dimensions of social apartheid, it is difficult to consider it, particularly in the hands of a white racist, as anything but a 'bullet'. It is designed to injure, cajole, and contain, and thus *maintain* a particular set of social relations. The word, thus, challenges the very core of Mill's thesis – that words, in essence, are the means to enhance liberty. But, it is also clear, that the word *is* used in other ways. For example, the LA-based rap band, *NWA – Niggaz With Attitude* – have been able to use it as a means to challenge its orthodox meaning. This is a powerful weapon; aimed at taking back the language of oppression in order to disarm its user, or, perhaps better, ensure that those being fired at are wearing metaphorical bulletproof vests.

Often referred to by postmodern theorists as an example of the 'linguistic turn', the n-word like all words can take on the quality of being, precisely, a *mere* word. Here, words do not *represent* reality. They are not signifiers but are themselves signs, that is the word 'nigger' (however spelt) does not represent an object – in this case a certain set of social relations – but has a linguistic freedom to present itself as meaning whatever its user intends. It is clear that the word is *currently* burdened by years of having a particular meaning foisted upon it, but we should not thus conclude that the word, in essence, means any one thing. It may be able to uniquely capture the history of slavery in the US, but this does not mean that the word was destined to do this, and thus *discovered* to do this, for it is possible that it may be commandeered for many purposes, indeed, in the future may even be able to imply an opposite meaning. In this sense its meaning is always *manufactured*.

This postmodern interpretation is clearly in evidence when we consider the fact that in some circles in the US it has become a term of endearment, and is used in much more playful and multifaceted ways. However, this playfulness tends to be exercised by individuals and groups with whom these language games are deemed acceptable, and thus, disarming the language of oppression can only be undertaken by those who have been its victims. Thus, black-on-black use of the word is acceptable, but white-on-black use is still largely unacceptable, even if the white person is clearly aware of the rules of the language game. It is as if any white person in the US carries, by nature of his or her skin colour, the collective memory of the derogatory use of the word, and thus cannot play with the word at all. In the same way that Jews can tell jokes about Jews but others cannot, membership of the disadvantaged group grants entry to the club and with the correct credentials one is then validated to be able to interpret meaning more freely. These are language games with club membership rules, and certainly not where 'anything goes'. And these games do not exhibit a thoroughgoing postmodern sensibility, but a carefully delineated one; a new form of politics, but one which clearly has significant birthmarks.

We should not be quick to dismiss the parental politics from which this playful postmodern child has emerged, for here, as before, there is still an unfinished battle between those on the left who do not believe that the US has produced a level political playing field, and those on the right who believe it has. In this context, 'finding a voice;' is not the same as 'having a voice' and 'distant voices', by definition, cannot be heard as well as 'foreground voices' on the political stage. Thus, although the right might be dismissive of most forms of 'protectionism', the left are divided on whether offering a helping hand onto the political stage will inevitably turn that hand into a parental (and dependent) one. And, in the context of higher education, we have perhaps begun to see some more enlightened or liberal parenting when it comes to the use of language. Thus, a university or college might now consider that its former speech code was a rather heavy-handed (parental) instrument, and instead begin to sanction the 'playing' of more postmodern language games, where, for example, an unwritten licence is granted for the use of the n-word amongst students, so long as the unwritten membership rules are understood. In effect this might be a tacit recognition of the effects of power inequalities; clearly not a 'nanny' state but equally not a policy of 'anything goes' either.

N-word debates are instructive for several reasons. Not only do they test how far one might consider words to be *mere*, and what exactly this might mean, but also how far words can be said to be owned by everyone, or just certain social groups. Furthermore, the n-word is an extremely useful weather vane of social and cultural change. For example, as Kennedy highlights, there are numerous cases brought to court where the prosecution was unable to persuade the court that their client had suffered sufficient injury from the n-word being used in their presence (Kennedy 2002). And, based on this, it could be argued that there will be fewer still in the future. However, the reasons might vary; between the fact that whites might increasingly stop using the term, and that blacks may increasingly refuse to grant the word the power to harm them. Thus, although it might once have been a 'bullet', like an old relic from a war zone, it is debatable as to whether it still has the ability to be fired and, if so, whether it might do any harm.

Clearly, in postmodern circles playing language games is a form of politics, where meaning is always figurative rather than fixed and representational, but are we all sufficiently clear about the membership rules, and what do you do when confronted with someone who is playing a different game, or with someone who doesn't believe that anything to do with the n-word is a 'game' at all? Even those most supportive of PC causes can be easily tripped up on these matters. For example when John Lennon said that 'woman is the nigger of the world' the meaning was reasonably clear at the time (1971), but in the light of subsequent debates about who owns words, and who has the authority to speak for whom, it is not clear whether this is now a PC or non-PC statement. Nor is it clear to many people how they should react to someone suggesting that they might 'become their nigger', or whether the phrase 'working like a nigger' could ever be considered truly ironic, rather than literal. And, of course, paraphrasing the words of the black writer McWhorter, just as the chances of him being referred to as a nigger by his head of department in 2003 is nil (McWhorter 2003), it still has to be said that this may not be the case in somewhat less enlightened circles.

The problem with oppositional cultures

N-word debates are troubling for the left, particularly those who would rather that politics was played out in more traditional ways, centred on the redistribution of wealth, and changing the material circumstances of people's lives. In this context 'verbal uplift is not the revolution' (Ehrenreich 1991), and messing with language, as we have already seen in the previous chapter, is just as likely to court the wrath of the radical left as it is the conservative right. But the importance of language in understanding the organic growth of culture should not be dismissed lightly. Although there is clearly a case for considering many PC euphemisms to be little more than a demeaning thesaurus for the oversensitive, and that 'verbal uplift' or 'verbal hygiene' (Cameron 1995) does little to change people's lives, it is also the case that many of these euphemisms have been produced by the critics themselves rather than reflecting terms which are used by the groups and individuals concerned. And, more significantly, the n-word can be demonstrated to be important in considering the ways in which black culture has been reframed in the US.

An excellent example of this is the discussion that ensued from the comedian Bill Cosby's concerns about the continued use of the n-word (Dyson 2005). On the one hand, it is open to misinterpretation by the white community, and thus, it can perpetuate the view that the word is still, generally, acceptable. On the other hand, it encourages a kind of separatist, oppositional mentality that will, ultimately, result in the continuation of forms of racial segregation, and hold back black achievement in American society. These arguments are premised on the belief that whites, in general, cannot differentiate between positive and negative uses of the term, that is, that they cannot understand the context, and, furthermore, that whites who wish to use the word in a negative way somehow need confirmation of their racist attitudes by reference to black usage of the term. This debate was also fuelled by the comedian Chris Rock's reappraisal of his routine 'Black People vs Niggers'. More importantly, however, this debate invites us to reconsider the broader sociological point that oppositional cultures exist precisely because of the material reality that gives rise to them. In this context, the sense that one is part of a self-generated thriving culture – be it based around the traditional youth interest in style (clothes, music, and cars, etc.), or the more intellectually based interest in adopting alternative forms of knowledge and community – is fundamental in explaining how people develop notions of self-identity and purpose.

At the heart of the Cosby critique is clearly a frustration that many more black students do not 'buckle-down' and become the kinds of successful doctors and lawyers that he portrayed in his famous situation comedy *The Cosby Show*. And this is also behind McWhorter's more academic critique of oppositional culture in the black community (McWhorter 2001, 2003). But, by embracing these ideas are we in danger of not fully understanding the organic ways in which cultures actually grow? As we have already seen, the ability to (re)appropriate language can be a powerful political act. And the very fact that the n-word is off-limits to whites might further heighten that power. Furthermore, much of the oppositional nature of black culture in the US is, in a very real sense, a critique of the very mainstream that Cosby and McWhorter, perhaps inadvertently, subscribe to. Here, understanding the power of language is also about understanding the liberatory potential to transform mainstream meanings of 'success'. This issue will be discussed in more detail in the next chapter.

Keeping it real and doing the right thing

This brings us to an aspect of PC which relates to its original Marxist–Leninist formulation, the extent to which what one says or does needs always to pay heed to a correct reading of a political agenda. In cultural politics this is a version of 'keeping it real' or seeking to 'do the right thing'. Part of Cosby's critique of oppositional black culture was his denigration of lifestyles which to his mind are going nowhere, or perhaps better, would not enable a black youth who embraced them to take a foothold on mainstream American culture. And of course here lies the (political) point. For if aspects of the mainstream are questionable, it is perfectly reasonable that these aspects might be symbolically resisted. Thus, although hip-hop music and dress, particularly when embraced as a lifestyle, may well offend Cosby's mainstream sensibilities, by the same token they can act to highlight the ironies and contradictions of the mainstream. For example, just as it is undoubtedly true that much of the dress code mimics prison attire and could thus be construed as a 'politics of despair', it may also be seen as deeply subversive.

Similarly, those who dislike many aspects of hip-hop culture often home in on the misogynistic and homophobic lyrics and the gangster lifestyle which it often celebrates. In reply one might argue that this helps to 'keep it real', because it reflects the reality of lives led, and to which one might add that all cultures have positive and negative attributes. To take an obvious counter-example, Christian religious fundamentalism in the US might be argued to be equally misogynistic and homophobic, but, in other respects, it upholds a deeply felt compassion for the 'brotherhood of man'. In this context to 'do the right thing' is always about knowing what is the correct thing to say in order to uphold the integrity of the cultural politics one espouses. This is a form of PC, for it deliberately, but for sound political reasons, highlights certain aspects of a cultural existence at the expense of others. In other words it asks that representatives of that culture understand its politics and the correctness that is required. Clearly those who oppose the culture will seek cultural capital by highlighting what is silenced, but, in equal measure, why wouldn't members of that culture seek to defend it particularly when the oppositional culture is struggling to maintain its foothold in hostile territory? Of course, to 'do the right thing' is not always obvious, because in the very nature of an organic culture it will have tensions, ambivalences, and contradictions, many of which might come to the fore at unexpected moments. And this is surely the main point of Spike Lee's film *Do the Right Thing* (1989).

For similar reasons it is understandable why Spike Lee was subsequently concerned about Quentin Tarantino's use of the n-word in the latter's films. Clearly Lee is troubled by the fact that Tarantino will not understand the subtleties of the ways that blacks have come to see the n-word in the late twentieth century, and he might thus not 'do the right thing' in using it. However, equally, it could be argued (in postmodern terms) that Tarantino's use of the word may bring new, alternative perspectives, albeit not necessarily the PC ones. It is interesting to note in this context that Kennedy sides with Tarantino, against Lee, in his analysis of the n-word (Kennedy 2002).

In some respects all these debates are peculiarly American, and probably have their roots in the pivotal role played by the legacy of the Civil Rights Movement in contemporary American society. For, surely, it is only in this context that one could hope to understand how someone could be fired for using the word 'niggardly' in a speech; or how Julius Wilson was castigated for emphasizing class disadvantage over race; or how numerous students have been able to claim that their sensibilities have been offended by the insensitivity of their teachers in their choice of language. In the light of these examples it is no wonder that even those who espouse the causes most commonly associated with PC have chosen to distance themselves from the term, thereby allowing it to fall into total disrepute. However, perhaps more importantly, all these examples indicate how the 'tripwire' of race operates in American society (see McWhorter's comments in Chapter 7). Indeed, it is such a sensitive wire that it might be wise for years to come to have these most sensitive issues discussed only by those within the appropriate communities. Of course, this is, itself, a form of PC because the normal rules of detached academic scholarship are hereby abandoned leaving us all with the choice between rallying against this in the name of free speech, or embracing it as a form of 'doing the right thing'.

One measure of the dynamic nature of these debates is how readily people pride themselves on being deliberately, and sometimes provocatively, non-PC. And, perhaps more interestingly, that they are aware that they have become a pawn in a PC game of chess and might now want to relieve themselves of the burden of always having to be seen to be doing the right thing. As Kennedy remarks at the end of his book, when speaking of black entertainers who regularly use the n-word:

'I don't give a fuck.' These entertainers don't care whether whites find nigger upsetting. They don't care whether whites are confused by blacks' use of the term. And they don't care whether whites who hear blacks using the N-word think that African Americans lack self-respect. The black comedians and rappers who use and enjoy nigger care principally, perhaps, exclusively, about what they themselves think, desire, and enjoy – which is part of their allure.

(Kennedy 2002: 173)

Here we see an important aspect of cultural identity, the sheer exuberance of creative energy, and unfettered by the contribution it might make to a political cause. In one way, of course, it is still political, but it is not where the politics comes first, or where the politics is a badge of approval. That is for others.

Conclusion

To a large extent the debate about words and actions is intractable. Either one believes that the two have sufficient similarities in their effects that they should be considered indistinguishable or one does not. And the legacy of J. S. Mill is substantial in this context, for who does not want to be on the side of 'liberty'? As before, the problem is rather more epistemological than political when it comes to PC, because if maximizing free speech takes us closer to the truth, this will inevitably collide with those who believe that what we will actually get is simply more perspectives. Furthermore, although Mill tries hard to reject the view that speech can be harmful, it is ultimately a utilitarian argument rather than a principled one, that is, there is more to be gained from freedom of speech than lost. Thus, in situations where there might be a case for more being lost, it is not clear at all that a principle of free speech would be upheld. And this is surely the main reason why the US has established exceptions to the First Amendment. When it comes to actions, Mill carefully articulates the difference between self-regarding and other-regarding actions, allowing the state the right to intervene in cases of the latter. Although notoriously difficult in practice to delineate any actions which are purely self-regarding, the PC problem seems to have become not just one where the same rule should apply to speech as action, but that the state (or proxy) interventions need to be punitive and protective. Furthermore, as in the case of hate speech legislation, that this should apply only in situations where a social group has been previously identified as vulnerable.

A troubling PC angle, particularly for the left, is how far any social change can be either instigated or brought about by reframing the use of language. And here the thought of Gates, a black university professor, standing on a New York street corner yelling 'It's only a trope!' at cab drivers who repeatedly ignore his attempts to hail them, is a reminder of what exactly is the nature of the politics behind various strands of literary theory (Gates 1992: 147). But, as we have seen, n-word debates are instructive in highlighting the ways in which cultural and countercultural forces play important political roles, and how wider notions of deconstruction might be employed. Here is also an example of where context is everything, and in two separate senses. First, subverting the very concept of race *is* a significant anti-racist strategy in intellectual circles where one has a grounding in a critique of essentialist thinking, but being a 'nigga with attitude' is equally subversive in wider cultural debate beyond the university seminar. Similarly, within the confines of a community of scholars who are engaged in the disinterested pursuit of truth there might well be some disquiet about the fact that one should be seen to be doing the right thing. However, in other communities one might well have to make difficult decisions as to whose side one is on when a particular argument ensues.

Although speech codes quickly became viewed as rather blunt and clumsy instruments, it is clear that colleges and universities did feel that they needed to respond to the kinds of provocations that some students were facing. It might also be said to be somewhat ironic that although the right put much of the epistemological blame for PC on the deconstructing tendencies of poststructural theory, the advocacy of a much more playful attitude to language does not sit at all squarely with a desire to police the use of language.

But, should Eden Jacobowitz have been reprimanded for uttering 'water buffalo'? Cleary, the term was directed at a 'vulnerable' social group, and given that he was forceful in wanting them to be quiet there was an element of 'fighting talk'. On the subject of the term itself, it appears that it has a Jewish root, as a derogatory slur aimed at lazy people. Thus, to see it as a racist slur would require some manoeuvring, either towards arguing that it has an alternative meaning, or that someone might hide a form of racism behind it. Whatever the merits of the case it is clear that it was soon to become fodder to the anti-PC campaign, and earned the president of the University of Pennsylvania at the time, Sheldon Hackney, the dubious honour of being named 'the pope of PC'. That Alan Kors also worked at the university at the time meant that the story had even more of an impact than it might otherwise have had. For Kors it helped forge the view that universities had become 'shadows' of their former selves (Kors and Silverglate 1998). For Hackney it meant he had to try to steer an almost impossible path between demonstrating that he was keen to be seen defending students from potentially harassing behaviours whilst upholding the intellectual integrity of the university (Hackney 2002).

Upholding the First Amendment as a fundamental principle in the US may have become more the responsibility of the right than the left in the past fifty years, but, from the *Flint* v. *Falwell* case alone, it is clear that the Supreme Court of the US would take some convincing of the need to abridge any speech. However, within the walls of higher education and in wider cultural debate it is clear that certain forms of abridgement do operate, and for good reason. Although the case against speech codes is generally sound, it is not clear at all that higher education is where one would expect to see the most free speech, because if it is a 'marketplace of ideas' it is a very unique one. Universities and colleges are there to promote a particular type of speech, speech in the form of ideas, to be tested, examined, questioned, and analysed. Thus, a racial epithet, at least in the form in which it is normally uttered, is not an *idea*. However, arguments that support forms of racial intolerance are ideas, they *are* there for the academic community to discuss, debate, and possibly debunk. Thus, the question to ask is not about the freedom to speak as one pleases, but to render that speech liable to critical analysis.

The principle underpinning this conception of the marketplace of ideas is a Kantian one: 'Man and every rational being exists as an end in itself, not merely as means for arbitrary use by this will or that; but he must in all his actions . . . be regarded at the same time as an end' (Kant [1788] 1909). What we have seen in the past twenty years is those who wish to promote the interests of powerless groups in society (and particularly in higher education) shoot themselves several times in the foot. Having, on numerous occasions, not been able to defend themselves from the accusation that they are unnecessarily policing speech and actions, and in the process breeding a 'nation of victims', they have also had to confront the fact that, in challenging the First Amendment, they are also un-American. With hindsight it might have been much wiser to consider that the problem lay not with particular words, phrases, or actions, but with their intention, and to defend a university as a place which demands that ideas are always rendered in ways which enable them to be debated and analysed. The First Amendment has turned out to be a significant club with which to beat PC causes; a Kantian categorical imperative centred on respect for personhood may have offered more resistance.

5

The end of civilization in California
Illiberal multiculturalism

Previously Stanford steered all incoming students through a core
curriculum – an examination of the philosophy, literature, and history of
the West, focusing on such thinkers as Plato, Dante, Machiavelli,
Voltaire, Marx, and Freud; and on such events as the ascent of Greece,
the fall of Rome, mediaeval Christian civilisation, the Renaissance and
the Reformation, the French and Scottish Enlightenment, and the
founding of modern states. The new CIV [Cultures, Ideas, Values] would
substitute a multiple track system, each examining an issue or field, such
as Technology and Values, through a cross-cultural survey of ideas and
mores. Such an approach would include Western perspectives, but also
African, Japanese, Indian, and Middle Eastern ones. Since the number of
texts that can be assigned and discussed in a semester is limited, the
relative importance of Western thinkers would be correspondingly
reduced. Some of them, such as Homer, Virgil, and Aquinas, would have
to make way for new non-Western voices. A special effort was promised
not to imply any superiority of western ideas or Western culture – all
cultures would be sustained on a plane of equality.

(D'Souza 1992: 61)

Introduction

Multicultural education has been an important *bête noire* for anti-PCers. Those
who promote the multicultural cause are often cast as agents of dumbing down
or purveyors of mediocrity and this was especially so in the debates that
surrounded the 'end of civilization' at Stanford University in the late 1980s, that
is, over the decision taken by the prestigious university to replace its Western
Civilization course with its CIV course. For many it epitomized what was wrong
with higher education and confirmed the need to defend the 'Western Canon'.

The debate at Stanford appeared to be bitterly fought. In the metaphorical
blue corner there was 'Western Civilization' representing the good and beautiful; a very substantial cultural heritage and concomitant realist epistemology. By
contrast, in the metaphorical red corner there was 'Culture, Ideas, Values'
arguing that not only had the blue corner created an 'incredulous' modern

canon but it was also having the effect of marginalizing other cultural works, particularly from those whose voices were either distant from, or antithetical to, the 'canon'. Not surprisingly these latter works were often Afrocentric, feminist, eco-friendly, gay, etc., comprising the 'usual suspects' of the political right in the US, and those groups most associated with PC. Major exponents of this *au courant*, as D'Souza (1992) refers to them, have been the deconstructive and decentring schools of poststructuralism, the epistemological and playful strands of postmodern thinking, and, in general, the radical political left, who are charged with seeking to discredit the very notion of canonical knowledge.

In this chapter I will be discussing the relationship between multiculturalism and PC and I will argue that the epistemological foundations of deconstruction and poststructural theory are a substantive foundation for forms of multi-cultural education. However, in helping transform the aims of higher education there is still a partial case to be heard about the impoverishment of higher education. In arguing this I will conclude that one should not be either pro- or anti-PC in debates concerning multiculturalism, but recognize what is actually being defended by those who take these positions.

As we have already seen, wresting famous authors from their canonical pedestal was bound to court controversy. The popular interpretation of postmodernism was that it seeks to establish a thoroughgoing relativism in all things cultural and epistemological, thus denying any credible or objective way to measure the quality of anything. Put simply, surely we should be able to say that Shakespeare's portrayal of King Lear is of a higher quality than little Johnny's poem about his parents, and the ceiling of the Sistine Chapel is a more worthy artistic product than an electric bulb hanging from a bare-roomed ceiling and being turned on and off? And as we saw in Chapter 2, Bloom (1987) arrived quickly on this scene.

Multiculturalism is a problematic term, partly because it has many dimensions, and also because it has been discredited by the left and the right: aside from its association with 'canon busting' it is also linked with a number of sociological concerns about the social construction of educational failure, a wider concern about competing axes of knowledge, and an allied concern about what education is for. In each case these concerns have been tarred with the brush of PC, and the notion has a chequered history in American academic literature (e.g. Sykes 1995; Katsiaficas and Kiros 1998; Sacks and Thiel 1998; Wiener and Berley 1999; Barry 2001). For some the term is relatively unprob-lematic. Indeed, Spring offers the following concise summary:

> Multicultural education programs have four important goals. The first goal is to build tolerance of other cultures. The second goal is to eliminate racism. The third goal is to teach the content of different cultures. And the fourth goal is to teach students to view the world from differing cultural frames of reference.
>
> (Spring 2004: 166)

However, almost immediately we find ourselves having to ask whether these goals should be pursued over and above other goals, and, more controversially, what is to be done when we are confronted with any facts that might demand some *intolerance*? For example, is female circumcision simply a case of *Que Sera, Sera*, and how fundamentally should we hold on to a belief in tolerance, particularly when we know that other cultures are often singularly *intolerant* of, for example, forms of blasphemy or homosexuality? Notwithstanding the ambivalence there is towards both in Christian circles in the US, it is clear that any number of similar examples will present a serious challenge to an education which rests on a rather loose and general notion of tolerance.

Furthermore, although Spring's second goal would obviously be lauded by most people in the US, it is not at all clear exactly what one needs to do in order to bring this about. And here is an example, once again, of where many on the left and right might agree, because it is not intuitively obvious that by teaching *about* racism one is thereby helping to eliminate it. Nor is it clear to what extent this should overshadow, or indeed become integral to, the teaching of the traditional 3Rs – reading, writing, and arithmetic. And, as will be discussed shortly, it is not clear, conceptually, that the first place to begin to confront the material reality of racism is the classroom. There is an obvious link here with issues raised in the previous chapter about whether changing the language and behaviour of the classroom is a sufficient determining variable in changing society at large. And here we also see an example of where many on the left would argue that forms of multiculturalism can have the effect of trivializing the analysis of racism, which is exactly the charge made by Sykes (1992) about PC in general.

However, at the most fundamental level multiculturalism encourages relativism in knowledge, and it is here where Spring's summary can be rendered the most problematic. In this context, multiculturalism's ideological stance is that cultural knowledge is precisely that, knowledge tied to cultural context. This often leads advocates to the conclusion that to attempt to judge, in some hierarchical fashion, the validity of cultural knowledge is simply a form of unacceptable cultural imperialism. Not surprisingly therefore it is not uncommon to ally this type of thinking with broader postmodern ideas, and the critique of 'modern' forms of knowledge: 'there is a huge disparity between the claim of Reason to be independent of ideology and the pedigree of any of the reasons you might think to give' (Fish 1994: 17). Naturally this is itself roundly criticized by those who argue that Modernity, through its epistemological grounding in positivism and Reason, is *precisely* about being able to make hierarchically based judgements concerning the validity of knowledge: 'Cultural relativism succeeds in destroying the west's universal or intellectually imperialistic claims, leaving it just be another culture. So there is equality in the republic of cultures' (Bloom 1987: 39).

Multiculturalism as a war on poverty

Multiculturalism has a long history in the US. Indeed it might be argued that it is implicit in the very notion of a 'melting pot' (Zangwill 1909). The more modern conception of multiculturalism began to take shape in the context of debates which surrounded President Johnson's 'War on Poverty' in the early 1960s, and is often linked with its most successful programme, Head Start – the series of initiatives aimed at improving the educational attainment of children from poor families. Although it is debatable how successful the Head Start programme has been, it is generally perceived in a positive way – and it also spawned the popular TV show *Sesame Street* (Office of Head Start http://www.acf.hhs.gov/programs/hsb/index.htm; accessed 17 January 2007). However, the original 'War on Poverty' did spark significant intellectual controversy about the notion of 'cultural deprivation' and how this was perceived as the primary cause of the low educational attainment of many children from 'impoverished' families, particularly in the years surrounding their early schooling. Generally speaking, it seemed to imply that cultural poverty was a bigger problem than financial poverty, and thus that the latter might be masked by the former.

Furthermore, as many sociologists were quick to point out, a key concern quickly became whether this was not so much a deprivation of culture *in general* (for how could someone be deprived of all culture?), but one of deprivation from a *particular* set of cultural values (Ryan 1972; Keddie 1974; Valencia 1997). Or, to put it more politically, cultural deprivation came to be viewed as the need for certain pupils, mainly black and working class, to trade in their own values for those of their white, middle-class counterparts. This was seen as being fuelled by the unconscious imposition of middle-class values by the teaching profession who simply could not see their own values as anything other than 'culture' itself. It was a short step from this thesis to seeing 'cultural deprivation' as a thinly veiled disguise for forms of unjustifiable cultural imperialism. It not only helped cement the feeling in many black communities that success in school simply meant 'acting white', but it also added some significant rationalizing fire to the growing Afrocentric movement, which contrasted traditional Eurocentric knowledge with its own (Asante 1997). This is the background context to much of what Bloom presented in his defence of 'Western Civilization' (Bloom 1987), and also the decision by Stanford University to remove its course of the same name.

Competing axes of knowledge

Once the curriculum had been politicized in this way it was a short step to ask: 'In *whose* history do we want to invest our belief?' In the more radical forms of multicultural education this became allied with the idea that, by investing in the 'facts' of Eurocentric knowledge, this *itself* contributed to the continued subservience of those who did not benefit from these 'facts'. Here we have a form of Marxian cultural hegemony combined with a dose of 'false class consciousness'. And the solution to this bourgeois deception is to see education as a form of 'consciousness raising', in order to give subservient groups the voice to further develop their own forms of knowledge; forms which will promote *their* interests. As will be discussed shortly, this is not strictly speaking a Marxist position, as it gives the kind of 'relative autonomy' to superstructural institutions which would undermine the central Marxist tenet that these must 'reflect' the mode of production. And we have already seen these concerns expressed by many on the left in previous chapters. Furthermore, it has led many to conclude that education would very quickly become hopelessly relativistic, where no knowledge would be independent of human vested interest. On both points it is easy to see how multiculturalism quickly became associated with PC: on the one hand it was not political enough, but on the other it made education intrinsically a political process. For authors like Rorty (1989) it also confirmed the postmodern position that the truth is made not found, and thereby asked us (somewhat ironically) to look to the original Latin root of the word 'fact' – as in *to manufacture*.

The contours of this debate can be seen most starkly in the early 1990s controversy concerning City College of New York's Chair of African American Studies, Leonard Jeffries, and his teaching of history on the basis of the distinction between 'sun people' and 'ice people' – the former being people of African descent who have developed a more cooperative lifestyle, to be contrasted with a more European form of competitive individualism. The controversy this sparked is very much a PC controversy, not just because cooperative lifestyles are judged to be superior to forms of competitive individualism, but, more importantly, because even in the light of significant factual evidence which undermines the whole credibility of the thesis one can still be asked to invest one's belief in it because it is *politically* the right thing to do. That is, as we saw in the previous chapter, doing the right thing requires that one be willing to rank knowledge according to whether it is *politically correct* rather than factually correct. This also neatly ties up a number of threads in PC debates, namely: the questioning of facts which are deemed independent of human interpretation; the use of education to promote the interests of subservient social groups; and, perhaps most significantly, the idea that political 'truths' are more important than 'natural' truths.

It also provides a firm foundation for the consideration of a broad range of knowledge bases. From this perspective 'factual' knowledge is brought down from its metaphorical Mount Olympus and is asked to find a spot on the salt plains of Nevada, alongside a plethora of alternative forms of knowledge, from voodoo, faith, and forms of pagan wisdom at the more traditional end, all the way to more recent concepts of 'standpoint' knowledge, feminist voices (Gilligan 1982), emotional intelligence (Goleman 1995), and perhaps even forms of 'beauty' as a kind of knowledge. And many of these will not be rooted in the cognitive domain, but the affective, and the kinaesthetic. In this context challenging Eurocentric knowledge is not just about challenging its content, but also its epistemological and (lack of) emotional foundation: 'The Afrocentrists insist on steering the minds of their readers and listeners in the direction of intellectual wholeness' (Asante 1997: 180).

Multiculturalism, postmodernity, and epistemology

The wider intellectual context of these debates is often linked to work of the French philosopher Foucault, who demanded that we view all knowledge as the defence of vested interest, be it witting or unwitting, which itself is often linked to the literary deconstruction movement, popularized in the writings of Derrida, and which has its most cogent representative in the US in the work of Stanley Fish. Indeed, in the book which brings together most of his ideas on matters relating to PC he mockingly begins with: 'Do you hear what they're saying? Words have no intrinsic meaning, values are relative, rationality is a social construct, everything is political, every reading a misreading' (Fish 1994: 4).

The connection between radical multiculturalism and these postmodern ideas is an important one because the latter have a double-edged subversive quality. They lend support to the view that all knowledge contains vested interests, and also, thereby, that there is no higher authority to which one can appeal when seeking to advance one's position; none that is apart from rhetorical dexterity (Fish 1994). The consequences of this conclusion have serious implications for the way that the word 'political' should be understood in PC debates. For if all human knowledge is *thoroughly* political, this becomes a substantial epistemological stand upon which to defend multicultural education. From this perspective multicultural education need no longer depend on a normative imperative to defend its position, for, in having an epistemological foundation there truly is 'equality in the republic of cultures' because there is no longer a Platonic 'divided line' between different forms of knowledge (Plato [360 BC] 1955).

If everything is a footnote to Plato this argument also suggests that PC is actually as old as *The Republic*. For, in arguing that *epistemic* knowledge is of a higher order than the *doxa* of opinion, Plato was seeking to establish the original higher authority that Bloom was resurrecting, and he is doing so in the face of considerable democratic sophistry, the likes of which are currently embodied in the work of Fish. If we take this strand of PC to be important, it thus becomes possible to argue that there has always been *political* correctness. That is it is one thing to argue that PC politicizes the classroom in allowing overtly political causes to be taught as part of the curriculum (whether this be at an ideological level or in an effort to raise self-esteem), but it would appear to be (literally) of another 'order' to argue, on epistemological grounds, that all knowledge is thoroughly political in its very nature. And although the former argument came to dominate much of the debate about PC in the late twentieth century, it would appear that radical multiculturalism offers us a significant window into understanding a deeper set of roots.

Multiculturalism and the left

Returning to Spring's summary definition of multiculturalism, it is obviously understandable why, given the history of race relations in the US, he refers exclusively to race in the second point. But eliminating other forms of discriminatory behaviour (e.g. sexism and homophobia) could easily sit comfortably alongside. Apart from the Pavlovian reaction that many on the right seem to have when these 'usual suspects' of dominated groups are listed, it is clear, as we have already seen in previous chapters, that the left have had some considerable problems in deciding the appropriate theoretical status for the 'rainbow alliance' of the disadvantaged. Indeed, Marx himself may have had some concerns about the 'lumpenproletariat' but, generally speaking, he had a clear conceptual notion of the proletariat; that they should be defined by their relationship to the means of production, and they should understand their historical and universal mission. Thus, Marxist theory generally does not sit comfortably with much of the multicultural agenda. One of the main issues is the extent to which one wishes to adhere to a strict Marxist position on the correct relationship between 'base and superstructure' (i.e. that the economic base must always be seen as the determining variable, and that the social, legal and cultural institutions of the superstructure – the Church, schools, etc. – must be seen as the ideological means through which the base is reproduced).

This Marxist formula was given its most comprehensive airing in the work of Bowles and Gintis (1976). Operating with what they refer to as a strict 'correspondence theory' they produced a catalogue of evidence to suggest that students from working-class homes in the US experience schooling as little more than a preparation for the kinds of low-paid, low-status jobs which help to sustain a capitalist economic structure. Much criticized in subsequent years in both the UK and the US for its somewhat crude reproduction theory, and often by the left itself and other Marxists (see Willis 1977), their work has proved to be remarkably resilient to empirical refutation. Indeed, twenty-five years on they were confident in being able to reassert the validity of much of their original thesis (Bowles and Gintis 2002). This is relevant to a discussion of PC in a number of ways. First, if we take Bowles and Gintis to be modern representatives of the strict Marxist position on 'base and superstructure' then their conclusion (that reforms in the education system are unlikely to bring about the kinds of changes that would substantially alter the life chances of working-class youth) suggests that the forms of multiculturalism advocated by many liberal theorists would actually make very little headway into seriously challenging inequality in the US.

In this regard, both the left and right can agree once more; that changing the curriculum and being more sensitive to the needs of students who are not 'white, middle class, and male', is at best a trivial enterprise, and a worst a distraction from the heart of matter. Of course, whereas the heart of the matter for a conservative would be functional numeracy and literacy, inculcation into a cultural heritage, respect and deference for American ideals, and so on, for a radical it would be the wholesale transformation of an economic structure which demands that millions must earn their living in low-paid, low-status, dead-end occupations. Once again we can see here how PC stands, on the right, for activities which act to subvert mainstream American values, and, on the left, for activities which detract attention away from the reform and transformation of the capitalist economic structure.

Hidden means and ends in the curriculum

Although Willis's notion of 'counter-school culture' ultimately results in working-class youth colluding in their own exploitation, Giroux, following Freire considers how forms of 'critical pedagogy' can offer prospects of empowerment for those who are currently distant from the more traditional corridors of power (Giroux 1981; Freire 1970). Both 'counter-school culture' and 'critical pedagogy', as concepts, invite us to reconsider not just what mainstream schooling is for, but also just how contestable more traditional notions of schooling *as culture* are, and how 'cultural literacy' and a 'literary canon', in reality, simply reflect the values of a comfortable bourgeois existence. In this context, investing in 'cultural capital' is literally an investment in a middle-class lifestyle (Bourdieu and Passeron 1977).

As we saw in the previous chapter, a thorny PC matter is the extent to which one views this investment as valid. Those who support it escape the label PC, but those who don't are quickly prepared for PC ridicule. For Willis, in the UK, the working-class pupils who undertake the investment have to suffer the derogatory label 'ear 'oles' by their counter-school peers, 'the lads'. In the more racially divided context of US education the former are said to be 'acting white' by their black peers, and in wider society are often referred to as 'Uncle Toms' (Ogbu 1988). However, in all cases, intellectuals who support any one of these stances have to suffer the less ignominious label of being 'PC'. Regardless of the labels, however, the notion 'counter-school culture' does raise important educational questions, and the most important of these is whether it demands that we put more effort into countering the countering, or consider the ways in which the curriculum might become more meaningful to those who resist it. Clearly forms of 'critical pedagogy' are predicated on the latter response, but this is complicated by asking whether the word *pedagogy* (in 'critical pedagogy') is a reference to the *methods* by which one might engage alienated pupils, or the *content* of the curriculum itself.

Just as we have to ask whether the real purpose behind a 'critical pedagogy' is to find ways of simply *engaging* those who are disillusioned or whether it is really about changing the content of the curriculum, the same needs to be asked about multiculturalism in general. Underneath the concern that all students should be able to see their own cultures, backgrounds, and experiences reflected in the curriculum is a deeper one about whether this is being provided as a stepping stone to embrace what many other (middle-class) students already possess, or whether it is the first step towards a more broadly based curriculum, or even, an alternative, separatist curriculum (and even an alternative conception of knowledge altogether). Naturally, as one makes one's way down these alternatives the more likely one is to be cast, in derogatory manner, as PC.

The issues raised here have been of concern in American education for some considerable time and can clearly be seen in the debates about the merits of encouraging forms of bilingualism, particularly in early schooling. Indeed, the key dilemma can be traced back to the seminal text on the use of standard English in American schools (Labov, in Keddie 1974). This article can be read in one of two ways. First, as a powerful indictment of the, so-called, superiority of standard English over other forms, but second, as a mild endorsement of an assimilation project, which simply asks teachers to accept the 'logic of non-standard English' as a first step towards the gradual adoption of mainstream forms of communication. The crucial difference between a traditional assimilation position is that here 'standard' English is not considered superior, simply conventional. This debate has proved difficult to resolve and it resurfaced with a vengeance in the controversy over the use of 'ebonics' in Oakland Schools in the late 1980s (McWhorter 2001).

Liberals against radicals on multiculturalism

Just as multiculturalism is too conservative for the radical left, it is equally too radical for the conservative right. But the more interesting observation is surely that the concept of multiculturalism has brought the liberal left much closer to the conservative right. United in opposition to a *radical* multicultural agenda, whose ultimate aim would appear to be the destruction of the Enlightenment project, the term PC has become an important axis for this debate. This can be seen most clearly in the PC-dedicated edition of *Partisan Review* published in the autumn of 1993. Here we see a rallying call to the *liberal* left to unite in opposition to a radical left. Using the language of the conservative right (see Chapter 2) many of the authors castigate the radical left as tyrannical, Orwellian, and Stalinist: 'PC is a form of groupthink fuelled by paranoia and demonology and imposed by political or social intimidation' (Dickstein 1993: 543).

But, more significantly, the deeper concern is the epistemological foundation for forms of multicultural education. The radical left's form of multiculturalism is thus cast as an anti-Enlightenment project, an epistemological attack as much as a political one. In this context it is objectionable, not simply because it constitutes a 'dictatorship of virtue' (Bernstein 1994), a form of obedience to a party political position, but equally because it runs roughshod over the Enlightenment principle of the rational individual in pursuit of truth and human progress. Put this way it is easy to see why such an interpretation of multiculturalism could not appeal to a traditional liberal mind:

> Central to this slowly emerging and often contested way of thinking has been the idea of an autonomous individual who, not inherently embedded in religion, nature, and community, is capable of overcoming the constraints flowing from them and even of turning against them. These cognitive predispositions have provided fundamental communalities to the civilizations of the West, in spite of vast differences in history and culture and the many bloody wars fought among them.
>
> (Berger 1993: 519)

Although at one level teaching children to tolerate, or even celebrate, cultural differences, and in higher education allowing them to further this exploration by concentrating on the local and the particular might be viewed as simply an inferior education, at another level it is clearly the avenue to a completely different conception of what an education should be for. Not only does it open up the possibility that children become unable to discriminate between what is good and what is not, but as they grow older and enter higher education they become unable to see what is common to the human condition, and ultimately find themselves having simply validated their own existences. This is a PC world because there is no notion of education as the search for the truth; no notion that there are objective criteria for making judgements as to something's worthiness; no notion of a shared higher education commitment to agreed rules of scholarship; and, ultimately, no notion of a common humanity. Clearly for some commentators all these features are also uniquely un-American.

Liberals as conservatives on multiculturalism?

In the view of Schlesinger, multiculturalism has helped to bring about the 'disuniting of America' (Schlesinger 1998). Following on from themes we have already encountered (Bloom 1987; D'Souza 1992; Sykes 1992), multiculturalism is accused of hijacking the more worthy aims of education in favour of the celebration of cultural identity. Rather than seeing programmes such as *Sesame Street* as a means to assimilate ethnic minority children, the whole of education from pre-school until university graduation has begun to be used to positively affirm ethnic status:

The militants of ethnicity contend that a main objective of public education should be the protection, strengthening, celebration, and perpetuation of ethnic origins and identities. Separatism, however, nourishes
prejudices, magnifies differences, and stirs antagonisms. The consequent
increase in ethnic and racial conflict lies behind the hullabaloo over
'multiculturalism' and 'political correctness,' over the inequities of the
'Euro centric' curriculum, and over the notion that history and literature
should be taught not as intellectual disciplines but as therapies whose
function is to raise minority self-esteem.

(Schlesinger 1998: 22)

Although Schlesinger dissociates himself from some of the more conservative
attacks on PC, his own attack on forms of multicultural education is rooted in
some familiar conservative concerns:

Let us by all means teach black history, African history, women's history,
Hispanic history, Asian history. But let us teach them as history, not as
filopietistic commemoration. The purpose of history is to promote not
group self-esteem, but understanding of the world and the past, dis-
passionate analysis, judgment, and perspective, respect for divergent
cultures and traditions, and unflinching protection for those unifying
ideas of tolerance, democracy, and human rights that make free historical
inquiry possible.

(Schlesinger 1998: 104)

This is not, therefore, an attempt to resurrect Western Civilization but simply a
plea that traditional forms of scholarship be applied to the newly emerging
curricula content. If there is a problem with the curriculum it is not so much
what is being taught, but *how* it is being taught. The problem is thus truly a
pedagogical one. A further dissociation with many on the political right
follows from his recognition that much of what constitutes traditional history
is little more than ideological defences for the powerful – enabling them,
through educational means, to stay in power. But, having learnt this lesson, what
merit can there be in the discipline of history simply becoming the means by
which powerless groups seek some sort of revenge. All that we do, if we allow
this to happen, is replace 'exculpatory history' with 'compensatory history'
(Schlesinger 1998: 54–55).

Schlesinger's critique is cogent, particularly in arguing that 'compensatory
education' is the means by which notions like esteem have been able to infiltrate
even the higher education curriculum, and how the study of history has become
a form of retribution, but we should be careful to separate this strand of PC from
its more epistemological one. For, it is one thing to argue that the discipline of
history is in danger of losing its sense of criticality, quite another to argue that
there are rules of method by which historical analysis can be rendered objective
and free from propaganda. Indeed, in concluding that it is important to practise

'respect for divergent cultures and traditions' it is troubling that he then proceeds to condemn female genital circumcision; troubling not because we should be celebrating the latter, but because it is not clear at all, in the light of anti-foundational arguments, that one could unquestionably separate the facts from the values in these situations.

The other significant strand in Schlesinger's critique is the reconsideration of the means by which we measure success. Like many others he is extremely worried about the extent to which the ultimate aim in multiculturalism is the replacement of the traditional ladders of opportunity in American society with an alterative separatist edifice. Given its ability to chime with many who oppose PC causes the relevant section is worth quoting at length:

> Even if history is sanitized in order to make people feel good, there is no evidence that feel-good history promotes ethnic self-esteem and equips students to grapple with their lives. Afro centric education, on the contrary, will make black children, as William Raspberry has written, 'less competent in the culture in which they have to compete.' After all, what good will it do young black Americans to take African names, wear African costumes, and replicate African rituals, to learn music and mantras, rhythm and rapping, to reject standard English, to hear that because their minds work differently a first class education is not for them? Will such training help them to understand democracy better? Help them to fit better into American life? 'General Powell did not reach his present post,' Jacques Barzun reminds us, 'by believing that Black English was sufficient for the career he wanted to pursue.'
>
> (Schlesinger 1998: 99)

Here we see the validity of three important pillars of radical multiculturalism undermined: the validity of arguments in favour of raising self-esteem in education; the validity of claims in support of 'the logic of non-standard English'; and the validity of alternative axes of knowledge. Of course, the original foundation for the critique itself rests on the worthiness of striving to succeed within the existing institutions of the US. And, in accepting that the three multicultural pillars might be made of salt, it does not logically follow that one should thus seek 'life, love, and the pursuit of happiness' in traditional American ways.

Ultimately, for Schlesinger, the problem with multiculturalism is that it undermines the notion of 'common culture'. It disunites Americans, by detracting attention away from what is 'common' to the American way of life: 'The future of immigration policy depends on the capacity of the assimilation process to continue to do what it has done so well in the past: to lead newcomers to an acceptance of the language, the institutions, and the political ideals that hold the nation together' (Schlesinger 1998: 127). Thus, in a time-honoured fashion, Americans are asked to see themselves, first and foremost, not as black, female, or gay, but as American, and to accept the validity of the institutions which support that nation. Multiculturalism is simply not assimilationist enough in its aspiration. On too many fronts it supports either the celebration of difference, or the promotion of forms of separatism.

Conclusion

From the perspective of 'the US as a nation of immigrants' multiculturalism is hardly a controversial term. Whether one takes the 'melting pot' or the 'salad bowl' as the metaphor the US is clearly a multicultural society. Even in discussions of the more contentious term 'inclusion' multiculturalism has been able to avoid controversy. However, in its association with PC it has been tarred by a very thick brush. One of the key themes in anti-PC literature is how the causes associated with the term have been rendered un-American, and this is the case with much of what has been written against multiculturalism.

However, it would wrong to assume that only conservatives are against forms of multicultural education, for its critics can be found across the political spectrum. That said, it is important to understand the different reasons for the objections. For the right, to question received wisdom on the contributions of Western civilization to art, literature, and politics is simply too much to bear; to run roughshod over agreed rules for aesthetic taste, literary criticism and appreciation, and to find the vested interests of class, race, and gender throughout all that has been written, and in all political institutions, is a challenge that simply must be risen to. And the term PC has proved very powerful in both defending these standards, and promoting forms of 'cultural literacy' centred on them.

Concerns about forms of multicultural education can also be found on the political left. One of the clear effects of PC debates has been to create a chasm between the liberal left and the radical left. In subscribing to a postmodern sensibility and adopting forms of anti-realist epistemology radicals have incurred the wrath of those liberals who have seen such manoeuvres as an onslaught on the basic principles of the Enlightenment. The thought that rational individuals can no longer make valid judgements about the enhancement of the human condition is simply too much for them to bear as well. And in promoting alternative axes of knowledge, and extreme forms of cultural tolerance, the liberal enlightened mind has been quick to try to rescue us from this relativistic quagmire.

Although some of these liberals have tried to associate the postmodernists with the Marxists in a united affront, the association is not well founded. Apart from the fact that many who adopt forms of postmodern thinking are sceptical about politics in general, it is important to consider what else is at stake. Forms of radical multiculturalism, from 'critical pedagogy' to separatist forms of Afrocentrism, all grant educational establishments the power to effectively transform people's lives, and in strict Marxist terms this is suspect both empirically and theoretically. As part of the superstructure of capitalist relations of production the education system simply does not have the 'autonomy' to bring about the necessary changes, and therefore forms of multicultural education can do little beyond ameliorate the effects of structural inequalities. Furthermore, in generating their own unique conceptual frameworks, including 'sex classes' and 'sun people', it is not clear how higher education degrees in women's studies and black studies subscribe to any 'common dream' of a future egalitarian humanity; only justifications for why certain forms of knowledge require a particular lived experience in order to be understood. That this understanding could be more intuitive rather than strictly cognitive might also lead us to conclude that, when it comes to the Enlightenment, Marx himself was clearly much more a liberal than a radical.

One of the most damning criticisms of multicultural education is that concerns for students' self-esteem have taken such a precedence that they have undermined the more worthy aims of education. As we saw in the work of Sykes, some of this concern is rooted in the belief that throughout the last century we slowly came to believe that Americans were vulnerable people, and they might thus become stigmatized, or even traumatized, by their inability to succeed in a competitive educational environment. Better therefore that students be perceived as 'needing development' rather than 'failing', and be praised for their efforts, rather than their achievements. For authors like Bloom and D'Souza this quickly culminated in a higher education curriculum which was more concerned to positively affirm the status of one's identity than engage in critical discussion and analysis (Bloom 1987). Furthermore, in a link with the critique of separatist axes of knowledge and political ideologies it was likely to create university 'enclaves', with no notion that higher education was an initiation into a universally shared community of scholarship (D'Souza 1992).

As we saw in the last chapter, it is somewhat paradoxical to argue that if the best weapon against hateful speech is speech itself, we should not therefore invest some time and energy in developing people's confidence to 'fight back', but there is a much more troubling aspect to the onslaught on self-esteem. It is one thing to argue that these concerns have had a corrupting influence on education, but quite another to link this concern with the encroachment of radical forms of multiculturalism in the curriculum. Thus, although there might be some general disquiet about the inability to make judgements on the dubious activities of various cultures, and that we should look for value in all art forms, it does not follow from this that all forms of postmodern thinking lead one naturally into a relativistic celebration of everything cultural. For, at the heart, forms of literary deconstruction and sociological constructivism are deeply subversive. Thus, far from celebrating ethnic identities, both intellectual tools are much more likely to lead one to see *all* literature as partial and flawed, and *all* notions of self as historically contingent and fragmented. Put in these terms it is much more likely that the traditional 'modern' axis of knowledge would lead one to celebrate some 'essential' knowledge, as opposed to engage in high order forms of criticality.

PC debates about multiculturalism are extremely instructive. They neatly forge a link between sensitivities concerning the use of language, the perceived need to include all people's experiences in the classroom, and the desire to raise people's self-esteem. At the political level, they highlight just what is at stake in the alternative conceptions of what education is for; competing axes of knowledge; and what it might mean to forge change. Thereby, they also raise the wider question of whether one believes that widening the cultural scope for education is the means to motivate alienated students, or the door through which alternative notions of education's purpose and knowledge might be developed. And behind this lurks the question about whether success is always sweeter in winning a game where the odds are staked against you, or in being able to design a new game altogether. However, the most significant lesson to be learnt might well be that in seeking to put criticality back at the centre of the higher education experience one does not necessarily have to reassert the importance of the traditional methods of enquiry, because within forms of postmodern thinking there are methods which are just as powerful, if not more so.

6

A day at the races in Michigan
The victims of reverse discrimination

Behind many a modern injustice lies a good idea gone bad. 'Affirmative Action', the 1960s scheme whereby Blacks were given special consideration for university places (and other things), was a wise attempt to redress a grievous discrimination. For a time it worked well; it helped, for instance, to create America's growing black middle class. But it has since been extended to various other minorities, such as Latinos, Pacific islanders and, absurdly, women. Now the idea of racially based preferences has become an Orwellian monster – outdated and ineffective at best, profoundly illiberal at worst.

This week the Supreme Court agreed to consider a case brought by three white students with good grades whose places at the University of Michigan were, they claim, given to black and latino students who had done no better. The university's defense rests on the idea that there is a 'compelling state interest' in maintaining diversity. . . .

At the bottom, affirmative action comes down to a poor piece of social policy and a profoundly illiberal principle. Social policy should be based on identifying the unfortunate by income, not colour, and helping them by direct support – making poor schools better – not by dropping standards in universities. The illiberal idea is the notion that your identity – let alone your capacity to contribute to university life – is decided by your race. That is a malignity Americans have fought wars to kill. The Supreme Court should not tolerate it.

(*The Economist* 2002: 16)

Introduction

This Supreme Court case refuelled the debate in the US about whether universities were operating with 'quota' systems in their admissions procedures (i.e. the reserving of places for particular social groups, and which is illegal). For many, such cases are seen as indicative of the way that standards have been allowed to drop in the interests of producing a more diverse student population. This is a double-edged argument, for while the fall in standards is lamented, in the process very able students are being denied places, thus a double whammy of injustice.

In this chapter I will be discussing the relationship between affirmative action and PC. There have been several excellent edited texts which look at these issues from a number of competing perspectives (e.g. Curry 1996; Beckwith and Jones 1997; Cahn 2002). One conclusion is that the principle of affirmative action is becoming increasingly difficult to sustain in the light of changes in the relative positions of disadvantaged social groups in the US, and arguments in favour of forms of affirmative action now hang much more strongly on individuals rather than social groups. However, there *are* compelling arguments for broadening the basis upon which individuals are given access to higher education, and none of them depends on lowering academic standards in order to be acted on.

Although affirmative action controversies seem to coincide neatly with the rise of PC in the mid- to late 1980s and early 1990s the notion itself has a much longer history. The essence of the argument was well put in the 1960s by President Johnson:

> Imagine a hundred yard dash in which one of the two runners has his legs shackled together. He has progressed 10 yds, while the unshackled runner has gone 50 yds. How do they rectify the situation? Do they merely remove the shackles and allow the race to proceed? Then they could say that 'equal opportunity' now prevailed. But one of the runners would still be forty yds ahead of the other. Would it not be the better part of justice to allow the previously shackled runner to make-up the forty yard gap; or to start the race all over again? That would be affirmative action towards equality.
>
> (Johnson 1965, Executive Order 11246)

Regardless of any ulterior political motives, the metaphor clearly had a resonance at that time, and, presumably, it is upon this basis that *The Economist* (quoted above) lent its support for the original notion. Although President Johnson's metaphor of the running race is powerful it has its limitations. For example what if we argue that the runner who is behind is shackled by laziness and simply hasn't trained? And at what point do we cease with the strategy of stopping the race and argue that unfairness has been addressed? And, perhaps most controversially, if we start the race again how far might we want to go in ensuring that both runners actually finish the race together, that is, how strong is the case for an egalitarian equality of outcome?

Just like 'multiculturalism' it is also difficult to neatly define affirmative action. Indeed, it could be argued that its meaning *has* changed over time. Rather than a definition it is perhaps better to speak of its many dimensions. With reference to higher education, the two key dimensions appear to be: a perceived need for forms of direct action to address the unequal representation of various social groups on the campus; and a further perceived need to question the 'objectivity' of the criteria used to determine the scholastic aptitude and/or achievement of the student population.

One of the most difficult stumbling blocks with affirmative action is whether one sees it as a necessary and permanent weapon of social justice, in the face of entrenched social inequities, or as a set of short-term political strategies, to address a historically specific social problem. Or put another way, how far *does* the social structure of the US offer sufficient and meaningful equality of opportunity to all its citizens? And here, once again, we find ourselves returning to the left–right political dichotomy, with those on the right defending the meritocratic principles of the US and arguing that affirmative action is largely unnecessary, and those on the left arguing that without sustained interventions aimed at social justice we will inevitably continue to see the self-perpetuation of over-privileged and underprivileged social groups (or classes). If we add into this equation the complication that any particular intervention may result in unforeseen, unintended, or unfortunate consequences we can also see that all the foundations for a PC debate are now in place, and it is therefore not surprising that affirmative action became associated with PC.

The changing face of affirmative action

When President Johnson spoke of shackled runners as a metaphor for the effects of social disadvantage the message was clear: the impediments to economic success for many in the US were so great that it was a *simple* matter of social justice that they be addressed, and addressed through forms of intervention which are now readily called affirmative action. And the social costs of doing nothing were high, not just for the disadvantaged, but also for the advantaged, who might suffer in a climate of fear (from potential social unrest, street crime, etc.). Taken alongside the rallying calls of the Civil Rights Movement and Martin Luther King's famous 'dream' speech in 1965, it was clear that the rhetoric of social justice *was* resonating loudly throughout the US. Put in this context affirmative action is just a natural adjunct to these calls, as opposed to the anti-American PC rhetoric with which it is often associated today.

It is here, indeed, where we can also find the key PC point, that the transformation of affirmative action from a progressive force to an anti-American one was an important rhetorical battle, to ensure that affirmative action resonated with the right connotations – to create a more just society (for those on the left), or, as a dangerous infringement on the principles of meritocracy (for those on the right). In this context the right clearly had a problem, for how does one wrest affirmative action from the civil rights rhetoric with which it had been associated? This was clearly necessary, because to denigrate affirmative action as an adjunct of the Civil Rights Movement would have been a dangerous political strategy, but to argue that affirmative action was, in essence, not born of that movement at all, would enable those on the right to be seen to be supporting civil rights, while at the same time castigating forms of affirmative action. And the term PC proved the perfect weapon with which to achieve the necessary switch: it is not the right who are out of touch with the American people, but the left.

But, perhaps the notion of affirmative action has changed over the years anyway, thus making the rhetorical battle a much easier one to win. Searle makes the point well:

> Originally, affirmative action was a way of implementing the principle of equal opportunity, and the 'affirmative actions' we were supposed to take were a matter of affirmatively encouraging members of groups who had previously not competed for university positions to begin to do so. But as interpreted in recent years, 'affirmative action' is no longer consistent with equal opportunity, since the operational meaning of affirmative action is that in a competition between a white male and a member of a targeted minority, the minority person is given preference. The basic change is that originally, race, sex, and ethnicity were grounds *for encouraging someone to compete*; now they are among *the criteria for judging the competition*. There is a traditional term for such policies; they are called racial and sexual discrimination.
>
> (Searle 1993: 709)

If affirmative action did once chime with the Civil Rights Movement this is clearly no longer the case: from taking steps to ensure that everyone can compete fairly and equally, we have actually moved to a situation which is fundamentally unfair, and with no clear sense that there is even a competition. Put in these terms it is easy to see why affirmative action might simply be regarded as 'reverse discrimination', and on the grounds that 'two wrongs don't make a right' it would be difficult to consider this a form of social justice. More fundamentally, this might also be a basis upon which any number of the intellectuals and commentators who have featured in previous chapters might be united by a common allegiance to King's 'dream' of judgements being made about a person precisely *not* on skin colour, but on the content of character (or in the case of higher education, ability).

The social construction of educational reality

The quote from Searle above also raises the highly contentious issue of what exactly should be the test of people's abilities, and this issue has a number of dimensions. Not only is there the question about whether the tests are administered in a *fair* fashion, but also whether they *objectively* measure the ability in question. Furthermore, even if their reliability and validity could be assured, there are still questions to be asked about equal access to appropriate test preparation, and whether tests of the same ability might be measured in different ways. In a variation on the Marxist adage, used in Chapter 2, that there is little point in being free to dine at the Ritz restaurant in London if one has no money, equally, there is little point in arguing that because a university's entrance test is the same for everyone, thereby everyone has an equal chance of gaining entrance. And, once again, we are never far from traditional political ideologies in seeking our answers to these questions.

One way to consider Searle's point is that, regardless of the trustworthiness of the tests themselves, there is a simple and compelling logic to arguing that those who were most successful in those tests should be the ones who are admitted to higher education. To do otherwise simply undermines the whole idea of there being a competition for places, and it would destroy the whole notion of seeking to maintain a standard of excellence. For example, how could one decide who has won a race if one person decides to run 100 metres, and another to run a 400-metre steeplechase? Although the logic is simple the practice is more complicated, for what would happen if one year only a few people applied for a particular university course and the quota of places could not be filled? In this regard it is difficult to conceive of university admissions being solely based on a criterion-referencing system because, in reality, some form of norm referencing is inevitable

Radical 'constructivist' thinking that draws on the earlier work of the interactionist and ethnomethodological schools of sociology in the US and the more Marxist work of French sociologists like Boudon and Bourdieu have helped substantiate the claim that an educational test cannot be said to be testing some innate or 'essentialist' ability, and also that what it does test is only ever a reflection of the values of those who design, administer, and interpret the results of those tests (Choi and Murphy 1992). From the critiques of psychological testing and the IQ movement (Kamin 1974; Lewontin *et al.* 1984) to the more sociological work on the pernicious effects of social class on educational attainment, and the social construction of educational concepts (Ryan 1972; Keddie 1974), it is clear in a climate of attempting to keep politics out of education that these ideas would soon all be tarred with a PC brush. But radical thinking is split on the implications and conclusions one should draw from this research. For some it provides the evidence that we need more intervention to boost the chances of the disadvantaged to perform better on those 'constructed' tests, but for others here was the evidence to justify alternative conceptions of what might be valued in an educational experience. Sitting somewhere in the middle was also the view that expanding the fold of educational success might be best served by simply recognizing that there are many different ways in which people might display their intelligence. This might also be said to reopen the broader question of what exactly is higher education for?

In all of this one of the most intractable problems remained just how could forms of compensatory education actually compensate for the effects of an unequal society? (Bernstein 1970). The question takes a twist in affirmative action debates because if affirmative action is said to be unfairly discriminating in favour of certain social groups, is this not, in reality, no different from the discriminatory effect of privileged social groups being able to sponsor *their* offspring's educational success? In a simple form of logic, if the former is fair then so is the latter; also, if the former is unfair, then so is the latter, so what difference does it make either way? Of course, the logic might be simple, but this is a dangerous slippery slope. Whereas in the case of the former at least those sponsored by private means will actually be prepared to take on the challenges of higher education, but this could not be said for the latter, for although they will have gained access through a justifiable compensatory policy of a university, there is no evidence that they will then be able to cope with what is now in store for them. This argument is difficult to win one way or the other because, as Carter (a black affirmative action baby) has argued, if someone does excel in higher education, regardless of how they got there, this is the real point (Carter 1991). In this line of reasoning although affirmative action might be a clumsy tool it is being applied to an extremely complicated social order, and if it has some measure of success, then it will have been worth it.

Affirmative action as a black problem

The fact that black students throughout the US do not perform as well as they might, or should, is almost a national obsession in the US. On almost every measure black students do not perform well on any test when compared with other social groups, and these figures are at the centre of the argument *against* affirmative action put forward by McWhorter (2001). At first glance it might be assumed that a black professor of linguistics armed with such alarming statistics might use them to support the case for affirmative action; that some direct intervention is required to address this national epidemic. However, for McWhorter it provides evidence of the very 'victimology', and untenable separatism, we have met in previous chapters. And, for him, it also provides evidence for a 'cult of anti-intellectualism'. He argues that all the traditional reasons put forward for why black students do not do as well as others – from poverty, teacher racism, bias in tests – simply do not stand up to critical scrutiny. Put simply, the uncomfortable fact is that black students really are their own worst enemies. All that affirmative action has done is fuel the feelings that to be black in the US is to be a victim, which has, in turn, fuelled oppositional black cultures and, in addition, in some quarters, a deep feeling that mainstream education needs to be contrasted with something more authentically black. As we have already seen in the previous two chapters, this latter development is often allied to alternative conceptions of knowledge, and the accusation that black affirmation and testimony have replaced traditional forms of scholarship. Here, the affective domain takes prominence over the cognitive, where being in touch with one's feelings and experiences is seen as a more authentic form of knowledge, particularly when compared with the rather cold and detached forms of cognitivism associated with more traditional scholarship.

It is tempting to agree with the *Journal of Black Studies* that McWhorter is a contemporary D'Souza, but in many respects this would be unfair. For a start McWhorter is at pains to produce a series of reasoned arguments as to why the traditional claims of racism in education do not stand up, whereas D'Souza, being more concerned to critique multicultural curricula, devotes little attention to this. Also, McWhorter discusses the self-righteousness that he argues is endemic to forms of oppositional black culture, whereas D'Souza is quick to blame the mood of left-leaning intellectualism in colleges and universities. In conclusion, McWhorter has a very real sense that black communities have *themselves* fostered the mood which rejects forms of mainstream schooling. However, there is also a very real danger here that in pursuing this line of argument he simply ends up repeating the *cultural* message of Murray and Bernstein, that many communities actively embrace welfare dependency, rather than seeing this as the result of the socio-economic position in which they find themselves (Murray and Bernstein 1994). And this is surely the association that has damned him in some quarters.

Leaving this contentious issue aside, what seems fundamental to McWhorter's argument is that *time moves on*; it is simply not acceptable to argue that racism in the early twenty-first century is as endemic as it was thirty, or even ten, years ago. For example, whatever one believes about whether Rodney King *was* inappropriately restrained/beaten by white police officers in 1991, and whether this was racially motivated (Fiske 1996), this should be seen, at worst, as a racist *incident*, and not as indicative of a pattern of racist brutality or institutional racism. And, utilizing the level playing field metaphor, we should now be talking about divots and occasional bunkers rather than a steep slope from one end to the other. Of course, how much the 'levelling' attitudinal change and social mobility are due to affirmative action and whether these would have happened regardless is well nigh impossible to judge.

Much of McWhorter's direct experiences of affirmative action come from his days as a professor at Berkeley. Indeed he was employed there for the five years that immediately followed the passing of Proposition 209, which effectively banned affirmative action from Berkeley admissions practices:

> The State shall not discriminate against, or grant preferential treatment to, any individual or group on the basis of race, sex, color, ethnicity, or national origin in the operation of public employment, public education, or public contracting.
>
> (State of California, Proposition 209, 1996)

It could be argued that Prop 209 simply reflected the fact that, indeed, the playing field was now so sufficiently levelled, in university admissions at least, that it simply was no longer justifiable to continue with any admissions policies that sought to filter students based on social grouping. Or it could be argued that it simply represented a backlash against the unacceptable unintended consequences of affirmative action itself; that, in practice, it was simply reverse discrimination, and thus that many eligible students were losing out on a place even though their test scores were higher than many of those who did get a place?

However, it could also be argued, given that only one black law student attended Berkeley in 1997 (and he was a deferred student from the previous year), that this itself was enough to claim that Prop 209 was a retrograde step in civil rights. Indeed, even in 2005 the figures for Berkeley freshman entry show that only 110 of the 9,000 new recruits were classed as African American (see Chapter 7 for a fuller discussion of these issues). However, it is unlikely that any argument can be convincingly won with reference to such statistics. For a start we would need to know much more detail about why people apply to Berkeley, what percentage come from the neighbouring Bay Area, and California in general, as well as information on whether some black students felt that Berkeley was not a welcoming campus and simply did not apply, and whether, in the meantime, other universities had been able to attract black students who might otherwise have gone to Berkeley.

What seems to be far more significant is how Proposition 209 and similar cases, such as the Supreme Court case cited at the beginning of this chapter, were able to reopen debates about whether a raw test score should be the sole basis upon which one makes a judgement about eligibility. There are a number of considerations here, any one of which might be referred to as affirmative action: the weighting of grade point average (GPA) scores against scholastic assessment test (SAT) scores; the weighting of achievement in a public school as opposed to a private school; an application form indicating that a candidate has much to offer university life, etc. In this regard it is interesting to note the decision taken by the University of Chicago to abandon the use of its own entry test in favour of a more standardized one, and to speculate whether this was for PC reasons, that is, the fear that the old test might be interpreted as being biased in favour of certain 'coached' social groups.

When is a quota not a quota?

There is little doubt that the biggest controversy which surrounds affirmative action in universities and colleges is the extent to which it amounts to a form of 'race quotering'; that a certain number of places each year are earmarked for certain social groups. In reality the question is more complicated and is often referred to as 'race norming' rather than quotering. Here it is not that there is no competition for places, but the competitive scores are weighted between the various social groups, and the score of each individual is only ever compared with the scores of other individuals from within the same social group:

> Imagine that four men came into a state employment office to apply for a job. One is black, one Hispanic, one Asian and one White. They take the standard test . . . All get a composite score of 300. None of them will ever

see that score. Instead the numbers will be fed into a computer and the applicant's percentile ranking emerges. The scores are group weighted. Blacks are measured against blacks, whites against whites, Hispanics against Hispanics. Since blacks characteristically do less well than other groups, the effect is to favor blacks. For example a score of 300 as an accountant will give the black a percentile of 87, an Hispanic of 74 and a white or Oriental [sic] a score of 47. The black will get the job as the accountant.

(Pojman, in Beckwith and Jones 1997)

This form of 'race norming' has been illegal in the US since 1991, but the general accusation that something like this still persists is the main reason why affirmative action is often associated with forms of reverse discrimination. In this line of argument if you happen to be a member of a very successful social group then it is right that members of less successful social groups should be compensated in some way for this fact when they are in competition with you for a university or college place. Of course, for the individual who sees his or her higher test score resulting in someone else, with a lower test score, receiving a place at his or her expense, quite naturally it looks like a case of unfair discrimination. In general, this is precisely the sort of evidence that is used to claim that standards in universities and colleges must be falling, and that the meritocratic principle is being undermined. The Supreme Court case concerning the University of Michigan turns precisely on how one interprets the status of American meritocracy, because if unfairness is itself undermining the meritocratic principle then universities surely have the right to produce some kind of interventionist policy.

In one version of a critical response to the Court ruling (that the University of Michigan *had* acted inappropriately), it is tempting to say that the university's policy was reflecting a simple fact of life, that competition for places everywhere and always rarely produces the kind of fairness that one would ideally like to see. And given the tortured history of race relations in the US if affirmative action reads like a form of reverse discrimination it is a price worth paying. Using a simple language of reparative compensation the black community are collectively saying to the three white protagonists in this case that life has not been fair to us, so why assume that it should always be fair to you. But of course the problem with reparations arguments is that they tend to be couched in terms of social groups, rather than individuals, and also that today's generation become direct representatives of past generations. But, equally, when was the time that privilege and reward were distributed fairly? Or, as Wasserstrom has argued, affirmative action does not prevent us from having a desirable meritocracy, because we never had one to begin with (Wasserstrom, in Beckwith and Jones 1997). Somewhat ironically, perhaps, the more one accepts that some kind of unfairness is inevitable the easier it becomes to accept the use of quotas: 'Because they [white males] are the ones who stand to unfairly gain the most without preferential treatment, it is fair that preferential treatment be aimed at preventing their unfair gain' (Beckwith and Jones 1997: 173).

The principle of the level playing field

Given what has been argued above, it is unsurprising that the concept of affirmative action has attracted the attention of philosophers in the US and the UK. As one might expect, many of the arguments hang on whether it is possible to mount a *principled* case either in favour of affirmative action or against it, and this is itself usually couched within a wider argument about the nature of social justice. Pojman has succinctly summarized the essence of these arguments:

> The seven arguments for affirmative action are (1) the need for role models; (2) the need to break stereotypes; (3) the 'unequal results reveals discrimination'; (4) the compensation argument; (5) compensation from those who have innocently benefited from past injustice; (6) the diversity argument; and (7) antimeritocratic deserts arguments to justify reverse discrimination: 'no one deserves his talents.' The seven arguments against affirmative action are (1) affirmative action requires discrimination against a different group; (2) affirmative action perpetuates victimisation syndrome; (3) affirmative action encourages mediocrity and incompetence; (4) affirmative action policies unjustly shift the burden of proof; (5) and argument from merit; (6) the slippery slope, and (7) the mounting evidence against the success of affirmative action.
>
> (Pojman, summarized by Beckwith and Jones 1997: 168)

If there is no sound logic as to why certain people end up more capable than others then any admission policy to higher education will have unfairness etched between the lines of its rationale. Also, there is surely a form of social justice in trying to repair the damage caused by this arbitrariness, particularly if it can be proved that there is a consistent pattern of under-representation in higher education from certain social groups. Fundamental to these arguments, and clearly seen in debates about affirmative action, is the question of the 'level playing field'. If one believes that the US has a level playing field every case for affirmative action seems to fall apart very quickly. But it is also a question about things moving on, and asking to what extent forms of discrimination from the past have now so sufficiently evaporated that we should view present-day examples merely as isolated incidents, rather than examples of entrenched, and predictable, patterns of behaviour.

For commentators like Searle it is clear what is happening: a form of reverse discrimination *is* now in operation, and this has violated the basic meritocratic principle that there should be a fair competition between all individuals for university places (Searle 1993). For D'Souza this is crippling in two ways because the reverse discrimination also operates through a privileging of quotered groups: 'Proportional representation for ethnic groups directly violates the democratic principle of equal opportunity for individuals, and the underlying concept of group justice is hostile both to individual equality and to excellence' (D'Souza 1992: 55). But this problem *is*, at root, a level playing field problem because what both commentators are trying to ensure is that there is fairness in the competition for places (i.e. equality of opportunity). Both authors have no time for those who would want to question the nature of the testing (be it for fairness, or to widen it), or whether the competition ends up reproducing a particular type of intelligentsia – so long as the competition to be in that intelligentsia was fair. Thus, if there is a case for affirmative action it would simply be to boost (or level) the chances for everyone to take part in the initial competition.

This model is one of 'weak' affirmative action, to be contrasted with 'strong', which 'involves more positive steps to eliminate past injustice, such as reverse discrimination, hiring candidates on the basis of race or gender in order to reach equal or near equal results, proportionate representation in each area of society' (Pojman, in Beckwith and Jones 1997: 178). This is a form of egalitarian affirmative action, based on an equality of outcome model, and underpinned by a very different notion of social justice. Those subscribing to such a left-wing ideology would maintain that the 'weak' model is fundamentally flawed, because one generation's equality of opportunity which results in an inequality of outcome, will, for the next generation, inevitably lead to an *in*equality of opportunity. Here, a level playing field requires that we take steps to ensure that the distribution of societal rewards and resources cannot become so uneven that equal opportunities are thereby unbalanced for the next generation. This is ultimately always a question of political ideology, and, once again, one clearly centred on traditional notions of left and right.

The compelling case for diversity

In 1996 President Clinton spoke publicly of his support for the compelling case for diversity – 'Mend it, don't End it' (Clinton, in Curry 1996). The philosophical debate which led to this conclusion dates back to the Supreme Court of California ruling in the case of *Bakke* v. *the University of California*, and discussed in the collection of readings edited by Cahn (2002). Bakke, an applicant for the University of California at Davis Graduate School of Medicine was denied a place on their programme, and claimed that this was unfair to him on the grounds that 16 of the 100 places could only be competed for by students who were classified as 'black'. The Supreme Court upheld his complaint, that his rejection was unconstitutional, that Davis was using an unwarranted racial quota system, and that he should be admitted to the programme. Seen at the time by many as *the* death knell for affirmative action, it raised a number of troubling issues.

The most outspoken critic at the time was the Oxford philosopher Dworkin (see Cahn 2002): 'In spite of popular opinion, the idea that the Bakke case presents a conflict between a desirable social goal and important individual rights is a piece of intellectual confusion' (Dworkin 1973, in Cahn 2002: 108). What Dworkin is alluding to is the unsubstantiated appeal being made to the Fourteenth Amendment (concerning equal treatment). We have seen Fish previously making a not dissimilar claim about the First Amendment; that it is so cherished as a principle that one often forgets the rhetoric required in order to make a substantial case in its favour. In the case of Bakke, Dworkin argues that there is a sleight of hand in the argument in favour of the Fourteenth Amendment, and that Bakke was not discriminated against in the way that the Fourteenth Amendment *should* require:

> Allan Bakke is being 'sacrificed' because of his race only in a very artificial sense of that word. He is being 'sacrificed' in the same artificial sense because of his level of intelligence, since he would have been accepted if he were cleverer than he is. In both cases he is being excluded not by prejudice but because of a rational calculation about the socially most beneficial use of limited resources for medical education.
>
> (Dworkin, in Cahn 2002: 111)

The University of California, thereby, did have some strong grounds for the use of racial categories in its admissions policies. That is, if it is clear that the percentage of black doctors is tiny and showing no signs of increase, even when the black population is growing and, furthermore, that medical schools have become white enclaves, then surely a compelling case for producing a more diverse medical school population is now upon us? Or, at least we might say that there is a compelling case for a series of emergency, short-term measures. The University of California's defence in the Bakke case rested, in part at least, on the argument that they *were* responding to this urgent social need, and that affirmative action which did not include some targeted quotas was unlikely adequately to address the problem. Clearly, the university was caught in a difficult dilemma: either it abandoned its affirmative action and got criticized for not meeting an urgent social need, or it continued with its affirmative action and got criticised for introducing racial discrimination in its admissions procedures. Of course, what was implied throughout the case, and since, is that if an institution wishes to act affirmatively then it should, but it must not be seen to be using a quota system.

Widening the net of university admissions

If quotas are unconstitutional, but there remains a compelling case for diversity, it leads to the obvious question 'What is to be done?' For those on the political right the answer is straightforward: encourage everyone to believe that higher education is an aspiration that can be fulfilled, and the higher education population will gradually begin to reflect the population at large. That said, even conservative thinkers like D'Souza are willing to concede that some interventions may be necessary: 'Universities seem entirely justified in giving a break to students who may not have registered the highest scores, but whose record suggests that this failure is not due to lack of ability or application but rather to demonstrated disadvantage' (D'Souza 1992: 251). This statement needs to be qualified by adding that this should always be done 'individual-case-by-individual-case' and not by a system of social group preferences.

For those on the political left the problem is more complicated. Not only is there the deep-seated problem of nihilism in some black communities, which universities would find very difficult to take account of in an admissions policy, no matter how compensatory, but there is also the problem of what is to be done about the cultural bias in the nature of the values, knowledge, and scholarship which is traditionally found in the university. Of course, for the right the problem is non-existent because almost all these traditions are taken to be 'American', whereas on the left they are variously described as: 'middle class', 'bourgeois', 'imperialistic', and so on. That said, even if one accepts the implication that education is 'middle class' there is still a decision to be made, as we saw in the previous chapter, about whether there is more to be gained by winning a game which is not of one's making, or trying to play an alternative game.

In effect, universities have always used entry criteria that go beyond strict adherence to a test score. Indeed it could be said that the whole point of any application form (for a job, club membership, etc.) is not just to list one's academic qualifications, but to state a case concerning one's general aptitudes and ability to assimilate into the life of the organization one aspires to join. At this point, radicals may feel as comfortable as conservatives agitated, because doesn't this introduce an unwarranted value base into what should be an entirely objective exercise? And ultimately wouldn't this compromise the academic standing of the university and the community of scholarship within it? Of course, having already questioned the validity of the canonical knowledge and scholarship of Western civilization (see previous chapter), many radical scholars might actually welcome the latter.

Under the heading of affirmative action universities and colleges might widen the net of admission in three separate ways. First, one might concede that the implications of radical arguments concerning 'abilities' are substantial. After all, what is the measure of someone's ability, and thereby their merit, if, by chance of birth, they have been hothoused by middle-class parents, both of whom are university professors, coached to pass tests by private tutors, taught in a private school with a low teacher–pupil ratio, and afforded every resource to help in scholastic attainment? Or put another way, at what point would one concede that this 'sponsoring' of ability is unfair, so unfair that it is another student's constitutional right to claim that s/he has been discriminated against by not having had these advantages afforded to him/her? It is also interesting to note here that this discrimination might be argued to be far greater than any suffered by Bakke in his initial rejection by UC Davis. Put in these terms any amount of affirmative action short of a quota might be argued to be not only constitutional, but also highly desirable.

Second, a university might introduce an application form which widens the criteria for entry. Although success in traditional scholastic tests would still be included these would sit alongside a broader range of criteria, including, for instance, judgements about potential as well as existing achievements, and a chance for potential students to offer a testimony as to their wider achievements, and what they might bring to university life. Again, if there is compelling argument for diversity this might include an ability to mentor future prospective students, or a willingness to further embed a culture of diversity in the university community. This is not a quota in the illegal sense, but it might certainly expand the quota of certain types of students in the university population. Obviously, this might infuriate some conservative scholars because of its perceived wilful contempt for traditional notions of academic excellence, to which it might be retorted that these notions are only radical versions of a 'boost' notion, and all students would still be expected to develop their scholarship in much the same ways as ever. In effect, these measures only seek to balance the effects that already distort university entrance through forms of privileged access. Of course, one might also add that there's always been more to university life than simply academic achievement anyway.

Third, it could also be argued that many of these radical measures are simply additions to those that already exist for tie-breaking situations where competition for places is keen. And, echoing the point made by Carter in Chapter 3, one should surely reserve judgement on people's abilities until they have been given the chance to prove themselves (Carter 1991). Or, as in the old adage that 'the proof of the pudding is in the eating', we should perhaps be paying more attention to students as they leave university, rather than as they enter. Furthermore, in the absence of clear statistical correlations between the initial entry scores on tests and the final degree results of all students, it remains an open question as to what is the best predictor of performance, particularly when there is a real concern, even amongst some conservative scholars, about who is presenting themselves for admission to higher education.

Consequentialism and the case against affirmative action

Somewhat ironically the strongest case against affirmative action might well turn out be one based on its unintended or undesirable consequences. As we have seen throughout the previous chapters this is a common concern in all PC debates, and this is no less so when it comes to affirmative action. For conservative scholars it perhaps matters very little whether the dumbing down of standards generally in higher education is intentional or not, but for radical scholars it poses a difficult dilemma. For those scholars who would argue that alternative notions of knowledge and scholarship are not dumbing down the problem is simply to defend these alternatives. However, for those who wish to see disadvantaged groups compete equally in the more traditional forms of higher education it has become hard work dodging the accusation that many of those now in higher education did not compete equally to achieve their place. And, perhaps more pertinently, it has become extremely frustrating for the individuals who have been the beneficiary of affirmative action to have to spend a good deal of their time defending their right to be in higher education, or, indeed, even their right to be doing the job they might subsequently secure (Carter 1991).

Radical scholars who look to promote alternative forms of knowledge might find they can win some intellectual battles, although closer to the lecture theatres and seminar rooms of higher education this might easily be perceived as producing minority enclaves. This can create a sense of distance between 'us and them', and thereby fuel a feeling of 'majority' resentment. Cases like Bakke and Michigan might be bad publicity for affirmative action, by confirming a public sense of 'majority backlash', but it could well be that one of the most insidious elements of affirmative action is the more daily sense that universities and colleges are increasingly perceived by students themselves as being divided between those who are pursuing traditional forms of scholarship and those who are engaged in something which looks rather pernicious and threatening (D'Souza 1992). For others the insidiousness comes in a different form, that of 'group infighting'. In a society increasingly centred on entitlements rather than rights (Samuelson 1995), it is inevitable that minority status will become a battlefield. In part this is because there is much to be gained in the first place by having 'victim' status, but increasingly it becomes important to ensure that one's own minority has more of the ingredients to confer that status when compared with others who are also vying for the same status (Sykes 1992). This is not only a dangerous slippery slope in its own right, but also reminds us of Gitlin's previous warnings to the left about losing sight of any sense of 'common dreams' (Gitlin 1995). And, of course, this minority infighting could easily spill over to include more majoritarian concerns: 'Person P may be harmed and rendered less able to compete because his parents were discriminated against. But person Q might be harmed by his parents being killed; person R because her parents were defrauded' (Beckwith and Jones 1997: 171).

Although Sykes's solution, that we should seek to restore in families a sense of personal responsibility, might be unpalatable for many on the left, there is no universal agreement on the left that some form of affirmative action is the solution. For example the very real sense that there are forms of black nihilism amongst some black communities indicates that both Sykes and affirmative action are merely scratching at the surface of a deeply entrenched problem. 'Nihilism is a "disease of the soul" that must be cured by affirmations of one's worth fuelled by the mutual concerns of others' (Beckwith and Jones 1997: 27). And if an unintended consequence of affirmative action is that it breeds notions of inferiority amongst its recipients, affirmative action can only make things worse: 'Victimisation, like implied inferiority, is what justifies preference, so that to receive the benefits of preferential treatment one must, to some extent, become invested in the view of one's self, as a victim' (Steele, in Beckwith and Jones 1997: 28).

Conclusion

Just as one needs to ask what exactly is PC about multiculturalism the same question needs to be asked about affirmative action. Similarly, what proponents of affirmative action are accused of is politicizing education in unwarranted ways. Put simply, the criteria upon which one enters higher education should not be a question of politics, but one of academic ability. Furthermore, tests of that ability should not be interfered with so as to engineer a particular type of college or university population. Although the reasons for doing this might be worthy these should not be allowed to compromise academic standards and traditional notions of scholarship. The problem with this argument is that it assumes that these traditions are not themselves political. It assumes that testing is not only objectively administered, but in the choice of content and in the nature of scholarship there are not only agreed rules, but they are, somehow, of a higher Platonic order, certainly than that of the mere opinion of the political world. In the most extreme form of this argument this Platonic knowledge and understanding is also argued to be fundamentally American, and those who would challenge it are damned for a lack of both epistemological and patriotic faith.

An important article of patriotic faith is a belief in the meritocratic principles of the reward system of the US. It is not surprising therefore that those who question it should be labelled PC. The critique is double-edged because it questions not just the equality of the opportunities that are afforded to American citizens, but also the inbuilt bias towards the cultural interests of the middle class in the very tests which are the measure of merit. Radical scholars have several ways of dealing with these issues. First they might argue that without a much firmer commitment to equality of outcome, any notion of equality of opportunity will be hopelessly compromised. Second, they might seek to replace the inbuilt bias with new and alternative forms of knowledge and understanding. But in deciding whether there is more to be gained in helping people to be successful in the traditional conceptions of ability, or in subverting them, there is no one clear message or mission. Thereby, affirmative action debates also raise the important question of what higher education is for, and whether colleges and universities have duties to the wider society which they serve. At one extreme it could be argued that the 'disinterested pursuit of truth' is the most worthy of duties and that we all benefit from this in some way, not least because it is likely to be the only place where this is possible. At the other extreme it could equally be argued that colleges and universities are there to serve the taxpayer, the fee payer, and all other stakeholders, including the state and the economy, and therefore they should be willing to embrace any number of aims. Not least of which might be the urgent social need to ensure that certain professions do not become enclaves of a particular socio-economic group, and the recognition that the social cost of not investing in 'diverse' institutions is simply too high.

One of the lessons of the Supreme Court rulings on affirmative action is that while acting affirmatively is constitutional and legal, using quotas is neither. Also, given that conservatives can recognize the need for some action on disadvantage, and that some radicals can concede that the consequences of much of the action has been counterproductive, it raises the obvious question of what *is* desirable and, at the same time, not likely to lead to the accusation that it is 'PC gone mad'. If affirmative action were based on individual cases rather than membership of social groups it might well help to eliminate the view that it is simply a form of reverse discrimination, and that everyone is simply a personification of a former social ill. But this could also be qualified by it being 'permissible for a university to employ an admissions program in which "race or ethnic background may be deemed a 'plus' in a particular applicant's file"' (Justice Powell – ref: *Regents of Univ of Cal.* v. *Bakke* 1978). Here, a compelling case for diversity is not overrun by the sense that a quota system has been introduced via the back door. Affirmative action is difficult to justify when it is seen to be replacing a fair system with an unfair one, but if all systems are founded on particular values, each will be seen as fair if one believes in them and unfair if one does not. But at least in these situations the argument is one based on rhetoric, and the worthiness of one's values, and not one which contrasts a political commitment with one which is beyond politics (Fish 1994). Affirmative action as 'political correctness gone mad' makes sense if one will not concede Fish's point.

7

Talking about political correctness
American conversations about political correctness and higher education

Introduction: the what, why, and whether of PC

This chapter is almost exclusively empirically based. It is the result of an analysis of eight interview transcripts with academics, leaders, and administrators in American higher education. The interviews were semi-structured – revolving around a short series of headline questions, and followed up by more general conversation which flowed naturally from the direction each interview took. The headline questions were: (1) How would you define political correctness? (2) How do you feel about questions of freedom of speech? (3) How do you feel about aspects of multiculturalism? (4) How do you feel about forms of affirmative action? These questions were used in part to create a structure and sense of consistency between the interviews, but the aim was not to make judgements about the validity of what was being said in comparison with other responses. Neither should these interviews be seen as an attempt to measure the amount of political correctness in higher education, but rather as an attempt to consider the ways in which people talk *about* political correctness. More specifically, with what did the term resonate, and what role did it play in their thinking and understanding of issues in higher education, and in their own work. In this regard the interviews should be considered very much as conversations. From a methodological point of view they were an attempt to create a space in which to view a transcript as a consistent narrative *about* political correctness.

The quotations in this chapter were carefully chosen to reflect those places in the transcripts where the interviewee appeared to be either the most animated about an aspect of political correctness, or the narrative appeared to reflect a particular stance or articulation of a general point. I did not ask the interviewees to tidy their narrative accounts for the purposes of written prose. Other than some editing, removal of the most colloquial of speech terms, and some tiny insertions – all for the purposes of clarity in exposition – the text is left as was said in the original interviews. This was done to maximize the sense that this was how people naturally spoke about the relationship they have with aspects of political correctness. The interviews were conducted in San Francisco and New York in April and May of 2005.

The following eight people were the academics, leaders, and administrators who provided the empirical evidence for this chapter. The post they held at the time of the interview is also listed.

- **John Searle**, Professor of Philosophy at the University of California, Berkeley, and author of 'The Storm Over the University', *New York Review of Books* (6 December 1990).
- **Robin Lakoff**, Professor of Linguistics at the University of California, Berkeley, and author of *The Language War* (2000).
- **Genaro Padilla**, Vice Chancellor, Student Affairs at the University of California, Berkeley.
- **Philip Day**, Chancellor of the City College of San Francisco.
- **John McWhorter**, Senior Fellow of the Manhattan Institute, New York, and author of *Losing the Race* (2001).
- **Jonathan Zimmerman**, Professor of Educational History at New York University, and author of *Whose America?: Culture Wars in the Public Schools* (2002).
- **Allen McFarlane**, Assistant Vice President for Student Diversity Programs and Services at New York University.
- **Todd Gitlin**, Professor of Journalism at Columbia University, and author of *The Twilight of Common Dreams* (1995).

Talking about the term 'political correctness'

All the interviews began with a simple question about the term political correctness itself: how it might be defined and with what did it resonate. As this was the opening question I made no attempt, in this case, to discern a wider narrative, but simply to document what appeared to be key aspects of each person's response:

> There is a certain cultural milieu, especially in universities that tends to impose cultural conformity on its members and the leading feature of this cultural milieu is its opposition to what they take to be mainstream American culture. So it is an oppositional culture. So I can tell you what the politically correct views are but you will not understand political correctness by looking at the content of the views. There is something else though about politically correct people which is itself very interesting and that is they are so lacking in intellectual independence that if you know their opinions on two or three questions you can pretty much predict all the rest.
>
> (Searle, 19 April 2005)

Clearly, for Searle, the key issue revolves as much around the *correctness* as the politics, and the cultural process at work in producing forms of conformity.

Both Lakoff and Padilla also responded in cultural terms, but emphasized the more ironic resonances of the term:

> From the beginning when it was left against left – us in the family – we can tease each other and people do sometimes say 'I hate to be politically correct, but . . .', so they can kind of use it of themselves but always in a self deprecatory way.
>
> (Lakoff, 20 April 2005)

> Political correctness as a term, as a phrase, has I think successfully been appropriated by the political right to derogate a number of programs and projects and initiatives not only in California but across the country . . . Most of the people that I know that have been affiliated with initiatives to help create greater, in this case, campus access or multicultural curricula or multicultural centres or gay and lesbian locations and safe spaces, and that kind of thing, do not use the term political correctness, although they unwittingly have, I think, been brought into the argument in a rather reactive and too often defensive way.
>
> (Padilla, 26 April 2005)

It is as if the positive connotations that the term *might* have once had have been slowly stripped from it, as a more wholly negative and derogatory sense came to dominate discussions. This perspective was taken a step further by Day who, by reference to the institutions in which he had worked, wanted to distance himself from the term altogether:

> We don't talk about political correctness issues. We don't even identify with the term. People who might be looking at organizational behaviour from an outside-in standpoint might say – when somebody is denied a scholarship, and let's say that the person that got it happened to be a person of colour, as opposed to somebody who got denied it – they will say: 'Well, you know, they are playing that affirmative action game', which may not have anything to do with the actual core decision that was made.
>
> (Day, 26 April 2005)

Here, the inference seems to be that the term political correctness is something imported *to* higher education, and not something which is a *modus operandi* for the people who actually work on the causes with which it is most commonly associated.

For McWhorter, too, although political correctness might have taught us several things, it has also derailed us:

> Sadly, I think what has been learned is (a) by many, that education and enlightenment can consist of being taught that some people have more power than others and often abuse it – ultimately a rather simple lesson that derails too much supposedly intellectual work, and (b) by many, that

a certain cohort exaggerate victimhood and bias – such that they become wary of any mention of 'identity' issues.

(McWhorter, 30 May 2005)

Several interviewees allude to the fact that political correctness, in the US at least, appeared to be on the wane, but Zimmerman emphasized how this might simply be a move from a more overt to a covert form:

I think the phrase is decreasingly used but to me that doesn't necessarily mean that PC is not operative. Indeed, it may well be the opposite, that a certain kind of code has become so much a part of our kind of social and cultural DNA that it no longer requires a name. There are certain things you say, there are certain things you don't say, so I don't hear people use the term PC very often but I wouldn't therefore conclude that it doesn't operate or exist.

(Zimmerman, 17 May 2005)

McFarlane understood this movement differently and suggested that new terms have increasingly become its more appropriate and enlightened substitute:

I think it has been supplanted by two new phrases, and that is, diversity is still hanging on there, and then the other issue that is really emerging is the whole area of social justice. And social justice is really about looking at a person's or a group's condition and examining what those challenges are and rallying the community to address those challenges.

(McFarlane, 19 May 2005)

It is as if the work that has been done over the last twenty years to promote access and equal opportunities for disadvantaged groups has continued unabated, but whilst its detractors have wanted to label it 'political correctness' in order to denigrate it, those who have been working on developing the strategies and interventions are now simply working with less tainted terms. That said, Gitlin re-emphasized the sense that is found in much of the literature on political correctness:

I think I would mean by it the imposition of a linguistic orthodoxy upon tangled matters of public or private speech. No more, no less. It is a simple imposition of a code of legitimate and illegitimate speech.

(Gitlin, 19 May 2005)

Interestingly, and as it emerged more fully in the Gitlin narrative later, it is clear that he felt this wasn't merely an academic question, for it is too easy to find examples where some form of unwarranted conformity has been foisted on higher education faculties. And, thereby, we find confirmation here that conservative and radical thought does have much in common when it comes to the question of *correctness* (Searle 1990; Gitlin 1995).

Talking about freedom of speech

Three key themes were apparent from the conversations about freedom of speech. First, what might be referred to as 'the delineation problem', that is the difficulty in iterating the boundaries of free speech. Second, and related, the problem of distinguishing between one's role as an academic and as a wider professional figure. And, finally, and related again, what might be referred to as 'the reality of everyday life problem', that is, the reality of the disjunction between principles and practice.

The complex nature of the delineation problem was perfectly illustrated in the following from Gitlin:

> The First Amendment is, of course, a restriction on the powers of government to infringe upon language and that is there for good reason. I am a great defender of it and Britain could use it, and if so you wouldn't have these awful libel suits. But the right to cry fire in a crowded room is not a right I am prepared to affirm. There is a very vexed question about what constitutes speech. Currently, we are having this debate whether there should be a shield law for journalists, and I have a lot of sympathy with the argument that what the First Amendment defends is not the freedom of professional journalists, it is the freedom of the press – of anyone who communicates publicly. That said, I think that the attempt to circumscribe categories of speech should be a last resort.
>
> (Gitlin, 19 May 2005)

Here we see a short abbreviation of much of what has perplexed scholars about protecting freedom of speech. It is not so much that one ends up being ambivalent about the whole subject but one needs to recognize the full implications of working with a *principle* of free speech. Careful not to be seen to be arguing that, *absolutely*, 'anything goes', Searle drew a very wide boundary for free speech:

> If you want to publish an article on this campus saying that people who are exactly of my racial make up – I happen to be 1/64th Cherokee, and English and Dutch – that those people are inherently inferior, I would think it is an idiotic article but you have a right to publish it, of course. You see there is [a] logical mistake that a lot of people make and that is if you have a right to do it, it must be the right thing to do, and if it is not a right thing to do then you don't have a right to do it, but of course I have a right to do all kinds of things that are just dreadful. But a lot of Americans and a lot of people internationally [say] if it is a terrible thing to do or a wrong thing to do then you cannot possibly have a right to do it. And that is wrong. Now there is a deep philosophical reason for that distinction and that is that you have to guarantee people a field of rights which is larger than should be exercised. Otherwise you don't have the

flexibility that society requires, so that all kinds of things that I have an academic right to do, that I wouldn't think of doing, should entitle me to do them. If I did something outrageous intellectually, then it seems to me the university has no right to send the police in to stop me, even though I am doing something idiotic.

(Searle, 19 April 2005)

The other conversations all seemed to revolve around not so much the *principle* of free speech but how people are constantly working with a very broad *notion*; and one which requires ongoing dialogue, negotiation, compromise, and professional constructions of meaning. Lakoff seemed to capture the nature of these new contours:

Whether we should have anti-hate speech legislation on campus is a very charged and complicated issue. Some people would say even though the use of epithets as such is not 'political ideas' speech, and therefore a cut below it, but they would say that any restriction of speech is dangerous. Or any restriction of speech encourages the next restriction. It is important to understand that normal people always restrict their speech. So, if you are talking to someone more powerful than you, you are going to be very polite. If you want something from someone you are going to be direct or maybe even obsequious. So everybody knows, everybody who is older than two or three knows, that you have to restrict your speech and while, by the time we're adults, that kind of speech restriction isn't something we are necessarily conscious of, it is not as though speech codes are absolutely something nobody ever has to do except in this rarefied academic context.

So one way to look at hate-speech restriction is to say we are trying to extend the notion of a decent society or decent behaviour. What we do with friends and family members because we are members of the same group and we have to expect to be nice to each other as members of an in-group. We are trying to sort of symbolically recreate that in-group to include everybody and some of the opposition to it is really about, covertly, we don't want them in our in-group; we want them to stay as an out-group. But I am not at all convinced that anything in rigorous academic discourse is lost, strictly, by anti-hate speech codes, and you know, one part of the argument in favour of them is that when people, especially people whose groups have histories of discrimination, when they encounter discriminatory language it makes them less able to do what they come to the University to do – to learn, to participate in vigorous discourse themselves. So, in other words, those people who complain that hate speech restrictions inhibit their vigorous discourse need to take account of the opposite position which is that for those on the receiving end, hate speech itself may impair their possibilities of vigorous discourse.

(Lakoff, 20 April 2005)

Day was most forthright in this regard, arguing that it is a form of professional duty for academics and teachers to intervene when they come across forms of discriminatory language:

> I think hate speech is violent and it does abuse people and I think it does affect them. It may not affect them physically but it certainly can affect them psychologically and have pretty long-lasting, long-term effects. In colleges and universities if it is not written down there certainly is a code of conduct that we abide by, that is driven by the principles associated with academic freedom. But even within the context of academic freedom, it doesn't provide you with a license to spew forth with all kinds of racial epithets and justify that behavior on the basis of your freedom to express a point of view.
>
> If you hear some things, and I have done this myself where I have been in the cafeteria, or walking across the college campus, and I hear something that I think is just not in keeping with the standards of conduct and the values of our institution, I will stop the person cold in their tracks and say: 'Look, you have every right to talk about what you are talking about, the way you want to talk about it, but you are in an academy – you are in a college campus – and there are some standards that we set for ourselves. The values of the institution are not reflected in the way you are conducting yourself right at this moment and my responsibility is to inform you of that violation, and if your behaviour persists, to take the necessary action to address it.'
>
> (Day, 26 April 2005)

As we have seen in previous chapters it is clear that many fear that such interventions can easily escalate into the use of highly circumscribed and restrictive speech codes, and encourage a culture of dependency in 'victimized' groups, but here we find ourselves being asked, what academic would say nothing of an advisory nature when overhearing abusive language on a college campus? And, to take an example from Day's campus, who would not think to intervene if they overheard the term 'towel head' being used to refer to a Muslim student, perhaps just to advise that even in the context of a joke it is apt to be interpreted very differently?

Zimmerman too, questioned the validity of holding too tightly to a principle, for its logic might well compel one towards some unfortunate consequential inferences:

> You know, there are certain things that you say and you don't say. That is not to say that there isn't a speech code [at NYU] but I have never heard of it and I have never heard of anybody being penalized for violating it. The only kind of speech code that I have heard of people violating, and one that I heartily endorse, is a speech code surrounding what we call

sexual harassment. After all, those are speech codes as well, and my students who are absolute libertarians, First Amendment libertarians, think that people should be able to say anything. I would say to them that should a professor be able to say to a student: 'Well, sleep with me and I will give you an A', and if they say no then they believe in a restriction on speech.

(Zimmerman, 17 May 2005)

Professionals are often forced into positions where outcomes will need to be negotiated, and where dialogue and judgements are required, rather than strict adherence to a principle. This was most evident in the example offered by McFarlane, concerning the controversy over, so-called, 'bake sales':

The affirmative action bake sale is essentially taking cookies and pricing them for Asian Americans at 25c, for African Americans 50c, for white males it might be a dollar. Same cookie. The point that the bake sales are trying to make is that the same dollar that a white man might spend, they have to spend more to get the same cookie, whereas the African Americans only by 50c, etc., etc. Well, that actually happened at NYU. That occurred and the students who were present and saw this – a particular student called – and they were outraged about it, they were very upset about and yes, they did appear in my office, they appeared in other professionals' offices, they filed a grievance, and that is where strategies come in.

It is more of an advisement perspective in terms of that and addressing how they feel and what they think went wrong and acknowledging that the way you are feeling is – I mean you want to have some empathy to that. At the same time we are talking about free speech on our campus and also at the same time what other policies may have been broken? In other words there is a New York State law where you can't sell.

The other thing is that these things do not happen over night. What is so critical about situations that occur on campus is the speed in which the university responds. Very critical – I think that is a whole new research area in terms of how to handle the communications between the group that actually had the bake sale, the students who are upset and angered about it. And so what are you going to do? And they want to know what are you going to do now? So there has to be an infrastructure within the university community to actually look at, and come up with, strategies to deal with these issues, and one of the main things is to keep an open line of communication with students.

(McFarlane, 19 May 2005)

However, it was also clear, particularly in the light of a broader reflection on the delineation problem, that in seeking to produce broad policies and strategies, particularly concerning complicated matters, this has not been without serious irony:

What really troubled me was when there was a women empowering conference here at the campus and in that case I was not allowed to go, because I was a man and I thought that was just preposterous. So the reason I gave that example is because I am a Latino who has worked very hard to help to build access for minority students and for women and for gays and lesbians, and so I was put in a position of being the male, and so a sort of twisted position, I typically felt I was able to occupy.

And so it occurred that there were going to be many other examples in which white students, for instance, were asked not to attend a certain kind of event or discussion, I think in many cases people are engaged in the politics of exclusion based on a sense of coming from a dis-empowered background and these events or locations or discussions needed to take place in what is often called 'safe space'. The whole category of safe space seems to me to be interesting but troubled by this expectation that certain groups are required and have the right to a certain, to that kind of a, privilege.

(Padilla, 26 April 2005)

Here we see complicated, and perhaps unintended, consequences, but it also highlights the need for serious critical reflection, and it is when the latter is lacking that the charge of 'political correctness gone mad' would appear to have the most credence. Later in the conversation Padilla articulated this well with reference to the tendency for groups to calcify in their thinking (see below). This aspect was not lost on McWhorter also:

Hate speech is hard because while the intentions of the policies are good, in real America today, the policies are so subject to abuse that I would eliminate all hate speech provisions. The policy wants to protect black people from being called 'nigger' – but too often for my taste, what really happens is that a black person blows the whistle when the word 'niggardly' is used (this has happened no fewer than three times on record) or a black student who doesn't like her campus forges threatening hate notes to blacks so that her parents will withdraw her from the school thinking it is a racist campus (that actually happened at a small school two weeks ago). Maybe words can help define the world – but another perspective is to teach people to resist this, rather as was expected in less enlightened times, we might say.

(McWhorter, 15 May 2005)

Lest we might be able to conclude, convincingly, that more has been lost rather than gained in seeking to legislate over some restrictions on speech, Lakoff reminds us of some of the broader political contours of the debates:

There is this funny thing where the strongest groups in society, the white, middle and upper class males, start behaving like victims. A word they despise when it is used of someone else. They: 'Oh boo hoo, we are so afraid of being victimized by these people who are going to come and, you know, listen to our every word and record our speech and hall us off to prison and give away our jobs as a result', but in fact those things never happened. And . . . the Orwell thing is used as a way of scaring people, but it really doesn't represent the reality. Now, of course, it is true that if you are a member of that group that has always had the power to do whatever it wants, to whomever it wants, and you say to them: 'Well you now have to start thinking about possible consequences when you do whatever you want to whomever you want' then it seems like a constriction. It seems like you are being deprived of rights that you have. But you shouldn't have had those rights in the first place.

(Lakoff, 20 April 2005)

And Gitlin reminds us that what is so disappointing about what has happened in higher education is that we seem to have lost a sense of perspective, that, too often, it is not a question anymore of professionalism, but adherence to rules. Questions of freedom and speech and restrictions on speech should really be matters for ongoing professional dialogue:

It is a matter of decorum. This is, I think, a social function; I mean it is a legitimate social function to secure decorum. You don't need the formality of rules. You don't need law and certainly the worst way of policing these things is through the media, which have their own stake in inflammatory processes.

(Gitlin, 19 May 2005)

Talking about multiculturalism

As we have already seen throughout the previous chapters, the arguments for and against forms of multicultural curricula are the widest ranging, particularly when it comes to questions of political correctness. This was reflected in the ways the people in these interviews spoke. That said, two clear themes were apparent: first, on the question of the nature of academic knowledge and the role of the university in its production and dissemination, and second, on some of the limited and limiting effects of multiculturalism in addressing educational questions.

Unsurprising perhaps, the role of the university and the nature of knowledge produced a wide range of animated responses. In response to a line of questioning about whether multiculturalism could be seen as some kind of threat to a university Searle said:

I would go so far to say that it is a threat to the university if you make it; if you admit to the idea that you can have all kinds of languages and all kinds of traditions in the university. But as far as higher education is concerned, in our civilization, you are not an educated person if you cannot speak and read English and if you don't know something about the historical and cultural background and the present social, political culture. That is the point I would make. Now there is a more interesting question about this and I don't really fully understand it, but if we take the definition of multiculturalism to be: there should be no such thing as a preferred language or preferred cultural tradition, in, let's say countries like the United States and Britain, my worry would be I can't think of any successful multicultural countries in history.

(Searle, 19 April 2005)

This was followed by animated concern over some of the more postmodern claims that have been made about knowledge in higher education:

I look at my own life history and I have never engaged in an intellectual enterprise with the idea that I am forced to do this in order to serve some imperialistic end; that is ridiculous. . . . As far as knowledge and people are concerned I perceive on the basis of certain actual fundamental assumptions. One, there is a reality that is totally independent of us. It doesn't give a damn about us and one of our roles as intellectuals is to represent [it]. Now two, there is a socially real reality. A reality of government, property, rights, economy, and so on, but even there you have an epistemic objectivity, that is to say, the subjectivity of the domain, the fact that it is socially created, doesn't mean that you can't have objective knowledge about it.

(Searle, 19 April 2005)

Although Gitlin's more radical political agenda might be apparent in the following response, it is also clear, again, particularly towards the end, that there are similar resonances with Searle's concerns:

I have been teaching the last two years at Columbia. I have been teaching one of the core courses, Contemporary Civilization, the so-called Great Books course, *Plato to Nato*, as we call it informally. I'm a great believer especially after having taught it. I was already for it. It has been by far the best teaching experience I have ever had. Do I think there is a good reason to read certain texts from outside the West?: Yes. Do I think that the curriculum should be radically revamped towards that end?: No, I would be perfectly happy to stipulate that Plato was black if those who think it is important to know he was black would read him, and take him on. I despise that sort of shallow Afrocentrism and I despise the arguments of those who think that the teaching of Western civilization is intrinsically an imperialistic act.

(Gitlin, 19 May 2005)

Gitlin was also forthright about the intellectual credibility of some forms of multiculturalism in the university curriculum:

> My impression is that the defence of multiculturalism as an intellectual enterprise has stagnated for a number of years. I see articles about the shrinking number of black studies majors and the like. There has been both the process of normalization but also of shrinkage partly because of the economic pay-off pressure for students and partly because of the shortfalls in intellectual life. I may be ignorant, but I'm not aware of breakthroughs in women's studies. Maybe people are making break-throughs in the sex specific, race specific qualities of the genome and their bearing on certain physical qualities. Outside the hard sciences I don't know what the feminist theory of anything is these days.
>
> (Gitlin, 19 May 2005)

Lakoff emphasized that knowledge is intrinsically multifaceted, and thus, what forms of multiculturalism have done is simply raised the profile of a wider approach to knowledge:

> I think very little in a university is disinterested and I think it is kind of good if we can acknowledge it on the surface from the start: 'here are my prejudices, here is what I prefer to think and, you know, if you students or colleagues object, it is your job to raise your objection reasonably.'
>
> But I also think that part of human knowledge is emotional knowledge. That the vanishing of feelings and opinions, and so on, and different evaluations from the business of the university distorts what knowledge is about and distorts the university experience. There are some kinds of things you study, like mathematics, that don't have a large feeling component with them, and you don't study them that way, but if we talk about America as being composed of a wide array of diverse people you have to talk about things like the immigrant experience, what people have gone through, and how different cultures perceive the world in different ways and this is represented in their language, and these are first of all intellectual ideas. Very responsible people have talked about them and given interesting evidence for them which can be argued about and contraverted, and various stuff, and the fact that it does involve the possibility of personal testimony, I think enriches it.
>
> Very often there is no thing called truth which everybody has to agree to, and I think it is a very important part of one's intellectual university experience as a student, to understand that the world is full of ambiguity. That there are some things that you are not going to absolutely determine and that nobody can tell you this is right, this is wrong, this is true, this is false; can't now, and often will never be able to. And if you can't learn to appreciate uncertainty and undecidability, indeterminacy, and all that

kind of thing, you will never be able to think your way through some of the really most interesting and distressing issues of our time.

(Lakoff, 20 April 2005)

Having also taught on multicultural courses Lakoff also defends them, but on this line that they offer a wider understanding of what exactly knowledge is:

Berkeley, probably some 15 years ago, instituted its American Cultures course, which every undergraduate has to take one, and those are, kind of, our explicit moves in favour of multiculturalism. Basically it is the recognition that America comes together from a wide array of different cultures, of different cultural experiences, and rather than trying to do the old melting pot where you obliterate those differences as quickly as possible, multiculturalists talk about a mosaic or a salad for each member, who retains its own identity so what a university would try to do is instil in all its students this notion that each of us carries a particular ethnic identity that by itself contributes to the richness of the culture, you know, that it is better that it is not being obliterated and that this would have to do, first of all, with what it is in your curriculum, in a world literature course, how you teach a world history course. In the case of literature you extend the canon to include people who never would have been in it. We teach a course, Linguistics 55, which is part of this curriculum in which we try to teach students first, a sense of the complexity of the linguistic scene in America. Where these different languages and dialects come from, how they differ, how they are similar, and how each one borrows from the ones around it. So the notion that cultures, multiculturalism, or being multicultural contributes to the richness – each one contributes to others rather than that it is something to fear, as something to obliterate.

(Lakoff, 20 April 2005)

These notions might be taken further to imply that higher education has a duty beyond the strictly academic. In the extreme this might be argued to be one of generating forms of social cohesion in society at large, or at least recognizing that higher education should not be divorced from the communities beyond it. On this aspect of multiculturalism McFarlane was particularly forthright:

Any university that is not looking at how they are a microcosm of the real world challenges is in trouble. What's really wrong with feeling good about being connected with members of the community, is that a bad thing? That is on one level. And the other level is, aren't we training future leaders . . . when they move out to the community? Our community, the US community, depending upon where you go, is diverse. So the whole cultural competency thing is about how can we get folks to get to the point, or become engaged with one another, so that they can actually exchange ideas, help come up with solutions, even if they do want to make money on Wall Street. Okay, alright, so you want to make money on Wall Street, that is a good thing, but if you are not thinking about how you need to lead other folks you are cutting short your own intellectual capacity. That would be my argument.

(McFarlane, 19 May 2005)

Zimmerman, however, raised the question of how changing the curriculum to reflect a more diverse American society had not in the process necessarily brought about a more critical engagement with questions of identity and culture. Thus although a wider range of social groups are now represented in American History courses:

What a lot of those movements wanted is a kind of compensatory history. They would compensate for the very real and obvious slights that they have received and continue to receive across our history and it seems to me if you open up the official narrative today, the official story, you get that. You know, from Frederick Douglas through Martin Luther King. Not only are African Americans there but they are celebrated and their tremendous achievements are celebrated and I want to be very clear that given the outright neglect and distortion and really, slander, of African Americans in our history you have got to count that as progress and it is a very recent vintage. We are almost too close to it to see how recent it is, but gains come with costs. All gains come with costs. Americans don't like to say this but that doesn't make it any less true. Is it progress that our text books are now quite literally multi coloured? I think it is enormous progress if you look at how lily white they were before. But what hasn't changed is the story itself. Look at the title of the books and you will see that: *Rise of the American Nation, Quest for Liberty*. What is different is that it is 900 pages long and it's a rainbow, and it is a beautiful rainbow, and if you want your differently-abled Uzbekies we have differently-abled Uzbekies. We have a side bar, and you will see the great heroes that the differently-abled Uzbekies contributed to this wonderful national story.

But I think really the problem, when it comes to history, is that, for our entire history we have regarded the entire enterprise as the wonderful story of us, and in the past 30 years we may be us much more diverse and that is a good thing, but it is still the wonderful story of us and you can't really have an analytic history on those terms because again that substitutes answers for questions. What is wonderful about us? Would other people agree? What is your measure of wonderful? And if the goal of history is to promote a certain feeling, either a certain national feeling or a certain racial feeling, you won't get to those questions.

(Zimmerman, 19 May 2005)

For Gitlin, however, the question is perhaps a much simpler one. For, how could we even aspire to have such debates when, in reality, it is still too easy to find debate stifled just at the point where you would hope that it might be opened up:

> But every time I think that we have wised up and collectively matured I have run into another absurdity. Two years ago I was one of the lecturers in a series . . . in Indiana, where the political scientist who organized this series, had large questions in mind of a theoretical nature about the relation between university life and democracy, but by the time we got to deliver these lectures a committee of post-60s faculty had taken command of the curriculum reform committee and had eliminated the common core part. And I heard one of these people speak and I was horrified. It's an appalling thing when you discover that what you have described on paper is real. And this wasn't 1994, this was 2003, and there it was in the heartland of Indiana, the rejection of the white male-ocracy, and one occasionally hears it. Today you are much more likely to hear it from that generation of faculty and those who followed along in their wake than from students. I think there's very little student interest. In fact on the whole there is a negative interest.
>
> (Gitlin, 19 May 2005)

This brings us naturally and more squarely to the question of the limitations of the multicultural agenda. Again there is evidence in the responses of the ironies that have been produced; unintended, perhaps, but ones which have put academics and administrators in difficult positions. Padilla provided a pertinent example:

> Especially after 9/11 and then with some of the immigration issues in California, whether it is a campus Republican magazine, or the newspaper, political cartoon, and so on, there have been either articles or cartoons that have been very offensive to – whether it is – Muslim students or Latino students or black students, and they want us, the administration, to go and do something, to go and shut down the publication and to stop this, and on the one hand it seems to me to be our responsibility to try to promote an environment in which people feel comfortable, but that is not what a university is, never has been, and should never be. And I have students who argue against me about this. I say listen, political cartoons have a long history of doing just what is happening to you. That is their job, okay; their job is not to be nice about this. It is to caricature, I mean you are going to have faces that have a nose this way or eyes this way or colour that way.
>
> So it seems to me one way to handle that would be to have a campus symposium or dialogue in which you talk about the history of political lampooning, or satire, or caricature as that is exactly what it is meant to do. So let's think about the forms that response can take to that which are more reasoned than stealing all the newspapers, hiding them, hoarding them, or

something, or asking for this place to be shut down, because when you do that – and that sometimes comes up as a form of political correctness – I think it is unfortunate because rather than teaching students how to respond to an event, that they are going to see over and over again as they go into adulthood, and to help them shape ways of thinking about it and responding to that, sometimes the conversation just gets shut down.

(Padilla, 26 April 2005)

Echoing some of the comments of McFarlane before on freedom of speech Padilla outlined how events can quickly escalate, particularly when wider, ideological, forces come into play:

Things do happen that are hurtful and harmful and insulting. Unfortunately, but with no surprise to me, the event undergoes a series of transformations. And I think that the water buffalo story is in that genre. In other words, something indeed happened, a confrontation between white students and black students over nonsense probably, and then it is racialized, and probably it didn't start as a racialized incident but became racialized because I would say that the power of racial consciousness in this country has this tendency to, in fact, create a wider set of meanings and interpretations from events that are in their local context *fairly* unsurprising. I wouldn't say *not*, because they *are* surprising. So I think that is probably true, and I know that has happened with us.

But I think that is again one of the problems with the political correctness and its attribution, its connection with the left, is that, frankly, I sometimes see that it tends to calcify with the left more quickly than I think it should, so that rather than people on the left saying: 'Did this really happen, or what happened, or who was there, or how do we know it happened in that way, or shouldn't we think this through?' It is almost always: 'That *did* happen and that is the reason why this campus is so messed up.' We have come to expect it here but it certainly happens everywhere and it has become very, very difficult to deal with, whether it is from the left, from the right, whether it is Muslim, Jewish, African American and Korean. We have become so racially sensitive in this country that is it very difficult to have a conversation. I mean we are consumed by race but we can't talk about it. We can't have a probing, real discussion about it.

(Padilla, 26 April 2005)

Again, this was echoed more broadly by McWhorter:

It is definitely true that my saying something about blacks carries a certain weight because I'm black: namely, the idea is that I cannot be called a racist, which is the first thing that many aim at negative evaluations of black culture from whites. Of course, I have also commonly been said to 'not like black people' and the like, although I sense that people said this more in 2000 and 2001, when I was best known for *Losing the Race*, than lately, when people have started to understand that I am more moderate than they may have thought. But in general, whether or not someone is a racist is a tripwire issue in modern America, as much as whether or not one was a witch was such an issue in Salem back in the day.

(McWhorter, 13 May 2005)

The notions of 'calcification' and 'tripwire' would appear to offer significant insights into the nature of the problems that have been experienced on many US higher education campuses. Again, McFarlane offers a pertinent example:

You have a situation where you are trying to build the campus community, helping students feel connected to the campus, in their own identity, in their own culture, but then you may have a white student or a white professor, and we have done some break out sessions on diversity for a student affairs conference and one of the sessions was called 'diversity revealed' and just very quickly we asked the question – it was very multi-racial in terms of who was there – 'What was your greatest concern about working with or talking to and meeting other folks of colour?', and one of the things was 'I am afraid if I make a mistake or say the wrong thing that somebody is going to view me as a racist. And then, you know, I am branded for life. You know, I am the racist on campus.' So the problem with that fear is that it keeps people from crossing over into trying to learn more about other races and other cultures and interacting with them because, for many folks they are afraid that: 'Well, I don't know if I know enough, or feel confident enough or supported enough and if I make a mistake, I mean can I make a mistake?' I mean no one is even talking about the term forgiveness. I think if we are going to connect with each other as a multifaceted, multicultural society, there has got to be room for error and we're, as a society, not giving each other much room for error.

(McFarlane, 19 May 2005)

And, of course, this is not unrelated to the nature of knowledge either because it raises the question of whether one needs to be an advocate of a political position or social group in order to advance and disseminate knowledge of that position or group. In the extreme it raises the thorny question of whether a white person could ever be considered to be the head of an ethnic studies curriculum, or a male the head of a women's studies curriculum. Zimmerman echoes this point but takes the conversation into new territory also:

You walk into a room at NYU and there is just an assumption that at a minimum everybody hates George Bush, and that assumption is true, and I think that for me that is the root of the problem, that we are all trying to make a university that is more diverse, along the axes of race and gender, which is again something that I absolutely endorse but there is almost no intention to making the university diverse in other ways. And the only people frankly who seem to want to do that are themselves conservatives, which is why whenever I write on this subject people presume I am a conservative, which speaks exactly to the problem. The only reason you would ever express sympathy or solidarity with a group is that you are of that group. You can't make a democratic politics on those terms. But the same thing happens when I write about gay rights. I am not gay myself but whenever I write about the subject I get all kinds of emails. And everybody, pro and con, assumes I am gay. You sort of strip away the logic or illogic of all this and what you are left with at the end of the day is to be a geologist you have to be a rock. To express sympathy with a group you have to be of that group, and we will not create social progress in this country on those grounds. We cannot. It is illogically and politically impossible.

(Zimmerman, 19 May 2005)

He pushes the point even further in the following:

I do want an intellectually diverse faculty and the way to do that is not necessarily to hire more women and blacks, it is to stop being prejudiced against conservatives. I have written about this in the press and you can find it. I am not a Republican. I have never voted for a Republican in my life, but I would like to have more Republican colleagues. I just think it would make for a more fruitful and a more diverse faculty. And whenever I suggest this people respond in ways that I find profoundly anti-intellectual. People will say to me when I say: 'Yeah, I wish there were more Bush voters in the faculty', and they will say: 'Well, we don't hire Bush voters because we are smart.' I find that a moronic remark. I mean Milton Friedman and Saul Bellow voted for George Bush, I think, and maybe you are smarter than they are, but I am not.

(Zimmerman, 19 May 2005)

Zimmerman was also very animated about how multiculturalism, even for its advocates, has managed to detract attention away from what are, perhaps, the real causes of the problems in American education:

If the question is 'Are American students woefully inadequate in basic literacy and numeracy?' well, that is not a question at all, that is a fact, they are. But to lay this at the door of multiculturalism, it just denies huge structural realities, especially economic and equality that we are faced with everyday. That is not to say that I am an unequivocal defender of multi-culturalism but to impute all these other problems to something called multiculturalism I think is a wilful distortion of reality. The most cynical reading of multiculturalism is that it is a way to paper over these much more real and enduring differences, so okay, this school is very poorly funded and it is falling down and none of its teachers are trained, but we have got black history day. 'Right, I am somebody, somebody who can't read by the way, but I am somebody nevertheless.' And there is absolutely no amount of multiculturalism that is going to help kids in school where none of the teachers have sufficient training and where the school itself is not safe. There is no amount of multiculturalism that is going to solve that. That is not a curriculum problem, it is an economic one. With respect to the way that we fund schools, historically schools in the United States have been a local enterprise. This is why 'no child left behind' is actually a radical act. It is a radical act in the sense that it is historically disjunctive. The way we fund schools is, I think, the pre-eminent issue in education because it is the source of the inequality.

(Zimmerman, 17 May 2005)

Almost everyone responded at some point about how schools are funded, and the ways that higher education is often forced into a position of having to play catch up. This will be looked at again in the following section on affirmative action.

Talking about affirmative action

Two main themes emerged in the discussion of affirmative action. First, the rather obvious question surrounding what exactly the term actually means, and how this is translated into meaningful institutional action. And second, discussion of the ironies and contradictions that forms of affirmative action have highlighted, and how one might perceive the implications.

Searle was quick to point out just how much the term has actually changed meaning:

As always, you have got to tell me exactly what you mean by affirmative action, and that is a non-trivial question because the definition changes. What happened is that in the early days I was all for affirmative action because the idea was that we were going to take affirmative action and make sure that any folk who had not been able to compete in American life were given a chance to. That they were raised up to a level in the high schools where they would be able to compete for admissions, that they would be raised up to a level in other parts of American society so that they would be able to compete along with anybody else. But what happened was, and I guess this was inevitable, was that instead of affirmative action being an encouragement and assistance in competing, it became a criterion for judging a competition. So you did not have to win the race if you were black or Hispanic or, in the early days, Oriental-Asian. You were given a leg-up – it wasn't a level playing field.

(Searle, 19 April 2005)

As we have seen several times before, in earlier chapters, these comments raise the fundamental question about whether we should be putting the emphasis on helping people to take better part in an existing competitive game, or changing the nature of the game itself, or indeed, in the extreme, challenging the very idea that all games must, necessarily, be competitive. From his experience of Berkeley admissions Searle also questioned whether the notion of 'fairness' was being understood in all its complexity. On the surface it would appear that Berkeley admits very few black students, and this might be interpreted as blatantly unfair. But:

> Of the 36,000 applicants, we send out letters of acceptance to 9,000. Of those 9,000 only 4,000 actually come – a little less than 50 per cent. Now I would like to know how many blacks were in the 9,000 and I will tell you the problem in very simple terms. The kind of people who can get admitted to Berkeley can also get admitted to much more snobbish public schools, and if they are black they will be subsidized. Their way will be paid. So, you are an intelligent black kid from a slum area in Los Angeles and you get admitted to Harvard and Berkeley, and Harvard offers you bags of money, where are you going to go? There is no question. So I think there are two questions I want to [bring] to the Chancellor – how many did we admit – not how many actually accepted but how many got admitted, and secondly how many got admitted to the whole university system because it turns out that there are other campuses that are less demanding than Berkeley that will provide you with a leg up so that you can eventually make it to Berkeley or you can go to Junior Colleges and transfer to Berkeley. So . . . I think the figure is misleading. If that was the only statistic then I would say that we have to do something about that. But I don't believe that. I think what actually happens is that we admit a sizeable amount of people but our criteria says that anybody admitted here is going to be admitted to other places and they would rather go to these other places – more snob value. The truth is, people admitted to both Harvard and Berkeley, about 90 per cent go to Harvard. If they have got the money to do it they will do it.
>
> (Searle, 19 April 2005)

Much of this might be read as an irony built into the way that access to elite schools in the US has played itself out. Zimmerman outlined what he saw as the driving force here:

> The elite schools do everything they can to get as many kids of colour and they compete vehemently with each other for the kids who have the educational background to do this. It is fierce out there because everyone wants their numbers to be better so they are in a war for a very small pool of African American, mainly, kids. The amount of attention devoted to that compared to the amount of attention devoted to why are there so few

kids in the pool, that is the question. And our view is so skewed and narrow and jaundiced, it's where we live. We are all fighting for that small pool and nothing will change until the pool gets bigger. I think everybody knows that. Indeed, the vehemence of the competition reflects the small size of the pool.

(Zimmerman, 19 May 2005)

From his own experience of working with Berkeley admissions Padilla drew attention to some of the means by which the 'pool' is being enlarged. Just like many of the terms associated with political correctness he began by questioning whether *the term* 'affirmative action' has much value anymore:

It's so contaminated with a variety of meanings that I would put it aside and start in a different way such that we are able to think of a university like Berkeley thinking clearly what the student body should, not so much only look like, but how the variety of intellectual strengths or social locations or language groups or income strata that students represent are brought together in a way that helps us to fashion an undergraduate student body that we think will come together to generate the kind of intellectual and social vitality that you want at a university. So, it seems to me that when you do that what you think about is at Berkeley we have approximately 36,000–37,000 applications for freshman class and we typically admit 9,000 or 10,000 students for an entry class of 3,800 to 4,000 freshman and then we also do the same for transfer students. So, when we had that conversation there is no question that if we wanted to just do this by academic index alone we could run the applications through a computer base. It would be done within five minutes and you would take some scatter of criteria, feed that in and that would be that. Well I don't think any good university does that. Harvard doesn't do that, Stanford doesn't do that, Yale doesn't do that, not Michigan.

As I say it is really important to think clearly about what kind of student body you want to fashion along the contours of what you want the campus to be on a day-to-day basis and then therefore we have committed our intellectual energy and a great deal of resources into trying to figure out how best to select students such that, for instance, there are some eligibility benchmarks that students have to meet, a certain GPA. But what we have done at Berkeley is we find a measure of how students do in their context, and in the context in which they do their work by looking at their high school we have a kind of thick description of every public high school in California so that we can tell you that high school X in Los Angeles county involves about 4,800 students, there are three different time calendars for the students, maybe as many as 45–57 per cent of them are on some form of public assistance, we can tell you that there are a certain percentage of the teachers who are not credentialed in the field of instruction but emergency credentials, over and against high school X in Walnut Creek, or suburbia somewhere, and where the profile is exactly the opposite.

(Padilla, 26 April 2005)

In the first paragraph here we have a version of the compelling case for diversity, but in the second we see that this is not being engineered by a simple open-door policy, but one rooted in a sophisticated selection process based on school context; what in the UK is often referred to as an index of 'value-added', that is an attempt to weight the achievements of an excelling student from a poor school neighbourhood differently from the more moderate achievements of a student from a privileged private school.

Lakoff was particularly animated about the broad picture, and how we need to assess any admissions policy with this in mind:

> I think what we need to try to do, somehow, is make people of all ethnicities feel more comfortable living in a pluralistic society and I sort of think whatever it takes is a good thing to do. Now, again, whites – who are middle-class whites – have for a very long time sort of seen that the university was theirs, it was their pie and they got to have practically all the slices of it, by right. And one of the things that multiculturalism, and feminism, and affirmative action all do is say no, somebody else is entitled to some of these slices and they say 'but then we are being deprived, we are being denied our rights because we have a right to those slices'. Other people say no. Now it is sort of interesting here because Asian Americans have been getting more and more of that, of the Berkeley pie, so it is now about two-thirds of the Berkeley population and you know, the whites sort of don't know what to do about that. You know the problem is that the Asians get in fair and square.
>
> But you really have to say what is best for the entire community, and you have to sacrifice maybe. It's too bad but somebody's got to sacrifice and giving this lot to a black person is ultimately in the greater good so you've got to sit back and say I'm not going to fight for it. That would be the non-individualistic position, I think. And you know, it always sort of interests me that here are all these white guys who say 'oh boo hoo, my right to a slot is . . . quotered out', but I went to a university as an undergraduate 45 years ago, and it was a prestigious university and slots were very scarce and the rule was four males were admitted for every female and that was a quota, 4:1, that was it, and I never heard any of those guys say boo. If they are so sensitive now, how come they weren't sensitive, or their counterparts weren't sensitive, back then? So I don't feel too sympathetic.

(Lakoff, 20 April 2005)

Here, Lakoff alludes to the fact that all achievements will be sponsored in some way, and thus it would be almost impossible to engineer a completely fair meritocracy. Better, therefore, that we concentrate on asking where are the most obvious cases of inequality and injustice in society and see that as a sound, moral, general rationale. The fact that it might produce some undesirable consequences for those who have been privileged in the past is not sufficient ground for being deflected from the soundness of the original stand. However, McWhorter reminds us of how some of the, perhaps unwitting, consequences here might bring us to question the validity of some of the arguments rooted in notions of social justice:

> Two wrongs don't make a right; the legs up that whites have had exempt people from trying their best. So be it. But this means that affirmative action can't be justified on the same basis. Especially when in practice, affirmative action creates a culture in general. The true evil of racial preferences is less the specifics of admissions algorithms than the sense it creates among guilty whites (i.e. most of them in any education setting) that black people are to be applauded for 'being there' rather than what they actually do or how well they do it.
>
> (McWhorter, 13 May 2005)

He also made the wider point:

> It seems to me that whites have always been a majority, will always be a very large portion of the population, and have always had the most power. The salvation of black America will not be to upend this but to thrive despite it. Interesting – a lot of the dialogue on blacks and 'power' seems to proceed upon an assumption that blacks are about half of America. But if blacks were proportionally represented at the levers of power, then it would be at the rate of about one person in eight nationwide. Certainly blacks are more concentrated in some places like certain cities – which is exactly where blacks have often been the main people in power on, say, school boards and municipal governments, for thirty years. So I am not sure what the actual point of the 'white privilege' argument is – other than that it gives people something to complain about that they can be sure will never go away. That kind of race dialogue is not my cup of tea.
>
> (McWhorter, 13 May 2005)

As an educational leader, Day took a more pragmatic stand. Using the example of staff recruitment, rather than student recruitment, he outlined how forms of affirmative action can be implemented in uncomplicated ways:

> If the statewide workforce availability pool says that there are sufficient numbers of people of colour who have prepared themselves to be in the workforce similar in scope to your own, then you can use that data to assess the differences between what is available and the profile of your own faculty and staff. If there are significant differences then we can be legally on solid ground to aggressively recruit and to close the gaps and

specifically, for example to hire more people of colour to teach in such areas as Math, Science or any other discipline area where there are apparent gaps between what is available statewide, regionally, and locally and your current workforce profile. The goal is to close the gaps and hire faculty who reflect the profile of your students and the community you serve. But you have got to have the database available to justify your pursuits otherwise you can't do it and you don't meet the legal test.

(Day, 26 April 2005)

Of course, given that Day was working in the State of California, where Proposition 209 (discussed in Chapter 6) operates, employers are now, effectively, asked to select appropriate candidates from application pools only. With respect to student recruitment, Day was clear that he saw it as normal duty of any college to constantly monitor the make-up of its student body:

Given the huge growth in the Hispanic/Latino population we are necessarily expanding our recruitment efforts with this group. We are focusing on this effort not because we want to experience more enrollment growth but because the needs of this group (and others) are so critical and lagging behind when you compare them with others and particularly their white counterparts. They are, for example, significantly behind the achievement levels of African Americans in both secondary and post-secondary education; and, when you take a look at dropout rates from the K–12 system, Latinos are much more over-represented in school dropout rates than African Americans. So our mission is to try to work and position ourselves with clusters of students and with individual students to be their safety net or their springboard for a first-time (or second) opportunity for academic and career success.

(Day, 26 April 2005)

Gitlin was somewhat surprised that a, seemingly, practical and pragmatic principle outlined by Carter (1991) had not been taken more seriously. Gitlin began with reference to the famous Bakke case (discussed in Chapter 6):

Is medical school admission a right that pertains to individuals by virtue of their test scores or is it a social good that should be allocated with applying to outcome? I was persuaded by Stephen Carter's argument that the way to think about affirmative action was in what he called the pyramid, which I thought was the most original thing in his book and nobody paid any attention to it. Mainly, the notion that the claims of affirmative action are strongest at the bottom of the pyramid. That is affirmative action for admission to college has a degree of legitimacy. Affirmative action for professorships has less, far less. Affirmative action for a tenured professorship is altogether illegitimate.

(Gitlin, 19 May 2005)

Some of the conversations offered interesting insights into how questions relating to affirmative action are often deeply personal. Day and McFarlane gave particularly interesting testimonies in this regard:

> When suddenly somebody observes that as a result of our diversity initiatives or a variety of other programmes and services that we put in place – somebody is getting some special treatment, they look at it on two levels. Even though they might say it is not a big deal, they harbour some concerns, internally, that say: 'I wish somebody had dealt with me when I was coming up, because I had to do it all on my own.' Okay, and then they say: 'If I had had those same opportunities would I have been any further along than what I am?' And that's very internal types of ongoing thinking about to what extent one may have advantaged over another based upon one's own history and pattern of getting to a certain place in their lives, versus the way they see others holding their hand, supporting them, providing for a lot more of a nurturing, supportive environment. I think that below the surface that is what goes on. Above the surface, the way people relate, they basically accept the notion that the price we pay in our society for not creating a better climate, a better opportunity, a better context for these students to be successful, if that doesn't happen, then we all lose. And I think that they get that.
>
> (Day, 26 April 2005)

> I am bombarded by individuals who want to be successful – I am just in that environment. And then I am also outside of the environment, we are talking about a situation where it is not just the culture, we have got to look further back. We just can't do a research project on college students and try to determine whether or not they are motivated, equipped. Let's not forget about what happened in the first 15 years. I sometimes speak to elementary kids, third graders. Some of them, I am telling you, the capacity to succeed is there. Something is happening. It is in many ways it is not because it is a will *not* to succeed. That is the most insane thing I think, the will not to succeed. I just don't believe that there is no will not to succeed.
>
> (McFarlane, 19 May 2005)

Finally, Zimmerman reminded us of how affirmative action, like multicultural-ism, can act to deflect attention away from other, perhaps, more deep-rooted issues, and issues that Americans find it difficult to even talk about, let alone address:

> Just like multiculturalism is in some ways a convenient way to avoid talking about the unequal funding of schools. In some ways affirmative action is a very convenient way to avoid talking about class. The logic, or illogic behind affirmative action is that if only we could rid ourselves of

the stain of racial inequality, then we would be an equal society, but of course this is not true. The vast majority of poor Americans are white. I have a former student who did Americor, which is a volunteer project in Kentucky, and the poorest county in the United States. It has no African American citizens. It is the poorest county in the United States. Also the vast majority of poor Americans live in rural areas, not in urban ones. Affirmative action does nothing for those people, nothing, except possibly reinforce whatever racial anger and hatreds that they have inherited from their own history.

But I should add that in some ways [it is] legitimate [for affirmative action to have a race connotation] and here is why. First of all African Americans are quite obviously over-represented among people who are poor. That is the most obvious one, but here is the one that people talk about a lot less but is also true, this is right now the most depressing fact in American education. African Americans do worse in school, K through 12 schools, even after you control for income and education of the parents. I wish it were not true, I really wish it weren't true. It is a fact, even the black kids that come from wealthy families do worse in school than the white kids who come from wealthy families and that is a really hard nut to crack. We don't like to talk about that. We want it all to be about opportunity.

(Zimmerman, 19 May 2005)

Zimmerman also made the more general point about how difficult it is to talk seriously about discrimination in the US. Remembering McWhorter's 'tripwire' it is as if the ultimate irony is that to seek to make any discriminating statement is liable to render the speaker a racist, in some shape or form:

Racism has given discrimination a bad name. Discrimination in a dictionary sense is at the heart of every intellectual enterprise. We cannot live without it. The problem is that racism, which is an invidious kind of discrimination, has given other kinds a bad name. You cannot have an intellectual project unless you are willing to award more strength and more credence to certain ideas than to others. Even the claim that all ideas have equal strength is itself a claim which you have to defend against other claims. Nobody really believes that line, even people who spout it at me. For me the beginning and end word on this subject is an essay that Clifford Geertz, the anthropologist wrote 30 years ago called 'anti anti-relativism', which I absolutely love, where he just points out, look, he is an anti anti-relativist in the same way that Humphrey Bogart was an anti anti-communist. That is Humphrey Bogart was not a communist, he hated the communists in Hollywood, but he also hated the ridiculous things that were done against communists. But Geertz is not a relativist but he goes on to say that actually nobody is. He says maybe in Times Square, Rodeo

Drive, somewhere you will find this sort of pure relativist, this person without any principles whatsoever, but if you look at human beings you will find that actually they don't operate that way, so in some degree it is a red herring.

(Zimmerman, 19 May 2005)

General conclusion

The purpose behind this chapter was to report the conversations I had with a group of American academics, administrators, and leaders concerning aspects of political correctness. The main aim was to try to capture some of the ways in which people talk about political correctness. In essence, with what does it ordinarily resonate, and on what do people put the emphasis when confronted with direct questions on the subject. To repeat, what is reported here is not an attempt to measure the amount of political correctness in higher education, but rather how people grapple with the issues that have been raised while working in higher education during a period when the term was in the ascendant.

The broad themes correspond with much of what has been written about political correctness over the past twenty years. This is not surprising given that all these individuals would have been broadly familiar with the contours of those debates. What is more significant is how much of what was said relates more directly to their work as employees in schools of higher education. And in this regard the chapter offers insight, literally, into how people *work* with the term, and aspects with which it is associated. To use Berger and Luckman's (1967) phrase, the chapter has been about the social construction of everyday professional realities, and ones where the term political correctness has been apt to intrude.

If it confirms anything that has come before, then it is surely that political correctness is all about politics. But what seems to be more to the fore here is how people rationalize their thoughts and behaviours, and work with the term, even if this involves trying to distance themselves from it. Hopefully, this chapter also highlights the complex nature of professional decision making, and although, at one level, these decisions might be seen as inherently political in nature, it is not at all clear that this always flows inexorably from a rigid standpoint. If confirmation were needed that media coverage of events can have the effect of distorting a far more complex reality, this chapter might be read as an attempt to capture more fully some of that complexity.

8

Green sheep in London
The Loony Left and British PC

Introduction

There is much to support the claim that whatever becomes big in the US will arrive in the UK a few years later – from standardized testing in schools and colleges to the McDonaldization of society at large (for a fuller discussion see Hyland 1994 and Ritzer 2000 respectively). With regard to political correctness there is no doubt that discussions of the appropriateness of speech codes and codes of conduct have made their way to the UK. There has also been much discussion of political correctness in the leading weekly newspaper for academics, the *Times Higher Education Supplement* (*THES*), and some authors (e.g. Furedi 1997; Hayes, in Lea *et al.* 2003) have invoked much of the conceptual language found in earlier literature in the US, such as in *A Nation of Victims* (Sykes 1992) and *Culture of Complaint* (Hughes 1993). The tone of much of the discussion is disparaging, and, in the case of some popular media articles, implies that political correctness is as unwelcome an import to the UK as a McDonald's restaurant would be in a leafy English village.

The broad aim of this chapter is to trace the connections between PC debates in the US and the UK in the last twenty years, and to ask whether there are distinct cultural differences at work, and the effect that these might have had on the nature of debate in the latter. The main method adopted for this purpose is a review of relevant literature in British academic journals, books, and news magazines. Wherever possible this review is limited to publications that are focused on post-16 education, unless a discussion lodged elsewhere touches explicitly on educational matters, or the discussion is sufficiently noteworthy for its insight into political correctness in general. This survey chapter will be followed by a more detailed analysis (in Chapters 9 and 10) of the key themes which are most relevant to post-16 education in the UK.

Loony Leftism and the British tabloid press

There is some evidence that the newly adopted use of the term political correctness by many conservative commentators in US educational debate in the mid- to late 1980s began to make its way to the UK in the early to mid-1990s. The first use of the term in the *THES*, the house newspaper for UK HE academics, was in 1990, and a steady stream of articles appeared in the following five years. A critical discussion of these articles will be a central part of this chapter. However, there are good reasons to begin this discussion with the two general elections which took place in the UK in the 1980s – 1983 and 1987. Indeed a major contention of this chapter will be that the anti-Labour Party campaign orchestrated by politically right-leaning news media in both election campaigns contained many of the ideas seen *subsequently* in the conservative anti-PC campaign in the US.

Popularly referred to as *Loony Leftism* at the time, the campaign ran by many newspapers – most notably by *The Sun* and its sister paper the *News of the World,* and the *Daily Mail* and its sister paper *The Mail on Sunday* – contained much of the invective that was seen in the popular US-based *Time* and *Newsweek* a few years later. The underlying message was much the same: there is a tyrannical left-wing conspiracy at work and its extreme politics should be resisted by right-thinking people everywhere. There are some references to the connection between the Loony Left campaign of the 1980s and the subsequent discussion of PC in the 1990s in the UK (most notably in Dunant 1994), but little attempt to systematically draw together the similar threads in the former campaign and the right-wing campaign in the US in the same period. The most comprehensive analysis of the British campaign was undertaken originally by the Goldsmith's Media Research Group, led by James Curran (Goldsmith's Media Research Group 1988), which subsequently became part of a wider discussion of the media and the British left (Curran *et al.* 2005).

A good starting point for understanding the nature of the campaign was the by-election held in February 1983, in the constituency of Bermondsey, South East London (due to the death of the standing Member of Parliament), where the Labour Party candidate Peter Tatchell found himself at the centre of a mounting campaign by right-leaning tabloid newspapers, whose aim was to expose extremism in British politics. Tatchell, known to be gay, claimed his sexuality became a feature of this campaign (not something he was promoting at the time), but he was also cast more generally as a 'folk devil' of the left – a personification of middle-class intellectualism which had been infected by a Trotskyite brand of Marxism, and which could be portrayed as completely alien to the interests of ordinary working-class voters. In the process he also claimed, in two self-penned newspaper articles, that he had become the subject of enormous personal vilification, and subject to hate mail and other intimidating behaviours, and, furthermore, that he felt these effects long after the by-election was over (*The Guardian*, 18 April 1983, and *The Independent*, 25 January 1989). Of course, he may have lost the by-election vote to the Liberal candidate Simon Hughes due to the effectiveness of his opponent's campaign, or, indeed, to the ineffectiveness of the Labour Party in general in the early 1980s. However, there is little doubt about the intention behind the more general tabloid campaign against the left in British politics at that time. This period coincided with a growing number of tabloid stories which sought to discredit the activities of many Labour-controlled local councils, and the Greater London Council (GLC), whose leader Ken Livingstone was christened 'Red Ken'. In an early reference to 'Loony Lefties' *The Sun* carried a full-page story on local councils which it claimed were wasting taxpayers' money and promoting minority interests against the mainstream majority (*The Sun*, 9 May 1983: 9).

This campaign contained much of what was to inform the subsequent Loony Left campaign particularly in the run-up to the 1987 General Election, namely a deep-felt anti-intellectualism, and claims of infiltration by extremists in all matters of education and of a sinister desire to control people's everyday lives. This was typified by variations on a headline theme established in 1983: 'The Crazy Things They Do With Your Rates' (*Daily Mail*, 16 February 1983), and stories peppered with references to the fact that the minority interests of blacks, women, and gays were being put above the mainstream, were working against the mainstream, and were, in some way, ludicrous. For example, 'Loonies Put Ban on Wife Jokes' (*The Sun*, 13 March 1987). Although the term political correctness was not the focus for the campaign, it is clear that much of what has come to be associated with the term was being invoked and, indeed, after the election the term increasingly came to be used when these issues were discussed. As if the term Loony Left was considered appropriate for the overtly political arena of two general elections, it subsequently became subsumed under the more general term political correctness, but mostly for the same purpose of pursuing and persecuting the perpetrators of so-called tyrannical thought. In this light it is not clear that PC in the US pre-dates PC in the UK, for the concurrence of the campaigns against left-leaning (particularly intellectual) thought indicates the presence of cross-fertilization, and a growing awareness of what was needed successfully to discredit the left on both sides of the Atlantic.

In an attempt to analyse what lay at the heart of this campaign the researchers at Goldsmith's College, University of London, led by James Curran, presented their findings in an *Open Space* documentary broadcast by BBC2 under the title *Loony Tunes* (Goldsmith's Media Research Group 1988). They concluded that of the stories they were able to investigate all of them were either exaggerated or fabricated in some way. This included the story that several local councils in London had banned black coffee and black bin liners on the grounds that they were racist, and, what for many became the most famous example of loony behaviour, the alleged banning of the nursery rhyme 'Baa Baa Black Sheep' for fear that it might be racially offensive. This prompted the famous *Daily Mail* headline 'Baa Baa Green (Yes Green) Sheep' (*Daily Mail*, 9 October 1986). Utilizing the phrase 'there's no smoke without fire' the researchers were able to pinpoint the grain of truth upon which the stories built great edifices of loony, and, what today we would call, PC behaviour. The key principle at work seemed to be the desire on the part of some tabloid journalists to highlight, to the point of ridicule, sensitivity about language, which, at best, was perceived as unwelcome, and, at worst, was policed with a tyrannical zeal. And there is a clear connection here with what was about to be said about PC in news magazines in the US. Thus, just as 'the water buffalo' case was able to enter the lexicon of PC folklore in the US, the banning of this nursery rhyme in the UK seems to be the British equivalent. Indeed as Curran and his colleagues point out, the story seems to just keep giving, for it has resurfaced on a number of subsequent occasions (Curran *et al.* 2005). Indeed, even in 2006, almost twenty years later, the nursery rhyme was back in the *Daily Mail* under the headline 'Baa Baa Rainbow Sheep' (8 March 2006), this time with nearly one hundred, mainly anti-PC, bloggers' comments attached to it (http://www.dailymail.co.uk/pages/live/articles/news/news.html?in_article_id=379114&in_page_id=1770&in_page_id=1770&expand=true; accessed 4 January 2008).

However, on closer scrutiny, there are subtle differences between the anti-PC campaign in the US and the preceding Loony Left campaign in Britain. In the text of many of the British stories there is a much clearer thread of anti-intellectualism compared to the American stories, that is not only were those on the political left loony, but also the perpetrators were middle-class intellectuals who were acting as a misguided vanguard of true working-class feeling. Indeed, in the case of Peter Tatchell, he was accused of hiding his middle-class credentials and thereby *masquerading* as an authentic Labour supporter. If this was a deliberate strategy then surely its purpose was to drive a wedge between an intellectual wing in Labour politics (portrayed as overrun by middle-class Trotskyites) and a more authentic sensibility rooted in traditional working-class communities. In what is often referred to as the summer 'silly season', *The Sun* ran a number of stories in 1983 about the alleged infiltration of the British Leyland car plant by Trotskyites, culminating in a jokey guide for its readers entitled '10 Ways to Ferret out a Red Mole' (*The Sun*, 18 August 1983). It is difficult to gauge whether the true intent here was to steer these working-class voters more towards the Conservative Party, or simply to drive a class-based wedge between different types of Labour voter. Either way the zeal with which this aspect of the campaign was mounted is in part explained by the rich vein of anti-intellectualism one finds generally in tabloid newspapers in Britain, as popularized by headlines that preface stories about university research findings with variations on a theme of 'Boffins have discovered the bloody obvious again'.

Furthermore, what seems to distinguish the Loony Left campaign in Britain from the anti-PC campaign in the US is the overtly political nature of the British campaign, that it relates directly to *party* politics, as opposed to the US, where it was more clearly part of a wider cultural debate, or 'culture wars' (Hunter 1991). And, perhaps most significantly, the right's campaign in the US was very successful in associating the left with un-American thinking. It is not clear that a similar association was clearly established in the UK, where the purpose was more to associate the left with having gone 'mad' rather than being un-British. Given the common perception that the US is a more patriotic country compared to the UK, this variation in strategy is perhaps not surprising. However, it is clear that the left are being associated with a form of deviant behaviour, and perhaps this is the real point. The overtly political nature of the British campaign can also be seen in the conclusion to the Goldsmith's research television broadcast, which was that the most significant effect of the Loony Left campaign was to give credence to the view that local councils and local education authorities (most notably the Greater London Council), needed to be 'called to heel'. And thus, the Loony Left campaign gave popular consent to a legislative call to curb the activities of many of the political institutions that were seen to be orchestrating the increasingly progressive equal opportunities ethos of the schools and colleges which came under their jurisdiction (Curran *et al.* 2005). Indeed, many of them might well have gone on to oversee the introduction of codes of conduct in the UK, had they been able to continue to wield significant political power. The fact that the newly re-elected Thatcher government of 1983 announced its intention to abolish the GLC certainly lends credence to the view that the tabloid media were important in creating an appropriate climate for this legislative call to be validated

Moral panics and folk devils in PC debates

This link between media campaigns and government legislation could be argued to be one of the most significant features of the early anti-PC climate in Britain, and might well offer us a model example of how to produce a *moral panic*. Drawing on the seminal work of Cohen and his study of 'Mods and Rockers' and their relationship with the agencies of law enforcement and the media in Britain in the 1960s, and the subsequent work by Hall *et al.* in the 1980s on 'black youth muggings' and McRobbie in the 1990s on 'single-parent families', it is clear that the Loony Left and anti-PC campaigns are textbook examples of the dynamic interplay of forces one witnesses in a moral panic (Cohen 1972; Hall *et al.* 1978; McRobbie 1993).

The key player in a moral panic is the *moral entrepreneur*, the disgruntled individual or group who wishes to curb the behaviour of a social group who are engaged in what is perceived to be either offensive, immoral, or reprehensible behaviour. What is fundamental from the outset is how the reprehensible behaviour is then exaggerated with regard to its true social significance. In this way the culprits can be cast as *folk devils*, and thus can be quickly deemed responsible for a whole host of other reprehensible behaviours (Cohen 1972). The folk devil is then able to detract attention from what might be the real social problem, and act as a scapegoat, both for the purpose of blame and to ensure that the wider social problem is not dealt with in any other way than through curbing the behaviour of that social group (Hall *et al.* 1978). This curbing of behaviour is usually achieved by the folk devil having been demonized in popular media sources, most of which are happy to increase their circulation figures on the back of the public's desire to be informed about a threat to their safety or general sense of decency. Once the public is alerted in this way it triggers the agencies of the law to be seen to be acting in the interests of the public, and to be clamping down on the activities of the folk devil. In the final piece of the dynamic jigsaw, legislators may feel they need to be seen to be doing something about the new menace, and the wheels of the legislative machinery may thus begin to turn.

Much of the dynamic of a moral panic appears to have been present in the Loony Left campaign in the UK and in the anti-PC campaign in the US. Some of this is evident in the speech given by President Bush (senior) at the University of Michigan in 1991, in which much of the language of the preceding anti-PC campaign in the US was invoked:

> What began as a crusade for civility has soured into a cause of conflict and even censorship. Disputants treat sheer force – getting their foes punished or expelled, for instance – as a substitute for the power of ideas.
>
> Throughout history, attempts to micromanage casual conversation have only incited distrust. They have invited people to look for an insult in every word, gesture, action. And in their own Orwellian way, crusades that demand correct behavior crush diversity in the name of diversity.
>
> (Bush 1991 http://bushlibrary.tamu.edu/research/papers/ 1991/91050401.html; accessed 14 May 2007)

Thus, we might read a moral panic in more conspiratorial terms. That is, one might not need to wait for the happy 'coincidence of wants' between the players to manifest itself because a key moral entrepreneur might be able to orchestrate the whole campaign to some considerable extent. In this reading, it might be possible for the final piece of the jigsaw, the legislator, to act as an *instigator* of the moral panic, in order to create the climate of urgency needed to justify the legislation that they themselves have already decided is needed; to act *proactively* in instigating a moral panic, rather than reactively in the face of, largely manufactured, popular concern. Furthermore, to the extent that one could establish some firm links between any of the players who would be needed to take part in a moral panic, it would be possible to argue that the moral panic is actually a political strategy, and not just a happy coincidence between various interested parties (McRobbie 1993).

In conclusion, by utilizing the work of Cohen (1972) on Mods and Rockers, Hall *et al.* (1978) on black youth, and McRobbie (1993) on Conservative Party attacks on single parents, it could be argued that the Loony Left campaign in the UK and the anti-PC campaign in the US, in the same period, are not just excellent examples of moral panics, but they also demonstrate the potential to manipulate public opinion for political advantage. Indeed, in the final analysis, there might be times when it is necessary to invoke a moral panic if one wishes quickly to instigate legislative change, be it welfare reform, going to war, or curbing the excesses of politically motivated progressive thinkers in education. If one combines the evidence from authors like Wilson (1996) and Feldstein (1997) in the US, and Curran *et al.* (2005) in the UK, it could be argued that the anti-PC campaign in the US and the Loony Left campaign in the UK have a similar sense of orchestration by key moral entrepreneurs. If there is a difference between the UK and the US here it is not in the nature of the pieces of the moral panic jigsaw, but in who the moral entrepreneurs were, to what extent they were able to marshal support, and what their political purposes were. In the case of the UK the answer seems to be that popular right-leaning newspapers were the key moral entrepreneur, but this was quickly seized on by politicians who were looking for support to concentrate more power centrally in Whitehall, as opposed to local council chambers. In the US the moral entrepreneur appeared to be a narrow coalition of right-leaning funding organizations, whose aim was not legislative change but a perceived need to invoke a more rigorous defence of the First and Fourteenth Amendments, that is, the need to alert members of Supreme Courts to use these amendments to 'call to heel' the *folk devil* that is the politically correct university, be it Pennsylvania, Stanford, or Michigan.

From 1988 onwards in the UK the notion of Loony Leftism slowly waned as the term political correctness became its substitute. Tabloid newspapers have continued to use the term ever since, usually to signal an unwarranted political intrusion into a perfectly sensible status quo. Indeed, so successful has this association become that the term PC began to be used freely in a headline to indicate 'bad', 'wrong', or 'stupid', and without any need of further explanation. Furthermore, the term seems to have become a shorthand for an ongoing moral panic about unwarranted political intrusion, particularly in education, and one which can be invoked at any convenient point. This has also resulted in an ever growing cast list of the PC folk devils, which in the UK has included both the former Mayor of London (Ken Livingstone), and the former Director General of the BBC (Greg Dyke).

Reports on the state of the PC nation

In order to find explanations rather than accusations of PC we need to go beyond the British tabloids and, in the absence of much serious scholarly writing elsewhere, a key source is the *Times Higher Education Supplement* (*THES*), which ran a series of stories on PC in the period 1990–1995. Taken collectively they might be grouped under four headings: reports on the state of the PC nation (i.e. the US); a tale of two national cultures; academic adventures in British PC; and profiles of American PC protagonists.

Many of the early *THES* articles were simply reports on what was happening in US universities at that time, the majority of which came from one reporter, and the remainder from a selection of academics based mainly in Britain but some in the US (Hodges 1991, 1992, 1993a, 1993b, 1994a, 1994b, 1994c, 1995a, 1995b; Hofkins 1992b, 1992c; Lewis and Altbach 1992; Annette 1994; Patterson 1995). Given the nature of the invective often used by US commentators at the time what is most striking about the *THES* reports is how moderate and balanced they are. The first report was on the existence of various activist groups in the US who were either designated pro- or anti-PC (Hodges 1991). Lewis and Altbach (1992) reported on their survey of full-time academics in American universities, and argued that they seemed to be more concerned about *debates* about PC, rather than the political causes that underpin the debates; that there was general agreement about the desirability of pursuing forms of affirmative action and battling with bias and prejudice in its many forms. They found a general liberal consensus, with little evidence for a tyrannical vanguard, and in general a sense that PC arguments are like any other organizational debates: 'as the manifestation of natural social processes – of good faith and bad faith, of faulty communication, of expectations too high and expectations too low, of over-conformity to norms or under-conformity to norms' (Lewis and Altbach 1992: 17).

In June 1992 the sister publication to the *THES*, the more broadly based *Times Educational Supplement* (*TES*), produced a two-page focus on PC in US colleges and universities, which was followed up six months later by a further symposium of articles in the *THES*. In the latter Hodges again reported 'from America where it all began', this time highlighting the case for affirmative action:

> When pressed, university officials admit that . . . ethnic minority students are often admitted on lower academic scores than others and that their presence in an institution keeps out white or Asian students who are better qualified. But they are convinced that it is preferable to engineer the racial mix in pursuit of social justice, a more dynamic intellectual environment, and a richer undergraduate experience than to do nothing.
>
> (Hodges 1993a: 20)

Echoing what was referred to in Chapter 6 as the compelling case for affirmative action, she leaves open the question as to whether the students with lower scores are offering anything as an alternative, but follows up with the statements from Davis Ray (director of public policy at the Association of Governing Boards of Universities) that: 'many students are in badly run and equipped schools in urban areas and it's a wonder they learn anything. So, if you have a standardized test that everyone takes, of course they're not going to do as well' (Ray in Hodges 1993a: 20). Whether the solution is to admit these students simply on the grounds of social justice and/or as compensation for lack of opportunities, or whether we should be seeking to enhance their initial education such that they could perform better on the standardized tests themselves, is not considered.

The *TES* two-page focus was a report by Hofkins on PC in US colleges and universities, which contained three articles (Hofkins 1992a, 1992b, 1992c). She begins with a discussion on the policing of language, leading on to a discussion of the means by which the so-called literary canon might be expanded. The conclusion is noteworthy for its reference to the fact that whatever one does to produce or discredit a canon there will always be a case for students to make up their own minds about what they take from an educational course, and that a canon's authority will always be questionable due to the lack of 'totally objective criteria for excellence' (Suleiman, in Hofkins 1992a: 12).

The second article begins by focusing on the work of an outspoken opponent of all things PC in the US, Alan Dershowitz, and highlights the subtle ways in which professors in the US are made to conform to the prevailing orthodoxies (Hofkins 1992b). This is mainly achieved, on the one hand, by the desire to be popular – student evaluations being a major form of teacher appraisal – and, on the other, by university administration teams, who have helped create a climate in which students are encouraged to complain if they are offended. This kind of 'victimology', first popularized by Sykes (1992) and then by Hughes (1993) was latterly to become a feature of much of the anti-PC academic literature in the UK (see below), and is summarized cogently by Dershowitz in this article:

> We are miseducating a generation of students to run to Daddy Dean and Mommy President for paternalistic protection when someone offends them. The students want to be treated as adults sexually, and want to be treated as adults in relation to what they eat and drink and where they live, but when it comes to what they hear they want to be infantilized. It's patent hypocrisy.
>
> (Dershowitz, in Hofkins 1992b: 13)

However, the article is balanced by quotes from Ruth Perry, head of Women's Studies at MIT, to the effect that there really isn't anything very sinister about asking people to think about the language they use; and that, echoing a common theme in PC literature in the US, we should be extremely wary of the political funding of educational causes, particularly from those who support right-wing causes (Perry, in Hofkins 1992b: 13).

This theme resurfaces a year later in the *THES* in an article on the newly formed First Amendment Coalition from Harvard, a group opposed to '"ideological conformity", speech codes, double standards in grading and a curriculum bias in many humanities and social science departments which denigrates the Western tradition and American institutions' (Hodges 1994a: 11). The article concludes with Horowitz's defence against the accusation of funding by politically motivated conservative organizations with the fact that the money involved 'was "nothing" compared to the millions spent annually by colleges on minority student associations' (Hodges 1994a: 11). This issue of funding is further echoed in the article by Annette a few months later, when he compares the National Association of Scholars with Teachers for a Democratic Culture, and cites the accusation that the former's power base comes from traditional conservative sources, namely the American Enterprise Institute, the Olin Foundation, and the National Endowment for the Humanities. This is countered by the restatement of 'the conspiracy-of-1960s-radicals-now-in-postions-of-power-theory' as an attack on the latter group (Annette 1994: 16). This article and Patterson's (1995), which came soon after, are noteworthy for being able to articulate many of the subtleties that surrounded PC debates in the US. In particular, Patterson offers concise summaries of many of the more complex themes of PC: the ability of enlightened language to effect positive change; the tension between preserving distinct cultural heritages and the forces of assimilation; and the tension between identity affirmation and detached academic study.

All these articles are in stark contrast to the hyperbole often seen in many US news magazines between 1990 and 1995; and they stand as testimony to the fact that most of the more analytical discussion of PC in British-based media was balanced and informative. What is perhaps more noteworthy however is the extent to which the British-based articles began to reflect on the underlying social and cultural forces at work in the two national contexts and the effects that these might be bringing to matters of PC. Annette's final sentence alludes to this shift when he signals that social inequality is at the heart of serious debate about political correctness, and that this is clearly not just an issue in the US 'but also in Britain where numbers are increasing and universities are facing the challenge of providing a socially meaningful education for a mass public' (Annette 1994: 16).

This theme of 'a tale of two national cultures' is clearly evident in Bygrave's article in *The Guardian* (1991), to which Parker makes reference in his *THES* article (Parker 1992). Bygrave argues that PC makes 'sense against the back-ground of the Reagan/Bush [senior] era' (Bygrave 1991: 15). Parker reiterates by quoting Bygrave: 'PC is the politics of despair, or even irrelevance. Changing the curriculum is what you do when there is no hope of changing the government' (Bygrave 1991: 15). This alludes to the presence of a more radical Marxist tradition in British academe, and one which we have seen before, somewhat ironically, in the work of the American sociologists Bowles and Gintis (1976):

> PC is Marxism without the economics, a revolution made with words instead of weapons. It's a new attempt to change society by changing the way people talk and think; yet its concern with the political power of language harks back to the Middle Ages. Its opponents likewise attack PC in medieval terms, calling it 'theological' and 'a new witch hunt'.
>
> (Bygrave 1991: 14)

And, by reference to the Loony Left campaign discussed earlier, the article goes on to mock the American substitution of 'language games' for real political action: 'It sounds as if the loony left are at it again only, being Americans, they're twice as loony. Roll over Beethoven and tell Plato and Shakespeare the news – you were nothing but a bunch of racist fascist oppressors' (Bygrave 1991: 14).

The article is prefaced by a menacing cartoon by Colin Williams of an Orwellian, storm-trooping character emblazoned with 'PC', echoing the tyrannical theme of much of the conservative writings in the US at the time, and has an appendix which mocks the emerging PC glossary. For example: 'ABLEISM – oppression of the differently abled by the temporarily abled.' No dwarf jokes, either. 'GYNOPHOBIC – anti-womyn.' 'PHALLOCENTRIC – anti-womyn with knobs on' (Bygrave 1991: 15).

However, Parker concludes his article by indicating that Britain does need to take seriously the notion of PC, because the population of post-16 education is changing, to include 'large numbers of people from the ranks of communities whose antecedent experiences, as well as expectations, are very different from those of the generations of the recent past' (Parker 1992: 18). It is not clear why this fact alone should be so important, for it could easily be countered that if all students had the necessary study skills and the universities and colleges reiterated the importance of the 'marketplace of ideas' and the nature of academic debate, then any problems of a changed population could be ameliorated in these ways. However, his second point is much more fundamental and relates to the nature of the knowledge that students are likely to be engaged with: 'For educational institutions, offensive as it may sound at first, empowerment for not-Europe (as well as for the oppressed within the ranks of Europe) may well have to begin with a serious look at the vested interest we have in emphasizing the works of Dead, White, Males' (Parker 1992: 18).

This theme, common in PC literature in the US whereby values inherent within the 'American way of life' are defended or denigrated, is here played out with a new 'We' and 'Other'. And the theme is extended by MacGregor a year later to include African studies, and the ways in which PC has stifled debate (MacGregor 1993: 22). She cites Davidson's book (1992) as an example of this form of PC which 'attributes things that have gone wrong in African politics since independence . . . to European influence' (MacGregor 1993: 22), thereby effectively ignoring other contributory factors. In order to make the point potent, she quotes Richard Jeffries of the School of Oriental and African Studies, University of London:

> It would be unthinkable for almost any scholar working on African studies to, say, blame poor economic performance on laziness or poor management capability, and yet anyone living and working in Africa knows that these are basic problems. . . . Though the reasons for political correctness can be understandable – European academics feel guilty about the colonial exploitation of Africa and the slave trade, and African academics feel the need to fight a continuous battle against racism – it can

have a profound effect on university research and teaching, as well as on African countries.

(MacGregor 1993: 22)

MacGregor concludes her article by reiterating the point made earlier by Bygrave (1991) and Parker (1992) and subsequently by Annette (1994) that British academic life has been able to sustain an influence on social affairs which had been eroded in the US. This is ironic given the role that American universities traditionally have played in the general socialization of the population, and particularly when compared with the somewhat detached tradition which has prevailed in Britain. Quoting Stuart Hall (from the Open University) she concludes:

> Political correctness has also had less impact in Britain than in the United States where, says Professor Hall, it to some extent reflects the larger scale of universities, which are far more politically active than the UK's quiet campuses. 'There is frustration among Americans at not being able to act politically elsewhere. University politics replaces politics on the larger scale'.

(MacGregor 1993: 22)

Thus, British academics, it is claimed, have more confidence about their ability to directly influence policy makers, without any need to resort to indirect mediation through more obtuse cultural and intellectual debate, particularly through the reframing of the dictionary of everyday life.

From the mid-1990s to the present the steady stream of articles reporting on the 'State of the PC Nation' began to dry up, to be replaced by those from various British-based academics reporting on their own perspectives on PC debates. The first of these was Fairbairn, who argued that behind much of what is referred to as PC there is a desire to silence the unfashionable. In his case his anti-abortion stance is perceived as being un-PC, implying that he would be wise to keep these particular views to himself. He argues that not only should this have no place in higher education, it is also, generally speaking, unpalatable and unprincipled, resulting 'in an increasing number of people spend[ing] their lives saying one thing, believing another and doing something quite different altogether' (Fairbairn 1995).

Thomson's article is a very balanced piece on politically correct language, arguing that society has changed for the better by making 'people more aware of their responsibilities in using language' (Thomson 1999). Using Cameron's work (1995) by way of support, both Fairbairn and Thomson suggest that much of the downside to matters PC are caused by its unintended consequences, for example in how the term Ms came to represent a third term rather than replacing the old Mrs and Miss, and thus in the process fell into some disrepute. Thomson suggests that British universities may not have suffered in the ways that American ones have from cases of PC due to the fact that widening participation amongst non-traditional learners had not significantly tipped the balance of the student population in ways that forced many American universities to introduce speech codes. The article is followed by examples from *The NATFHE [National Association of Teachers in Further and Higher Education] Guide to Politically Correct Language*, which appears to have the effect of enabling its readers to turn language debates from the serious to the absurd and vice versa depending on what one brings to one's reading. For example the guide offers advice about sensitivity in the use of words associated with 'disability', and then proceeds to contrast phrases like 'old fogey' with 'more experienced', without recognizing either the subtleties or the jokes implicit in the use of both terms. The effect, intended or otherwise, seems to be to undermine much of the associated article's credibility.

The final article is also explicitly related to The National Association of Teachers in Further and Higher Education, this time on its pronouncement 'that academics should not have to teach BNP [British National Party] members' (Baker 2003). This raises once again, but in a British context, the question of what exactly is the purpose of a university education. If it is purely academic, then surely there is a case for NATFHE to answer here. However, if universities actively espouse other values, such as the need to forge 'social cohesion', then their pronouncement is not without considerable merit. Indeed, if their aim was to seek to protect their members from threats and intimidation from BNP members on campus, then once again there would appear to be a clear case, not just for the pronouncement, but also for the exclusion of BNP members from the campus altogether. That said, it could be argued that universities already have the powers to exclude any student who engages in intimidating behaviour, and in this respect the pronouncement could be argued to be inflammatory, for it implies either that academic debate cannot be separated from deeply held views or that members of the BNP are problematic on a university campus simply by their very presence and before they have behaved in any particular way. The article also raises the question of whether the best way to address racism is to encourage debate about it, no matter how disturbing, for fear of driving it underground or simply elsewhere:

> But surely there's an irony in the fact that while many attribute the growth of the BNP to a lack of education among their supporters, Natfhe is set on denying an education to those who possibly need it the most. 'We're very aware of this dilemma,' Gledhill admits. 'How can we expect enlightenment unless we're prepared to tackle this issue? In an ideal world, we should deal with it like that. But unfortunately in this situation, we're not dealing with people who are just speaking their mind, we're dealing with people who are forcing their agenda on the rest of the country in an extremely organised and hateful manner.'
>
> (Baker 2003: 21)

The remainder of the articles in the *THES* are profiles of leading intellectual figures who have some prominence because of their associations with PC debates in the US, including two key protagonists from the intellectual right and left in the US: Lynne Cheney and Stanley Fish. The first article on Cheney, captures succinctly the essence of her arguments concerning 'truth', the politicization of the curriculum, and the need to reinstate the classics of Western civilization in the university curriculum:

> 'The whole question of whether there is such a thing as truth is behind political correctness', she says. Many academics, particularly in the English and history departments, and in the 'soft' social sciences, regard truth as a cultural construct, she argues. It empowers some and oppresses others. Because professors see the truth as relative, they feel perfectly justified in using the classroom to advance their political views.
>
> (Hodges 1994b)

By contrast, the article on Fish contains his reflections on his academic career, as he contemplates removing himself from the intellectual limelight: 'The reason that academics want and need their complaints is that it is important to them to feel oppressed, for in the psychic economy of the academy, oppression is the sign of virtue' (Fish, in MacFarquhar 2001). The article confirms his status as 'the grand wizard of political correctness – the man who hired Marxists and supported campus speech codes – and was held up as an example of everything that had gone terribly wrong with higher education' (MacFarquhar 2001).

There are also profiles of Judith Butler and Condoleezza Rice, the latter being of particular interest due to her subsequent appointment as Secretary of State in the Bush Administration of 2004–2008. In Rice's previous role as provost of Stanford University she had first-hand experience of many of the controversies at the university which related to political correctness, and supported the principle of affirmative action: 'Although she is against quotas, Rice is in favour of affirmative action, that is, voluntary action to broaden the pool of people you look at to find people who are first-rate' (Hodges 1995b). She also confirms that on matters of PC the issues are more complicated than some would have us believe, as if to confirm that much of what one hears and reads about university campuses is often simplified in order to promote particular ideological positions.

The article on Butler summarizes her intellectual achievements to date and emphasizes not just her articulation of gender as 'performative' rather than 'essential' but also her embracing of the 'linguistic turn' in the humanities, and the ability of oppressed groups to 'restage' harmful speech:

> The way to prevent people being victimised by insults and the violence of pornography according to McKinnon and Dworkin is to ban pornography and curb unlicensed, injurious speech. But according to Butler, this

only represses the problem without confronting it. McKinnon has under-estimated 'the power people have to change language and to be changed by language'. So how would Butler deal with violent and degrading pornography? 'I'd like pornography as a genre redefined. I'm not even sure I would want to call it pornography. I think there needs to be a shame-free exploration of sexuality in art.'

(Wallace 1998: 17)

At a time when PC debates were at their most feverish and ferocious in the US, by contrast, most of these articles from the *THES* (and some from *The Guardian* and the *TES*) were well balanced. The most marked contrast seems to be that British academics appear to have more confidence in their ability to directly affect national political debate, and their more Marxist concern that PC debates are something of a distraction from 'real' political action. Indeed, the very fact that so many of the stories about PC were rooted in what was happening in the US is perhaps evidence that British academics in general appears to have been somewhat indifferent to the whole question of PC.

The British right and PC

With the amount of space given over to debates concerning PC in conservative news magazines in the US it is perhaps surprising that very little of this can be found in their British equivalents. Of course this could in part be explained by the fact that much of the ridiculing of PC in Britain has been left to the tabloid newspapers. One of the key conservative news magazines, *The Spectator*, has run a few articles on PC, one of which mocked the PC credentials of the Scottish Parliament (Cochrane 2001), and this was preceded a year earlier by a witty account of right-wing PC by Parris (2000). A damning article was written much earlier by Johnson, who summarized for British readers what had been happening in American universities in the early 1990s (Johnson 1993).

Johnson pulled no punches in producing a British attack on PC every bit as vitriolic as many conservative American commentaries of that time. Singling out Sheldon Hackney (see Chapter 4), and described in the US at the time as 'the pope of political correctness', Johnson adds his own brand of vitriol:

Hackney is a prime example of the high-placed liberal appeasers and stringalongs who are making it possible for Political Correctness to bulldoze the American education system into rubble. He is president of the University of Pennsylvania, the once great institution founded by Benjamin Franklin, now a hell-hole of PC and racial hatred.

(Johnson 1993: 22)

Furthermore, echoing again much of the commentary seen in the US at the time, Johnson goes on to offer his own general assessment and solution:

The object at the University of Pennsylvania seems to be to create an atmosphere of terror in which whites will keep a low profile and cringe, while the black militants rule the roost. . . . Some famous Ivy league places like Princeton, Yale and Harvard have been badly bruised by PC and weak leadership, but none of them is indispensable and plenty of them are only too eager to appropriate their reputations by displaying first-class objective scholarship, tolerance and freedom of thought.

(Johnson 1993: 22)

By distinct contrast Parris's article highlighted the extent to which language and culture are essential to all political and social groups, and serve to ensure that their members can be easily recognized, and distinguished from others. In a vein of writing on PC which seems to be singularly absent from the right in the US, Parris captures the subtle ways in which language and manner cajole social group members of both the left and the right to adopt obvious badges of approval. In the form of a dictionary for the British right Parris advises on what one should and should not be seen to be thinking and saying (i.e. what is 'politically sound', or PS). For example:

B is for Blood Sports. Don't. The word is deeply unPS. Say 'country pursuits' or 'field sports'. An engulfing concern for the 'rural way of life' and 'rural employment' is PS. Concern for the coalminers' traditional way of life is unPS.

Q is for Queer. When the word is used to describe homosexuals it is not PS to complain (as PS speakers do in the case of 'gay') that English has been robbed of a perfectly useful little word. The Sound do not want this word 'back'; we 'homosexualists' (PS-word) can have it for ourselves. Incidentally, 'sexuality' is non-PS, as is 'gender' and 'ethnicity', the correct expressions (in reverse order) being 'race', 'sex' and 'which team is he playing for?'

(Parris 2000: 12–13)

However, given the way the tabloid press in the UK (which is predominantly right-leaning in its politics) has been able to commandeer the term PC, it is perhaps not surprising that many commentators on the right have not felt the need to explore or exploit the PC landscape. Preferring instead to give the occasional endorsement of the 'tabloid take', the term appears to be used by the right as an unproblematic reference to the unacceptability of a raft of left-wing initiatives and ideas. In an early and now perhaps infamous reference, Margaret Thatcher, in the 1987 Conservative Party annual conference, scathingly denounced 'anti-racist maths' by implying that the instigators of such a notion had somehow taken leave of their senses, and the term PC seems to have become a shorthand way of implying much the same sort of sentiment about a whole host of left-wing ideas ever since. Indeed, the oft-used phrase 'political correctness gone mad' clearly implies that one is not in one's right mind.

One clear exception to this is the British based 'Campaign Against Political Correctness' (CAPC) (http://www.capc.co.uk/; accessed 14 May 2007). Its website has brought together a wide range of anti-PC thought, mostly British-based, and it has elicited support both through a national petition as well as through sympathetic MPs. Although the group appears to be clearly connected with the British right, what is perhaps most interesting about the campaign and its concerns is that many of it views could be shared by some on the political left in Britain, including (if the phrase 'pride in country' is removed) the following:

Political correctness encourages offence to be taken where none is intended, encourages the re-writing and re-thinking of history along with the abandonment of pride in country, is a serious threat to free speech and, despite being portrayed to be in the name of tolerance, is completely intolerant of anyone who does not act in a politically correct fashion.

(http://www.capc.co.uk/faqs.htm; accessed 14 May 2007)

New times for the British cultural left

Given that the volume of discussion about political correctness in UK scholarly media is low in comparison with the US, and the evidence that British academics tend to view PC as something of a political sideshow, it would be easy to conclude that PC is a peculiarly American phenomenon. However, as we have already seen, there is much in the notions Loony Leftism and moral panics to indicate that there has been a cross-cultural fertilization of ideas. Furthermore, although *the term* is not invoked very often, many of the debates particularly on the cultural left do have a distinctly PC flavour. Indeed, there is no doubt that the cultural left in Britain have been divided for some time about how they should articulate what is at the core of their political struggle. Prompted by several significant political events in the 1980s, most notably the defeat of the miners' strike in 1984, and the collapse of the Berlin Wall in 1989, it became increasingly clear to many on the left that a politics based on the collective ownership of the means of production had little credibility anymore. Indeed, the Labour Party finally removed the 'collective ownership' (clause four) component from its constitution in 1995. And, just as we saw the cultural left in the US finding refuge in the humanities departments of American universities, where some at least embraced new forms of literary criticism as their political weapon of choice, we saw this mirrored in Britain, where intellectual radicals began to embrace new forms of identity politics as the locus for political struggle. This was most clearly evident in the burgeoning study of sexuality, where authors like Weeks (1985), Butler (1990), and Giddens (1992) began seeing the body as a subversive home for political struggle.

Despite the claim that an 'Urban Left' in Britain 'were attempting to extend Labour's core base of the organised, white working class by adding to it, not reducing it' (Curran *et al.* 2005: 19), the broader context of intellectual debate on the left seems to indicate that the political events of the 1980s helped cement the view that the left would have enormous difficulty maintaining a belief in the ability of class-based mass social movements to bring about significant social change. With hindsight both beliefs were probably true. Although the left may have had little influence on *central* government politics at that time, in towns and cities like Liverpool, Sheffield, and London (where they had a significant hold on *local* politics) it is clear that local councils did attempt to significantly sway the distribution of resources away from the rich towards the poor. At the same time, many newer intellectual debates about the rights of individuals and groups to pursue particular, non-conventional, lifestyles were also finding influence on the more traditional political landscape. This was, of course, the crack that the British tabloid press so mercilessly sought to widen throughout the Loony Left campaign.

Much of the intellectual energy invested in discussing the need to capture the essence of these leftist shifts was concentrated in a few left-wing news magazines and academic journals, most notably *Marxism Today* and the *New Left Review*, which, in the early 1990s, contained numerous contributions from figures on the cultural left in Britain, including Hall, Hobsbawm, Jacques, and Murray, and their articles were peppered with their use of a new 'post-industrial', 'post-fordist', and 'late-modern' language and concepts in place of more traditional Marxist notions. For example a defining article was produced by Murray entitled 'The State After Henry' (Murray 1991). Three years earlier *Marxism Today* had christened this shift New Times, which was summarized by one of its architects as: 'the passage from a homogeneous, mass-produced society to something more flexible, differentiated and segmented' (Jacques 1991: 29). Throughout these debates the term PC was conspicuously absent; nonetheless it could be argued that the groundwork was being laid for a political agenda which was reformist rather than revolutionary, where personal identity politics was more to the fore than the traditional class-based social movements, and where the centre of left-wing debate was rapidly taking place in the field of consumption and the cultural, rather than in the field of production and the economic. In this respect the intellectual left in Britain was busy, perhaps unwittingly, creating the space where the issues most commonly associated with PC could thrive. Authors such as Hobsbawm were clearly aware of this, and without reference to the actual term he sought to critique its impoverished politics:

Since the 1970s there has been a tendency – an increasing tendency – to see the Left as essentially a coalition of minority groups and interests: of race, gender, sexual, and other cultural preferences and lifestyles, even of economic minorities such as the old getting-your-hands-dirty, industrial working class have now become. This is understandable enough, but it is dangerous, not least because winning majorities is not the same as adding up minorities.

(Hobsbawm 1996: 44)

In an attempt at synthesis, Butler (1998) sought to reinvigorate the old Marxist debate about the importance of the economic base of society taking precedence over the 'merely cultural' by arguing that the relationship between the two is always more dialectical, revolving around a complex interplay of social forces, rather than the simple determinism that Marx himself once famously dismissed. She warns of the unacceptable consequences for intellectual debate on the left of having to choose between forms of crude economic determinism and forms of poststructural cultural theory, arguing instead that what might appear as 'merely cultural' is usually intimately connected with the material facts of the reproduction of certain social relations and a mode of production:

> To the extent that naturalized sexes function to secure the heterosexual dyad as the holy structure of sexuality, they continue to underwrite kinship, legal and economic entitlement, and those practices that delimit what will be a socially recognizable person.
>
> (Butler 1998: 44)

The war of the British words

In what turned out to be a rare British book on political correctness, the Dunant (1994) volume of articles captured much of the essence of these New Times, but with explicit reference to PC. Although many of the articles repeat arguments that were prevalent in the US at the time, a number of them help significantly in identifying a distinctly British take on PC. Furthermore, they articulate well just how much PC represented a crisis for the left in British politics, and also how much this was very much of the left's own making:

> With its emphasis on the rights and demands of minorities, it is often cited as one of the guilty parties in the growth of what has become known as victim culture. The great fear about victim culture is the effect it will have: that the cacophony of voices demanding attention will, far from achieving a richer cultural mix, only succeed in breaking apart any notion of a cultural whole.
>
> (Dunant 1994: xii)

The use of the phrase 'cultural whole' is illuminating. For, as if to accept that one of the main cultural consequences of the fall of the Berlin Wall was to acknowledge that one can no longer speak about 'state socialism' or the 'working class' as convincing political concepts, the left in Britain seemed content to start using a range of euphemisms which only hinted at the former confidence that once existed for mass, class-based, politics.

In the two articles that are the most analytical both authors allude to the fact that there appeared to be an unhappy coincidence of social forces at work in Britain in the early 1990s. First, the break-up of state socialist societies which gave renewed confidence to those on the right who were proclaiming 'the end of history' (Fukuyama 1992). Second, the emergence of a clearer sense of post-industrial conditions of work, fuelled by a continuing enthusiasm for Friedmanite free-market economics (Friedman and Friedman 1980). Third, what might be referred to as a triumph of the humanities over the social sciences in academia, and the general acceptance of a poststructural epistemology instead of a more traditional realist representational form. And, of course, this itself had been fuelled by left-wing intellectuals (many of whom had been Marxists) who were promulgating the view that grand narratives (such as Marxism itself) were at best historicist and at worst incredulous (Lyotard 1994, Baudrillard 1994).

In this regard one of the key distinguishing features of PC debates in the US and the UK was the extent to which the cultural left in the US was more entrenched in their acceptance of the Enlightenment notions of truth and the ability of words to reflect and represent reality in contrast to the cultural left in the UK, where many more were willing to embrace the so-called 'linguistic turn' (Hall, in Dunant 1994). Concomitant with this was the acceptance of the inability of words to describe in value-neutral ways the reality of the social world, and in recognizing the reframing ability of language one was also able to recognize the ability of language to effect real and significant social change. In what is probably the most significant and epistemologically grounded of the articles Cameron alludes to this throughout her article:

> The kind of verbal hygiene characterised as 'PC' rejects the simple Orwellian opposition between neutral terms and loaded ones, drawing attention to the fact that all words come with values attached, and moreover that these are variable depending on who is speaking, in what context and within what structure of power.
>
> (Cameron, in Dunant 1994: 28)

Thus, we find ourselves returning to a tradition in sociological thought of demonstrating how words and labels are about to invoke 'self-fulfilling prophecies'; how they reflect the conventional understandings of those who invoke them; how they can act, perhaps unwittingly, to reflect traditional power structures; and, in general, how language is able to frame reality as much as reflect it. It is surely here that we reach the heart of this PC matter: that those who are most disparaging of PC matters are usually those most disparaging of infusing words with these powers, and those most supportive of PC matters are those most persuaded by the ability of language to reframe the nature of reality. This is probably because there appears to be much more scepticism towards poststructural, and, generally, postmodern, forms of thinking amongst liberal intellectuals in the US compared to their UK counterparts.

Also significant about Cameron's article is the way in which she confirms some of what had been previously argued in the US, that it is extremely difficult to decide whether one is pro- or anti-PC because the term has a 'straw man' status. Clearly, if one subscribes to the notion of 'the linguistic turn' one would want to distance oneself from a speech code that sought to ban words, and in this respect one would find oneself being anti-PC. However, in order to distance oneself from those who are seeking 'value-neutral' language it might be sensible to allow oneself to be referred to as pro-PC in this context. Somewhat paradoxically, however, it might also be wise to distance oneself from the term PC altogether for fear that its loaded, derogatory overtones would cast one's arguments as untenable. Cameron succinctly puts the case:

> Like the classic example sentence illustrating presupposition in semantics textbooks, 'The King of France is bald', 'are you politically correct?' depends on a false and contested proposition (that there is a King of France, or that 'political correctness' refers to a real phenomenon with such-and-such characteristics.
>
> (Cameron, in Dunant 1994: 16)

The articles by Alibhai-Brown, Grant, and Syal when taken together strike a similar chord. The first discusses the ways in which multicultural education has made great strides in opening up Western literature to ideas from elsewhere, the second looks at the controversies surrounding date-rape, and the third considers the author's own background in the Arts. With the benefit of hindsight there appears to be, in all three articles, a social history lesson to be learnt about the battles against racism and sexism in the second half of the twentieth century in the UK. The argument is relatively straightforward. In the face of numerous forms of discrimination in post-war Britain we should not be surprised that many of the ways to confront them might appear somewhat strident and draconian, and somewhat exclusive in the way they promoted social change. Nor that the unfortunate consequence of this was that everything female or black became 'good', and everything 'white, male, and middle class' became 'bad'. Again, with the benefit of hindsight this can be seen much more as a necessary evil and a phase through which liberatory politics must pass. It is only when a minority group has 'found its feet' that debate can then become subtle and nuanced, and begin to reflect the fact that all cultures, in reality, have inconsistent and contradictory elements. In this way it might be argued to be a sign of maturity when one can debate these issues free from the accusation that one must be racist, homophobic, misogynistic (etc.) if one dares to question the orthodoxy.

Mind your multicultural language

Perhaps reflecting the fact that the cultural left in Britain engaged more with forms of French-inspired postmodern thinking, the few academic articles which have explicitly discussed political correctness have largely been concerned with the position of language and its relationship with political action. For example

Corbett looked at the way the language of 'disability' has changed over the years (Corbett 1996), but more importantly she does so in the much wider context of the 'struggle to match words with actions' and the PC difficulties that can result (Corbett 1994). People naturally feel anxious when they are not sure whether they are using the 'correct' words, but more importantly she argues that the language we use is more likely to *reflect* changing attitudes rather than vice versa, and that changes in language are not usually intended to change behaviour. The specific example she uses is the way in which the phrase 'special educational need' has slowly fallen out of favour, not because a new word or phrase has become a more politically correct euphemism, but because it has been increasingly accepted that a more integrated and inclusive approach to educational provision has replaced earlier forms of (at the time enlightened) segregated thinking. And thus, new terms are used to reflect, not bring about, these changing attitudes.

This does not mean that there won't be those who might seek some cultural capital out of policing miscreants who are still using the older language, and in such cases it could be argued that it is not so much the politically incorrect language of the miscreant which is the problem but the politically correct attitude of the so-called enlightened user of language or vanguard cadre who is often invoked in anti-PC literature in the US. Indeed, Corbett alludes precisely to this mentality when she reports on the discomfort she experienced at a conference where a speaker appeared to be castigating those in the audience who were still using the phrase 'learning difficulties' in the mid-1990s, when, obviously, the correct term was 'learning disabilities'. And this raises the question whether it is advisable, analytically, to hang on to a language–action dichotomy. In a variation of the traditional mind–body dichotomy, the way to avoid the crude and obvious charges of PC would appear to be to seek a more dialectical relationship between the two, thus leaving the charge of PC for situations in which the dialectical unity appears to have become a dichotomy.

Ecclestone questioned whether the language about competency-based education and training in post-16 education was fast becoming mantric in its effect (Ecclestone 1995). That is, that its talk of empowerment was ironically becoming a means by which debate and discussion were being closed down, and that increasingly it is state quangos who define what practitioners will teach and assess and what learners will learn (Ecclestone 1995). The argument is also *double* double-edged, because some of the more andragogic language adopted by the profession itself seems to present itself in the form of a politically correct orthodoxy, and that students are not necessarily having their horizons widened in consequence. These themes will be explored in more detail in the next two chapters.

A thorough 'discourse-analytical' perspective was brought to the question of political correctness in the PC dedicated edition of the journal *Discourse and Society*. In that edition Fairclough's article charts the relationship between 'representations, values and identities', or, in broad terms, the nature of the relationship between culture, language and social change. In refusing to adopt a dichotomous position between language and action he articulates the subtle and reflexive ways in which culture, language, and social change interact with each other: 'We need a balanced view of the importance of language in social change and politics, which avoids a linguistic vanguardism as dismissing questions about language as trivial, and an incorporation of a politics of language within political strategies and tactics' (Fairclough 2003: 27–28). Here the real power of language lies in its ability to capture the essence of a new and emerging set of social conventions, but we should be careful to distinguish between the 'enactment' and 'inculcation' of language:

> there is a stage short of inculcation at which people may acquiesce to new discourses without accepting them – they may mouth them rhetorically, for strategic and instrumental purposes, as happens for instance, with market discourse in public services, such as education.
>
> (Fairclough 2003: 28)

The articles by Johnson *et al.* (2003) and Mills (2003) continue the theme of 'linguistic reflexivity' in order to understand the nature of contemporary (or late modern as they refer to it) discourse analysis. In the article by Mills her main research focus is an exploration of issues raised for women in their choice of surname and title. However, in the accompanying theoretical discussion she couches her argument within a much wider framework of the ways in which language requires complex sets of negotiations. Utilizing Bourdieu's notion of 'habitus' (Bourdieu 1999), she explores the ways in which particular types of social practices do not simply act as constraints, but as places in which negotiations will take place about what an individual believes is appropriate behaviour for her, for example as to whether to take a particular surname in marriage. As Mills clearly points out, to take on the title 'Ms' or 'Mrs' and, moreover, to move between the two is often a complex process involving negotiation with many people and institutions. It simply is not a matter of being 'feminist' or 'traditional', or pro-PC or anti-PC, because what these terms mean and how one relates to them is ongoing and negotiated.

As we have already seen, one of the implications of a more thoroughgoing acceptance of the implications of the 'linguistic turn' is that a simple representational model of language and reality becomes increasingly problematic. For example it might have been considered perfectly reasonable for a university or college code in 1985 to state that words and phrases such as 'chairman', 'mankind', 'black sheep', 'dyke', 'queer', 'nigger', and so on, are unacceptable, and although the same might still be said twenty years later, it probably would not be said in quite such a categorical way, thereby reflecting the more nuanced way in which the use of any of these terms might now be negotiated. Cut loose from representational moorings, it is inevitable that language games will become not just more prevalent, but also more subtle and multilayered. And, of course, it is precisely in this context that one is prone not to get the joke, or even to understand the joke, or whether there is a joke.

Finally, Johnson *et al.* (2003) conducted a key word analysis of the use of the term 'political correctness' and directly allied phrases in the British newspapers *The Times, The Independent,* and *The Guardian* (each taken to broadly represent the political spectrum in Britain, from right to left respectively). In drawing out the subtle differences between the ways in which the three newspapers used the term in three periods in the 1990s, what is perhaps far more striking from the newspaper quotations they use is the way that the term seems to imply that the reader already understands what it means, for in almost all cases it appears as a derogatory slur, either against an individual or a political position. In discourse terms, one might say that the phrase 'political correctness' is a linguistic gift which just keeps giving – it is able endlessly to signify without ever needing to specify what exactly is being signified.

The diminished self in post-16 education

Just as we saw in the US, there have been some attempts by the left in the UK to defend a more traditional conception of political action. Particularly in the work of Gitlin and Scatamburlo we saw how the politics of PC had impoverished the left's most vital and vibrant claim to unite those disadvantaged by capitalism in a 'common dream' of a more enlightened future (Gitlin 1995; Scatamburlo 1998). In the UK echoes of these sentiments can be seen in the work of Furedi and Hayes, who ridicule PC for its empty political gesturing, and those who have embraced a postmodern sensibility, which grants a power to words and their meanings that they do not or should not have (Furedi 1997; Hayes, in Lea *et al.* 2003). That said, what is more interesting about both British authors is that instead of making a direct appeal to more traditional Marxist notions about common political struggles, they invoke much of the same conceptual language of conservative authors such as Sykes (1992) and Hughes (1993) in the US, and suggest that the real problem with PC is not how it has helped dismantle 'common dreams', but how it has helped to see 'people as victims of their circumstances rather than as authors of their lives' (Furedi 1997: 147). In this context it is perhaps hardly surprising that the UK-based Institute for Ideas, with which Furedi is often associated, has been accused of being a breeding ground for ex-Marxists, who now want to embrace a new brand of rather reactionary, and right-wing politics (Bunting 2005).

Furedi refers to PC as 'the new etiquette', and one which clearly has a strong moralizing agenda. Although it is the political right in the UK that usually speaks of the 'nanny state' it is clear that Furedi has the same target in mind, and in this respect 'PC provides a new language with which to express traditional moral themes concerning the regulation of human conduct' (Furedi 1997: 157).

Indeed it could be argued to be worse than in the past for 'the new etiquette' is far more intrusive than traditional Victorian moralizing, for it is much more clearly backed by state sanctions on behaviour, rather than being based on the more traditional forms of moral suasion. These developments, Furedi argues, are pernicious in the way they mystify their true intent. Masked in a language of protecting the powerless, in effect they keep people in a powerless state, albeit one in which they are encouraged to feel protected: 'The outcome of these developments is a world view which equates the good life with self-limitation and risk aversion' (Furedi 1997: 147). This containing, moderating, and controlling of people's behaviour is thus legitimated as a form of 'risk aversion', in the name of protecting people from an ever growing set of menaces, embracing everything from forms of pollution and disease down to what sometimes appears to be the sheer presence of other human beings. There is a direct parallel here with J. S. Mill's discussion of human behaviour in his essay *On Liberty* (1869), where he makes it clear that the state should have no right to seek to protect individuals from themselves.

An interesting dimension to Furedi's work is the extent to which he is promoting the view that PC's ability to disempower in the name of empower-ment is not an unintended consequence of a set of enlightened strategies either to combat the abuse of power or to seek to redistribute power, but is part of a *concerted effort* to seek to direct and contain an increasing array of human behaviours. Herein, of course, lies the connection with an agenda more traditionally associated with the right, that if people are left to their own devices they will develop forms of self-responsibility which will be far more liberatory than any notion of the state as the people's protector. Furedi subsequently expanded these ideas to include the way in which a more broadly based therapeutic culture has now enveloped people in the UK; a culture in which people have become increasingly dependent on an army of professionals, and in which 'Intuition and insight gained from personal experience is continually compromised by professional knowledge' (Furedi 2004b: 101).

This leads naturally to the question whether post-16 education has, for better or worse, taken a 'therapeutic turn', that is, has it become more interested in seeing students as people in need of nurturing, as opposed to seeing them as learners interested in knowledge? Indeed, has knowledge increasingly come to be viewed in therapeutic terms, defined more in terms of what nurtures self-esteem and self-worth? Clearly this is a loud echo of the work of Sykes (1992) in the US, and subsequently of Sowell (1993) and Schlesinger (1998), and in the UK is most clearly articulated in the work of Hayes (see Lea *et al.* 2003), and subsequently by Ecclestone *et al.* (2005). Stimulated by the broader thesis of Nolan (1998), Hayes considers the ways in which a 'therapeutic state' has been made manifest in post-16 education; and utilizing the ideas of both Bloom (1987) and Sykes (1992), Hayes considers the ways in which the 'disinterested pursuit of truth' has been hijacked by a so-called humanism which is more concerned with forms of personal self-discovery. The general thesis is that students are increasingly viewed as 'vulnerable' and in need of therapeutic forms of pedagogical intervention. These ideas will be considered in Chapter 10. The significant point at this juncture is that although such ideas have been associated with conservatives in the US (see Chapter 2) these authors write within a much more avowedly left-wing position. This is well articulated by Hayes in the following:

> The horizons managers and professionals set for us and our students are lowered because the social antagonisms that drove society forwards and produced big ideas such as 'socialism' are absent. The consequence is a turn towards the personal and subjective, and if we are not aware of the political context of this change, the belief that all we can do is improve inter-subjective communication quite naturally follows.
>
> (Hayes, in Lea *et al.* 2003: 99)

This neatly crystallizes the crisis for the left which was discussed above. For Hayes, in a period where mass social movements have lost much of their material foundation, and, in consequence, their appeal, and even credibility, we have retreated into a type of crass reformism, centred around getting 'people to feel better about things' (Hayes, in Lea *et al.* 2003: 99). In Marxist terms we might say that we have returned to a rather primitive form of Young Hegelianism, where we have managed to put Hegel back on his head. In strict educational terms by turning away from a content curriculum model and towards a process model we have not just encouraged the view that education is, or should be, seen as a form of self-development, but increasingly in an impoverished form.

The roots of PC revisited

Just as several American authors have sought to trace the roots of PC, both the use of the term itself (Perry 1992) and its deeper meaning (Schwartz 2003), this is mirrored in the UK in the work of Ellis (2004). In one of the most original lines of argument in PC debate Ellis takes us beyond both the new right interpretation of PC from the late 1980s in the US and the Western new left interpretation of the late 1960s and early 1970s, and leads us back to its Soviet interpretation in the 1920s, as used to castigate those who held an incorrect understanding of the party line (see the second half of Chapter 1). Through this argument Ellis is able to contend that the defence of left-leaning intellectuals that PC is a recent phenomenon, and a myth manufactured by the right, is itself a myth. For there is much evidence that the term was used, or at least implied, in left-wing thought throughout most of the twentieth century (Ellis 2002, 2004). Furthermore, and by way of confirming many of the conclusions (if not the analysis itself) of the new right interpretation, it *always* had a tyrannical heart running roughshod over any dissent to the *correct* interpretations of history events. Also, by implication, if it is true that the term PC took on a mocking, ironic interpretation in Western left-wing circles in the late 1960s and early 1970s, this is clearly a mocking *precisely* of its more literal and original interpretation. To which it might be added, at the same time that its ironic sense was being cemented in the West, this could not be said in the East, where in the Chinese Cultural Revolution of the late 1960s it still very much retained its original literal sense, along with its associated dire consequences for dissidents. Ellis, however, is clear that a connection can be made:

> Western versions lack concentration camps for re-education and reform through labour, yet they indisputably involve wholly unacceptable levels of censorship and intellectual violence to those who dissent from multi-cultural orthodoxy. Race awareness courses in American universities are just one example.
>
> (Ellis 2004: 38)

However, if there is a PC culprit in this analysis, it is not Mao, nor Stalin; for Ellis the key figure was always Lenin.

> In the Manichean mindset created by Leninism a term was required, which unlike partiinost, contained an explicit reference to right/wrong, correct/incorrect from a political or ideological point of view, one that could be used to indict those deviating from the party line in an authoritative manner. Politicheskaya pravil'nost, that assertive, impressive sounding and approving criterion of orthodoxy, satisfies this requirement very well. We might see political correctness as a practical solution to a problem arising from the theoretical discussions surrounding partiinost.
>
> (Ellis 2004:11)

The term political correctness is thus simply a translated term from Russian, but in a much more important theoretical sense it captured for Lenin the importance of having a correct interpretation of historical events, and which, thereby, created a distinction between politics in the ordinary sense of that word, and political correctness, implying that one could *read* political events correctly. Two crucial consequences follow naturally from the logic of this distinction: either one's understanding of historical events is correct or incorrect, and, perhaps more importantly, *these political truths have a greater status than truths discovered through more traditional means*. For Lenin, however, Ellis contends, the situation was much simpler: 'To be politically correct meant to be consistent with, not deviating from, the party line or any given issue. To be politically incorrect was to run the risk of being denounced as engaging in "revisionism", "factionalism", being a "wrecker" or "an enemy of the people"' (Ellis 2004: 15). Thus, it was not the job of the intelligentsia to engage in *interpretation* of history, simply to *comply* with the interpretations already undertaken by the party vanguard.

The question of truth here is also of vital importance, because it is not just a question of utilizing a non-realist epistemology, or 'linguistic turn', but more of having elevated political truths above natural truths; or seeing progressive truths, as opposed to reactionary ones. The Russian language is again instructive here by distinguishing between:

> *pravda* (truth which is socially, morally or ethically just) and *istina* (the truth, the empirical state of affairs, that what nature makes possible or impossible). For the Marxist-Leninist, and more recently the multi-culturalist and feminist, empirical reality (*istina*) is the enemy, since the Soviet ideologue and his current imitators are pursuing a socially and morally higher truth (*pravda*).
>
> (Ellis 2004: 20)

Hereby is revealed precisely what is at stake in post-16 college and university education, particularly in the humanities and the social sciences. For what is it that makes the study of these disciplines critical? For those cast as PC it is very often that they champion a form of liberatory thinking, which distinguishes between a politics of containment and a politics of change. For Ellis the roots, and subsequent folly, of such thinking are grounded in a correspondence not between facts and reality, but between ideas and virtuous forms of political action. Ellis locates support for this interpretation in the memoirs of the Soviet dissident, Berger:

> [*Istina*] denotes the correspondence between the notion and the objective reality. *Pravda* is a unique and specifically Russian concept: it means the highest concept of truth, a truth elevated to the rank of an idea. It is etymologically linked with *pravo* ['right' or 'law'] and with *pravosudie* ['process of justice']. A Russian who 'stands for *pravda*', or who 'struggles for *pravda*', does not stand or struggle for the sum of all kinds of truth, big and small, but for the truth which needs to be attained, truth in action, the ideal of conduct, the correspondence between acts and the demands of ethics.
>
> (Berger 1971: 52, in Ellis 2004: 21)

In this analysis the roots of PC turn out to be very deep, and via a different journey the conclusion is similar to Schwartz's (2003) that PC makes Nature a social construct. The effect here is also to tie up a clear connection between this interpretation of history, and forms of identity politics centred on the body, and how forms of sexuality are performative and constructed (Weeks 1985; Butler 1990). The difference, of course, is whether one believes this to be a positive or negative intellectual endeavour. For Ellis this is 'Lenin's revenge' (Ellis 2004: 51). Not only is it dangerous in intellectual terms – because it distorts facts and values – but also it is precisely what has granted the new PC cadres in higher education in the West their moral self-righteousness and sense of superiority:

language is not primarily used to communicate ideas but rather to signal the speaker's willingness to submit to the politically correct register ('gay', for example, in place of 'homosexual', or 'gender' in place of 'sex'). Language is power not for the masses but for the party intellectuals who are to instruct us on correct usage. Contemporary political correctness pursues the same policy by dominating public discourse and creating a climate of fear such that 'incorrect' opinion is declared 'illegitimate', 'extreme' or 'racist' and so on.

(Ellis 2004: 23)

Although the point here is clear, unfortunately the examples chosen undermine it, because the word 'gay' was long since adopted by 'homosexuals' themselves before it was imposed by anyone else, and this was surely for sound political and practical reasons (i.e. 'homosexual' had taken on a derogatory meaning, and it was used mainly to refer to a form of male sexuality only). And the term 'gender' was adopted by sociologists in order to distinguish conceptually between the biological sexes male and female and the socially inscribed behaviours of masculinity and femininity, and this was surely despite its more 'incorrect' and popular interpretation on application forms which require one to state one's 'gender' when clearly the form simply requires one's 'sex'. Ellis is thus half-right, in indicating that there is a tendency to prescribe and dictate a particular form of language when other forms are perfectly acceptable. But it would be a mistake to argue that this is always imposed, in the form of a downward *party* dictate, because the examples he chooses indicate that the use of language is actually much more negotiated, and can be equally empowering as disempowering.

What is also problematic in Ellis's analysis is the extent to which it is fair to compare the 'correctional' techniques of the Soviet and Maoist regimes with those used in higher education in the West:

Agreeing to some blatant fabrication, the victim damages and eventually destroys his ability to think for himself, which is consistent with the Maoist view that '"Self" is the origin of all evil'. His inner self destroyed or broken, the victim ceases, finally, to be an independent, thinking human being.

(Ellis 2004: 28)

That said, D'Souza was keen to paint a picture which was not dissimilar for US universities, as witnessed by his reference to the soon to become infamous 'red flag' case of the word 'individual' being scrutinized for its political insensitivity (D'Souza 1992). And Ellis pulls no punches in concluding that the new right interpretation of PC in the US is actually much more accurate than many of them may have realized:

Whatever cause the left-wing radical supports in the rainbow coalition – and these days he need not be very left or very radical – his relativist approach to knowledge, his commitment to the 'truth that ought to be' rather than the one that is, his barely concealed loathing of individual excellence, the belief that in the collective or community resides superior wisdom, his loathing of free speech (which he naturally exploits to the full) and his ready acceptance of a completely politicised education system, are demonstrably the offspring of communist systems. Political correctness provides the deep structure, the base on which the superstructure of multiculturalism et al can be raised. Political correctness, in other words, is something serious.

(Ellis 2004: 40–41)

Fundamentally, it is serious because its epistemology invites a view of knowledge where one does not discover the secrets of Nature, but seeks to free oneself from its constructed shackles (Rorty 1989).

There is however a far more apocryphal component to Ellis's work, because two years later he found himself under threat of dismissal from his lecturing post at Leeds University, on the grounds of holding and disseminating views that might be described precisely as '"illegitimate", "extreme" or "racist"' (Ellis 2004: 23). Either this was itself a very extreme way to prove a point, or it is deeply ironic that in rallying against forms of PC, he should become the victim of it within such a short space of time. Before his case ran its full course he took early retirement so we cannot be sure what might have been the outcome had he stayed on to fight it, but we do know that the climate of discussion which surrounded it was very divided, from those who wished to defend his right to free speech, to those who felt that his views were simply unacceptable in a twenty-first-century British university. What brought about the case in the first place was reported in the Leeds University student magazine *Leeds Student*, in an interview he gave, followed up by an edited version of his own authored piece which appeared a week later. The full text, entitled 'Time to Face the Truth about Multiculturalism' is available on the web (e.g.: http://devilskitchen.me.uk/2006/03/frank-ellis.html; accessed 12 November 2007).

From an academic point of view this is a classic case of PC and for two important reasons. First, he was disseminating views which were clearly unpopular to most of the liberal university community, and in this sense he was unorthodox. This presents the anti-PCers with a good test case of how tolerant a community can be towards its dissenters. Second, it is also a test of whether a university really is a 'marketplace of ideas', and whether one's duty as an employee to an organization and its values should be greater than one's allegiance to a wider notion of academic enquiry and 'the disinterested pursuit of the truth'.

Echoing the work of Fish, it is difficult to imagine that such cases could be unambiguously considered from a position of first principle. For example the article Ellis wrote was a mixture of references to academic research and his own punchy political polemic, and it could be argued therefore that he wrote the article as much as an *individual* as an academic. It is not clear either that any of the views relate directly to his area of expertise – Russian and Slavonic studies. But what complicated the case enormously was the question of whether as an *employee* of Leeds University he had broken a contract to adhere to the values of the institution in which he worked, and the state legislation to which Leeds University must adhere. The two obvious referents here would be the Equality policy of the university and the UK Race Relations legislation of 2003. It would appear that the actual case against him, as opposed to the 'bloggers' case, is that the university were concerned precisely about his position as an employee. (See, e.g.: 'University Suspends Lecturer in Racism Row who Praised BNP', *The Guardian*, 24 March 2006: http://education.guardian.co.uk/racism/story/0,, 1738570,00.html; accessed 12 November 2006.) And reflecting back on Kors and Silverglate's (1998) concern that American universities have become 'shadows' of their former selves (see Chapter 4), cases like this highlight that the principled allegiance to freedom of scholarship and honouring a contract of employment are very often two sides of the same coin, rather than two, easily separable, coins.

Conclusion

In both Ellis's academic work on PC, and the separate case against him for inappropriate behaviour, we see important aspects of PC. Most significantly, in his academic work he convincingly argues that the roots of political correctness are much deeper than we might be led to believe, particularly if we remain focused on much of the discussion which emerged in the US in the 1980s. That this analysis also signals that the adherence to 'the party line' is at the core of PC will be instructive throughout the next two chapters. And although he is critical of the view that the word *pravda* might be considered to be a more important basis for truth, we can also see sound evidence here that multiculturalism need not always be grounded in moral self-righteousness, but that it can be demonstrated to have a much firmer epistemological foundation.

More generally speaking, and in the light of the economic and political upheavals of the 1980s, it is clear that the left in Britain have had enormous trouble seeking to reconcile a desire on the one hand to restate a fundamental belief in the central importance of overturning the material basis of capitalism as an economic system, with, on the other hand, a burgeoning sense that more localized and particularistic forms of struggle are increasingly becoming the locus for many people, be they, for example, small-scale experiments in sustainable living, or the celebration of more plastic forms of sexuality.

We can also glean here some evidence that the gap between those who wish to adhere to some of the more traditional Marxist concepts and those most willing to make a 'linguistic turn' appears to be much wider in the UK than in the US – there being many more intellectuals sitting between these positions in the US. There is also some evidence here that because of this many more British academics (from both extremes) seemed concerned to ensure that language was very clearly afforded its correct position in being able to bring about social change. Although the term PC itself may not have been invoked anywhere near as easily as in the US this does not mean that the debates themselves have not had clear PC overtones.

There are simpler explanations of why matters relating to political correctness have not been of great concern in intellectual debate and discussion in the UK. Chief amongst these might well be the fact that almost all the polemics that were rallied against PC in the US (see Chapter 2) were directed precisely at left-wing colleagues working in US higher education, and this produced bait which was very difficult to resist. As a consequence, political correctness, as a label, was very quickly attached to a host of issues in intellectual discussion in the US. This does not mean that many of the same or similar discussions were not taking place in the UK, simply, again, that the term itself was not so readily invoked. That said, what seems to be the most significant difference between the US and the UK is the way in which conservative polemics were used to steer debate much more towards *what* was considered to be politically correct, such as a belief in harmful speech, multicultural curricula, and forms of affirmative action, rather than the *form* that politically correct debates take. In taking us back to its deeper historical roots in Leninism and Stalinism, Ellis's work is extremely instructive on the latter. And this interpretation will be a central feature of the following two chapters, which will seek to embed these more general concerns in a discussion of recent reforms in post-16 education in the UK.

9

PC and the panopticon principle
Quangos, surveillance, and scripted communication in the academy

It is obvious that . . . the more constantly the persons to be inspected are under the eyes of the persons who should inspect them, the more perfectly will the purpose of the establishment have been attained. Ideal perfection, if that were the object, would require that each person should actually be in that predicament, during every instant of time. This being impossible, the next thing to be wished for is, that, at every instant, seeing reason to believe as much, and not being able to satisfy himself to the contrary, he should *conceive* himself to be so.

What is also of importance is, that for the greatest proportion of time possible, each man should actually *be* under inspection. This is material in *all* cases, that the inspector may have the satisfaction of knowing, that the discipline actually has the effect which it is designed to have: and it is more particularly material in such cases where the inspector, besides seeing that they conform to such standing rules as are prescribed, has more or less frequent occasion to give them such transient and incidental directions as will require to be given and enforced, at the commencement at least of every course of industry.

(Jeremy Bentham, *The Works of Jeremy Bentham*, published under the Superintendence of his Executor, John Bowring (Edinburgh: William Tait, 1843). 11 vols. Accessed from http://oll.libertyfund.org/title/1925/116372 on 26 October 2007)

Introduction

Although written over a century and a half ago and concerning the principle of a panopticon design for a prison, many people working in post-16 education in Britain in the late twentieth century might have been forgiven for thinking that it was describing the systems of inspection that were introduced at that time. Bentham also wrote about extending the idea to institutions like hospitals and schools, where the 'inmates', be they patients or pupils, might be supervised in the form of omnipresent surveillance. If we extend the principle one step further we can see that those conducting the initial surveillance might themselves become the subject of surveillance, and logic dictates that this might eventually become a chain. Twisting the old dictum 'who educates the educators?' we would then find ourselves asking 'who supervises the supervisors?'

It is clear from Bentham's own drawings that the principle of the panopticon was to be understood as a literal form of architectural design rather than as a metaphor for surveillance in general. In this chapter I will be looking at the extent to which a metaphorical understanding is not only valid, but might also be referred to as a form of political correctness. Furthermore, that the form of political correctness implied by this perception has more in common with its roots in Soviet-style Leninism, and Stalinism, in opposition to much of the writing about political correctness in the US during the 1980s and 1990s. Whereas the latter invoked images of totalitarianism the clear implication was that this was being perpetrated by the cultural and intellectual left, mainly located in US universities, rather than the state itself. The focus for this chapter will be on whether it is possible to argue that the state's broad policy framework for post-16 education in Britain over the past twenty years has produced a distinct form of political correctness.

The road to Orwell

As we have already seen, much of the early anti-PC literature in the US invoked images of American higher education as having become an Orwellian nightmare, where Big Brother is monitoring the indoctrination which has been perpetrated by an army of New Left revolutionary cadres. In keeping with a traditional rendering of *1984* and *Animal Farm* as anti-Soviet treatises, these images reinforced the general view that Americans need to be on constant guard against such threats to their freedoms. However, in her book *Killing Thinking*, Evans reminds us that Orwell's warnings were much more Weberian; they were a warning about oligarchic tendencies in general in the twentieth century (Evans 2004). Thus, both Orwell books are actually about how elites in all societies wrestle with ways in which they might seek to maintain their power, or, perhaps better, ensure that in a climate of democracy and equality some at least will always be more equal than others. The point is a significant one because it raises the question of the tension between universities being controlled by power elites, whilst simultaneously seeking to maintain a degree of autonomy from those elites.

It could be argued that the past twenty years in Britain has seen post-16 education more surveyed by power elites than ever before. Indeed, to such an extent that it might be integral to a more serious undermining of the role and very meaning of education (Abbs 1994; Maskell and Robinson 2002). When public sector professionals first came under the critical spotlight in the Thatcher governments of the 1980s the case was usually made by reference to the fact that the taxpayer deserves to know precisely what his or her money is being spent on, and that it is being spent efficiently (Lea *et al.* 2003). As we saw in the previous chapter, this was no doubt helped enormously by the fact that it coincided with a tabloid media campaign, aimed at curtailing what was seen as the wasteful use of public resources. And much of this waste was perceived as spending on 'loony' educational initiatives, such as anti-racist maths, and the promotion of homosexuality as a normal lifestyle.

The next chapter will consider some of the implications of the British state promoting certain aims for post-16 education. In this chapter the focus will be on the means of surveillance employed by the agencies of the state and to what extent they might be referred to as forms of political correctness. Evans is disparaging in her indictment of the type of surveillance one now sees in the British university, but she also highlights exactly *why* it is difficult to resist. With reference to a Teaching Quality Assessment (TQA) undertaken by the Quality Assurance Agency for Higher Education (QAA) at the university where she works, she comments:

> it was not conscience that made cowards of us all, but fear of doing badly in that loathsome and deplorable exercise. Across the country other academics, people who have spent years on specialist research and cared with some passion about it, have also had to adopt what can only be described as the Winston Smith position: telling a bunch of lies because the alternative is a bad mark, and a bad mark means, if not physical torture, then public failure, and even more assessment and even more regulation. Moreover, the very process of assessment is legitimized in terms of reference to 'open-ness' and 'accountability'. To challenge this orthodoxy immediately lays critics open to the charge that they are in favour of, not the sensible spending of public money, but practices of secrecy and exclusion.
>
> (Evans 2004: 61)

Later in the book she repeats the question Paul Newman asks Robert Redford of their pursuers in *Butch Cassidy and the Sundance Kid*: 'Who *are* these people?' (Evans 2004: 122). An obvious clue lies in the euphemism often given to inspection visits, that they are a form of 'peer review'. That is those conducting the surveillance are very likely to be other academics, ex-academics, or retired academics, and thus, although there might well be a large measure of self-policing at work, this is being aided by colleagues who are on hand to help others to see more clearly the merits of a transparent system of public accountability. Nearly ten years earlier Hyland had succinctly summarized the more general change in value system that this was premised on: 'Seducing and cajoling the public sector middle class into the embrace of the market has been a key objective of public sector reforms' (Hyland 1996: 76–77).

In Chapter 1 a Soviet understanding of political correctness was outlined: either the Party understands history correctly, in which case someone who does not follow this line is politically incorrect, or, in more ironic terms, someone understands it, does not believe it, but pays lip service to it in order to avoid an extended stay somewhere in Siberia. Thus, in the case of the 'audit culture' (Rustin 1998) and the more general 'social market' philosophy (Elliott 1993), which have emerged in British post-16 education, the question becomes: Is it possible to argue that both demand either a literal or ironic acceptance, and that both options clearly resonate with an understanding of PC as 'toeing the Party line' or 'lineism'? (Perry 1992).

Self-censorship in public discourse

In his article and subsequent book the American author Loury presents a theory of political correctness as a form of self-censorship (Loury 1994, 1995). In keeping with most writing in the US it suggests that the academic community itself demands forms of self-censorship. However, in shifting the argument to the context of the audit culture in British post-16 education we might be able to see another significant resonance. Loury sees political correctness 'as an implicit social convention of restraint on public expression within a given community' (Loury 1995: 147), and one where 'the velvet glove of seduction' is a much more powerful metaphor than the more traditional 'iron fist of repression' (Loury 1995: 147). In essence it is a game theory of strategy where players must consider the impact of the words they choose on their intended audience. Thus, it is never just the words themselves which are important in communication, but the assessment of how they might be received. In this regard speech is never entirely free because it is always constrained by these strategic assessments. As Loury points out this must include his own assessment of how the words chosen in his own book might be received, and thus, by implication, the words chosen throughout this book also. This is a form of political correctness, again, not because of the actual words a person chooses, but because of the perception she must have of her intended audience.

Naturally, where there is a power imbalance between sender and receiver the strategies have the potential to become more complicated, subtle, or even subversive. Morris, following Loury, considers the implications of this in interview situations, where someone wishing to ensure that their information is utilized may have to make some strategic decisions about the nature of their communication, even lie, but only as a means to ensure that their end-truth will have its desired impact (Morris 2001). Thus, we might argue that even in the case of an interview for an academic post – where one might expect a large degree of forthrightness in the communication – it is clear that an interviewee might perceive a need to lose some battles in order to be allowed to go on and fight a larger war. Returning to Evans's 'deplorable' experience of QAA inspection, quoted above, we can clearly see why outright resistance might be unproductive for the academics in question, but we can also see that there is, in fact, a large space for a range of subtle and subversive strategic language games to be played out in these contexts. At one extreme this can be exemplified by members of Warwick University's Economics Department, who dismissed the validity of the whole QAA inspection regime, but only after having received a score of 24 out of 24 in the exercise itself (Macleod 2001). But much more subtle forms of strategic game playing might also be in evidence. For example the research undertaken by Coffield *et al.* on the use of 'learning styles' in post-16 education indicates that it has become something of a mantra, and which might lead to an inspection scenario, with inspectors deciding that they like the notion, and colleges knowing this, in which case a simple exchange of the term ensues, without any question of the term's true validity or effectiveness in enhancing the student learning experience. As Coffield *et al.* point out, the effect is to have certain notions 'accorded the status of "best practice", without always making clear the evidential basis for the claim' (Coffield *et al.* 2004: 137).

Both these cases might be understood as ironic forms of political correctness; as 'toeing the party line', but not always out of direct fear of the consequences if one does not, but sometimes as forms of subversion, aimed at maintaining some professional autonomy whilst recognizing an immovable controlling force. The ethnomethodologist Garfinkel drew attention to this forty years ago in his study of hospital doctors. The title of the article succinctly makes the point, that there are often 'good organizational reasons for "bad" clinic records', based on the 'ties between the social system that services and is serviced by these records' (Garfinkel 1967a: 114). He argued that doctors will often produce deliberately poor patient records in order to engineer more time to get on with what they see as their real job, that is patient care, but will pay the documentation just such sufficient attention that it will guarantee continued funding for the hospital. This results in 'informal and hidden recording practices that permits the recorder to maintain the priority of his other occupational obligations while keeping the front office appropriately misinformed' (Garfinkel 1967a: 118). And this seems to describe precisely the process that many public sector professionals are involved in when time is short and inspection regimes are intrusive, or the 'terrors of performativity' (Ball 2003) are most apparent. Clearly, there is bound to be a large amount of endemic insincerity in these forms of communication (Lea, in Hayes 2004).

Scripted communication in an audit culture

'*What* was going on? A roar of laughter from the aphasia ward, just as the President's speech was coming on, and they had all been so eager to hear the President speaking' (Sachs 1985: 76). Here, Sachs draws attention to the fact that President Reagan's speech was inevitably going to be 'seen through', as an act, a performance, and as a piece of inauthentic theatre. Ironic of course in the obvious sense that Reagan was an ex-actor, but in more subtle ways it highlights how people are often forced into situations where their performance becomes a necessary masquerade. Hopefully, the audience will not perceive it in this way, or if they do, this perception will only be by those who understand both the nature and necessity of the game. Unfortunately the aphasiacs were not intended to see the joke, but their condition is such that this is what they always see. If this aspect of aphasia is seen as a metaphor it could be argued that colleges and universities now employ many people with this condition.

The pervasive nature of inauthentic speech is neatly captured in the fast-food valedictory comment: 'Have a nice day!' On the one hand it is simply another way of saying goodbye and, following Garfinkel, is just an example of shared meanings in a common-sense everyday world (Garfinkel 1967b), but, on the other hand, it niggles as a form of irritation because of its false sincerity. Taken from the employee's point of view it is just a simple enactment learnt in training, where one learns not just the technical aspects of operating machinery, and how to accomplish a series of physical tasks, but also how to communicate. However, these are not communication skills where one learns the need for judgement, or even etiquette or politeness, but where one learns a literal script and repeats it on every occasion. Thus, it is not uncommon now in British supermarkets to be asked whether one needs help in packing even if one has only bought a newspaper.

Given that the employee is likely to be earning the minimum wage it is perhaps not surprising that the lines might sound rather insincere, particularly when they are repeated ad nauseum, but why exactly does the employee need a script? Following Ritzer, it offers customers the knowledge that they are in safe territory – a comfort zone where everything is predictable – and it protects employers from inappropriate comments that might be uttered by employees, which might harm sales (Ritzer 2000). We might take this argument further by suggesting that learning a script is an oft-overlooked part of employee skills training. Furthermore, that it is the retail sales equivalent of 'deskilling'. Thus, why trust employees to learn to communicate effectively when you can control them directly through a script: 'The managers assume the burden of gathering together all of the traditional knowledge which in the past has been possessed by the workmen and then of classifying, tabulating, and reducing this knowledge to rules, laws, and formulae' (Taylor 1947: 36). In his seminal work, Braverman, utilizing the notion of deskilling, looked at how routine non-manual work had fallen prey to this inexorable part of capitalist logic in his example of key-punch computer operators (Braverman 1974). The question here is: How far might the *professional middle classes* also be deskilled by these processes?

The problem with pursuing this line of argument is that, by definition, middle-class professionals *are professional* and their need to make judgements must preclude the possibility of scripted communication: 'Professional judgements and decisions are ethical and not simply technical in character' (Elliott 1993: 67). But, as colleges and universities in the UK have slowly become more managerial in their approach to service provision (Randle and Brady 1997; Avis

2000; Deem and Brehony 2005), and as government quangos have increasingly taken on the role of ensuring that they perform in ways which comply with these values (Keep 2006), it raises the obvious question of how much the communication between academics, their managers, and outside agents of surveillance has become increasingly scripted in nature.

An early example of the need to adopt new forms of language to reflect a change in values was provided in the aptly titled book *Further Education in the Market Place* (McGinty and Fish 1993). An obvious connection with political correctness in the US can be made here, that is, we can see how the new educational terms which increasingly became popular in the early 1990s in Britain, performed exactly the same task as the more generally recognizable PC terms in the US. Thus, just as 'handicapped' became 'disabled', so 'student' became 'learner', and 'college' became 'learning provider'. And just as the 'people first' movement transformed 'disabled' into 'person with disabilities' (Titchkovsky 2001), this was mirrored in marketized education by references to 'teachers teaching' increasingly becoming 'learners learning', and references to 'teaching and learning strategies' being hurriedly reversed to become 'learning and teaching strategies' lest the 'learning provider' be perceived as one which puts its employees before its clients. Indeed, it was not uncommon before the term 'learner' became ubiquitous to see British colleges and universities experimenting with the use of words like 'customers' and 'clients'. This could also be used as confirmation of Ritzer's general observation about American education, that increasingly students have been invited to see themselves as consumers of educational products, and to see the university system as a series of shopping malls (Ritzer 1999). And whether any of these changes in language actually changed the nature of one's educational experience, or just euphemistically distorted its reality, was precisely the question asked by anti-PCers in the early 1990s about changes in the American lexicon of PC at that time – be they real or imagined (Hughes 1993; Leo 1994).

In the wider context, what might be called 'the aphasia judgement' thus becomes deciding whether someone working in a college or university actually *believes* in what they are saying, and sees the words as authentically appropriate, or whether one is making a strategically appropriate judgement, based, at one extreme, on the possibility of a dire consequence if one does not pay appropriate lip service, or one makes a more subtle assessment, that life might be a little easier if one sticks to the script. And sandwiched in between might be a range of more subversive opportunities, requiring a permanent ability to 'read between the lines'. A significant consequence of the audit culture surveillance of post-16 education is thus a much greater need for more scripts for professionals to learn. Indeed, to use the metaphor of the theatre, not only does the prospect of inspection require that one prepare the set, giving the impression of fresh paint, but also it requires that everyone has thoroughly rehearsed their lines. In this regard the educational consultant becomes little more than an old-style theatrical prompt. But also it demands that each person becomes adept at working out what is the appropriate way to respond *in the context*, and to begin to see everything through an aphasic's lens.

From a sociological point of view it is important to document the ways in which the behaviour of professionals might be modified by these developments in surveillance. If Garfinkel's observation that 'keeping the front office appropriately misinformed' now has a much greater resonance forty years later, it could also be argued that 'flying beneath the radar' also has a renewed and pertinent resonance. Thus, the first question asked of any request for information becomes: 'Who needs to know?', and the first whispered question in any meeting is the one popularized by the comedian Joan Rivers: 'Can we talk?' (Loury 1995). And finally, borrowing the term 'the return of the repressed' from clinical psychoanalysis, this might also be utilized as a convenient metaphor for how the more scripted a person's speech becomes the more he or she might be repressing what they really think and believe, and this needs an outlet. This prompts the obvious question, how many politically incorrect jokes are actually told by the very professionals who were being politically correct not two minutes earlier? This should not be taken to imply that all public sector professionals routinely dismiss the value systems of their professions, only that as behaviour becomes more systematically policed it creates a real desire to 'come off stage' whenever one can.

Quango land

> In a considerable number of countries which, for about a hundred years, have enjoyed practically complete freedom of public expression, that freedom is now suppressed and replaced by a compulsion to coordinate speech with such views as the government believes to be expedient or holds in all seriousness.
>
> (Strauss 1952: 22)

This view is supported by the British journalist John Pilger, who has campaigned throughout his career for people in so-called democratic countries to take a more critical stance towards their mass media, and to consider the ways in which the media is often little more than a public relations tool for ruling elites. He regularly quotes the Czech writer Zdner Urbanek, writing in 1977, about life in the Soviet bloc: 'You in the west have a problem. You are unsure when you are being lied to, when you are being tricked. We do not suffer from this; and unlike you, we have acquired the skill of reading between the lines' (Pilger 1994: 58). In this regard what is interesting about the Loony Left campaign, discussed in the last chapter, is not just how the government and the tabloid newspapers were able to coalesce around the notion, but how it became a politically correct line. That is, it became difficult for individual journalists who were serving this agenda to report in any other way (Curran *et al.* 2005). This is ironic because the main purpose of the campaign was, of course, to claim that the cultural, or 'urban', left were the ones who were being politically correct. This campaign is also interesting because although there is evidence that many of the stories were fabricated or exaggerated, and its aim was ideologically motivated, this should not be understood as implying that by removing this bias one necessarily arrives at the truth, because political stories are, by their very nature, *political*, and thus it might be better to argue that revealing the truth is actually about revealing the politics. This is again ironic, because this was precisely the aim behind those who proposed an epistemological understanding of multiculturalism, and which was much criticized by anti-PCers in the US (see Chapter 5).

In an analogous way it might also be argued that academics and teachers working in post-16 have been routinely asked to support a series of state-sponsored politically correct positions. This has included a wholesale adoption of a 'learning outcomes model' for teaching (Gosling and Moon 2001); the desirability of externally monitored frameworks for professional development (HEA 2006; LLUK 2007); acceptance of the view that universities should accommodate at least 50 per cent of 18–30 year olds (Thomas and Quinn 2007); that universities and colleges should see themselves as 'skill providers' (Leitch 2006); and more recently espouse a 'green' or 'sustainable' value system (Butcher 2007). Some of these issues will be looked at in the next chapter. Their relevance here is to consider the *means* by which post-16 professionals are asked to embrace these notions and their relevance to political correctness. For, not only is it difficult to challenge their validity, but that validity in the first place often rests on their marketized promotion by state quangos.

For example, in an early document from Lifelong Learning UK (LLUK), the quango charged with reformulating the professional standards framework aimed mainly at teachers working in further education, it is argued: 'There is a strand of opinion that regards ... prescription as impinging on the autonomy and professionalism of the sector. However, other professions have stringent require-ments on their members where this is appropriate' (LLUK 2005: 5). Reading between the lines it could be argued that this is actually the view of the quango, not the profession itself. Regardless, there was no hard evidence presented one way or the other. Similarly, when the HEA put their case for an appropriate framework for those working in higher education, their consultative document appeared to have no evidence-based references other than to official government documents (http://staffcentral.brighton.ac.uk/clt/home/documents/Academy_Standards_Report_.pdf; accessed 20 November 2007). Indeed, the mixed messages which can be seen in the responses to the consultation may provide sound evidence as to why the HEA found it very difficult to present a prescriptive final framework to the university sector, which itself undermines the LLUK case for stringency.

Of course, the very fact that there is consultation may be taken as evidence that there is no inherent motive to cajole and control academics and teachers and to seek to undermine their professional autonomy in the process, but it is in the nature of such consultation that the quango has the power to frame what will be consulted on. For example in a recent consultation on 'FE improvement' a case was presented for a new quality body whose aim was to promote more self-regulation in the sector, whilst at the same time being clear that 'regular and open assessments of their [colleges] performance through inspection by Ofsted' would continue, and where 'inadequate provison' is found 'the LSC will act to secure improvement'. Furthermore, 'government departments would continue to grant-fund specific programmes of work to support major national policy reforms' (http://www.dius.gov.uk/consultations/con_1107_feimprovement. html; accessed 28 January 2008). In this climate it would appear to be some time before any serious measure of autonomy could be envisaged.

Keep has argued that there is a broader political strategy at work here, and it is integral to the New Labour 'project': 'Ofsted, Adult Learning Inspectorate (ALI), the Quality Improvement Agency for Lifelong Learning, and the Learning and Skills Council (LSC) and its 47 local learning and skills councils are all quangos, financed primarily by central government, with governing bodies or councils appointed by, and solely responsible to, the Secretary of State for Education and Skills. They do not work *with* the DfES [now DIUS] (LSC 2005: 11), they work *for* it' (Keep 2006: 50). There is an even wider context here, and one which asks to what extent the eighteen years of Thatcherism (1979–1997) gave rise to ten years of distinctive Blairism (1997–2007), or whether the latter was just a revamped version of the former. If the post-war Keynesian social-democratic model was the First Way, and the free market model of Thatcherism was the Second Way, there is a simple logic to referring to Blairism as the Third Way. But the Third Way was also intended as a political model which saw people neither as atomized individuals, nor welfare dependents, but people who would be supported and 'incentivized' to become active citizens. Although jokingly referred to as 'Thatcherism without the handbag', Anthony Giddens, the British intellectual guru of Blair's Third Way, outlined its distinctive approach to government, which was to steer, rather than row (Giddens 1998, 2000). With hindsight it seems clear that the education quangos have become the hidden rowers. Or, in the context of the themes of this chapter, it might be better to argue that just as the quangos mark out the blueprint of the infrastructure for post-16 education, and then set about monitoring it, so the government of the day has the same relationship with the quangos. Thus, just as universities are autonomous institutions, which are merely steered, so are educational quangos. This is therefore a multistorey panopticon, requiring a new Benthamite diagram. And the implications are clearly not lost on those who work for the various quangos, who may themselves operate with their own aphasic judgements (Baty 2002).

Furthermore, just as Thatcher was often reported as asking whether people were for or against her reforms, implying that the latter were 'enemies within', so professionals working in post-16 education are now apt to be cast in similar black and white terms. Thus, to be against learning outcomes is to be against students; to be against professional standards is to be against professionalism; to be against widening participation is to be elitist; and to be against the greening of the university is to be decadent, uncaring and wasteful. And to be able to be cast in such ways is perhaps indicative of how much the university, in particular, has been transformed from an open community of scholarship into a culture of compliance. But what is perhaps more troubling is the way in which this has been achieved through a language of openness, and that the whole exercise is simply one of enhancing transparency, accountability, and, in broad terms, producing a system to re-reward institutions with a degree of autonomy. In a mirror of the arguments presented by conservative commentators in the US about the New Left's cultural coup in the American university, we see a direct parallel in Britain but this time the coup has been enacted by the government, in seeking to steer, or row, more directly the activities of the British university or further education college.

The impoverished professional

Returning to the Stalinist interpretation of political correctness, and the work of Loury and Morris, it is clear that strategic game playing has a sound rationale. But if we take the literal interpretation that a correct understanding of events is the real PC position we find a world divided between believers and non-believers. Thus, the 'dry' members of Thatcher's cabinets throughout the 1980s might equally have been referred to as PC as any member of a 'loony' local government council at the time. For both sets of people might be viewed as having adopted an unswerving alliance to an ideological position; and one where to waiver is apt to have one cast as a blasphemer. In this understanding of political correctness it is, quite literally, the correctness of the politics which is to the fore, and not the content of the political position itself. Thus, although political correctness throughout most of the 1980s and 1990s, particularly in the US, came to be associated with an unswerving allegiance to a series of strategies aimed at enhancing the relative standing of a number of disadvantaged social groups, we can see, particularly from the British context, that it could equally be understood more broadly to apply to *any situation in which a party (or Party) ensures that its interpretation of events will prevail.* Furthermore, that there will be forms of PC behaviour in two senses: first, unswerving belief in the correct interpretation from the party and its agents; and second, some strategic game playing from those who perceive that ironically 'toeing the party line' is the most sensible option.

From the perspective of those working in post-16 education this might be seen as an impoverishment model of professional life. There is a strong sense that the power to determine what will be of value has been wrested away and placed in the hands of the state, and its quango agents, and, as a direct consequence, there is an equally strong sense that if one pays sufficient lip service to it, one might still be able to find some space to act as an autonomous educator. Indeed, without reference to the term political correctness itself there has been a steady stream of academic work which has discussed these tendencies, particularly in the context of further education (Carter 1997; Gleeson *et al.* 2005; Robson 2006). This is a form of PC with a direct parallel to life as described by many dissidents in former Soviet bloc countries, with the exception that there is no direct equivalent of the salt mine: 'The term persecution covers a variety of phenomena, ranging from the most cruel type, as exemplified by the Spanish Inquisition, to the mildest, which is social ostracism' (Strauss 1952: 32).

Strauss's book on persecution and writing demonstrates precisely how *reading* between the lines is a necessary skill if one is to fully understand the *writing* between the lines of many authors:

> literature is addressed, not to all readers, but to trustworthy and intelligent readers only. It has all the advantages of private communication without having its greatest disadvantage – that it reaches only the writer's acquaintances. It has all the advantages of public communication without having its greatest disadvantage – capital punishment for the author.
>
> (Strauss 1952: 25)

Thus, just as one might view a newspaper story or a government document with a degree of scepticism, the same critical eye must now also be brought to bear on an increasing amount of writing in academic circles. This might range from carefully worded emails, and the perception of who might read them, to large-scale public documents which detail the past and predicated activities of a university or college, as witnessed by the mission statements which talk a lot about 'striving', but little about 'promising', and produce a lot of 'offers', but are reluctant to commit to 'entitlements'.

Although these strategic approaches might enhance the sense of impoverishment, they might also simply highlight what is always implicit when one addresses an audience. As Loury elegantly points out, the famous Shakespearean 'Friends, Romans, Countrymen' speech is carefully crafted to convey multiple meanings (Loury 1995: 149). It also highlights the extent to which most people naturally learn to curtail their right to free speech for political purposes. But what is perhaps the most troubling is the extent to which the enhanced sense of surveillance in post-16 education has forced teachers and academics to spend more and more time on strategic writing, leaving less and less time for more purely academic writing. Furthermore, where more time needs to be spent on working out whether people are writing and speaking in ironic terms. This is particularly troubling for workshop and seminar settings where topics like racism or sexism are being discussed because in a surveillance culture it will never be immediately obvious whether someone has adopted a PC euphemism because he or she believes it is the right thing to do, or for more strategic reasons. This is also an impoverished environment because it leaves little room for the exploration of these processes themselves, and might simply split the workshop between unswerving believers and ironic believers. Once again, this is a PC environment not because racism and sexism are being discussed, but because of the strategic decisions that people make about how they will present themselves, and how they might be perceived. At one level this is inevitable in the process of presenting oneself in everyday life (Goffman 1959), but at another level it takes on a more paranoid PC form in a culture of surveillance.

Conclusion

Throughout this chapter there has been no intention either to celebrate or denigrate those who do or do not support the various causes which have been promoted in post-16 education over the past twenty years. Rather, the point was to consider whether the means which have been employed to ensure that they are implemented and, more broadly, whether the enhanced forms of account-ability now used in the sector might be considered as an unwarranted form of surveillance and, more importantly, one which has significant resonances with forms of political correctness.

Couched in terms of political correctness the discussion also highlights some of the similarities and differences between the British and American contexts. Whereas the sense of surveillance in the US was intended to portray the true totalitarian tendencies behind the so-called enlightened cadres who would promote the interests of the disadvantaged, the *form* of argument could work equally well when the state and its quangos are intent on monitoring the work of public sector professionals. Although this might be *presented* as a straight-forward call for more accountability and transparency, for both taxpayers and stakeholders, and as the means by which a Third Way between a wholly private market and welfare model might be engineered, it might also be considered as a form of political correctness, both in the sense that many might perceive the state's intervention as an unwarranted call to conformity, and also in the way it invites appropriate lip service. In this model, government quangos are actually the underwater tentacles of the state, and once they are firmly wrapped round each ship, it is highly debatable as to whether this is really the means to enable those ships to navigate or steer themselves.

These arguments follow naturally from the association of political correct-ness with forms of totalitarianism. Whether the argument had much weight was the essence of the critiques presented mainly by those on the cultural left in the US (Wilson 1996; Feldstein 1997). Similarly, one might speculate about whether one might say the same about the more conspiratorial readings of Third Way politics (Hayes, in Lea *et al.* 2003). That said, the evidence that British pro-fessionals working in post-16 education are surveyed in very comprehensive ways is perhaps not really that controversial. That this is done in a manner which invokes images of a panoptical approach to the disciplining of social life in general is perhaps much more so (Foucault 1977). But what is perhaps most obvious is the extent to which this is a world which invites people to align themselves as believers or non-believers. Put simply, to what extent is the discourse of 'corporations, customers, and mission statements' a script if it is believed in? And to what extent is the language of 'learning outcomes' just lip service paid by many academics in order to be left alone to pursue their own more existential notions of the learning process? The answer is an obvious one: the more that one believes that this has been *imposed* the more heightened will be the sense that one is often reduced to having to rehearse a politically correct script.

This is an impoverished world not simply for those who are affronted by this assault on their professionalism, in terms of both the means and content of the assault (Beck and Young 2005), but also because it makes it extremely difficult to have an authentic conversation. In an extension of the irony much exploited by the right in the US, where enlightened individuals were accused of bullying tactics, it becomes increasingly difficult to imagine situations in which believers and non-believers might be able to sit in the same room and engage in debate. Furthermore just as it has become difficult in the US to engage in any authentic conversation about race, a less emotionally charged version of this could now be argued to operate throughout post-16 education when it comes to notions like 'learning outcomes' and 'learning styles'. These terms now have a literalness about their meanings which mirrors the way that terms like 'nigger' and 'queer' became fixed and representational in advance of enjoying some measure of liberation in more poststructural circles.

In this context it is clear that all conversations must indeed be increasingly prefaced by the question: 'Can we talk?' The phrase 'Have a nice day!' is not intended to be delivered with irony, but the fact that it might be highlights the importance of tolerating such subversion for fear that language and debate might calcify. It must surely be that much more troubling if *professional* dialogue is stripped of these figurative, ironic, and subversive dimensions. And what is most interesting about seeing these issues in terms of political correctness is not that professionals have been prevented from being ironical in their use of language but how much more time is spent on the subversive deconstructing of quango mantras as a form of critical debate, as opposed to the more traditional free exchange of ideas.

Where academics and teachers have to be at their most strategic in their use of language is when the forms of surveillance are at their most direct, and where the threat of more surveillance is the most real. And here the valedictory phrase 'I'll be back!' is the one that nobody wants to hear from an inspection team. Using the metaphor of the panopticon, this is the equivalent of checking before one speaks or writes that the guard is looking in another direction, or that one is in the shadow of a searchlight rather than its full beam. Here, even if the call to public accountability is perceived as being long overdue, its reception is bound to be greeted very differently by those who feel that more organically grown value systems and forms of professional accountability have been completely undermined in the process. These themes will be explored in more detail in the next chapter by looking not so much at the means by which the state has surveyed post-16 professionals but what type of provision it has sought to engineer.

10
PC and the attenuated academy
Social engineering, widening participation, and professional allegiance

I say, a University, taken in its bare idea, and before we view it as an instrument of the Church, has this object and this mission; it contemplates neither moral impression nor mechanical production; it professes to exercise the mind neither in art nor in duty; its function is intellectual culture; here it may leave its scholars, and it has done its work when it has done as much as this. It educates the intellect to reason well in all matters, to reach out towards truth, and to grasp it. . . .

I say that a cultivated intellect, because it is a good in itself, brings with it a power and a grace to every work and occupation which it undertakes, and enables us to be more useful, and to a greater number. There is a duty we owe to human society as such, to the state to which we belong, to the sphere in which we move, to the individuals towards whom we are variously related, and whom we successively encounter in life; and that philosophical or liberal education, as I have called it, which is the proper function of the university, if it refuses the foremost place to professional interests, does but postpone them to the formation of the citizen, and, while it subserves the larger interests of philanthropy, prepares also for the successful prosecution of those merely personal objects, which at first it seems to disparage.

(John Henry Newman (1982 [1852]),
The Idea of a University, pp. 94, 126)

Written within ten years of Bentham's various texts on the idea of the panoptican (referred to at the beginning of Chapter 9), Newman's thoughts would appear to strike a similar chord of resonance amongst the academic community in Britain today. In producing a passionate defence of what is often referred to as the Liberal educational creed, Newman outlines an essential quality of a university education: first and foremost, a university should be a place where knowledge is pursued for its own sake. Although it is highly debatable whether there has ever been a university which upholds this purely and exclusively, it is, nevertheless, still held by many as a cherished belief. We saw this previously throughout Chapter 2 concerning the American academy. In this chapter I will be considering the ways in which post-16 education in the UK has increasingly been asked to accommodate itself to a series of social engineering projects, and to see itself, first and foremost, as a servant of the economy and society; and asking whether there is any validity in seeing these projects as forms of political correctness.

The nature of the disgruntlement about these social engineering projects is exemplified in many of the punchy polemics produced by Furedi in the *Times Higher Education Supplement (THES)* (Furedi 2004c, 2004d, 2005b, 2007a, 2007b). In this series of disparaging attacks on attempts, mainly by the Higher Education Academy (HEA) and the Quality Assurance Agency for Higher Education (QAA), to enhance the status of learning and teaching in the university, Furedi seeks not only to critique what he sees as the bureaucratized understanding of key educational concepts, but also mounts a concerted effort to reassert the right of academics to control their own profession. On both counts he thereby seeks to undermine the false authority of these state-sponsored bodies, or quangos. In the light of the discussion in the previous chapter we can see that this argument is double-edged; it is both a critique of *what* such bodies seek to implement, but also the *means* they employ to do so. If we inextricably connect the two it is perhaps not surprising that educational concepts must be rendered as objects which have quantities (rather than attributes which have qualities) because how else could the state easily monitor, measure, and compare? (Hartley 1995). In the process Furedi also directs some of his anger more generally at the way academic knowledge has been reduced to a mindless form of 'skill', and the dire consequences of seeing students as customers of educational products. This chapter will address each of these issues, but, in contrast to the previous chapter, it is less about the *means* to call public sector professionals to account, and more about *what* should be the purpose of their endeavours, who should decide this, and how this relates to political correctness.

Faith in the soul of learning

Many of Furedi's concerns stem from his reading of the 1997 Dearing Report into higher education (Furedi 2007b). At that time Dearing was making a number of recommendations about the future of both higher and further education (Dearing 1996, 1997). This was interpreted broadly as a call to make more transparent the purposes of educational encounters, mainly for students, but this also had the effect of making it clear what might be specified for the purposes of review, or inspection. The obvious manifestation of this was in the wide-scale adoption of a learning outcomes model for curriculum development and session planning (Gosling and Moon 2001), and an implicit understanding that effective learning and teaching was to be understood as a form of 'constructive alignment', which demands that assessed outcomes and learning and teaching strategies be aligned explicitly with the learning outcomes (Biggs 1999). Dearing's recommendations were also instrumental in broadening the understanding of the nature of learning, and that this might be better expressed as a series of skills rather than simply subject content. In higher education the generic academic skills were subsequently made manifest in the QAA's level descriptors which detailed exactly the nature of the skills that a student would expect to be able to demonstrate at the end of each of the three years of a UK undergraduate programme, a Master's programme, and a doctorate (http://www.qaa.ac.uk/academicinfrastructure/FHEQ/EWNI/default.asp#annex1'; accessed 28 January 2008). A group of wider 'key' or 'transferable' skills were also included, many of which have subsequently been subsumed under the notion of 'graduate skills', and which can be explicitly demonstrated and documented by students in an ongoing progress file (http://www.qaa.ac.uk/academicinfrastructure/progressFiles/default.asp; accessed 28 January 2008).

Furedi has no time for such a bureaucratized rendering of teaching in higher education: 'Predictable and measurable outcomes have no place in an intellectually engaged environment' (Furedi 2004c); 'Somehow we have become more comfortable with template teaching' (Furedi 2005b); 'the attempt to forge a shared corporate culture through the institutionalisation of "behavioural statements" violates the spirit of university life' (Furedi 2007a). The message is a consistent one, and includes a dismissal of the view that higher education can be expressed as a series of skills or reduced to a technical exercise, and that 'corporate culture' can make universities more effective. Ten years before Dearing, Abbs succinctly critiqued the mindset which he saw at its foundation, asking provocatively 'what right does a government have to decide the actual nature of educational activity' and that 'we must free ourselves from the crippling assumption that the first task of teachers is to serve the economy, to turn out skilled robots and uncritical consumers for the "hi-tech" age' (Abbs 1986). A few years later this became a passionate defence of liberal education from a Socratic perspective:

> The first principle of Socratic education is that it cannot be simply transferred. Education is not an object (a mass of knowledge or information or skills or know-how) that can be unambiguously handed from the teacher to the student. Education is, rather, an activity of mind, a particular emotional and critical orientation towards experience.
>
> (Abbs 1994: 17)

Utilizing the Stalinist understanding of political correctness from the previous two chapters it is clear that the argument is indeed double-edged. For, on the one hand, there is the question of *what* exactly the state is proposing and, on the other, there is the question of the validity of the state *to* propose anything in the first place.

The academic community is clearly divided on the merits of a more transparent system of accountability for public sector professionals (Hayes, in Lea *et al.* 2003; Lomas, in Lea *et al.* 2003). The idea that learning outcomes are the most appropriate way to render learning transparently has also been equally defended and critiqued (Gosling and Moon 2001; Hussey and Smith 2002). But key here is asking whether agencies of the state know best what teachers need to be accountable for, and whether the systems of accountability need to be implemented and monitored by state quangos. As demonstrated in the last chapter, with such an incursive framework it is perhaps inevitable that many who are proud of their tradition of professional autonomy should be affronted, but also that it might cause forms of strategic game-playing and appropriate lip service, particularly by those who feel that subversive activities might be the simplest way to ensure that they maintain some measure of professional autonomy. Inspection agencies have been quick to defend themselves on the grounds that they only hold institutions accountable for what they say they are doing. But when the stakes are so high, in terms of national grading and the threat of further review, it is surely only a very brave university that would present any of its courses as having no learning outcomes, no references to agreed academic levels and subject benchmark statements, and no graduate skills. If inspection for some simply means paying the appropriate lip service there is a precedent in referring to this as a form of political correctness, but we should also consider upon what basis the state feels justified in requiring that colleges and universities not just submit to outside forms of inspection, but also to particular educational aims. In this context, having 'faith in the soul of learning' (Furedi 2004d) is not just about what an act of learning is, and who has the right to determine it, but also what the evidence base is for such decisions.

The skills revolution

The issue of the evidence base is particularly pertinent to the gradual envelop-ment of post-16 education by the notion of 'skill'. Throughout the 1980s and 1990s one might have been forgiven for thinking that the notion of 'competence' was set to become the term by which all educational encounters would eventually be defined. Despite the enormous efforts of the then director of the National Council for Vocational Qualifications (NCVQ) to mastermind this revolution the term has remained largely within the confines of NVQs (Jessup 1991). Dogged by claims that it is based on a flawed theory of learning; that the assess-ment regime unduly ignores the question of reliability; and that it has been the means by which young people have been contained rather than liberated by education (Bates et al. 1984; Bailey 1984; Hyland 1994; Wolf 1995), this form of 'outcome' model for post-16 education has not actually turned out to be the main means by which the curriculum would be 'vocationalised'. Instead, the allied 'outcome' term 'skill' has been rediscovered for this purpose. And, rather than concentrating on preparing people to enter particular occupational fields, and enhance their abilities within them, vocational preparedness has increasingly become seen as a more general form of 'employability'.

Since the turn of the century almost every government document aimed at post-16 education has been dominated by the notion of 'skill', and the idea that the country's future success is principally connected with plugging skills gaps (e.g. DfES 2002; DfES 2003a, 2003b; Foster 2005; Leitch 2006). The effect of being bathed in this rhetoric is that the term has become a mantra, and one which has replaced the popular Blair sound bite 'Education, Education, Education' with 'Skills, Skills, Skills', and the term has come under critical academic scrutiny precisely for these reasons (Hyland 2001; Williams 2005). The notion of key skills has certainly been a troublesome term (Hodgson *et al.* 2001), not helped perhaps by an ongoing change in the use of allied terms, for instance from core skills to basic skills, and from transferable skills to key skills. The instigators of the terms in each case were always at pains to carefully delineate the various meanings, and although some people might have been confused by the difference between, for example, a basic skill and a key skill, the delineations usually had a clear rationale. Thus, basic skills came to be associated mainly with numeracy and literacy skills, whereas key skills came to be associated with a much broader, and more advanced, range of communication skills. Both terms have themselves been more recently supplanted by what, for many, might be taken as a mere euphemistic transformation of basic skills into 'skills for life', and, in some universities, key skills into 'graduate skills'. In the case of the latter, this might be taken as a form of appeasement for recalcitrant academics. Taken together, the changes might be seen as a simple form of political correctness, in the form of 'verbal hygiene' (Cameron 1995). But there is a much broader question at stake concerning the validity of seeing educational encounters in terms of skills in the first place, no matter how they are defined, delineated, or labelled.

In the commissioned 'Review of Skills', Leitch reports on the challenges that the UK economy will face in the years running up to 2020 (Leitch 2006). Almost all these are couched in terms of the need for more 'skills'. However, in a 150-page document it is very hard to find any references to what exactly are the skills that one acquires in further and higher education that could be deemed so necessary to the economy's success. Without a sound epistemological grounding one might just as well say that the economy will do well if everybody works really hard over the next ten years. On two counts this criticism is unfair, because Leitch does offer a definition of skill at the beginning of the document and, further on, he has a sound rationale concerning *basic* skills. Unfortunately the general definition has a rather tautologous implication because it says that the most obvious measure of the degree of success in achieving a high skill economy is having lots of highly qualified people: 'The most common measures of skills are qualifications' (Leitch 2006: 11). This notion can only have any significant educational meaning if it is unequivocally clear that all qualifications are, in fact, collections of skills. If this *is* the case then one might just as well say 'highly qualified' whenever one wants to say 'highly skilled', and thus the argument is merely a rhetorical one. The case for more effort on the achievement of basic skills is more soundly argued, but beyond this it is difficult to see why a more explicit understanding of 'skill' in further and higher education, in general, is what is going to make the key difference in terms of the economy's success.

The main intention here is not to undermine the validity of arguing for a successful British economy, but to question the basis for trying to fashion a particular set of purposes for post-16 education without reference to sound educational arguments. This is a form of political correctness to the extent that it encourages sceptics to see the case as, literally, 'politically correct', that is, it is in keeping with a correct understanding of an agreed political, or ideological, agenda, and it is defended on the grounds that one has the power to impose it. And, once again the parallel with arguments in US higher education in the late 1980s and early 1990s is a strong one, but again, whereas authors like Cheney, Bennett, and D'Souza were arguing that this had been perpetrated by an *au courant* made up of the intellectual left, we see in Britain that the accusation might be similarly levied, this time at agents of the state. It is politically correct precisely to the extent that one feels that more soundly argued principles are being undermined; that it is zealously pursued by its believers; and one has little option but to comply.

Similarly, the concurrently produced Foster Review follows a similar line in outlining the need for further education to concentrate the core of its activities on producing a skilled workforce. The report is careful in outlining a number of traditions in further education, which are summarized as:

building vocational skills – providing a range of courses and qualifications to prepare learners for employment and upskilling those in the workforce.

promoting social inclusion and advancement – delivering courses that meet learners' personal aspirations or promote social integration.

achieving academic progress – including GCSE and A-level work, often 'second chance' and providing vocational, as well as academic, pathways to HE.

(Foster 2005: para. 47)

However, in response to stakeholders who have argued that FE has suffered from a lack of focus the report concludes that FE would be best advised to see its role as mainly an economic one. The report rests some of its support for this conclusion on the consultative work of Perry, who quotes evidence from Ainley and Bailey, Hughes, and previous work from himself (http://www.dfes.gov.uk/furthereducation/index.cfm?fuseaction=content.view&CategoryID=20&ContentID=19; accessed 28 January 2008). Unfortunately the quotation from Ainley and Bailey lends support only to the view that FE suffers from lack of focus. It does not follow directly from this that the focus should be an economic one. Indeed, it could be argued that if perception is the problem, then this might be solved by a marketing exercise in promoting the desirability of seeing FE as a broad church. Furthermore, in the light of Ainley's previous work on the relationship between social class and educational qualifications it would surely be incumbent to say something more here about the status of skills in this context (Ainley 1993). The point here is not to argue that FE should have a different focus from the one provided in the report, only that whatever view is promoted it is likely to be normatively based. Indeed, the position paper produced by Hughes in support of the economic solution is more of an impassioned plea for FE rather than an objective assessment. It is persuasively argued, but those who oppose an economic mission for FE will surely view the evidence as support for an ideological position, and thus question the validity of its evidence base. And it is precisely in such contexts that a key ingredient in a politically correct scenario is introduced. If this ideological position is then subsequently endorsed by the state, and echoed in a large range of further documentation and reports, the second key ingredient, of its correctness, is now in place. If this is subsequently monitored such that those working in the sector are steered to correct interpretations, the final ingredient would then also be in place.

It might be argued that this scenario takes the notion of political correctness to its breaking point, because we would now be able to see PC in almost every aspect of decision-making. At one level this is itself instructive because it helps draw attention away from *what* is being argued to be politically correct towards *how* things can become politically correct. But also, it demands a careful consideration of the exact nature of the evidence base for a political decision, and how a critical mass of similar evidence might be able to produce 'a mantra', and one which has the effect that 'distant voices of dissent' cannot then be foregrounded. In the same way that a moral panic is able to create a climate for a legitimate need to clamp down on certain behaviours, we can see how a critical mass of like-minded 'evidence' (*sic*) is similarly able to speed up a state-sponsored exercise in social engineering, and where, ultimately, it becomes extremely difficult to question its desirability without appearing hopelessly ill-informed.

Open access all college areas?

Arguably the biggest and most long-standing exercise in social engineering in post-16 education has been to raise the participation rate systematically. This has been more revolutionary than evolutionary, particularly with regard to access to universities; in one generation the university system has moved from being a long-standing elite one to a mass participation one. With such a short gestation it is inevitable that the revolution should bear significant birth-marks and the system might now best be described as a mass system with elite attitudes: 'Although British higher education is (quantitatively) mass, it is still (qualitatively) elite' (Scott 1995). However, the raw statistics are impressive: in thirty years the figures have risen from a participation rate of about 10 per cent to over 40 per cent, and the growth has been significantly sponsored by then Prime Minister Blair's support for a rise to a figure of 50 per cent for people between the age of 18 and 30 by 2010 (Thomas and Quinn 2007). At this point American readers might be forgiven for thinking that either British universities are now full to bursting, or there has been an enormous capital investment in the infrastructure. Evidence might be found to support both claims, but in reality the picture is complicated (Scott 1995). To a large extent the growth has been enabled by the conversion of a number of former polytechnics and colleges of higher education into universities, and a relaxation of the system by which an institution might apply for university status. Two other significant developments have been the much larger number of students who are studying part-time, living at home, and/or engaged in forms of distance learning; and a growth in the number of university qualifications which are franchised, or perhaps better, validated, such that they can be delivered in non-university settings.

The picture is also complicated by the fact that increased participation does not necessarily mean widening participation, and this reflects a long-standing concern that the variable 'social class' correlates much more strongly with all levels of educational attainment than any measure of 'intelligence' (Gorrard et al. 2006); indeed, to such an extent that it might be argued that intelligence does not cause social class standing, but vice versa. In this context, studies of social mobility throughout the last century seem to have confirmed the advice that if one wants to get on one should choose one's parents wisely (Halsey et al. 1980). The publication of the Kennedy Report (1997) also confirmed that these wider issues appear to be having a significant impact on the university population, and it is not uncommon for the THES and the press to produce stories each year to confirm that the problem of social class is somewhat endemic: 'Why I think universities need to acknowledge class as the final taboo' (Downs 2004); 'Education gap between rich and poor children has grown' (The Times, 25 July 2005). The picture in further education is much more encouraging: 'Colleges have more learners (both 16–19 and adult) who are relatively disadvantaged compared to the population as a whole and to learner populations in other educational establishment types' (Foster 2005: 93–94). That said, there is a long-running concern about whether the qualification structure itself is class-based and two-tiered (Ainley 1993; Avis 1996).

Universities and colleges routinely produce cohort-monitoring data, and are 'reviewed' on the actions they are taking to increase the participation rates of under-represented social groups on their programmes and qualifications. Indeed, it is not uncommon for academic staff to attend workshops on dealing with 'non-traditional learners', on the assumption that the learning needs of such students are likely to differ from those with more traditional forms of 'cultural capital'. Once again, it might be argued that such euphemistic labels are themselves forms of political correctness, and a veil to divert attention away from the more endemic structural problem of social class in British society, but they are also indicative of the fact that forms of affirmative action might be required in order to ensure that these students not only enter the college doors, but also stay in the buildings, and exit with the qualifications they aspire to. And, if one removes the highly charged US focus on race, the debates concerning the meritocractic credentials of students are much the same on both sides of the Atlantic. For some this prompts the charge that colleges and universities have changed their admissions criteria to such an extent that this must be evidence of a fall in standards, and hint that it is 'political correctness gone mad'.

This is clearly evident in accusations which have been levelled at 'the elite' British universities, such as Oxford, Cambridge, Bristol, and Durham. On the one hand they are accused of elitism when they do not admit a state school educated pupil who has excellent A-level results, but they are equally accused of dumbing down when they appear to have admitted a state school educated pupil above a privately educated pupil. The *cause célèbre* case for the former was Oxford University's rejection of the high achieving comprehensive school educated Laura Spence, who subsequently went on to study at Harvard; the media discussion at the time prompted *The Observer* to state that: 'All our national obsessions: class, education and elitism are represented in the experience of one shy schoolgirl' (*The Observer* 28 May 2000). For the latter, the *Daily Mail* produced a front-page headline: 'Backlash: Britain's leading schools to black universities that discriminate against the brightest pupils' (*Daily Mail* 5 March 2003). The latter case prompted one journalist to comment: 'Has Bristol become the most politically correct university in the country?' (Hodges 2003). In this climate it was difficult to resist the conclusion that it was merely party political point scoring, but the underlying ideological positions are significant. They mirror exactly the concerns of those in the US who have questioned the validity of the test scores that predict academic success (see Chapter 6). Here, not only was it questioned whether certain students would be able to command the resources to be successful, but there was also a deeper question about a lack of confidence in the reliability and validity of testing and screening for ability. This is the conclusion of Thomas and Quinn in their survey of *First Generation Entry into Higher Education*:

> The transformative approach to widening participation recognizes the ways in which higher education privileges and prioritizes the values and *modus operandi* of middle class students over students from under-represented and non-traditional backgrounds.
>
> (Thomas and Quinn 2007: 127)

They differentiate between 'academic', 'utilitarian', and 'transformative' models for higher education access, or what in more traditional political terms might be seen as conservative, liberal, or radical approaches, and raise the question as to whether we should be more interested in fitting the students to the university or the university to the students. They favour the latter, which returns us not just to underpinning political ideologies but also to ask whether the classical humanist model of the university with its emphasis on the cognitive and the strictly academic is the most appropriate aim for a university. Clearly this draws on the implications of Bourdieu's notion of 'cultural capital' (Bourdieu and Passeron 1977), and we can see that it mirrors exactly the concerns that authors like Bloom and D'Souza had in the US about designing a politically correct university, and one which undermines its most fundamental *modus operandi.*

However, more attention in Britain has gone into seeking to act on potential student aspirations and motivations, and on ensuring that the admissions policies themselves are not seen as a barrier to access, and several research reports indicate a large degree of success for universities in reaching out to potential students, most commonly through summer schools, forms of student mentoring, and visits to schools and colleges (see the Higher Education Empirical Research (HEER): http://heerd.open.ac.uk/; accessed 28 January 2008). Much of the effort has been directed via Aim Higher (http://www. hefce.ac.uk/widen/aimhigh/; accessed 26 January 2008), and a comprehensive review of university admissions undertaken by the Higher Education Funding Council for England (HEFCE), summarized under the acronym PQA (post-qualification admissions) (http://www.admissions-review.org.uk/; accessed 26 January 2008). The PQA review concluded that universities should seek to modify their systems of admissions in the period 2006–2012 in favour of enhancing the information that students can access in order to make a confident application; ensuring that students can make an accurate prediction of the financial support they are likely to receive; asking universities to provide reliable feedback where students fail to achieve a place; and, most importantly, giving students a chance to reconsider their applications in the light of their actual qualification grades, as opposed to those they were predicted to achieve (Wilson 2005; Schwartz 2006). The HEFCE also uses a funding carrot for widening participation which rewards universities for the number of students they recruit from socially disadvantaged areas of the country (http://www.hefce.ac.uk/ widen/fund/; accessed 26 January 2008). This includes funding formulae for the numbers of students entering university; further formulae based on a risk weighting of their likely early departure; and a further formula for rewarding universities for recruiting 'disabled' students.

In a direct mirroring of the arguments in the US about affirmative action, the very existence of such measures, and the accompanying financial inducements, is enough for some to claim that this is an unacceptable form of dumbing down, for how could universities really be choosing the most able students in such a climate? This was reflected in the brouhaha that surrounded press reports on Bristol University in 2003, and which prompted the conservative columnist Simon Heffer to tell readers 'Why we middle classes have had enough' (*Daily*

Mail, 5 March 2003:12). However, Bristol University has a transparent and comprehensive admissions policy, and it makes explicit what many people understand to be behind all university admissions systems (http://www.bristol. ac.uk/university/governance/policies/admissions-policy.html; accessed 12 February 2008), that is an exercise in judgement as to which candidates for admission would be most likely to benefit from their chosen degree course. Unsurprisingly, predicted and actual qualification grades, particularly in the gold standard A-level qualifications, remain crucially significant, but in reality these are always one criterion amongst many, including factors which might bear on a candidate obtaining an actual grade below what might, *ceteris paribus,* have been expected, and evidence that candidates have battled in some way in the face of adversity. Put in this light the accusation that universities like Bristol have suddenly become 'politically correct' is just a derogatory veil to distort what has been common practice for years.

If anything is new in admissions criteria it is the adoption of a more explicit recognition of the ways in which all universities may have, perhaps inadvertently, discriminated against those candidates who have no tradition of applying to university from within their family, or class, backgrounds. Here the widening participation strategy for Britain can be viewed simply as an attempt to target those individuals and groups who have the potential to succeed but either are not presenting themselves to the admissions processes, particularly of elite universities, or would benefit from some different criteria being taken into consideration during the admissions process. For example, it is not uncommon now for universities to make judgements of a particular candidate's potential against his or her school's overall performance. Thus, a candidate with predicted A-level grades well above the average for their school might be weighted above another candidate whose predicted grades were the same, but which were below the average for their school. It is here where we find ourselves once more at the heart of debates about political correctness, and for two important reasons. First, there is the problem that the widening of the admissions net will be perceived as an unwarranted politicization of the objectivity of academic tests of ability, and this must be a slippery slope towards a whole host of new criteria being added on a regular basis. This argument was clearly and forcefully stated by D'Souza in the US (D'Souza 1992). Second, there is the question of whether we would do better spending our attention and money to ensure that all potential candidates are provided with the maximum opportunities to do well in the existing standardized tests. And this argument was most forcefully put in the US by Searle (1993).

In this light there is a certain inevitability about widening participation strategies being tarred with a derogatory PC brush. But, once again in a direct mirroring of the arguments about affirmative action in the US, many of the deeper questions at stake are epistemological and ideological. For example many people might question whether Britain needs 50 per cent of its population to hold a degree on purely economic grounds, but in some cases this might hide a more deep-seated Platonic view that only a small number of people in any generation are, in reality, able to cope with the rigours of high-level study, and thus it is inevitable that the university curriculum would need to be dumbed down to accommodate the masses. Furthermore, if one is able to question both the validity of the knowledge contained in measures of ability and the reliability of its measurement it is inevitable that this will lead to a wholesale politicization not just of admissions policies, but also of the nature of the knowledge that one is exposed to within the university. Naturally this is simply too much to bear particularly for those who hold dearly to the Enlightenment project of discovery and progress of truth, and believe in the classical humanist aim for the university. This might also explain why conservative authors like Bloom in the US and radical authors like Furedi in Britain have a lot in common: 'the expansion of higher education will only lead to a fall in standards if widening participation is driven by concerns that have little to do with the promotion of the ideals of the university' (Furedi 2004a: 99). This quote beautifully encapsulates the idea that a classical humanist conception of the university is beyond a mere idea. And once this elevation is established it is easy to see why alternatives might be viewed as politically correct (see Chapter 2).

Academies of well-being

In Chapter 8 the notion of 'the diminished self' was used to summarize the idea that post-16 education far from offering a traditional liberal and liberating educational experience, by holding a diminished view of individual capabilities, was actually containing individuals in a state of vulnerability and dependency. The echo with much US–based literature is an obvious one, both within writings on multiculturalism and affirmative action, and more broadly in the work of Bloom, D'Souza, and Sykes (see Chapter 2). The issue might also be couched with reference to the three traditional broad curriculum models or aims for education, namely whether it is largely centred on knowledge and content; on personal self-development and process; or on vocational preparation and outcomes. These ideologies are important because they draw attention to the fact that there is a general concern amongst these authors that post-16 education has been slowly retreating from the first ideology in order to embrace not just the third, but crucially the second model. This can be viewed as a form of political correctness if two conditions are met: first, the idea that post-16 education has in the past rested on a foundation of the pursuit of disinterested knowledge or truth; and second, that the other two curriculum aims have been used in an ideological battle to hijack the first one. Thus if the QAA is perceived as the British Antichrist, it is not just because it administers the surveillance of academics, but also because it could be blamed for being instrumental in steering the British university curriculum away from the first aim towards the other two.

If Blair's 'Education, Education, Education' sound bite has any substance, it is surely that education is perceived as being the main means to ensure not just a productive society but also a just one. In a reversal of the sociologist Bernstein's original claim that education cannot compensate for society (Bernstein 1970), Blair, using Third Way rhetoric claimed that it can. A strong echo of this can be found in the Kennedy Report (1997) where education is seen as a weapon against poverty. For some on the left in both the US and Britain this is sufficient enough for a claim that it is 'political correctness gone mad' because it substitutes the need for a real and substantial overhaul of the economic and social infrastructure with a call instead for individuals to motivate themselves to aspire to succeed by using the education system. Thus, from both a curriculum perspective and a wider political perspective, these engineering projects can be demonstrated to have a resonance with wider debates about political correctness. But in the context of the specific issues raised in this chapter there is also a difficult question to answer concerning how much these transformations in the post-16 educational landscape are in fact exogenously determined, and then imposed.

An interesting case in point is the recommendations of the Tomlinson Report (1996), which looked at the ways in which further education might become more inclusive with respect to students with learning difficulties and disabilities:

> Put simply, we want to avoid a viewpoint which locates the difficulty or deficit with the student and focuses instead on the capacity of the educational institution to understand and respond to the individual learner's requirement.
>
> (Tomlinson 1996: 4)

Here we see an exhortation to institutions – which was being echoed in broader sociological literature at the time – that disability is a social construct, and we should view college environments as either 'abling' or 'disabling'; that is, individuals should not be viewed as disabled, in themselves, but that the environments in which they find themselves can be *disabling* (Barton 1996), and, in consequence, it is the college's responsibility to ensure that it is able to accommodate individuals, not the individual's responsibility. Naturally, this is dangerously close to a PC scenario, and one for which an institution is likely to be held up for ridicule, particularly if it then enables students to demonstrate their knowledge and understanding through means of their own choosing rather than by what is presented to them in a prescribed course outline. But what is not at all clear is whether the Tomlinson Report was simply reflecting an increasingly generally held view, or whether it was being imposed as a form of state-sponsored dictate. In this context it is not at all clear that the increasingly popular allied notion that colleges and universities should move away from assessment *of* learning towards assessment *for* learning is not of the academy's own making. However, just as one person might see consensus while another sees conspiracy, it is difficult to resolve these matters easily. Certainly, authoritative books on educational innovation do not give the *impression* at all that they are paying lip service to a state-sponsored agenda (e.g. Laurillard 2001; Bryan and Clegg 2006), and popular websites like the US-based Center for Applied Special Technology are filled with references to the academy's own established theories of learning (http://www.cast.org/; accessed 28 January 2008). The Tomlinson Report also has a loud echo in the work of Thomas and Quinn (2007) where their default position was also one of ensuring that colleges and universities do the accommodating, not the student.

A pertinent example of the issues this raises is the mixed reception that the so-called 'therapeutic turn' in post-16 education has received. Whereas authors such as Ecclestone, Hayes, and Furedi (individually, and collectively) have been vociferous in their castigation of the emphasis on self-esteem and emotional well-being, others such as McGivney and Hyland have argued that the criticisms are misplaced. For example in a published dialogue between them, McGivney challenges Ecclestone's assertion that an emphasis on self-esteem in education can be disempowering by arguing the exact opposite (McGivney 2005). Similarly, Hyland challenges Hayes's claim that there has been a distinct therapeutic turn in post-16 education by arguing that the sector is, in reality, 'grossly deficient' in this area (Hyland 2005: 17), and that if there had been such a turn it 'pales into insignificance alongside the damage wreaked by CBET and the behaviouristic outcomes movement' (Hyland 2006: 302). On a broader level there is also the question of whether a rather promiscuous use of some psychoanalytic ideas in wider cultural analysis is bound to annoy those who would rather they stayed restricted to more obviously clinical contexts. This also leaves unargued the deeper question as to whether psychoanalysis, as a discipline, is itself a rather conservative one, or a highly subversive one, and one steeped in questions of epistemology (Young 1994). In this context it is unfortunate that Furedi does not include any detailed discussion of the broader intellectual context of key Freudian concepts in his critique of 'therapy culture' (Furedi 2004b).

These criticisms aside, the arguments of Ecclestone, Hayes, and Furedi make much more sense when couched in more overtly political terms, and it is here where previous debates about PC in the US can be instructive. Whereas authors like Bloom, D'Souza, and Sykes were able to alert Americans to the dire consequences of shifting higher education away from its mooring in a cognitive theory of learning and a classical humanist conception of curriculum ideology, others were able to defend the shift on the grounds that the Bloom–D'Souza–Sykes conceptions were, in reality, simply an attempt to resurrect an increasingly discredited epistemology which privileged male knowledge and forms of communication (Gilligan 1982), and largely ignored other forms of intelligence (Gardner 1993; Goleman 1995), and a long-established tradition of education as a form of self-development (Rogers and Freiberg 1994). In Britain, Ecclestone, Hayes, and Furedi might be argued to be similarly reactionary. But the crucial difference is in the way the three British authors argue their case from a distantly leftist position, unlike the three key American authors who write from distinctly conservative positions.

This can be seen most starkly where the British authors make constant references to the way in which the therapeutic turn is integral to the embedding of a broader political culture which seeks to orient individuals successfully around their existing circumstances, rather than offering opportunities with true liberatory potential. This has further obvious connections with wider cultural and structural theories of human agency, and the extent to which Third Way politics in the UK is, in reality, no more than a concerted attempt to divert attention away from the need to transform the material circumstances, and infrastructure, of everyday life. As we have already seen, the confusion in underlying political ideology is not helped by Furedi's references to human agency which give the distinct impression that he is supporting a conservative call to roll back the state, and have individuals take full personal responsibility for their lives. However, dig below the surface of this reading and it becomes clear that his political vision is not one of atomistic individuals fending for themselves, but is a search for a re-energized form of community (Furedi 2005a). In terms of political correctness there is an obvious connection with this discussion and the call for higher education to re-emphasize its classical humanistic roots as we saw in Chapter 2. Furthermore, claiming that post-16 education has increasingly become a therapeutic space can be viewed as a re-statement of a double-edged political critique for those on the left who like to see their politics couched in more radical terms. For, helping individuals to reorient themselves to the reality of their existing circumstances acts to help contain rather than liberate, and to limit horizons rather than widen them. And this has much in common with Marxist critiques throughout the 1980s of the state's intentions behind its vocational reforms of education at that time (Bates *et al.* 1984). Aside from Hyland's criticism that there is little empirical evidence of a therapeutic turn, he would surely recognize the resonance here given his long-standing critiques of CBET in the UK (Hyland 1994).

It is in this context that these issues can be related to the rest of the arguments in this chapter. On initial inspection it is not at all clear that the evidence of a therapeutic turn is an exercise in social engineering, at least not one coming from the state. There is much more evidence that the terms of the debate have been developed from within the academy itself. For this reason there should perhaps be no surprise that the notion of a therapy culture, or therapeutic turn, with its concomitant emphasis in classrooms on self-esteem, should have caused much indignation from other academics. In the other cases discussed in this chapter it was much clearer that the concepts and notions were being brought *to* the educational community. Hayes might retort that there is still political correctness *within* the academy, from those who have abandoned more traditional forms of politics in favour of a misguided form of liberalism (see

Chapter 11), and Furedi might still bemoan the fact that too many educators have embraced the notion that education should be a place for safe and comfortable forms of ego massaging (Furedi 2004a). It remains a complicated question as to the exact relationship between the academy's advocates, state sponsorship, and forms of acquiescence and subversion. At one point Furedi is very clear who is the real culprit: 'What is worrying is not the role of the political class so much as the compliance of the world of art and education with a philistine social engineering agenda' (Furedi 2004: 156). But clearly Ecclestone *et al.* do want a more overt connection with the activities of the state: 'we have explored ways in which the state requires new ways to legitimise its framing of social and individual problems' (Ecclestone *et al.* 2005: 195).

For those who would agree with them it would naturally follow that this might be viewed as a form of PC, both from the perspective of the correctness of the rhetoric, and the false sincerity with which educators may feel they have to endorse it. This broader question returns us to a theme that can be seen throughout much of Ecclestone's earlier work referred to in the previous two chapters (Ecclestone 1995; Coffield *et al.* 2004), and particularly in the learning styles research, where the authors imply that the concept is politically convenient 'because it shifts the responsibility for enhancing the quality of learning *from* management *to* the individual learning styles of teachers and learners' (Coffield *et al.* 2004: 135). And thus, the message of much left-leaning literature is confirmed, that it suits the state to see individuals seeking to reorient themselves to existing social circumstances, rather than providing them with real material opportunities to move 'beyond the present and the particular' (Bailey 1984; Bates *et al.* 1984; Ainley 1993; McDonald 1997).

Conclusion

Given the general absence of the term political correctness in debates about the changing roles, aims, and purposes of post-16 education in Britain it is easy to draw the conclusion that it has been a largely American preoccupation. But if one looks more carefully at the *form* that many PC scenarios have taken in the US we can see that this conclusion is perhaps a little premature. Put simply, in focusing on the way in which the state in Britain has sought to call to account teachers and academics, and also how it has sought to engineer a reorientation of educational aims, these arguments can be used to demonstrate that we should not always focus on the *content* of what is said to be politically correct – be it freedom of speech, multiculturalism, or affirmative action – but rather the *form* of the argument. Principally, the key ingredient in a politically correct scenario is ideological imposition, followed by a mixture of slavish or subversive reaction. And this has much more in keeping with a Stalinist interpretation of political correctness. This is also a more literal interpretation because in the case of Britain 'the party line' is very often The Party line.

These arguments are considerably weakened by the extent to which one views the reorientation of educational aims as having been engineered largely by the academy itself, in which case the state might be viewed as simply endorsing a message which already has a sound educational and epistemological foundation. If this is true the case for post-16 education having become increasingly politically correct would have to rest on modified grounds. First, that those who believe in the reorientation of educational aims are resorting to the kinds of intimidatory practices that many conservative thinkers in the US had previously claimed were being perpetrated by the *au courant* of left-wing intellectuals in the US academy (see Chapter 2). And, indeed, in the following empirical chapter this is exactly the charge that Hayes levels at many in the British academy. Second, a re-emphasis of the argument that evidence for the validity of the reorientation away from a classical humanist model for the curriculum is weak, and not just from official state sources, but, more importantly, from within the academy itself (Ecclestone *et al.* 2005).

As we saw in the previous chapter this is fundamentally a question about believers and non-believers and a battle about the validity of the knowledge claims which are being made. The most vociferous non-believers appear to be those who are most concerned about the way in which educational aims have been systematically hijacked by ill-conceived alternatives. As we saw in the US, much of this case rests on the belief that a classical humanist, or liberal conception of educational aims is not only the most valid, but is also a strong foundation from which to defend an increasingly attenuated academy. But this case is severely weakened by voices in the academy who would wish to embrace a broader set of aims. In which case the classical humanist model of education must rest its case more firmly on the fact that it is more likely to produce the kind of critical citizenry that everyone could agree on – which, of course, was Newman's original aim. In this context the charge of political correctness has meaning when one rejects the imposition of an *unwarranted orthodoxy*, and particularly where that orthodoxy can be demonstrated to undermine a more solidly based one. And this is always a question not just of what an educational establishment is for, but also who has the most right to determine it, and what is the evidence base for it? In which case a traditional liberal conception of education might still be viewed as the best preparation for employability, if people could be persuaded that the most 'transferable skill' (*sic*) of all is the one which conceives of learning as an act of mind (Abbs 1994). If this is the case the question then becomes not so much one of changing the aims of the university but seeking the means such that everyone has an equal chance to experience education as something which moves them 'beyond the present and the particular' (Bailey 1984). That Americans are much quicker to refer to policies and strategies aimed at alternative forms of social engineering as 'political correctness' does not mean that Britain is not engaged in similar battles, simply that the term itself is rarely invoked beyond its most obvious use in the tabloid press.

11

Talking about political correctness
British conversations about political correctness and post-16 education

Introduction

As in the case of Chapter 7 this chapter is also almost entirely empirically based. It is the result of eight semi-structured interviews with British-based academics, administrators, and leaders in post-16 education. The academics were chosen because they are informed about issues relating to political correctness. This was to try to ensure that each interview would take the form more of a dialogue and conversation, rather than an artificially contrived set of responses on matters which were of little interest to the interviewee. As with the American interviews, I made no attempt to try to produce a particular quota of social groups in the interviewees. Their social identity make-up was taken as an accidental antecedent of either their knowledge or role, and agreement to take part. The interviews took place between November 2006 and July 2007 throughout England.

The same headline questions were used in the British interviews as in the American ones: (1) How would you define political correctness? (2) How do you feel about questions of freedom of speech? (3) How do you feel about aspects of multiculturalism? (4) How do you feel about forms of affirmative action? In each case the subsequent conversation moved in spontaneous fashion. The terms 'freedom of speech', 'multiculturalism', and 'affirmative action' were interpreted freely by the interviewees, and no attempt was made on my part to ensure that usage of the terms could be compared with American usage. This is in keeping with the general aim of both sets of interviews, that they are *literally about* political correctness, that is what the term and its allied causes invoke and resonate with for these individuals, rather than an attempt to measure how much political correctness there is in post-16 education, whether in the US or the UK.

The following is a list of those individuals who took part in the interviews, followed by the post they held at the time of the interview:

- **Kathryn Ecclestone**, Reader in Assessment for Lifelong Learning at Nottingham University, and author of *Learner Autonomy in Post-16 Education* (2002).
- **James Tooley**, Professor of Education Policy at Newcastle University, and author of *Reclaiming Education* (2005).

- **Dennis Hayes**, Head of the Centre for Professional Learning at Canterbury Christ Church University, joint president of the University and College Union, and co-author of *The McDonaldization of Higher Education* (2002).
- **Frank Furedi**, Professor of Sociology at the University of Kent, and author of *Culture of Fear* (1997).
- **Tony Booth**, Professor of Inclusive and International Education at Canterbury Christ Church University, and co-author of *Developing Inclusive Teacher Education* (2003).
- **Irfaan Arif**, Equality and Diversity Manager at the University of Kent.
- **Dame Ruth Silver**, Principal of Lewisham College, London.
- **Angela Milln**, Director of Student Recruitment, Access and Admissions at the University of Bristol.

Talking about the definition of political correctness

Each interview began with a straightforward question about how the term might be defined and/or with what does it resonate, and what are its connotations. Both Ecclestone and Furedi outlined the territory it covers. Political correctness is:

> usually associated with notions of social justice and not being persecutory, or discriminatory, or causing offence. There are political reasons for correctly using terminology and ways of speaking, or ways of phrasing things that are sensitive to particular groups. So it is kind of group-based reason. And that the groups that one is sensitive to are, in left-wing terms, groups that we would see as either oppressed or discriminated against. The groups that would come to mind would be women, black people, people with disabilities and even here I can feel myself starting to trip over words, in case there are new words that I have missed out and so on.
>
> (Ecclestone, 26 October 2006)

> Some of the important features are the idea that you mustn't offend people; the thought that you must recognize people and value them for what they are; for not insisting on any particular perspective being true. And I think in general, it's actually a very inflexible way of finding an alternative to a conventional morality.
>
> (Furedi, 30 April 2007)

Hayes charted how he thought the term's usage has changed:

> What *instantly* comes to mind is that people very rarely say it. A. A. Gill, in *The Angry Island*, makes a point that no one ever announces, or stands up, and says 'I am politically correct.' It is usually used in the negative: 'That's PC, that's PC gone mad.' It often refers to enforced uses of language in speech codes. So when people use it, I would always think they

were going to point out some absurdity or some prescription of using a certain language. But I think there is a slight shift in the meaning of it. Literally, it means it is the correct thing to do, and so literally it means *politically* correct. I think the trouble is now people *say* it, and I actually caught myself talking to a group of students the other week, saying: 'How can I put this in a politically correct way.' But it is partly you become sensitive to how to put things but I think the term has shifted now to mean something like it always meant: it is just *politically* incorrect to use that phrase. So in an open sense political, and I suppose that links to the depoliticization in our times; there are no contested ideas; it is just assumed that it is the right thing to do, so you do it. I think there is that shift.

(Hayes, 28 April 2007)

Later in the interview Hayes went on to discuss how he thought political correctness had filled a political vacuum, but on the subject of its definition he added the following:

If you think of Islamophobia and holocaust denial; if you use these phrases, you are almost ill, so there has been a sort of medicalization of political differences really. So, no normal, sane person – I'm not allowed to say such things – only a crazy person, or mental health service user, would be racist or have those ideas. But if you wanted my sound bite, my take on what it means, a dictionary definition: 'Don't speak about this; these are things we must not say – we must not think, we mustn't speak about it.' I always think political correctness means the imposition of silence.

(Hayes, 28 April 2007)

It is as if, somehow, we have all agreed that something is correct, and thus to disagree with it is to expose oneself as occupying an absurd position. This theme was continued by Tooley, who was animated about how the term was able to capture a certain quality of orthodoxy in academic communities:

Political correctness is about the community outlawing certain ways of expressing yourself or certain areas of interest. It most definitely has negative connotations. To me it is wholly negative. I cannot think of a positive instance of political correctness.

(Tooley, 9 January 2007)

The negative connotations were also to the fore in the other interviews, where each person highlighted how unhelpful the term was in enabling people to undertake their work – be it strictly academic, or, more generally, professional:

I think of it as a term that is used to try and avoid discussions – not just about the way in which we use language to devalue and discriminate

against people – but to avoid discussions of discriminations. That is how
I tend to see it.

(Booth, 3 May 2007)

'Oh, I can't talk in this particular way because one group of people might
read it wrongly or might think that I am in some way inferring that they
are a particular way because they belong to a particular group.' I guess it's
a sort of stereotyping, and not wanting to react to people because of
stereotyping.

(Milln, 10 July 2007)

One thing I hear more than anything else is: 'This is political correctness
gone mad' so it's already got a negative attitude towards it. So I try not to
use it in my day-to-day role, because sometimes people tend to use that
and, for example, give a negative perspective to equality and diversity, and,
kind of, try and mask it with 'political correctness gone mad'. So I try not
to use the word at all; it's got no meaning behind it. It's just like a masking
term to cover up what the deeper issues are. People might just be saying
it to cover their backs in certain instances: 'Yes, we've done what we're
supposed to do; this is it; this is how we are supposed to say it; we are not
doing anything wrong.' I try to stay clear of it as much as possible.

(Arif, 2 July 2007)

It always flags to me some inauthenticity, because political correctness is
really saying people are behaving the way that keeps them out of trouble,
rather than behaving from a value system, or an ideology, or a philosophy.
It is people covering their backs; it is slightly sneering in its connotations
and context.

(Silver, 2 July 2007)

Arif's use of 'masking' is instructive, for in many of the narratives that were to
follow there was a distinct sense that the term political correctness was often
used in a deliberately, and provocatively, negative way to avoid important
discussions about discrimination, and more fundamental educational values, as
if the term might be used to tar and discredit the validity of those discussions.
In which case, although all the interviewees implied that the term had, largely,
negative connotations, these were interpreted differently. For some the causes
with which it is associated were questionable, whereas for others the causes were
valid, it is just the term itself which is questionable.

Talking about freedom of speech

Taken together there were three main themes which emerged from the transcripts. First, the question of *orthodoxies* and the related questions of deference,
perniciousness, and managerialism. Second, the question of *professional realities*,

and allied discussions of dealing with metaphorical smokescreens, risk taking, and the complicated nature of human communication. And, third, the question of the shifting nature of political debate, and whether political correctness was a *poor substitute* for a more effective form of politics.

On the question of orthodoxy Ecclestone nicely captured the double-edged quality of feeling the need to be deferential at the same time as feeling the need to be rebellious:

> I think if the notion had been around in the 70s when I was very politically motivated, and feministy kind of inspired, I would have completely accepted the whole idea of it. I would have been picking people up for language, I would have been doing all of that. So I think what is quite interesting is how one's views of it has changed as the decades have gone on and now when people say things to me like 'you can't say that' or 'that isn't the right term' I get this really rebellious thing and say 'I can say exactly what I like and if it causes you offence I am sorry but I am still going to say it'. So I think my attitude has changed, but having said that, when I am teaching and people pick me up on something I usually feel guilty so then I do defer to it. If somebody said to me: 'You can't say – which is the latest ridiculous thing – brain storming.' That is ridiculous. Even epileptic people haven't said that it is offensive and yet I would be so guilty about it that I would stop and defer to it.
>
> (Ecclestone, 26 October 2006)

Hayes developed his argument that forms of political correctness have changed, and with that new, and intolerant, orthodoxies have emerged:

> There are two new forms of political correctness, which is emotional correctness, which is feeling the right thing and its sharing your emotions, and environmental correctness, which is the new *political* form of political correctness which is *much* less resisted. I mean there are motions playing on union conferences and policies in almost every university – the greening of the university. The whole issue about whether you can challenge environmentalism. So it is not just the sexism. So I suppose you could say that political correctness relates to an old set of politics whereas the new correctness is environmental correctness; it's almost a new religion. Remember the Royal Society have a sort of papal bull against climate change denial; you cannot deny that global warming is happening, or the need to recycle.
>
> (Hayes, 28 April 2007)

Tooley articulated the pernicious nature of academic orthodoxy, and how it operates within the confines of traditional academic conventions:

> Now whether it [freedom of speech] is being eroded, that is obviously a judgement developed over time. I honestly don't know whether that is the

case or not, but academic freedom, freedom of expression is not under
threat, if you like – no, it doesn't *exist* in British universities. Let's say that.
There is a big problem. I am not saying it has got worse or better. I have
been in academia since, sort of, 1990 and over that time I have been aware
that as an individual I cannot say certain things. I got two articles in 1992
published. From then on for a few years it was incredibly difficult to get
articles published, once I had, sort of, stated I was neo-liberal, pro market
education. I knew the people who were refereeing my articles and I knew
they were rejecting them on ideological grounds. This was not the sort of
thing that one could put in a journal for philosophy education. Although
I believe to this day those articles were of a high standard.

(Tooley, 9 January 2007)

Tooley went on to argue that such orthodoxies are endemic in organizational
life, and extremely difficult to resist:

'Get your professorship first and then you can say what you like, you
know, but just don't rock the boat until then.' So first thing: it is about not
rocking the boat; whenever there is an orthodoxy – this cultural orthodoxy is there – you have to go by that. There is a second sort of orthodoxy
which is about getting on in your career, so actually, this person I am
thinking of, he is on that panel, the RAE [Research Assessment Exercise],
and his institution loves him; he is now on an escalator all the way up,
isn't he?

(Tooley, 9 January 2007)

He then went on to pull no punches in connecting organizational orthodoxies
with forms of state control of professional academics:

I don't like the RAE standard, the QAA [Quality Assurance Agency]
standard. I think it is partly about government bureaucracy trying to get
us. I am going to be judged by peers but in my case these peers are the sort
of people who don't like my work. I know them, and I know they don't
like my work. A perfect example of political orthodoxy.

(Tooley, 9 January 2007)

Booth made the same kind of connection, first about how people can feel
compromised by, often rather routine, organizational contexts, and second, how
what might appear as a state agenda can quickly be translated into an organizational dictate:

People say they are afraid to lose their jobs but it can't be that because it
is very hard to lose your job, but I think it is tied to people's concerns
about the kinds of reference they get for the next job or whether or not
they get an increment. It is a rather lower level pack of concerns which, in
a way, they don't want to acknowledge, but it's probably to do with that.

And there are certain issues which people feel they couldn't speak about clearly which would be to challenge policy decisions. If everybody took their freedom of speech it would probably change quite rapidly.

But there is another kind of level where the language serves to control people. So, take the notion of these words that have been the cornerstones of managerial institutions – like quality, quality management – and the ways in which the word is used but it means something entirely different. So, one of the people who had that quality control manager, whatever he got called, in the faculty, at a conference, said: 'Yes, I am the quality control manager. Quality means ensuring that what is put in place is what the government wants us to put in place.'

(Booth, 3 May 2007)

In outlining what he saw as some of the differences between higher education in the US and Britain, Furedi also gave examples of how British academics are now cajoled by certain forms of organizational policy and practice:

In most disciplines we now have disciplinary based benchmark documents, so for example in my discipline, in sociology, we have a lot of documents that tell us what a sociologist should do but they also inform the sort of language that a sociologist should use and what language is beyond the pale, for example using 'chairman' – all of the usual suspects – where you can't say anything really negative. And within academia there is a taken-for-granted assumption that there are certain words that you don't use anymore. But not only that, I think it is important to go beyond the classical forms of political correctness – on identity and culture. If you are lecturing students on controversial subjects that might offend them – like euthanasia or abortion, or homosexuality – you need to be careful how you talk. In addition to that we also have codes of conduct on bullying and, by implication, bullying language, which basically could mean any words that might be critical of somebody.

(Furedi, 30 April 2007)

When pushed on the question of bullying Furedi went on to clearly articulate how the concept of bullying in British universities could be seen as an unwarranted organizational marshalling of behaviour:

The construction of the idea of bullying is really something that describes childish, playground behaviour in an adult setting, and its formalization into unacceptable behaviour is our version of political correctness – it is our form of sexual harassment. The way I see it is that there are forms of behaviour, that in the past we would have called office politics, or we have called boorish behaviour, or clumsy behaviour, or disgusting behaviour – there are all kinds of names for it – there is a whole kind of continuum. By abstracting certain forms of relations between man and a woman, to do with the ambiguity of relationships, and codifying it, you are creating something that is very, very new. It is interesting that the problem is defined through the subjective interpretation of the victim, so if somebody thinks that they are being bullied, they are being bullied. It might not have been the intention to harass but if somebody feels that they have been harassed, they have been harassed, so it is really just a way of giving recognition to the emotional vulnerability of people who decide that they have been the victim of something. So, in that sense, sexual harassment is a cultural affectation rather than a description of a physical or pure activity.

(Furedi, 30 April 2007)

Lest it might be concluded that such marshalling is more often than not one group of employees (usually academics) being cajoled by another group of employees (usually managers), Silver gave a telling example of how a whole college might feel they are being marshalled in an unwarranted manner:

This College has been famous for a long time for its work on equality and diversity, and we were doing great things, because what we were doing was exactly what this College needed to do. So, we would look at what *Lewisham* needs and how *we* were doing, and we chose to focus and prioritize matters. Then the Learning and Skills Council, about three years ago, brought in this notion called EDIMs – equality and diversity impact measures – which were *just* ridiculous, I mean ridiculous. I lost my rag and said we are not doing these, but actually we had to do them, and so that, kind of, reframed, and actually took the warmth, and the spirit, out of some of the equality work. Now I could have said: 'Well, actually you have ruined it and that is it.' But all that did was make me all the more dedicated to not losing the warmth. This work is not about *measures*; this work is about a fair and just society. They made it managerial actually, managerial rather than professional.

So the EDIM thing for us was a question of us doing the thing rightly, rather than doing the *right* thing. So we are doing the thing *rightly*, you are ticking all the boxes. But the right thing to do was to work at producing a fair and just society where there is respect being increased, and it was a very difficult moment for us in the college, very difficult indeed.

(Silver, 2 July 2007)

This example seems to capture, precisely, that element of political correctness where one feels that one is compelled to toe a party line for, strictly, political, or even bureaucratic reasons, and thus not with a true sense of belief. The example is telling because here this is not because one doesn't believe in the cause – in this case equality and diversity – but because one *truly* does. And this is surely what Booth was previously alluding to about a whole host of words; that they can easily become hijacked for bureaucratic purposes. And in cases where the bureaucracy is oppressively hierarchical this might easily result in forms of lip-service adherence. As if to echo the point Silver went on to give a further example, and one which again highlighted how college leaders often need to fight to resist bureaucratic practice themselves, in the interests of a more fundamental sense of professional worth:

> It seems to me that there is something in the writing of the record that is a Pontius Pilate on us as human beings. I can tell you off, if you are a member of my staff, and a record isn't done properly, but the real challenge for me is to know what it is like to be you; to be so busy with the distressed young people in your class; the paper work goes to hell. For me to tolerate the humanity of that, to own up to my own experiences of being in the same position; 'I am not marking that register now because I actually I have got this distressed person here'; and then when you go to mark it you can't remember who was in the classroom and so you err on the side of justice. It is much more helpful to me to be continually reminded of the painful choice, and when filling in the record is an easy way of distancing myself from the emotionality of the encounter between the taught and the teacher, and all the contradictions and all the choices they have to make on that. So, the record is a very easy thing to tell you off about. Much harder is for me to *not* do that and say: 'Yes, I have been there, I have been there when a piece of paper didn't matter as much as the person in front of me.' So I think it is a high horse; it is a high horse that people can get off on.
>
> (Silver, 2 July 2007)

On the second theme, several people talked about the complicated nature of human communication, and alluded to how the term political correctness can be unhelpful (perhaps deliberately so) in understanding what is at stake. Arif referred to this a lot, and how it makes his role extremely difficult. In the following we can also see elements of orthodoxy at work:

> Being in the role I still don't know what is right and what is wrong to say. For me it is more of an exploration thing. If I meet somebody I tend to ask questions a lot, and see what is right; what is right for the individual rather than kind of just saying 'Okay, well, this is right to say for the whole group.' It doesn't work for everybody; everybody is different. It is usually people in my role who are more positive – consultants or trainers in equality and diversity – they tend to be up to scratch with things like what you can say and what you can't say, and will be more politically correct, but maybe only for the training session. I have been with them in a completely different environment and they have completely relaxed. It is as if it is like a big burden off their shoulders: 'Right, we can speak freely.' When I am speaking to them it is as if they are kind of holding back as to what they really want to say; I am Asian, I am talking to a white male or a

white female who is also an equality and diversity practitioner, and I feel they are kind of holding back what they really think they want to say because they think that I might be offended in some way.

(Arif, 2 July 2007)

Arif spoke several times about having the courage to take risks, and inviting people to be as honest as they can in the way they speak, and to keep lines of communication open:

> In a workshop situation people expect me to be an expert on these kinds of things and I am not. I am just as kind of curious and as new to these kinds of things as everyone else. I try and give people the approach of being in there and asking people questions. If you see a gay person and you are not sure how to say, just speak to them and say: 'Look, you know, I don't want to be weird or anything else but I am just curious' – you need to be honest. And I think that people say that with me as well: 'Are you guys doing this, or why do you do that?', and I say 'Okay, now don't be afraid to ask the questions. I would rather you learn from me than the media.'

(Arif, 2 July 2007)

Booth also spoke in a similar manner, highlighting how disingenuous some people can be, and thus, perhaps, deliberately attempting to undermine open communication:

> I think that the idea that people should be wary of including disabled people because they don't know what to call them, I would say that is being less than sincere, because if you don't have a problem with disabled people you could just talk to them, you could just talk to someone and say 'Look, I'm really glad you're here but sometimes I get caught up in what I am meant to be saying', and then this person will say 'Look, actually I don't give a shit what you call me.' You're guided by what disabled people say to you, and that can change, so if disabled people feel it is negative to say that they are handicapped, then it is. Why use a word that people don't want to be called by?

(Booth, 3 May 2007)

Booth was particularly animated about how linguistic labels, no matter how positive their original intention, can end up with wholly negative associations, and perhaps, thus, be used precisely to close down communication:

> But actually my greater concern in that area was the way in which notions of special educational needs are used and have become a sort of derogatory notion because people refer to children as 'SEN'. When people start referring to children as SEN it seems to me as a thoroughly derogatory way of talking about people. So it's a distinction between the amorphous

group of *the* handicapped or saying somebody is handicapped; to refer to someone as part of this amorphous group of *the* handicapped is derogatory. In the same way is this kind of unthinking way of referring to massive large groups of children as SEN. And then the variant labels like EDD or ADHD I find disgusting and I am amazed that relatively few of my colleagues are similarly disgusted.

(Booth, 3 May 2007)

In the following Booth made it clear what might be happening in these situations:

Yes, it is complex but people are very adept at working out the complexities of language. I mean when they start simplifying it there is usually a political purpose for trying to simplify the argument in the discussion. But the other issue I wanted to mention is that it is not the words themselves, it's the activity that's associated with the use of words. Somebody said to me the other day: 'Oh, I have got to go to a meeting where we will be discussing NEETS' – Not in Education Employment or Training. And it's singling out; it's the dregs, it's another word for the dregs – 'Oh I am going to go to another meeting where we will be discussing the dregs.' They don't say 'the dregs' but they say 'the NEETS' and this has become pretty widespread and I kind of get a pain in my stomach when I hear something like that. From the person who said it to me, a sort of community and youth worker, I mean a really good person, who in their dealings with young people is nothing but respectful, but hasn't seen, in my view, hadn't thought through the implications, the negative implications of adopting this kind of terminology.

(Booth, 3 May 2007)

Silver clearly articulated the need to be constantly monitoring the border between free speech which works to open up communication, and free speech which is aimed at closing down communication. Silver was clear that the latter should have no place in a college community, or perhaps better, should have no place in a college with a commitment to a particular value system:

I am not in favour of curbing free speech but I am in favour of establishing a set of protocols for communications – the College has got 147 nationalities, average age being 31, 44 languages spoken – you can see the diversity I am handling – so what I am trying to do is to say what to do, what not to do, and to be the culture of respect for difference. So that is how I tackle it. I would be keen to make it a learning experience saying: 'Actually, the reason why that kind of notion might not go down well in Lewisham College is because of the values this organization has.' It crosses the line when it becomes abusive, or hierarchical, or in any way derogatory. So the promotion of ideas for discussion and exploration is quite different from the use of language for the diminishing of somebody who is different in the College. That is very hard to police because what you are policing there is intentionality, and that's impossible. So what you would do, what I would do here, I would talk about the outcome. I can't ever really get to the bottom of intentions but I can be educational about the outcome of language spoken. So: 'You might not have meant it to be offensive but actually the outcome is that somebody is offended; let's explore that – how you can change your behaviour in the future.' But it's a very difficult line to tread and one most people fear because it continually depends on the exercise of judgement. Not unframed judgement, judgement within the frame of an organization's value system, mission, primary purpose, but it is a tough call. It's like bullying; like beauty is in the eye of the beholder; and that is always a tough call, and open to abuse at both ends.

(Silver, 2 July 2007)

Here we see a very good example of where a particular exercise in judgement might give rise to an outside claim of 'political correctness gone mad', but, at the same time, one might better understand the situation if one sought the value system from within which all such judgements are made. Arif also provided some telling examples of how tightly balanced some judgements might be:

In the university, I think it is changing because there is a lot of new kind of blood coming in, with the younger generation; they have a different perspective. I have met lecturers and teachers who are really open-minded and kind of question, and I have had good debates with them, and then you get the other people from the past – slightly stuck in their ways – and it is difficult when you speak to them because you don't really know if anything is getting through. For them their bread and butter is their research and their teaching and that is all they care about, and that is fine, and that is how it should be; that is their job, and they shouldn't have to worry, but again it is the attitude. They probably think: 'Yes, I am equal to everyone; I am fine to everyone; I take everyone into account', but, when it comes to, for example, the RAE – putting someone forward in your department. They might automatically put the male forward before the female, just unconsciously. They might not take into account that the female has had a career break, due to so and so. That doesn't mean that person is sexist or, in any way, it is just a certain way of thinking. I think currently this kind of role in England tends to be seen as a policing role, a bit more than one that actually goes out there and gets an involvement, and kind of questions *with* them, interrogates with the people about what it is we are saying, not as: 'You're saying it wrong and I'm saying it right', but why we are saying these kind of things.

(Arif, 2 July 2007)

In this context it could be argued that if one wants to question the efficacy of any of these interventions it might be more sound to do so from the point of their aim, rather than their effects, which, given the complexity of human relationships, are bound to be found wanting on a number of occasions. And finally, Milln provided the following telling example, which highlights how difficult some judgements can be, particularly when value systems might appear to clash:

> Part of our responsibility is international recruitment and of course when dealing with a country where the media is not entirely free, in its ability to speak out, we have become aware that our website might be censored. So, prospective students might not able to access the website. In one case we realized that the reason for it was that there was an academic paper which was published somewhere on the website which made mention of an organization, which is basically *persona non grata*, and effectively, it became obvious that the easy way, if you like, to sort that out, would be to remove that paper and to remove the mention of that organization from the website, which, physically, wouldn't have been a desperately difficult thing to do. The academic concerned might have been a bit annoyed about it, but I don't think it was a desperately recent paper; I don't think it would have caused anybody a huge issue. But you then come up against the clash with the fact that Britain does have freedom of speech and, indeed, you're in a university and the whole ethos of the university is about being able to explore different attitudes, different views, etc., and to be able to express your opinions freely. And so, actually, to remove a paper of that nature from the university website, effectively, would be allowing ourselves to be censored by another government. So we didn't remove it in the end. We went round all sorts of other tacks to try and get the issue sorted out. We may or may not sort it out for the long term but we eventually decided that it just wouldn't be appropriate for us to allow ourselves to be that influenced.
>
> (Milln, 10 July 2007)

On the third theme, of whether we are witnessing the substitution of a particular type of political engagement by a weaker and ineffective form, Hayes painted a picture of the broader context:

> There has been a collapse, as everybody knows, in the Labour movement, the traditional political parties, and a collapse in contestation and a struggle for vision for another society has disappeared and it has been replaced. I always remember Mrs Thatcher: 'There is no such thing as society, only individuals and their families' and that is the way politics is. And in that situation, obviously, when there are no large-scale political movements, and no collective movements, then you will get a drift into personal politics. In that situation it may *seem* as if what has brought that about – you'd have to argue in some strange way that the collapse of the

Soviet Union and the collapse of the Labour movement – was *because* of the campaign for changed language but it isn't; it is *out of* the collapse of those that the campaign to change the language came.

(Hayes, 28 April 2007)

Ecclestone and Furedi spoke in the same vein:

Intellectually, I know that trying to change people's language and what they say publicly, does nothing to change what they think or feel and nor does it necessarily change their behaviour, so they might still act in very discriminatory ways even though they are using the desired language. So I no longer believe, as I might once have done, that by changing people's language you can then start to turn that into some political consciousness. I don't believe that anymore. So intellectually I am a bit more clued up, I think, that that is not the case. But then there is another layer of it, which is what happens on the left, that political correctness – and I can see it very strongly amongst feminists – has become censorious, moral, judgemental, in its own way, a way of just stifling debate. Intellectually, I see that as quite problematic and worrying. Why that happens I am not clear except I think it is because the left and feminists have given up on social change and now all they think they can do is just make everything nice and sensitive and as long as people aren't offending each other, in its way that has become a compensation for social action.

(Ecclestone, 26 October 2006)

I wouldn't underestimate the importance of language but I would argue that language really becomes powerful when it resonates with cultural change and is able to draw on cultural resources. So if you have a change of words from cripple to disabled, what's important there is that it isn't simply a change of language, but the fact that in a society we have normalized disability. But more importantly, we've re-defined human subjectivity, so that increasingly the distinction between abled and disabled is not that important.

(Furedi, 30 April 2007)

Furedi seems to capture the essence of the dialectic at work here, that language reflects culture, although it does have some status as an independent variable as well. Hayes was clear that the universities had a lot to answer for in promoting a form of total independence for linguistic forms of politics:

It is the left in the universities, particularly in British universities, who, having abandoned struggles in the work place, retreated into the academy. They're responsible, and often in the roles of administrators as well as academics, course administrators and college administrators, who have imposed these codes as a way of, basically, advancing politics. It is largely because they know best, sort of approach, and that is spreading. If you just think about having speech codes when you go to university – student unions have them in their manuals, and you are then told you mustn't say these certain things and vague reasons why; because you don't want to be sexist, racist, homophobic, Islamophobic; without any real discussion you accept the code. So you learn from the word go that there are these things that you mustn't say. So there is no debate; that seems to me to challenge the basis of a university. A university is where you can say anything and then people will argue against you; that is my take on a university. And you then say, if you have it in codes, that one thing, in itself, is the basis of political correctness, and then graduate students leave and go into businesses and get jobs in the public sector, and I think there is a diaspora from the university.

(Hayes, 28 April 2007)

Hayes referred to this as a form of 'gesture politics', and here we see how he is able to connect a number of developments: linguistic orthodoxy in the university, which has undermined the true mission of the university, and how this has spread outwards from the university to other professional and commercial contexts. Booth saw these aspects of political correctness differently. Rather than the left in the universities being the culprits he reminded us of how forces on the right were provocatively seeking to undermine the progressive educational causes that were being pursued by local educational authorities throughout the 1980s:

I can think of certain key speeches that Margaret Thatcher made about the changes that were brought in education. There is a speech, I can remember the beginning of it: 'Look at Bernie Grant'. So, *look* at Bernie Grant. If you looked at Bernie Grant what you saw was a black man . . . and then the next sentence was: 'What they are doing in our schools' – it was a sort of attack on the idea of having black people within the community. Then she talked about what they are doing to our maths text-books; this idea that there was this huge movement which was reshaping the curriculum in a way that was biased to the left, when actually the movement within the ILEA [Inner London Education Authority], the *small* movement towards developing anti-racist curriculum, or looking at bias, was trying to remove bias, not put it in.

(Booth, 3 May 2007)

For Booth, the significant shift in the nature of political debate seems to be the closing of the space for grass roots debate and discussion, and, in universities, just how little room there is to question their corporate nature:

I have just got back from Cuba and if somebody asked me here: 'Oh, what do you think about Cuba?', I would say there's more grass roots participation in Cuba than you find in this university. So if democracy has got something to do with participation. . . . Personally, I think people should participate in decisions about their own lives, that is what I see as being part of the purpose of education, but I think that the political systems are open to question because democracy, the kind of democracy we live in, seems very stultifying.

Every block in Cuba has its committee for the defence of the revolution which is their point of participation. Not every block in England has some kind of political participatory unit, and it is more than that, it's a kind of social welfare unit as well, and some work well and some don't. The problem I have with the notion that 'we know and you don't know' is that that notion encourages both groups not to know. So it is sort of anti-educational for both groups because it encourages, in its modern context, the managers and the workers, which you get in an institution like this. The managers constantly delude themselves about their knowledge and the workers get demoralized and their thinking deteriorates, and they start to rush around for appropriate supports for their thinking.

(Booth, 3 May 2007)

In conclusion, it is clear that the notion of orthodoxy is troubling. For some, this is an almost inevitable outcome of organizational life; for others that life is often very much a reflection of a broader attempt by the state to seek to control aspects of it. A further dimension is to consider the extent to which it is either the process of establishing orthodoxies which is the most troubling, or the content of the thoughts they promote. With reference to the term political correctness itself we find ourselves once again asking whether it is the politics, or the correctness, which is most troubling, and furthermore, whether the politics should be understood as the promotion of certain ideas, or a broader conception of a type of political behaviour.

What is also clear, particularly from the administrators and leaders, is the extent to which the term political correctness can be an unhelpful 'mask' to discourage exploration of the complicated nature of human communication, and the lesson here might be that one needs to articulate constantly the value base from which professional judgements are being made, rather than allow people to highlight some of the unfortunate effects of the decisions themselves.

Talking about multiculturalism

Two broad sets of themes emerged from the conversations about multi-culturalism. First, issues relating to the nature of the concept of culture itself, and related questions of objectivity and epistemology. And second, issues relating to the concept of 'the self' and the role of values in educational aims. This last issue has already arisen in the context of freedom of speech and will be returned to at the end of this section.

In a theme often found in anti-PC literature in the US, Hayes was quick to dismiss what he saw as the divisiveness inherent in a *multi*cultural mindset:

I gave a talk at black history month and I was the only white male on the panel, with three black women, and they said it was good to have another ethnic minority perspective; everybody is part of an ethnic group, even if it is not a minority group. And I thought it was entirely wrong and my response to them was to say what has actually happened in all these situations is you make people more sensitive. You actually start to racialize relationships so you become hypersensitive and it doesn't actually overcome any of the issues that may be between you, it just makes you more sensitive to the fact that somebody is Asian, one was Muslim, one was West Indian, one was mixed race, and then I'm white, so then I have to think of myself as white, primarily, rather than thinking of us all as human beings.

I have talked about this with members of UCU [Universities and Colleges Union], about whether we've slipped into identity politics and we are asserting identity as the most important thing, and that's divisive. And one of the things you are not allowed to do – it used to be the case that you could criticize 'the veil' as a symbol of oppression. It used to be, if I remember, historically, the left position on Islam and any superstitious religion, you would then say: 'This is a symbol of women's oppression and you should campaign against it.' And nowadays you are not even allowed to argue that, and so you have invited speakers – and this is when it is not just about language – because you would invite the speakers and you will have a woman who wears 'the burka' come to speak about how she feels positive and safe, but nobody will invite anybody anymore to speak on the opposite. So there is no debate, and an assertion of people's identities.

(Hayes, 28 April 2007)

He went on to develop the argument that this type of thinking can lead to dangerous forms of cultural relativity, and how the celebration of difference can be a kind of uncultured position. When asked whether he thought we should be against forms of multiculturalism, he said:

Well the answer is yes, you should be opposed to it. It seems quite nice. My definition of culture was always that any society that could be described as cultured would be interested in other societies. There are more primitive and backward societies out there – I have been criticized on many occasions for saying this – [which] don't change over thousands of years; just become closed and replicate themselves. Whereas societies that develop, that get dynamic, absorb other cultures. Japanese people in Western culture and Chinese people are now coming over in droves to absorb the music and literature. It is not because they are being swamped by Western imperialism, it is because they want to learn, and that has always been the case so in that sense every culture should be interested in other cultures and that is positive. But, of course multiculturalism means *affirming*; it means *accepting* diversity, which is sort of keeping things separate.

(Hayes, 28 April 2007)

He concluded his argument by spelling out the political folly in believing that an anti-multicultural position is necessarily a pro-imperialistic one:

I think the general issue about imperialism is that it is slightly complicated, in that I would want – now I would almost want – to say yes, it was a civilizing influence, as compared with what goes on now, because if you take people who want *not* to interfere with other cultures – if you take the sustainable development people – they tend to be: 'We'll encourage you to stay as you are.' So, although it seems that you are not interfering in those cultures, you are trying to preserve them, actually it is *more* imperialistic. We're not interfering in other cultures; we respect your identity and diversity, you remain poor. And I think it is the worst politics and the more dangerous politics partly because nobody sees it. The past is seen as imperialistic, well, it clearly was, it was there to exploit the wealth of the world but it did have with it a civilizing mission, whereas now you do want to exploit them still, and you don't want to civilize them; you keep them primitive.

(Hayes, 28 April 2007)

Coming closer to the curriculum, although Silver clearly articulated a position based on a respect for difference, she was also clear that this should not imply that one should thereby celebrate and encourage separate cultural identities:

The standard can change but as long as there is only the one. Learn the ways of the world. Join. Just like the Dutch did in The Hague some years ago when they said – and this is where we got it wrong in Britain – it is compulsory to learn Dutch. What had happened was they came across all these communities from the Suriname, who had been there twenty, fifty years, and not a word of Dutch was spoken. So they had come from Suriname to set up Surinamese communities in Holland, and they were utterly isolated – separate banking, a whole separate country really – and the Dutch decided they didn't want to do that anymore, and they made it compulsory to learn Dutch. You could not come in unless you signed that you would learn Dutch. You were not entitled to any benefits unless you learned a Dutch learning programme, and they said: 'You may not exclude yourself. We will include you in the learning. You don't have to use it once you have it, but you have excluded *yourself,* not that we want to exclude you.' I was very taken by that, as a notion; it's about that choice. You have to join the world, or to be able to; if you don't then you choose not to, but there are ways of the world for a reason. I mean even standards in exams are to test a certain amount of knowledge, skills and ability, and that is quite important.

(Silver, 2 July 2007)

Several people were concerned about maintaining common standards of judgement, and this will be returned to in the next section. As a precursor to that Silver spelt out what she saw as the necessary balance in a curriculum, between, on the one hand, a respect for difference, and, on the other, a common standard of aspiration:

I like the approach of the curriculum here, so the national curriculum in schools means that everybody is learning the same thing at their own pace. There is choice built into that, and there is a real awareness in teacher development of the use of differentiated learning, deploying different teaching strategies, and the amplification of the national curriculum covers for all sorts of things, race and history and gender, and so on, and I like that. I'd like to see it promoted more.

I think I would like to see the encouragement of themed learning around that, that looks at differences in society and my sense is that schools are much better than colleges and universities in doing that, primary schools in particular. So, I feel quite happy with that. I like the notion that all students are doing the same thing so there is no excluded group; they'll perform differently in that for all sorts of reasons, but it means we are able to track. I can track now through all my data on how Indian male students are doing in Business Studies, compared to West Indian women students, or British.

I would be very nervous about locking people into identities rather than opening up opportunities for them. The one place of hope for me is the vocational curriculum where talents are beyond race and gender and so on; identities may not be but these are; a kind of balanced curriculum where they are provided with the choice to explore that; where they are absolutely promoted and encouraged for a plural society to take those into their fields. As Principal, I would be very preoccupied if that wasn't happening. For example, in our beauty saloon we do black skin as well as white skin. Just as in construction, people will do comparative drawings of different kinds of roofs in different parts of the world to see, the kind of, climatic field. So, I would be looking for everybody to be making that kind of connection, because we are the College that we are, with 147 nationalities. Maybe in another place I would be less anxious about that but it is very crucial here that we value and respect difference and see the origins of difference, rather than just say: 'Well you are different from us.' I would like a curriculum that was geared to difference *throughout*, rather than say: 'We'll do black history.' Themes seem to give you the chance to do that better. But you need to check that your themes are touching.

(Silver, 2 July 2007)

For Furedi this question was addressed more from the point of view of epistemology:

I am actually not against people using the university in any way they choose to do, as long as it is based upon an integral approach towards the development of knowledge. I am a big believer in the taking of ideas into the public domain and being engaged in a rather more interactive process. What I am against is when you have a very promiscuous approach towards epistemology, so we have 'my way of seeing', 'your way of seeing', which then becomes completely disorienting and ends up lacking any real intellectual rigour, and ends up making it impossible to have a dialogue, because if you have different epistemologies, different ways of seeing, then we are not seeing the same picture, even.

(Furedi, 30 April 2007)

When he was questioned on whether sociology, as a discipline, was firmly grounded on a particular approach to epistemology, he replied:

I am open to the idea that the truth is not absolute, and in my work there are truths, but the truths are relative to the time. Which basically means that rather than having a transcendental sense of truth – that this is true – we look at what is going on today in England, and we can work out what is true for our times, rather than say that there are many ways of looking at it. The truth is relative to the times that we are living in and therefore I am quite happy to be flexible and open-minded. And also to know that the truth is something that is not given, it is something that we have to discover for ourselves.

(Furedi, 30 April 2007)

Furthermore, he did not see this Enlightenment philosophy as being at all at odds with a radical, left-wing politics. Indeed, he clearly articulated a defence of Marxism from the claim that it represented a radical mission to see the curriculum as the means to uncover the ideological foundations of all thinking:

You have to remember in the realm of the aesthetic, politics should have a regular role, and I think that is something that Marx recognized. I mean Marx himself, his favourite author was Balzac. You should read Trotsky on literature, which I think is brilliant. He is one of the few people that made the point that art has its own laws of beauty. So you can understand it politically, but you should keep the two separate. I think that we live in a world that has made it very difficult to make that separation. In universities people find it difficult to pick up Jane Austen and just go the novel. They feel they have to talk about Jane Austen, the Victorian empire at the time and imperialism, and I think that is really unfortunate.

(Furedi, 30 April 2007)

This line of thinking confirms that many on the left can be just as concerned as their conservative counterparts about some of the implications of a radical multicultural college or university curriculum (e.g. Bloom 1987):

If you read Lukacs on Goethe; if you read Trotsky on literature; if you read Marx on Shakespeare – he is not saying Shakespeare is a lackey of the bourgeoisie or whatever, he is saying: 'What a brilliant writer!' At the same time, to understand Shakespeare, you have got to understand changing social conditions that you write in – that's two different things all together, but the two things have been collapsed and a line between aesthetics and social critique has been lost.

(Furedi, 30 April 2007)

Thus, just because truths are relative to the times does not mean there are no truths, and also, although it is clear that political interests have ideological foundations, this does not mean that all knowledge is similarly constructed. Hayes shared this Enlightenment philosophy and saw these aspects of multiculturalism as undermining the mission of a university:

We are seeing the politicization of the university. The University exists as the place where you study subjects from which we, with certain degrees of accuracy, or for pragmatic reasons, divide up human understanding to pursue knowledge. To then say we should do certain other things, you know, promote greenness or promote anything, is to take away from the university.

(Hayes, 28 April 2007)

He went on to defend a 'disinterested pursuit of the truth' position for the university:

Vannevar Bush, who wrote *Science: The Endless Frontier*, for the American Government, during the Second World War, he actually argued that if you want to progress science, what you need in a university is a place where scientists are free to follow whatever they like, just follow what you are interested in. His argument about the consequences were: it's arbitrary. If there is going to be any consequence you have got to have that total freedom to pursue knowledge for its own sake.

(Hayes, 28 April 2007)

Once again, we see evidence here of radical left-wing thinkers adopting a much more conservative position on matters of epistemology.

On the question of perceptions of 'the self', Ecclestone, Hayes, and Furedi echoed their work on the notion that it has become 'diminished':

There is a strong bit of me that thinks that higher education, further education, should try to include more people to achieve. But I think that there is a lot of fobbing off going on and in the name of inclusion. I think that – and again it is very unwitting and I don't think people mean to do it – there are what I would call quite diminished images of those students; new deficiency labels under the guise of being very caring and very concerned; the idea they need all this support, that they are going to find university life very difficult. I think it all starts from a very negative view and I think that those sorts of movements, if you like, are leaning to a view that those students can't cope and that if you, therefore, challenge, or try and make things challenging and difficult, that that is somehow wrong. But I think that it is quite unspoken, and I suppose a lot of people who are overtly working in those areas, they would say: 'Well that is not what we are doing, we are just being realistic about what those students need', but I think that it is a really interesting twist of political correctness because it isn't part of the old sort of standard of political correctness that you could recognize. But it has got its own very subtle terms of debate and I have learned that you can tread on toes very quickly in debates around inclusion and if you even question why – I had this at a meeting the other day – widening participation for students from local schools – and I said: 'Well, why do we assume that our university is what we want, and view it as a good thing', and people were horrified and people immediately had me down as some sort of right-wing elitist who didn't want those students to come in. And that isn't it. My concern is actually, I suppose a left-wing one in its old terms, that in the past, when you wanted to attract working-class people or people who wouldn't normally go to HE, you didn't have this diminished view of them. You assumed that they could achieve on the same terms. But now I think actually deep down, people don't believe those students can achieve, but for social reasons they think they should be achieving and I think that that is not the same thing.

(Ecclestone, 26 October 2006)

When questioned on whether his vision of a culture of fear and culture of therapy is fundamentally similar to the American work of authors such as Sykes (1992) and Murray and Hernstein (1994), Furedi replied:

I have a fairly high opinion of human subjectivity. Their critique of victim culture is a very individualistic one: 'You should take responsibility for your life', and all that. Whereas, in my case, I see people as having a potential to transform their circumstances, and therefore I have a much more collective vision of solidarity. And I have got a sense of history. They basically see all these problems as history repeating itself time and again, whereas I see the period as being very specific and life can change in all kinds of different ways.

(Furedi, 30 April 2007)

But, is it clear the means by which such a transformation could take place?

> I now think that the potential for social change in the here and now is very limited, which is why I think it is very important for people like me to give a greater emphasis on, and affirm, the exercise of human subjectivity, which often takes the form of promoting individuals, but my sense of the individual is very different than the conventional, middle-class, bourgeois sense of individuals. To me individuals become strong through their relationships with other people rather than somehow an accident of volition. I just think that the two have got to go hand in hand. Currently we live in a very individualistic world but we live in a very feeble individualistic world; individuals are seen as being sort of powerless and lacking in resilience.
>
> (Furedi, 30 April 2007)

Once again, Silver brought the argument closer to the college curriculum, and she outlined how the college can promote the view that students should see themselves as agents, not victims (Furedi 1997):

> We are training in futures and one of the key values of our personalization agenda is to develop a sense of consequence and a sense of contribution from our learners, so we are, absolutely, about the breaking of dependency and I would be very hesitant of anything in any way that breeds dependency. I think that we are a group in this College, and I personally would say – my daughter says this to me: 'Get over yourself.' 'This is your chance; it's real in the world that you will be treated differently; how can you get ready to handle being treated differently; how can you get ahead of that?' One of my mantras for students here, and to staff, is, actually, it's kind of our duty to make ourselves desirable. I am talking here in the employment context, when the students leave.
>
> There has been a terrible hostaging I think of the term 'rights'; 'people's rights'; in that it doesn't address enough for our own responsibilities as well. So, as a clinical psychologist, as a parent, as a professional educator, I would be continuing trying to breed and address the responsibility part of that agenda. People do have their rights, enshrined in law – rather a lot of them in this country – and what happens is that everybody distances themselves through the procedures, so the pain of being insulted – that can be promotional pain – 'actually, I am not having this I am going to do something about it', is diluted by ready access to procedures, and that same ready access to procedures makes people defensive, and also puts them into a position – it's almost an anti-learning position – on both sides.
>
> So, I would be much more for a social justice model; we have a social justice model in this College; we have a group of new professionals called 'intervention support officers' who are there to try and deal with moving on to taking responsibility for the hurt, the insult, rather than just being

litigious about it. But it's easy to wash your hands of it and say: 'Well, go
to procedures.' Much more difficult to say: 'When you said that what did
you mean?'; really working at the communication bit. That is not to say
that they aren't wrong – some of them are wrong – and quite clearly
against the law, but I'm talking about those areas of discretion in organizational life where you can make somebody more dependent on rushing
to authority to say: 'They insulted me' or this kind of thing. It's also open
to abuse isn't it; it's a difficult terrain for leadership.

(Silver, 2 July 2007)

That said, Booth wanted to stress that the curriculum itself – course content –
should be viewed as the key educational resource, and we should not shy away
from espousing its value base, or arguing that the university curriculum does
not, nor should not, have a value base:

I think the underpinnings of any aspect of the curriculum – the
assumptions and values – should have been made explicit so that it
becomes part of exploring that area of study. There are values which we
appear to espouse when we promote education generally, and these values
would include something along the line of 'every life is of equal value', or
'every life, and every death is of equal value' which I see as a core principle
which is worth exploring. So I would see a course – a disabilities studies
course at a particular period, or a women's studies course – as being a way
of addressing that central principle.

(Booth, 3 May 2007)

Although Arif highlighted just how fraught discussions can be when arguments
ensue as to what exactly will be able to make it on to any particular curriculum:

Someone asked the question recently: 'Well okay, in economics and
finance economics, we teach in England, it's multicultural. You teach
interest rates, and especially now – it's such a big thing – what about
religious and Muslim finance, Sharia finance?' That is something about
inclusion, and there is a lot of confusion, and it is a difficult thing to talk
about. It is a difficult thing to do, make a curriculum inclusive. So where
do you stop?

(Arif, 2 July 2007)

In conclusion, we can see evidence to support the view that when it comes to
political correctness both radical and conservative thinkers can be united in their
concerns about forms of multiculturalism, and that these are often, at root,
concerns about how forms of multiculturalism can undermine more deeply held
views about the Enlightenment. We can also see how aspects of the conservative
political agenda in the US which has promoted the view that forms of left-wing
politics have produced a culture of dependency, are shared by many people on
the left in Britain, although the causes and prescriptions for change might be

different. And when it comes to the curriculum it is also clear that there is evidence here that the more radical forms of multiculturalism do not receive wide support. But, once again, in order to counter the charge that certain aspects of the curriculum are simply 'political correctness gone mad', there is a compelling need to ensure that the value base of a curriculum, or a college in general, is carefully articulated, if it is not to be readily undermined by anti-PC literature.

Talking about affirmative action

Three main themes emerged in discussions of affirmative action. First, the question of the desirability of widening the scope for the way students are assessed, whilst seeking to maintain the same broad standards for all students. Second, was the question of the best ways to open up access to further and higher education. And, third, the extent to which it is desirable to see colleges and universities changing in terms of the type of learning that students experience.

On the first theme, Silver expanded on her belief about respecting difference whilst setting the same challenges for all:

> I am not in favour of widening assessment modes, but I am absolutely in favour of diversifying input mode because everybody starts at a different place. So that the end point is a place of measure and standard and that should be worked towards, but actually how you get there should be personalized because you start off in different places. So there is a need for good initial assessment and placement, the need for identification of additional learning support is paramount, and that kind of regular review, but actually somewhere that has to stop, and has to have credibility. Now if you know the American Small School Movement that was designed for the over-aged and under-credited young people, and unlike here where there are twenty-five million doors to get in through into university, there is only one in America, it is the general education diploma, and everybody has to get through that door, and so they will work with the old, and no matter what the issues are, to get through the one door. The joy of that is that they all know the same when they start college, and I was very taken by how impressed I was by that. There is something about the egalitarian experience of walking through the same door as everybody else, having come through the same route. Talking to the young women in the projects, and young black people, and young Hispanics; they knew they were the same as everybody else, and that just felt really important. But, they were treated differently, all got different help, learning support, different welfare, because they all started differently, but they all ended up, by a certain phase, in the same place. Whether they stay there is another matter, but that felt very crucial.

> (Silver, 2 July 2007)

From his own experience of being a student, Arif felt that there was a case to be heard about widening modes of engagement in order to allow students more scope to demonstrate their learning:

> Doing my Master's, there were a lot of Chinese students in my class and they, for example, found the oral stuff, the presentations very, very difficult. It doesn't mean that they haven't got the same ability as someone from the Western side but the way they had been brought up, the way they have been taught, was always lecture, lecture, lecture, and exams. The whole oral presentation didn't work for them, whereas for myself I preferred the presentation more, and the essays more, than I did the exams. It is a different learning style, but I think everybody is strong on some things and weak on other things, so as long as everyone gets a chance at each one.
>
> (Arif, 2 July 2007)

That said, Milln was clear that we should be seen to be offering *support* for learning, and not, in the process, changing or lowering standards:

> You are setting up expectations and I don't think you can really bring in a student from a completely different culture who is used to a totally different learning style, dump them into our own approach to learning without appropriate support, and then sit back in surprise if they don't necessarily do terribly well because actually they are just struggling to get to grips with a whole different way of doing things. In some cultures, particularly in the plagiarism kind of issues, you can have a situation that the approach to learning that we would describe as plagiarism is actually the thing that gains them, kind of, additional points in their own educational culture, and to not explain that to them and not support them in actually making that transition and understanding – what it is you are valuing and what you actually don't accept and so on and so forth, and why – seems quite dishonest in a way. So I think you do have that responsibility and I guess the challenge is how you exercise it, in that very often what you are doing is that you are pulling students from a number of different cultures onto the same programme so it is not as simple as saying: 'Right, you know, the programme was like this but now we are going to make it like that because that will make it work for this group of students', because in making it work for this group of students, you've probably lost another group. Which is, I guess, partly where things like the foundation programmes, and so on, come from, where you are really in a sense trying to use that year as a vehicle for pulling together a whole range of different backgrounds and working out where they are at and what they need to do in order to kind of adapt to the new culture that they are within.
>
> (Milln, 10 July 2007)

Ecclestone saw some potential for widening assessment modes, but wasn't convinced that any general case has, or could, be made:

> I think, increasingly, assessment methods have been diversified and evidence is being seen in a much broader and looser ways, and that may not be a bad thing, depending if you are assessing certain types of learning outcomes. I am quite old fashioned and I am not very technologically open, actually, to other ways of assessing. I think that the intellectual skills of analysis and evaluation – or maybe I am just very unimaginative – I can't quite see the alternative to writing. The oral, the viva, was an example where you are showing your intellectual ability in a slightly different way but my hunch is that you can't do that orally unless you can do it well in the written form. So I am a bit sceptical about all this diversity.
>
> (Ecclestone, 26 October 2006)

Furedi spoke in a similar way, but was more forthright in his condemnation of some of the changes he had knowledge of:

> I have been teaching now for 30 years, or something; I have often introduced, for example, takeaway exams. The line is crossed when it ceases to be intellectually challenging, and when the integrity of the subject matter is compromised. For example, some of my colleagues are introducing exams with 'true and false'. I think that's terrible. Or in some universities, you get people to talk about their experiences, and they get marks for knowing how to tie their shoes. But I am not so old-fashioned that there is only one way. You have to remember that my opponents are arguing against essays; that's their big target, which I think is really culturally important. I think that's where the battle lies; it's the ability to write, to communicate, to analyse, all in one, rather than take it apart and see it as a series of skills.
>
> (Furedi, 30 April 2007)

When questioned on whether universities have reliable admissions procedures he replied:

> I wouldn't want to glorify its practices and often it is very arbitrary, but I would rather have the arbitrarily, neat, coherent form of choosing students than to introduce a double standard or multiple ones, which in a sense kind of creates a regime that has different standards, and I think that once that becomes the norm, it basically creates a dynamic that is very self-destructive in a university setting and where neither the students nor anybody else can benefit from that. I think that if you genuinely want to help people the way you do it is that when children are very, very young you throw a lot of money into nursery education, schooling, and I am quite happy for spending £30 for working-class kids, for every pound that's spend in a middle-class area; I am quite happy to do that. I am

happy to discriminate in their favour; in that way resource it, rather than morally or intellectually.

I also think that universities cannot solve the problems of society or education which is what it pretends at the moment. I don't think schooling can do it either, but I think that in so far as there is any potential for a meritocratic society it needs to create a level playing field when kids are very, very young. I think that you could create an infrastructure for young children to try in a more egalitarian way than it is at the moment and that is the point that we need to intervene, providing the opportunities to make their way.

(Furedi, 30 April 2007)

These comments spill somewhat naturally into the second theme concerning the ways one might best open up further and higher education to a wider range of students. Most people felt that more effort needed to be put into preparing students to study, rather than changing the university or college itself. Milln was clear what could be at stake if the balance is tipped too far:

I don' t think you are necessarily losing your standards by adapting the approach, or the way somebody undergoes that transition to it. Having said that I think we do have to recognize why people come to the UK to learn, because there are certain values within the education system and certain approaches which have resulted in UK education having a very strong reputation, and whether or not individuals really openly articulate it, it's the approach that they are coming to acquire. Why have UK graduates got a good reputation? It is actually because we have equipped them with a particular approach to learning and a particular set of skills, and so on. So, if we suddenly took an extreme, if we took our degree programme and changed it into exactly the same approach as a degree programme in a country on the other side of the world, what have we actually done? We have brought them over expecting to gain a skills set that actually they are not going to gain and given them the skill set that they could have quite happily got by staying exactly where they are – although perhaps they wouldn't have got that kind of broader internationalism.

(Milln, 10 July 2007)

Silver struck a cautionary note concerning the reality of the budgets in which one is forced to work:

We would hope that we could serve everybody who came through our door, but we have two problems: one is a restricted resource and one is the readiness of the candidate to proceed. Where somebody wanted to do something but they weren't at the right level I would hope that we would refer them on to something that would get them to the right level, and respect the intention, or to work with them in ways, or to refer them elsewhere. And in terms of restricted resource, I made it clear a long, long time ago that we are not here to spend all our resource on those who are most needy. We are here to spend our resource on those who have the most chance of success. And when we had money for additional support and all my staff got on to spend it on the most needy, it made no difference to them. But if there was a borderline group – with just a wee bit extra – could get in, and proceed onwards. And those kind of judgements, made by and held by the senior team, are quite important. I got a lot of flack for that one. So, it's something about most able to benefit – most able to progress the furthest – by the use of resource there. I'd like to be doing something different with the most needy. I would encourage my staff to say no to people who will not benefit from being here, and the benefits are clearly spelt out.

(Silver, 2 July 2007)

From his experience of working for the Open University, Booth was optimistic about widening access, and placed the emphasis on the culture of support for learning:

Having worked at the Open University for 20 years which did have open access, that aspect of it was a positive experience. I couldn't see any argument against, seeing as how successful the Open University was, how rigorous the courses were. . . . There were a lot of negative things about the Open University but I can see you don't need restrictions on access. In France there are hardly any restrictions on access; in Italy there isn't. Our system was one which rationed access. You get the other issue in France and Italy where you have got people who don't finish the course, and I think it's a price worth paying. What happened at the Open University, I think, was that people were pretty well selected; they would select a course that they could manage and if they did that all right they would carry on. A university can run so that it has open access, but where there's a sort of negotiation with students when they arrive for what course they'll do.

(Booth, 3 May 2007)

Furedi took the opportunity to continue to develop the theme that what might appear to be emancipatory could actually result in the exact opposite:

I am not against organizing a year-long transitional course to university, really give them a good schooling and a basis where they can go to university, and be challenged. I am all for stuff like that. Affirming people ends up usually flattering people, and instead of challenging, stretching people, basically it assumes that individuals from different kinds of cultural backgrounds have got certain emotional or intellectual deficits and therefore you need a double standard or a triple standard by which you engage with them. And you cannot have a university, academic life, which is based upon dual standards, because the minute you do that then you no longer have a community of scholars, nor do you have a dialogue or a discussion. All you have is a kind of ghettoized, parallel development, which basically pretends that the lowering standards is an act of emancipation, rather than a very pragmatic way of bypassing the challenge of how you deal with these people.

(Furedi, 30 April 2007)

Milln expressed similar sentiments, but ones which were more practically based on her own experience of working in university admissions:

I think what you are trying to do is say what are we about as a university. The ultimate aim is to recruit the best students, who are most capable of benefiting from our programmes and doing well on them, and so on. And that the best should be regardless of background, culture – of whatever variety. What you are really aiming to do is to make sure that you are not excluding particular individuals purely because of their background, and so on and so forth.

There are the kind of very easy answers that roll off the tongue which is about the outreach work that you do with students within your local community, within the schools that don't have a strong tradition of entry to higher education, and so on and so forth. And we have huge programmes, things like mentoring and tutoring, where we take our own current students and put them out into schools, or we bring students into the university on a regular basis, or bring them in on summer schools, where what you are trying to do is to, I suppose, support improvements in both attainment and aspirations, so that you end up in a situation where those students that perhaps weren't getting the same support, are actually now getting it, supported by us maybe; are actually now seeing themselves as having the ability to come to Bristol, and are achieving academically, such that when they come forward they will be considered and come across well, relative to other applicants. That's the easy bit – it is a long-term, perhaps time-consuming, resource-consuming activity.

It is about expectations, and seeing themselves as being: 'Yes, this is for me', and it is also about attainment because it may well mean, if you sit down and wait for these students to come forward at the age of 18, they might not be there by then, either because they didn't see it or because they didn't have the aspiration – they didn't have the motivation to really achieve – and so, actually they have been underachieving. So it is kind of aspiration and attainment.

(Milln, 10 July 2007)

Arif struck a similar chord whilst distinguishing between two different types of process:

I completely disagree with quotas. There are two different things, positive action and positive discrimination. Positive action is different. You look, for example, at low poverty areas, or wherever; you promote a bit more. It's about putting people on a level playing field. You put people on that level playing field, then they can compete on a level for this place. And now if it happens to be all white or if it happens to be all Asians who get through that depends on ability after that, hopefully.

(Arif, 2 July 2007)

When questioned further on admissions to Bristol University Milln outlined the current approach which was being taken there:

The two things that you particularly grapple with are what sort of weighting is appropriate. I think we would pretty categorically say it wouldn't be appropriate to look at, in simple terms, two applications and to accept one *purely* on the strength that it was somebody from a particular background, a particular school, etc., without taking anything else into account – that is the one extreme. The other extreme is that you don't take it into account at all. But obviously somewhere in the middle, there's a sliding scale, and it is where do I set it? If I am going to take a particular factor into account what priority does that factor have, relative to the rest of my selection criteria? And I would say, probably, where we are at the moment is factoring it in but not necessarily as a huge proportion, the main focus of the selection process is very much on academic achievement, and the whole personal statement type stuff, and what the person concerned has brought with them by way of life skills, but trying to factor in, I guess, what they have done with the lot that life gave to them, if you like. So we are not automatically expecting them to have played in every single school team, or whatever it is. But if they have done a huge amount with a relatively limited amount of opportunity they may have brought more to the table than somebody who has done not terribly much with everything. So there is a lot of subjective assessment around that. I think the second challenge is about what factor is the appropriate factor to put in there. Where we are at, at the moment, is that we actually use school performance, and so what we look at is the average A-level performance of the school that the applicant is coming from, and, in simple terms, what that means is if you have an applicant who has gained 2 straight As from a school where the average A-level performance is A grades, and then you have another applicant who has got, let's say, an A and 2 Bs from a school where the average performance is 3 Cs, it might be reasonable to say that the one who has got the actually slightly lower A-level score, but from a school where that isn't the norm, has actually achieved rather more.

(Milln, 10 July 2007)

The final theme, concerning the changing nature of the university, also flowed naturally from the discussions about admissions. Again, Milln made a significant point:

> When you are looking at a selection decision for a university, certainly for us, the primary factor would be academic ability and potential, and that is the whole thing about what university is all about, what it is here to do, the contribution to the learning, the academic community, and so on and so forth. But you haven't just got one place, you have got 60–100 places, or whatever, and the learning of that group will benefit enormously from the fact that each individual member of that group brings different things to the table. And so the line I use in schools, if I am out there talking, is that we don't want to fill a medical course with 6-foot rugby players, because that would actually be a very boring, very one-dimensional group of students, who will all come at things from exactly the same perspective. You actually want a whole range of different people and I think that is where your other achievements start to factor in because if you have got this highly able academic student, *and* they happen to have done very well sporting wise, or whatever, they are going to bring something both to the learning experience, and to the university community as a whole, that one of their colleagues who may be highly able musically doesn't bring, because they bring something different.
>
> (Milln, 10 July 2007)

Here we see a clear sense that a university is a community beyond simply a purely academic one. It may be a much smaller component, but it cannot be ignored. Silver expanded on this point, but with reference this time to staff recruitment rather than student recruitment:

> In a college like this, with the 147 nationalities, actually coming from that world is an employment bonus for me, a skill bonus, a kind of cultural bonus, so I am not saying that as a kind of racialism/quotas thing but saying: 'Actually you might be able to help me with my Somali women because you are a Somali woman and you will have different ways of helping them, and the organization, change.' So I can see why we could be accused of political correctness, but I would say that it is, absolutely, *not* what it is. This is about the delivery of a value system that says diversity is an important value in this College and I am delivering that value and working on that value that I make these decisions. But I have another value; the eleventh commandment at Lewisham is that you do not allow a colleague to fail. So I would not appoint somebody who was at *any* risk of failure, and I would almost be the opposite – I would be politically incorrect – by saying that: 'Failure for you has so much more ramification, for you and for me in running the organization', so there's caution around: 'What's the chance of failure here?' But I do absolutely see

disabled colleagues rebalancing the population in the College. Any characteristic from any of those groups is an employment tick for me in the overall judgement of things, but the bottom line is they have to be the best they can be in their profession. If I could prove anything I'd be doing it in pursuit of a value rather than in pursuit of a target, and that may be hard to tell the difference.

(Silver, 2 July 2007)

That said, Hayes was troubled by the ways in which forms of social engineering had crept into educational communities, and how they were undermining what should be their true mission:

My example is comprehensive education which always meant to me that everybody should have a liberal education and some skills, but a broad-based curriculum. Whereas then it got mixed up with the idea of social engineering and creating certain sorts of school communities. And I think there is this sort of tension between the progressive impulse behind that form of social engineering and the curriculum where now it seems to me that the social engineering part is put into the curriculum. The curriculum is much more about social engineering, mostly in schools and in FE but increasingly so in the newer universities anyway.

(Hayes, 28 April 2007)

He was also not convinced that universities had not changed in order to accommodate a wider range of students:

I went to one of their [City and Guilds] celebratory dinners, and they said: 'Do you know that our courses prepare people more for university, and lots of universities will tell us that our students do much better?' And I said 'It's a double-edged sword that because the universities have changed their courses; the courses are now less academic and demanding, therefore your students do better.' You do change the nature of the curriculum so you do start bringing things into the curriculum to make it more relevant to those groups so then it gets to an issue of relevance, so you make it more relevant.

(Hayes, 28 April 2007)

Finally, Milln recognized that the university curriculum *was* slowly changing to accommodate a more skills focus, but, actually, this was only really making explicit what had always been implicit:

It is about the wider learning experience; it is still learning, but it's about wider than a subject base learning. We have always, as a university, referred to it as, kind of, general transferable skills, life skills, but you see them very much as a spin-off of what they are doing at university. So, they are here to study their subject; they are here to gain their subject knowledge; but it just so happens that along the way they will pick up a lot of other skills because of the way they learn and because of the fact that they gain independence for the first time, in a sort of managed way. And I guess we've always signed up to that one. Instead of just assuming that they will happen along the way, that process of being able to say: 'Well, we need to make sure that particular skill happens, and how are we going to factor it in, what are we going to factor in to the learning experience, to make sure that it does?'

(Milln, 10 July 2007)

In conclusion, we can see here that affirmative action is largely justified on the grounds that it is offering support to groups of people who it is recognized might not even come forward for university admission, let alone succeed in achieving a degree. That said, most people seemed to want to draw a line at the point where such support might significantly change the focus of the traditional curriculum experience. In which case it might be concluded that there was a general air of conservatism about the need to change the curriculum itself and the ways in which students should be assessed.

General conclusion

When compared with the American interviews it could be said that many of the resonances of the term political correctness *are* very similar. What is perhaps most striking about the contrast is the way many of the British conversations turned much more quickly to the ways in which the state regulation of post-16 education has encouraged the view that much of the orthodoxy one finds in college life is not the result of an organic growth from the immediate communities of professional practice, but a rather artificial one imposed by exogenous agencies. Political correctness here might be much more clearly seen as the lip service that people feel they have to pay to these bureaucracies in order to continue to still enjoy a certain amount of autonomy in exercising what they perceive to be the true purpose of their professional lives. This confirms much of what has been considered in the previous two chapters.

12
Conclusion
PC as oxymoron

As demonstrated in Chapter 2, a lot of energy was invested by conservative thinkers in the US in the 1980s to shape the term 'political correctness', and to ensure that it became wholly derogatory in its meaning. The broad purpose was to use it to denigrate a series of political causes which were being pursued by what they saw as a radical left, made up mostly of intolerant zealots. Those causes were often associated with developments in higher education, most notably: restrictions on freedom of speech, the promotion of forms of multicultural curricula, and strategies aimed at affirmative action. However, it is clear that this is not a simple left/right debate because there was some measure of support for this critique from more liberal intellectuals, who saw within the conservative critique an attempt to resurrect the Enlightenment principles of reasoned argument by the autonomous individual, the disinterested pursuit of the truth, and the general idea of cultural, economic, and social progress. Furthermore, in what might appear on the surface as an irony, many on the more radical left also felt some measure of agreement with the critique, particularly when it argued against the misplaced establishment of an educational ethic of diversity, and one which promoted forms of affirming and protectionist strategies aimed at vulnerable students (Furedi 2004a). For some on the radical left this form of liberal politics became a distraction from the need for more authentic forms of political struggle, where the term political correctness came to symbolize the replacement of a programme of real social reform with a cosmetic exercise in papering over the cracks of social division and disadvantage (Scatamburlo 1998). Here the PC accusation is not that there is too much politics, but not enough. And, perhaps more troubling for some, this became the basis for all kinds of separatist thinking and, thereby, a dismantling of any sense of a common humanity, sharing a 'common dream' (Gitlin 1995).

Sometimes the bond between left and right appears extremely close. The work of Sykes and the work of Furedi is a clear case in point (Sykes 1992; Furedi 1997), as is the measurement of agreement between Searle and Gitlin in the conversations in Chapter 7. Indeed, it would appear that there is much for the left and right to agree on in the following two quotations:

> A defence of freedom of speech is particularly important in the compliant and politically correct atmosphere of contemporary higher education.

Increasingly being in higher education is about learning what not to say and not about allowing academics and students the freedom to think the unthinkable and say the unsayable.

(speech by Dennis Hayes, upon election
to the executive committee of NATFHE in 2005)

At the beginning of 2006 Anthony Browne, *The Times* European correspondent, began his book with a catalogue of examples from what he argues is a politically correct public discourse:

> In the topsy-turvy politically correct world, truth comes in two forms: the politically correct, and the factually correct. The politically correct truth is publicly proclaimed correct by politicians, celebrities and the BBC even if it is wrong, while the factually correct truth is publicly condemned as wrong even when it is right. Factually correct truths suffer the dis- advantage that they don't have to be shown to be wrong, merely stated that they are politically incorrect. To the politically correct, truth is no defence; to the politically incorrect, truth is the ultimate defence.
>
> (Browne 2006:7)

However, it would be misguided to believe that battling against a culture of dependency or a nation of victims requires the dismantling of a welfare state as well as a nanny or therapeutic state, and that epistemological conservatism necessarily equates with political conservatism. But equally it might be hasty to believe that 'Conflicting ideas about the paradigm of personhood are today equivalent of past clashes of ideologies and political alternatives' (Furedi 2006: 165), because what surely separates Sykes from Furedi (and probably Browne from Hayes) is not their shared belief in vulnerability, but the forms of community they aspire to engineer to take us beyond it; and the terms 'left' and 'right' would appear to be still very useful in keeping the authors' visions of common humanity apart. In this context 'culture wars' are always 'political ideology wars'.

That said, forms of identity politics have certainly split the left on both sides of the Atlantic. In the face of a crumbling Berlin Wall, and intellectual assaults on the 'incredulity' of historicist tendencies in Marxism, and grand theory in general, many found a more personal, local, and single-issue orientation the basis for sound political debate and discussion. Indeed, those who were able to embrace 'the linguistic turn' found what they saw as a far more radical political agenda than traditional forms of Marxism, because it became the means to *thoroughly* politicize all knowledge (Choi and Murphy 1992). Far from being able simply to reflect material forces, language became seen as the means by which reality was framed, and might be reframed (Smith 1988). Unfortunately many of these arguments appear to have become lost in the conservative assault on radical thought, where Marxism and poststructuralism became bedfellows. But, to some extent this was helpful because much of the assault centred not just on the unwarranted intrusion of politics in places where it did not belong, but on the zealous way in which a political agenda was being pursued. In this regard it is convenient that the term political correctness contains two words, because for many the correctness is equally as troubling as the politics. Of course it is here that the notion of there being a totalitarian heart at the centre of the reforming agenda in higher education came to the fore (Bennett 1984; Cheney 1992). This proved to be extremely valuable in the US because it enabled many on the right to associate the politically correct with a broader tradition of un-American activities.

In shifting attention more squarely to Britain what is immediately obvious is that the term political correctness has had nothing like the impact it has had in the US. That said, almost all the arguments about political correctness in the US over the past twenty years have surfaced in some shape or form in Britain (see Chapters 8 and 9). Furthermore, from evidence of the Loony Left campaign in the 1980s (Curran *et al.* 2005) it is not at all clear that the debates in the US predate those in Britain. Thus although the term itself might be an import, many of the arguments with which it is associated, and the political causes which have been denigrated by it, were well established in Britain in the early 1980s, and were beautifully captured in the film *Monty Python's Life of Brian* in 1979. What is perhaps more significant, however, is that the classic form that many politically correct scenarios take – unwarranted imposition and policing of an ideological agenda – are much more likely to resonate with the state's attempt to survey and reorient the aims of education, as much as any coup enacted by an *au courant* of left-wing and misguided intellectuals (D'Souza 1992). This is instructive for two reasons: not only does it draw attention away from the political causes themselves and towards the *form* that a politically correct scenario might take, but it also enables one to read PC scenarios more in keeping with a focus on the term's historical roots (Ellis 2004). In this way, what is interesting about the past twenty years is how PC came to be associated with certain political causes. To say that it was hijacked for this purpose might be too strong a word, but the implication here is that although many people in the US increasingly wanted to distance themselves from the term, for fear of being contaminated by it, once the term is released from this particular historical context, it is much clearer that it might have merit in helping to understand the dynamic behind a much broader range of political decision making (Loury 1995).

Unravelling the roots of political correctness is a complicated exercise. In part this is because the politicization of knowledge seems to have two separate sources. First, its Marxist-Leninist root, which emphasizes the higher order knowledge of *pravda* – knowledge that is beyond the natural, and therefore truly human (Ellis 2004). Clearly there are loud echoes of this interpretation in theories of sexuality which emphasize its plastic and performative nature (Weeks 1985; Butler 1990). Second, there is the more postmodern root, particularly evident in poststructural literary theory, which emphasizes the detachment of language from its representative role in describing reality, where signifiers become detached from signs, and knowledge thereby becomes partial, insubstantial, and contingent (Eagleton 1983). In this expression the post-modern sensibility finds itself seeking out the ironies, the slips, and the silences inherent within any language of representation, and its exponents often gleefully play with the subversive qualities of its liberatory potential – a liberatory potential which, of course, is very different from that which Lenin had in mind. Both roots however have clearly politicized knowledge, and both forms of politicization have found themselves unpalatable in almost equal measure to the conservative as well as to the liberal mind (Patai and Corral 2005).

In this context it is difficult to resist the obvious conclusion that the term political correctness must be an oxymoron, for if knowledge has been *thoroughly* politicized it is difficult to imagine how a correct orthodoxy could be sustained. Apart, of course, from the obvious paradoxical sense that to claim all knowledge is political is itself an authoritative stance. That paradox aside it is clear that Ellis castigates political correctness, as 'Lenin's revenge', he having imposed a more literal reading of politics to imply that one has either made a correct interpretation of the meaning of historical events or one is hopelessly 'incorrect' (Ellis 2004). And here the conservative attack on left-wing ideas in the American university in the 1980s and 1990s was perhaps even more accurate in understanding the roots of political correctness than was immediately obvious. However, that this same attack was levelled at authors such as Fish, who remained steadfast in his detachment from principled positions, indicates that many of the arguments were caricatured, and unsubtle (Fish 1994). In this debate the term PC neatly captures the difference between those who want to make the *apolitical* political, and those who want to do the exact opposite.

At its most epistemological, debates about political correctness are debates about the appropriateness of abstract nouns and pronouns. As Fish defended on a number of occasions, arguments from Principle always turn out, in reality, to be nothing of the sort (Fish 1994). In contra-distinction Bloom was extremely troubled that Reason had fallen off its perch, and that the study of Man had become the experience of men (Bloom 1987). Likewise Cheney was troubled by the fact that Truth had become people's opinions (Cheney 1992). Similarly, rather than seeking to discover Nature, we find that it is merely a social construct, and something from which we might be liberated, or simply manufacture knowledge about (Rorty 1989; Butler 1990). In all these cases the politically correct mindset is one which stubbornly refuses to use capital letters, and satisfies itself with the endless celebration of the particular, rather than the search to discover what is Universal. Put simply, this is culture, not Culture (Eagleton 2000); and the 'culture wars' are in fact not really moral (Hunter 1991), but epistemological. For Eagleton it is also a struggle to remove ourselves from 'that fetishism of discourse known as political correctness' (Eagleton 2000: 89), which might be read as a stubborn refusal by some to put language in its proper place. In this context it is worth noting that the more recent non-representational use of words like 'nigger' in the US (Kennedy 2002) indicates that the fetishistic tendencies are being 'cured'. What is also interesting here is how many British educational terms have become mantric rather than fetishistic, particularly in the face of the enhanced presence of the UK state in post-16 education.

The campaign against political correctness by the conservative right in the US was very successful. It was instrumental in successfully labelling a range of causes in higher education in a wholly derogatory manner, and in being able to align those causes with being un-American, including the undermining of the First Amendment; respect for individual liberty; and belief in the principle of meritocracy. Indeed, it was so successful that even those who believed in the causes which were being tarred with the PC brush became careful not to be associated with the term. But this was unfortunate if one was seeking to fully understand the roots and nuances of the term, and there are two significant consequences here. First, in arguing that only the politically correct are being political it bolstered the view that a classical humanist conception of the higher education curriculum and all that came to be associated with that was more than an idea and beyond political belief (Bloom 1987). And, second, it implied that only those who would mount a challenge to such foundations would resort to forms of indoctrination. This may well have been a smear in order to steer people away from the more serious political underpinnings (Wilson 1996; Feldstein 1997), but the consequence is that PC became clearly associated with certain ideas and certain groups. Furthermore it heightened the sense that political correctness is about choosing sides in a political debate and how ideas can become simplified and calcified. This served the anti-PCers well but helped substantiate a view that cultural arguments are not dynamic, and that all conclusions follow logically from intransigent positions (Zimmerman 2006).

What is valuable about taking a wider and deeper look at the term is how the focus can be taken off particular ideas and groups and steered more towards the general processes involved. Here the British context is instructive. Although it is debatable the extent to which the social engineering in British post-16 education over the past twenty years has been either exogenously imposed by state dictate or organically grown from within the academy itself, in focusing on the former it is clear that political correctness might be better understood in broader terms. This is particularly so where there is evidence of the unwarranted intrusion of ideas which have more ideological than educational merit, and where the clear means to establish conformity are in place. In this context the more general processes involved in establishing fixed orthodoxies come to the fore, and thereby show how the term 'orthodoxy' itself can acquire a derogatory meaning. There is an interesting implication here because if higher order knowledge is not understood as *pravda*, but more as *episteme* – as used by Plato – then the *doxa* (of opinion) with which he contrasts it, is extremely useful in making it clear just what an ortho-doxy comprises (Plato [360 BC] 1955). It is also interesting to note how the British conversations about political correctness (in Chapter 11) often turned to these issues, in contrast to the American conversations (in Chapter 7), which stuck, quite naturally, to the more traditional American terrain.

What is also interesting about the British context is the scope it offers to consider the contexts in which people do not exercise complete freedom of speech, but modify it for sound political or organizational reasons (Strauss 1952; Garfinkel 1967; Loury 1995). At one level there is a certain inevitability about this, indicating that there will always be a case for some politically correct speech. The specific context here is how the past twenty years in Britain have seen a concerted effort by the state to call post-16 educators to account, and to orchestrate a number of social engineering projects for colleges and universities. One of the results of this has been a heightened sense that communication has become more scripted. This is not a case of speech codes but coded speech; not a sense that certain terms have been outlawed, but a sense that one must frame one's speech and writing in a more strategic manner, and to be measured in the way that one embarks in the free exchange of ideas. In the extreme this might have to be a very subtle judgement if a form of surveillance is perceived as intrusive and not without potentially dire consequences. At one level this is clearly an impoverished environment for speech, but again, in contrasting the US with Britain, we can see how this is not just a matter of paying lip service to a politically correct register for diversity, but more broadly, it might apply to any situation in which ideological conformity is resisted. This is not just about being a believer or non-believer in creating a diverse college environment, but asking what is the essence of an orthodoxy and how it is maintained and challenged.

The questions that political correctness raises are not ones where one can simply look to uncover the truth about particular examples – did that happen; did he really say that; etc. It is not a question of uncovering the facts – whether it is looking for water buffalo in Pennsylvania or green sheep in London – because the important question is always about what is being invoked by the use of the term itself. And invariably this is a political question – requiring either that one digs below the surface to uncover more deeply held ideologies, or, increasingly, that one enquires into the perceived status of Enlightenment principles. In this debate, although many on the left and right are united in being affronted by the assault on the Enlightenment, equally it would be premature to equate this form of epistemological conservatism with a similar brand of political conservatism.

Throughout the conversations in Chapters 7 and 11 many people spoke passionately at certain points about deeply held convictions, but equally those conversations highlighted that professional *judgements* are exactly that. Thus, on the first point, just as one person spoke with passion about the role of a university as a place to pursue knowledge for its own sake, so another spoke equally passionately about the duty a university has to foster a sense of social justice. Furthermore, while one person spoke passionately about the need to widen the nature of the knowledge base for the university, another spoke equally passionately about the need to ensure that everyone has equal access to the traditional knowledge base. That some of these beliefs have come to be associated with political correctness is not really the important question, and they will continue to be debated regardless of the existence of the term.

On the second point, although appeals to the First Amendment, the idea of a common culture, and notions of a meritocracy, have been powerful slogans for conservatives in the US, the reality for many university and college administrators is that they have to confront cases of hateful speech; accommodate calls to widen the knowledge base and forms of assessment; and review their admissions procedures in order to maximize the pool of potential applicants. None of these aspects are necessarily indicative of a concerted *pro*-PC campaign, but are just the reality of working in an organic way to deal with matters of social justice and provide opportunities for as many people as possible to benefit from advanced study. In those endeavours mistakes have been made, and strategies have produced unintended consequences. For those who oppose the very purpose of those strategies the term PC has been an extremely useful derogatory label. For those who believe in the purposes it is perfectly reasonable that the First Amendment be balanced against a fundamental respect for personhood; that postmodern forms of knowledge be allowed to compete for curriculum space; and, in the absence of equalizing funding for all schools, that forms of affirmative action be pursued in the face of serious social and economic inequalities.

Discussions about linguistic euphemisms, therapeutic education, forms of affirmative admissions policies, and, in general, questions about the purpose of HE are mirrored in British literature and debates. The fact that the term PC is not so readily associated with the discussions does not mean that they are not PC debates. Equally, one may say that had the conservative agenda in the US not so readily invoked the label PC it is possible that many of the debates in the US could have continued without the label. What is most striking in the context of universities is the battle on both sides of the Atlantic for the soul of the nature of learning, and the ability of those who hold on to a classical humanist and Enlightenment vision for the university to claim that this is its rightful manifest destiny and not one idea amongst many. British authors have also echoed some of the deeper disquiet about the epistemological relativism one finds in anti-PC literature in the US. For example, Furedi spends much of his polemic in two recent books on the paucity of anti-Enlightenment thinking now found in British universities (Furedi 2004a, 2005a) invoking in the process recent American defenders of the Enlightenment philosophy (Himmelfaub 1999; Bronner 2004). In Himmelfaub's book she quotes one author's claim that such people suffer from a form of 'absolutophobia' (Himmelfaub 2001: 123).

This notion of being dis-eased in some way has also been mirrored by British authors, with the claim that multiculturalists suffer from 'oikophobia' (Scruton 1993), and relativists suffer from 'veriphobia' (Bailey 2001). The fact that most of the people who suffer from these conditions would be happy to do so indicates that many of the serious discussions about political correctness are battles concerning the nature of the knowledge that higher education should be dealing with.

Where these charges of having replaced a superior form of knowledge engagement with an inferior one hit hardest, particularly for radical thinkers, is in the claim that they merely act to affirm one's identity, massage one's ego, and help orient people (possibly through state sponsorship) to their existing social circumstances, along with a heightened sense of vulnerability, dependency, and a diminished sense of self. The fact that these arguments in the US, most commonly found in the work of conservatives like Bloom, D'Souza, and Sykes have come to be associated in Britain with radical authors like Ecclestone, Hayes, and Furedi is confirmation that although the diagnosis may be similar the implications and solutions demand that careful attention be paid to underlying political ideologies. Furthermore, that authors like Giroux and hooks would counter that forms of 'critical' or 'engaged' pedagogy can liberate rather than contain, and deconstruct as much as celebrate identity, also confirms that serious and scholarly engagements with knowledge can emerge from a range of curriculum models (Giroux 1981; hooks 1994). Finally, it is not at all clear that forms of relativistic thinking must inevitably lead to a less liberating educational experience because in pointing out just how 'constructed' notions like 'success' and 'intelligence' really are, epistemologically grounded versions of multiculturalism can be profound in subverting the ideological justifications for the status quo (Choi and Murphy 1992).

Political correctness is a useful term if one is willing to invest time in exploring some of the subtleties and nuances in its various meanings. Although the campaigns against forms of political correctness, in both the US and Britain, were successful in associating it with a string of ill-conceived, mainly left-wing, causes, the roots of the term indicate that it might easily serve other, broader, purposes. This is particularly apparent when one considers the processes involved in the unwarranted imposition of an orthodoxy, and in this context the Spanish Inquisition, and the allied notion of *auto-da-fé*, are apt metaphors and useful in reminding us of the broader contexts for understanding forms of political correctness. For they clearly indicate how often the world is split between believers and non-believers, and between those who are able to forge ideologically grounded orthodoxies, combined with an ability to police them, and the ways in which those who are subjected to them are often forced into forms of acquiescence or subversion.

References

Abbs, P. (1986) 'The poisoning of the Socratic ideal', *The Guardian* (13 January).

Abbs, P. (1994) *The Educational Imperative: A Defence of Socratic and Aesthetic Learning*, Washington, DC: Falmer Press.

Ainley, P. (1993) *Class and Skill: Changing Divisions of Knowledge and Labour*, New York: Cassell.

Anderson, M. (1992) *Imposters in the Temple*, New York: Simon and Schuster.

Annette, J. (1994) 'Present and correct', *Times Higher Education Supplement* 1143 (30 September): 16.

Aronowitz, S. and Giroux, H. (1988) 'Schooling, culture and literacy in the age of broken dreams: a review of Bloom and Hirsch', *Harvard Educational Review* 58(2): 172–194.

Asante, M. F. (1997) *The Afrocentric Idea*, revised and expanded edition, Philadelphia, PA: Temple University Press.

Atlas, J. (1990) *The Battle of the Books*, New York: W. W. Norton.

Avis, J. (1996) 'Learner identity: vocationalism and global relations', *British Journal of Education and Work* 9(3).

Avis, J. (2000) 'Policing the subject: learning outcomes, managerialism and research in PCET', *British Journal of Educational Studies* 48(1): 38–57.

Bailey, C. (1984) *Beyond the Present and the Particular: A Theory of Liberal Education*, Boston, MA: Routledge.

Bailey, R. (2001) 'Overcoming veriphobia – learning to love truth again', *British Journal of Educational Studies* 49(2): 159–172.

Baker, M. (2003) 'Is it right to refuse to teach a racist?', *Times Higher Education Supplement* 1592 (6 June): 20–21.

Ball, S. J. (2003) 'The teacher's soul and the terrors of performativity', *Journal of Education Policy* 18(2): 215–228.

Barry, B. M. (2001) *Culture and Equality: An Egalitarian Critique of Multiculturalism*, Cambridge, MA: Harvard University Press.

Barton, L. (ed.) (1996) *Disability and Society: Emerging Issues and Insights*, New York: Longman.

Bates, I., Clarke, J., Finn, D., Moore, R., and Willis, P. (eds) (1984) *Schooling for the Dole? The New Vocationalism*, Basingstoke: Macmillan.

Baty, P. (2002) 'Good teachers or great stage managers?', *Times Higher Education Supplement* (9 August).

Baudrillard, J. (1994) *Simulacra and Simulation*, Ann Arbor, MI: University of Michigan.

Beard, H. and Cerf, C. (1994) *The Official Politically Correct Dictionary and Handbook*, New York: Villard Books.

Beck, J. and Young, M. (2005) 'The assault on the professions and the restructuring of academic and professional identities: a Bernsteinian analysis', *British Journal of Sociology of Education* 26(2): 183–197.

Becker, H. S. (1952) 'Social class variations in the teacher–pupil relationship', *Journal of Educational Society* 25 (April): 451–465.

Beckwith, F. J. and Bauman, M. (eds) (1993) *Are You Politically Correct?*, New York: Prometheus Books.

Beckwith, F. J. and Jones, T. E. (1997) *Affirmative Action: Social Justice or Reverse Discrimination?*, New York: Prometheus Books.

Bennett, W. J. (1984) *To Reclaim a Legacy: A Report on the Humanities in Higher Education*, Washington, DC: National Endowment for the Humanities.

Berger, B. (1993) 'Multiculturalism and the modern university', *Partisan Review* 4: 516–526.

Berger, J. (1971) *Shipwreck of a Generation: The Memoirs of Joseph Berger*, London: Harvill Press.

Berger, P. and Luckman, T. (1967) *The Social Construction of Reality*, London: Penguin Books.

Berlin, I. (1958) 'Two concepts of liberty', in I. Berlin (1969) *Four Essays on Liberty*, Oxford: Oxford University Press.

Berman, P. (ed.) (1992) *Debating PC*, New York: Laurel.

Bernstein, B. (1970) 'Education cannot compensate for society', *New Society* (26 February).

Bernstein, R. (1994) *Dictatorship of Virtue*, New York: Knopf.
Biggs, J. B. (1999) *Teaching for Quality Learning at University: What the Student Does*, Buckingham: Society for Research into Higher Education and Open University Press.
Bloom, A. (1987) *The Closing of the American Mind*, New York: Simon and Schuster.
Booth, T., Nes, K., and Stromstad, M. (eds) (2003) *Developing Inclusive Teacher Education*, London: Routledge Falmer.
Bourdieu, P. (1999) *Language and Symbolic Power*, London: Polity.
Bourdieu, P. and Passeron, J. C. (1977) *Reproduction in Education, Society and Culture*, Beverly Hills, CA: Sage Publications.
Bowles, S. and Gintis, H. (1976) *Schooling in Capitalist America: Educational Reform and the Contradictions of Economic Life*, New York: Basic Books.
Bowles, S. and Gintis, H. (2001) 'Schooling in capitalist America revisited', *Sociology of Education* 75(2): 1–18.
Braverman, H. (1974) *Labor and Monopoly Capital: The Degradation of Work in the Twentieth Century*, New York: Monthly Review Press.
Bronner, S. E. (2004) *Reclaiming the Enlightenment: Toward a Politics of Radical Engagement*, New York: Columbia University Press.
Browne, A. (2006) *The Retreat of Reason: Political Correctness and the Corruption of Public Debate in Modern Britain*, London: Civitas.
Bruce, T. (2001) *The New Thought Police*, New York: Forum.
Bryan, C. and Clegg, K. (eds) (2006) *Innovative Assessment in Higher Education*, London: Routledge.
Bunting, C. (2005) 'What's a nice Trot doing in a place like this?', *Times Higher Education Supplement* (28 January).
Burgoon, M. and Bailey, W. (1992) 'PC at last! PC at last! Thank God Almighty, we are PC at last!', *Journal of Communication* 42(2): 95–104.
Butcher, J. (2007) 'Keep the green moral agenda off campus', *Times Higher Education Supplement* (19 October).
Butler, J. (1990) *Gender Trouble: Feminism and the Subversion of Identity*, New York: Routledge.
Butler, J. (1998) 'Merely cultural', *New Left Review* 228: 33.
Bygrave, M. (1991) 'Mind your language', *The Guardian*, Weekend Guardian (11 May): 14–15.
Cahn, S. M. (ed.) (2002) *The Affirmative Action Debate*, New York: Routledge.
Cameron, D. (1995) *Verbal Hygiene*, London: Routledge.
Carter, B. (1997) 'The restructuring of teaching and the restructuring of class', *British Journal of Sociology of Education* 18(2): 201.
Carter, S. L. (1991) *Reflections of an Affirmative Action Baby*, New York: Basic Books.
Cheney, L. V. (1992) *Telling the Truth: A Report on the State of the Humanities in Higher Education*, Washington DC: National Endowment for the Humanities.
Choi, J. M. and Murphy, J. W. (1992) *The Politics and Philosophy of Political Correctness*, Westport, CT: Praeger.
Cochrane, A. (2001) 'The smack of weak government', *Spectator* (15 September) 287 (9032): 22.
Coffield, F., Moseley, D., Hall, E., and Ecclestone, K. (2004) *Learning Styles and Pedagogy in Post-16 Learning: A Systematic and Critical Review*, London: Learning and Skills Research Centre.
Cohen, S. (1972) *Folk Devils and Moral Panics: The Creation of the Mods and Rockers*, London: MacGibbon and Kee.
Cope, B. and Kalantzis, M. (1997) 'White noise: the attack on political correctness and the struggle for the Western canon', *Interchange* 28(4): 283–329.
Corbett, J. (1994) 'Special language and political correctness', *British Journal of Special Education*, 21(1): 17–19.
Corbett, J. (1996) *Bad-mouthing: The Language of Special Needs*, London: Routledge Falmer.
Cummings, M. S. (2001) *Beyond Political Correctness*, Boulder, CO: Lynne Rienner.
Curran, J., Gaber, I., and Petley, J. (2005) *Culture Wars: The Media and the British Left*, Edinburgh: Edinburgh University Press.
Curry, G. E. (ed.) (1996) *The Affirmative Action Debate*, Cambridge, MA: Perseus Publications.
D'Souza, D. (1992) *Illiberal Education: The Politics of Race and Sex on Campus*, New York: Vintage Books.
Davidson, B. (1992) *The Black Man's Burden: Africa and the Curse of the Nation-state*, Oxford: James Currey.
Dearing, R. (1996) *Review of Qualifications for 16–19 Year Olds*, Hayes: SCAA Publications.
Dearing, R. [National Committee of Inquiry into Higher Education (NCIHE)] (1997) *Higher Education in the Learning Society: Report of the National Committee*, London: HMSO.

Deem, R. and Brehony, K. (2005) 'Management as ideology: the case of "new managerialism" in higher education', *Oxford Review of Education* 31(2): 217–235.

DfES (Department for Education and Skills) (2002) *Success for All: Reforming Further Education and Training*, London: DfES.

DfES (2003a) *21st-Century Skills, Realizing Our Potential*, London: DfES.

DfES (2003b) *The Future of Higher Education*, London: DfES.

Dickstein, M. (1993) 'Correcting PC', *Partisan Review* 4: 542–549.

Downs, C. (2004) 'Why I think universities need to acknowledge class as the final taboo', *Times Higher Education Supplement* (6 August).

Downs, D. A. (2005) *Restoring Free Speech and Liberty on Campus*, Cambridge: Cambridge University Press.

Drucker, P. F. (1994) 'Political correctness and American academe', *Society* 32 (November): 58–63.

Dunant, S. (ed.) (1994) *The War of the Words: The Political Correctness Debate*, London: Virago.

Dyson, M. E. (2005) *Is Bill Cosby Right? (Or Has the Black Middle Class Lost Its Mind?)*, New York: Basic Civitas Books.

Eagleton, T. (1983) *Literary Theory: An Introduction*, Oxford: Blackwell.

Eagleton, T. (2000) *The Idea of Culture*, Malden, MA: Blackwell.

Ecclestone, K. (1995) 'Perilous consequences of political correctness', *Adults Learning* 6(10): 298–299.

Ecclestone, K. (2002) *Learner Autonomy in Post-16 Education*, London: Routledge Falmer.

Ecclestone, K., Hayes, D., and Furedi, F. (2005) 'Knowing me, knowing you: the rise of therapeutic professionalism in the education of adults', *Studies in the Education of Adults* 37(2): 182–200.

Ehrenreich, B. (1991) 'The challenge for the Left', *Democratic Left* (July–August) 3.

Elliott, J. (ed.) (1993) *Reconstructing Teacher Education: Teacher Development*, London: Falmer Press.

Ellis, F. (2002) 'Political correctness and the ideological struggle: from Lenin and Mao to Marcuse and Foucault', *Journal of Social, Political and Economic Studies* 27(4): 409–444.

Ellis, F. (2004) *Political Correctness and the Theoretical Struggle*, Auckland: Maxim Institute.

Ellis, J. M. (1992) 'The origins of PC', *Chronicle of Higher Education* 38 (15 January): B1–2.

Ellis, J. M. (1997) *Literature Lost: Social Agendas and the Corruption of the Humanities*, New Haven, CT: Yale University Press.

Etzioni, A. (2000) *The Third Way to a Good Society*, London: Demos.

Evans, M. (2004) *Killing Thinking: The Death of the Universities*, New York: Continuum.

Fairbairn, G. (1995) 'A misconceived agenda', *Times Higher Education Supplement* 1205 (8 December): 20.

Fairclough, N. (2003) '"Political correctness": the politics of culture and language', *Discourse and Society* 14(1): 17–28.

Farrar, S. (2004) 'No sex, please, we're too politically correct (and a little prudish)', *Times Higher Education Supplement* 1628 (20 February): 1.

Feldstein, R. (1997) *Political Correctness: A Response from the Cultural Left*, Minneapolis, MN: University of Minnesota.

Firestone, S. (1970) *The Dialectic of Sex: The Case for Feminist-Revolution*, New York: Quill.

Fish, S. (1994) *There's No Such Thing as Free Speech and It's a Good Thing*, New York: Oxford University Press.

Fiske, J. (1996) *Media Matters: Race and Gender in U.S. Politics*, Minneapolis, MN: University of Minnesota Press.

Foster, A. (2005) *Realising the Potential: A Review of the Future Role of Further Education Colleges*, London: DfES.

Foucault, M. (1977) *Discipline and Punish: The Birth of the Prison*, New York: Pantheon Books.

Fox-Genovese, E. (1995) 'A Kafkaesque trap', *Academe* 81(3): 9–15.

Freire, P. (1970) *Pedagogy of the Oppressed*, New York: Continuum.

Friedman, M. and Friedman, R. D. (1980) *Free to Choose: A Personal Statement*, New York: Harcourt Brace Jovanovich.

Friedman, M. and Narveson, J. (1995) *Political Correctness: For and Against*, Lanham, MD: Rowman and Littlefield.

Frosh, S. (1991) *Identity Crisis: Modernity, Psychoanalysis and the Self*, London: Macmillan, New York: Routledge.

Fukuyama, F. (1992) *The End of History and the Last Man*, New York: Free Press.

Furedi, F. (1997) *Culture of Fear*, London: Cassell.

Furedi, F. (2004a) *Where Have All the Intellectuals Gone? Confronting 21st-Century Philistinism*, London: Continuum.

Furedi, F. (2004b) *Therapy Culture*, London: Routledge.

Furedi, F. (2004c) 'It's now no longer critical, and nor is it thinking', *Times Higher Education Supplement* (24 September).

Furedi, F. (2004d) 'Have a bit a faith in the soul of learning', *Times Higher Education Supplement* (5 November).

Furedi, F. (2005a) *Politics of Fear: Beyond Left and Right*, London: Continuum.

Furedi, F. (2005b) 'For accreditation, see indoctrination', *Times Higher Education Supplement* (6 May).

Furedi, F. (2007a) 'I refuse to jump through hoops', *Times Higher Education Supplement* (13 April).

Furedi, F. (2007b) 'The distorted vision of Dearing', *Times Higher Education Supplement* (10 August).

Gardner, H. (1993) *Frames of Mind: Theory of Multiple Intelligences*, London: Fontana.

Garfinkel, H. (1967) 'Good organizational reasons for "bad" clinic records', in H. Garfinkel, *Studies in Ethnomethodology*, New York: Prentice-Hall.

Garner, J. F. (1994) *Politically Correct Bedtime Stories*, London: Souvenir Press.

Gates, H. L. Jr (1992) *Loose Canons: Notes on the Culture Wars*, New York: Oxford University Press.

Gates, H. L. Jr (1993) 'Let them talk: why civil liberties pose no threat to civil rights', *New Republic* (20 and 27 September): 37–49.

Gates, H. L. Jr and West, C. (1996) *The Future of the Race*, New York: Alfred A. Knopf.

Giddens, A. (1992) *The Transformation of Intimacy: Sexuality, Love and Eroticism in Modern Societies*, Cambridge: Polity Press.

Giddens, A. (1998) *The Third Way: The Renewal of Social Democracy*, Cambridge: Polity Press.

Giddens, A. (2000) *The Third Way and its Critics*, Cambridge: Polity Press.

Gilligan, G. (1982) *In a Different Voice*, Cambridge, MA: Harvard University Press.

Giroux, H. A. (1981) *Ideology, Culture, and the Process of Schooling*, London: Falmer.

Giroux, H. A. (1995) 'Teaching in the age of "political correctness"', *Educational Forum* 59(2): 130–139.

Gitlin, T. (1995) *The Twilight of Common Dreams*, New York: Metropolitan Books.

Gleeson, D. and Shain, F. (1999) 'Under new management: changing conceptions of teacher professionalism and policy in the further education sector', *Journal of Education Policy* 14(3): 445–462.

Gleeson, D., Davies, J., and Wheeler, E. (2005) 'On the making and taking of professionalism in the further education (FE) workplace', *British Journal of Sociology of Education* 26(4): 445–460.

Goffman, E. (1959) *The Presentation of Self in Everyday Life*, London: Penguin.

Goldsmith's Media Research Group (1988) 'Loony Tunes', *BBC2*, Open Space Broadcast.

Goleman, D. P (1995) *Emotional Intelligence*, London: Bantam Press.

Gorrard, S., Smith, E., May, H., Thomas, L., Adnett, N., and Slack, K. (2006) *Review of Widening Participation Research: Addressing the Barriers to Widening Participation in Higher Education*, Report AWP254, London: Higher Education Funding Council for England (HEFCE).

Gosling, D. and Moon, J. A. (2001) *How to Use Learning Outcomes and Assessment Criteria*, London: SEEC.

Graff, G. (1992) *Beyond the Culture Wars*, New York: W. W. Norton.

Hackney, S. (2002) *The Politics of Presidential Appointment: A Memoir of the Culture War*, Montgomery, AL: New South Books.

Hall, S., Critcher, C., Jefferson, T., Clarke, J., and Robert, B. (1978) *Policing the Crisis*, London: Palgrave Macmillan.

Halsey, A. H., Heath, A. F., and Ridge, J. M. (1980) *Origins and Destinations: Family, Class and Education in Modern Britain*, Oxford: Oxford University Press.

Hartley, D. (1995) 'The "McDonaldization" of higher education: food for thought?', *Oxford Review of Education* 21(4): 409–423.

Hayek, F. A. (2001) *The Road to Serfdom*, London: Routledge.

Hayes, D. (ed.) (2004) *The RoutledgeFalmer Guide to Key Debates in Education*, London: RoutledgeFalmer.

Hayes, D. and Wynyard, R. (eds) (2002) *The McDonaldization of Higher Education*, London: Greenwood Press.

HEA (Higher Education Academy) (2005) *National Professional Standards Framework for Standards in Teaching and Supporting Learning in Higher Education: Consultation Document*, York: HEA.

HEA (2006) *The UK Professional Standards Framework for Teaching and Supporting Learning in Higher Education*, York: HEA.

Henry, W. A. III (1991) 'Upside down in the groves of academe', *Time* 137(13): 66–70.

Hernstein Smith, B. (1988) *Contingencies of Value*, Cambridge, MA: Harvard University Press.

Himmelfarb, G. (1999) *One Nation, Two Cultures*, New York: Alfred J. Knopf.

Hirsch, E. D. (1988) *Cultural Literacy: What Every American Needs to Know*, New York: Vintage Books.

Hobsbawm, E. (1996) 'Identity politics and the left', *New Left Review* 217: 38.

Hodges, L. (1991) 'Liberals organize for affirmative action', *Times Higher Education Supplement* 987 (4 October): 11.

Hodges, L. (1992) 'Room for politically incorrect as speech code is dropped', *Times Higher Education Supplement* 1038 (25 September): 9.

Hodges, L. (1993a) 'PC rivals learn to get on', *Times Higher Education Supplement* 1100 (3 December): 8.

Hodges L. (1993b) 'The importance of being earnest', *Times Higher Education Supplement* 1054 (15 January): 20.

Hodges, L. (1994a) '"PC" liberation front at Harvard', *Times Higher Education Supplement* 1123 (13 May): 11.

Hodges, L. (1994b) 'A lady fond of dead white males', *Times Higher Education Supplement* 1147 (28 October): 17.

Hodges, L. (1994c) 'Starboard wind propels change', *Times Higher Education Supplement* 1156 (30 December): 11.

Hodges, L. (1995a) 'Alumni launch PC fightback', *Times Higher Education Supplement* 1172 (21 April): 7.

Hodges, L. (1995b) 'Answers in the affirmative', *Times Higher Education Supplement* 1180 (16 June): 16–17.

Hodges, L. (2003) 'Does Bristol pick the best?' *The Independent* (6 March).

Hodgson, A., Spours, K., and Savory, C. (2001) *Improving the 'Use' and 'Exchange' Value of Key Skills. Debating the Role of the Key Skills Qualification within Curriculum 2000*, Lifelong Learning Group, IOE/Nuffield Series 4. London: Institute of Education, University of London.

Hofkins, D. (1992a) 'Uncle Sam's identity crisis', *Times Educational Supplement* 3962 (5 June): 12.

Hofkins, D. (1992b) 'Auto-censorship in the land of the free', *Times Educational Supplement* 3962 (5 June): 13.

Hofkins, D. (1992c) 'Adding a dash to everyone's culture', *Times Educational Supplement* 3962 (5 June 5): 13.

hooks, b. (1994) *Teaching to Transgress: Education as the Practice of Freedom*, New York: Routledge.

hooks, b. (1996) 'Postmodern Blackness', in W. T. Anderson (ed.) *The Fontana Post-Modernism Reader*, London: Fontana Press.

Hoover, J. D. and Howard, L. A. (1995) 'The political correctness controversy revisited', *American Behavioural Scientist* 38(7): 963–975.

Horowitz, D. and Collier, P. (1994) *The Heterodoxy Handbook: How to Survive the PC Campus*, Washington: Regnery Publishing.

Hughes, R. (1993) *Culture of Complaint*, Oxford: Oxford University Press.

Hunter, J. D. (1991) *Culture Wars: The Struggle to Define America*, New York: Basic Books.

Hussey, T. and Smith, P. (2002) 'The trouble with learning outcomes', *Active Learning in Higher Education* 3(3): 220–233.

Hyland, T. (1994) *Competence, Education and NVQs: Dissenting Perspectives*, London: Cassell.

Hyland, T. (1996) 'Professionalism, ethics, and work-based learning', *British Journal of Educational Studies* 44(2): 168–180.

Hyland, T. (2001) 'Skills, skills, skills', *Educa* 217: 8–9.

Hyland, T. (2005) 'Learning and therapy – oppositional or complementary processes?', *Adults Learning* (January): 16–17.

Hyland, T. (2006) 'Vocational education and training and the therapeutic turn', *Educational Studies* 32(3): 299–306.

Jacques, M. (1991) 'The Last Word', *Marxism Today* (December).

Jessup, G. (1991) Outcomes: NVQs and the *Emerging Model of Education and Training*, London: Falmer Press.

Johnson, P. (1993) 'A stampede of water buffaloes on the American campus', *Spectator* (29 May) 270 (8603): 22.

Johnson, S., Culpeper, J., and Suhr, S. (2003) 'From "politically correct councillors" to "Blairite nonsense": discourses of "political correctness" in three British newspapers', *Discourse and Society* 14(1): 29–47.

Kant, I. ([1788] 1909) *Critique of Practical Reason*, trans. T. K. Abbott, London: Longmans.

Katsiaficas, G. and Kiros, T. (eds) (1998) *The Promise of Multiculturalism*, New York: Routledge.

Keddie, N. (ed.) (1974) *The Myth of Cultural Deprivation*, London: Penguin.

Keep, E. (2006) 'State control of the English education and training system – playing with the biggest train set in the world', *Journal of Vocational Education and Training* 58(1): 47–64.

Kennedy, H. (1997) *Learning Works: Widening Participation in Further Education*, Coventry: Further Education Funding Council.

Kennedy, R. (2002) *Nigger: The Strange Career of a Troublesome Word*, New York: Pantheon.

Kesey, K. (1968) *One Flew Over the Cuckoo's Nest*, London: Picador.

Kimball, R. (1990) *Tenured Radicals*, New York: Harper Perennial.

Kogan, M. and Hanney, S. (2000) *Reforming Higher Education*, London: Jessica Kingsley.

Kors, A. C. and Silverglate, H. A. (1998) *The Shadow University*, New York: Free Press.

Kozol, J. (1992) *Savage Inequalities: Children in America's Schools*, New York: Harper Perennial.

Lakoff, R. T. (2000) *The Language War*, Berkeley, CA: University of California Press.

Laurillard, D. (2001) *Rethinking University Teaching*, London: Routledge Falmer.

Lazare, D. (1997) 'Ground rules for polemicists: the case of Lynne Cheney's truths', *College English* 59(6): 661–685.

Lea, J., Hayes, D., Armitage, A., Lomas, L., and Markless, S. (2003) *Working in Post-Compulsory Education*, Maidenhead: Open University Press.

Leitch, S. (2006) *Prosperity for All in the Global Economy – World Class Skills*, London: TSO.

Leo, J. (1994) *Two Steps Ahead of the Thought Police*, New York: Simon and Schuster.

Levitt, C., Davies, S., and McLaughlin, N. (eds) (1999) *Mistaken Identities: The Second Wave of Controversy over "Political Correctness"*, New York: Peter Lang.

Levy, J. (1991) 'The ennui of PC', *Brown Alumni Monthly* (October): 34–37.

Lewis, L. S. and Altbach, P. G. (1992) 'Political correctness, campus malaise', *Times Higher Education Supplement* 1008 (28 February): 17.

Lewontin, R. C., Rose, S., and Kamin, L. (1984) *Biology, Ideology and Human Nature: Not in Our Genes*, New York: Pantheon Books.

LLUK (Lifelong Learning UK) (2005) *New Professional Standards for Teachers in the Learning and Skills Sector: Draft Consultation Document*, London: LLUK.

LLUK (2007) *New Overarching Professional Standards for Teachers, Tutors and Trainers in the Lifelong Learning Sector*, London: LLUK.

Loury, G. C. (1994) 'Self-censorship in public discourse', *Rationality and Society* 6(4): 428–461.

Loury, G. C. (1995) *One by One from the Inside Out: Essays and Reviews on Race and Responsibility in America*, New York: Free Press.

Lucas, N. (2004) *Teaching in Further Education: New Perspectives for a Changing Context*, London: Institute of Education, University of London.

Lyotard, J. (1994) *The Postmodern Condition*, Minneapolis, MN: University of Minnesota Press.

McDonald, R. (ed.) (1997) *Youth, the Underclass and Social Exclusion*, London: Routledge.

MacFarquhar, L. (2001) 'Loudmouthed Milton man', *Times Higher Education Supplement* 1499 (10 August): 19.

McGinty, J. and Fish, J. (1993) *Further Education in the Market Place: Equity, Opportunity, and Individual Learning*, New York: Routledge.

McGivney, V. (2005) 'Are adult learners obsessed with developing self-esteem?' *Adults Learning* (January): 8–15.

MacGregor, K. (1993) 'The shifting sands of race studies', *Times Higher Education Supplement* 1054 (15 January): 22.

Macleod, D. (2001) 'Trial by Ordeal', *The Guardian*, Education Guardian (30 January).

McRobbie, A. (1993) 'Folk devils fight back', *New Left Review* 203: 107–116.

McWhorter, J. (2001) *Losing the Race: Self-sabotage in Black America*, New York: Harper Collins.

McWhorter, J. (2003) *Authentically Black*, New York: Gotham Books.

Mannheim, K. (1936) *Ideology and Utopia*, London: Routledge and Kegan Paul.

Marcuse, H. (1965) 'Repressive toleration', in R. P. Wolff, B. Moore, Jr and H. Marcuse, *A Critique of Pure Tolerance*, Boston, MA: Beacon Press.

Marx, K. and Engels, F. ([1846]1970) *The German Ideology*, edited by C. J. Arthur, London: Lawrence and Wishart.

Maskell, D. and Robinson, I. (2002) *The New Idea of the University*, Thorverton: Imprint Academic.

Matsuda, M. J., Lawrence, C. R., Delgado, R., and Crenshaw, K. W. (1993) *Words That Wound: Critical Race Theory, Assaultive Speech and the First Amendment*, Boulder, CO: Westview Press.

Midgley, J. and Midgley, L. (2005) *The Politically Correct Scrapbook*, London: John and Laura Midgley.

Miliband, R. (1969) *The State in Capitalist Society*, London: Weidenfield and Nicolson.

Mill, J. S. (1869) *On Liberty*, London: Longman.

Mills, S. (2003) 'Caught between sexism, anti-sexism and "political correctness": feminist women's negotiations with naming practices', *Discourse and Society* 14(1): 87–110.

Morgan, R. (ed.) (1970) *Sisterhood is Powerful: An Anthology of Writings from the Women's Liberation Movement*, New York: Vintage Books.

Morris, S. (2001) 'Political correctness', *Journal of Political Economy* 109(2): 231–265.

Moser, C. (1999) *A Fresh Start: Improving Literacy and Numeracy*, Sudbury: Department of Education and Employment.

Murray, C. and Bernstein, R. (1994) *The Bell Curve*, New York: Free Press.

Murray, R. (1991) 'The state after Henry', *Marxism Today* (May).

Newfield, C. and Strickland, R. (eds) (1995) *After Political Correctness*, Boulder, CO: Westview Press.

Newman, J. H. ([1854]1982) *The Idea of a University*, with an introduction and notes by M. J. Svaglic, Notre Dame, IN: University of Notre Dame Press.

Nolan, J. L. (1998) *The Therapeutic State: Justifying Government at Century's End*, New York: New York University Press.

Ogbu, J. U. (1988) 'Class stratification, racial stratification, and schooling', in L. Weis (ed.) *Class, Race, and Gender in American Education*, Albany: SUNY.

Parker, K. (1992) 'PC invokes the law in postcolonial scuffle', *Times Higher Education Supplement* 1003 (24 January): 18.

Parris, M. (2000) 'A lexicon of Conservative cant', *Spectator* (19 February): 12–13.

Patai, D. and Corral, W. H. (eds) (2005) *Theory's Empire*, New York: Columbia University Press.

Patterson, A. M. (1995) 'Free speech with kinder words', *Times Higher Education Supplement* 1159 (20 January): 16–17.

Perry, R. (1992) 'Historically correct', *Women's Review of Books* (5 February): 15–16.

Pilger, J. (1994) *Distant Voices*, London: Vintage.

Plante, P. R. and Eatwell, R. H. (1992) 'The opening of the American mind', *Educational Record* (Winter): 33–36.

Plato ([c. 360 BC] 1955) *The Republic*, trans. and introduction by D. Lee, Penguin Classics, Harmondsworth: Penguin.

Randle, K. and Brady, N. (1997) 'Further education and the new managerialism', *Journal of Further and Higher Education* 21(2): 229–239.

Richer, S. and Weir, L. (1995) *Beyond Political Correctness*, Toronto: University of Toronto.

Ritzer, G. (1999) *Enchanting a Disenchanted World: Revolutionizing the Means of Consumption*, Thousand Oaks, CA: Pine Forge Press.

Ritzer, G. (2000) *The McDonaldization of Society*, Thousand Oaks, CA: Pine Forge Press.

Robson, J. (2006) *Teacher Professionalism in Further and Higher Education: Challenges to Culture and Practice*, Abingdon: Routledge.

Rogers, C. and Freiberg, H. J. (1994) *Freedom to Learn*, third edition, London: Prentice Hall.

Roiphe, K. (1993) *The Morning After: Sex, Fear and Feminism on Campus*, Boston, MA: Little, Brown.

Rorty, R. (1989) *Contingency, Irony and Solidarity*, Cambridge: Cambridge University Press.

Rustin, M. (1998) 'The perverse modernisation of British universities', *Soundings* 8: 83–99.

Ryan, W. (1972) *Blaming the Victim*, New York: Vintage Books.

Sachs, O. (1986) *The Man Who Mistook His Wife for a Hat*, London: Picador.

Sacks, D. O. and Thiel, P. A. (1998) *The Diversity Myth*, Oakland, CA: Independent Institute.

Samuelson, R. J. (1995) *The Good Life and its Discontents*, New York: Vintage Books.

Scanlon, L. (1995) 'Political correctness: a victimless crime', *Academe* (May–June): 9–13.

Scatamburlo, V. L. (1998) *Soldiers of Misfortune: The New Right's Culture War and the Politics of Political Correctness*, New York: Peter Lang.

Schlesinger, A. M. Jr (1998) *The Disuniting of America*, New York: W. W. Norton.

Schwartz, H. S. (2003) *The Revolt of the Primitive: An Inquiry into the Roots of Political Correctness*, Westport, CT: Praeger.

Schwartz, S. (2006) *Fair Admissions to University: Recommendations for Good Practice*, London: DfES.

Scott, P. (1995) *The Meanings of Mass Higher Education*, Buckingham: Open University Press.

Scott, P. (2005) 'Mass higher education – ten years on', *Perspectives* 9(3): 68–73.

Scruton, R. (1993) 'Oikophobia', *Journal of Education* 175(2): 93–98.

Searle, J. R. (1990) 'The storm over the university', *New York Review of Books* (December): 6.

Searle, J. R. (1993) 'Is there a crisis in American higher education?', *Partisan Review* 4: 692–709.

Shiell, T. C. (1998) *Campus Hate Speech on Trial*, Kansas, TN: University Press of Kansas.

Singer, P. (1975) *Animal Liberation: A New Ethics for Our Treatment of Animals*, New York: Avon Books.

Smith, B. H. (1989) *Contingencies of Value*, Cambridge, MA: Harvard University Press.

Sowell, T. (1993) *Inside American Education: The Decline, the Deception, the Dogmas*, New York: Free Press.

Spender, D. (1980) *Man Made Language*, London: Routledge.

Spender, D. and Sarah, E. (1980) *Learning to Lose: Sexism and Education*, London: Women's Press.

Spring, J. (2004) *The Intersection of Cultures*, third edition, New York: McGraw Hill.

Strauss, L. (1952) *Persecution and the Art of Writing*, Glencoe, IL: Free Press.

Supreme Court of the US (2003) *Gratz* v. *Bollinger*, Washington, DC.

Sykes, C. J. (1992) *A Nation of Victims*, New York: St Martin's Press.

Sykes, C. J. (1995) *Dumbing Down Our Kids*, New York: St Martin's Griffin.

Szasz, T. (1972) *The Myth of Mental Illness*, London: Harper Row.

Tawney, R. H. (1931) *Equality*, London: Unwin.

Taylor, F. W. (1947) *The Principles of Scientific Management*, New York: Norton.

Taylor, J. (1991) 'Are you politically correct?', *New York Magazine* (21 January): 33–40.

The Economist (2002) 'Orwell and beyond', *The Economist* (7 December).

Thomas, A. P. (2005) *The People v. Harvard Law*, San Francisco, CA: Encounter Books.

Thomas, L. and Quinn, J. (2007) *First Generation Entry into Higher Education*, Maidenhead: Open University Press.

Thomson, A. (1999) 'Have you heard about the one-legged Irish dyke?', *Times Higher Education Supplement* 1380 (16 April): 18–19.

Titchkovsky, T. (2001) 'Disability: a rose by any other name? "People-first" language in Canadian society', *Canadian Review of Sociology and Anthropology* 28(2): 125–140.

Tomlinson, J. (1996) *Inclusive Learning: Report of the Learning Difficulties and/or Disabilities*, Coventry: FEFC.

Tooley, J. (2005) *Reclaiming Education*, London: Continuum International.

Valencia, R. R. (1997) *The Evolution of Deficit Thinking*, London: Falmer Press.

Wallace, J. (1998) 'What does it take to be a woman?', *Times Higher Education Supplement* 1331 (8 May): 16–17.

Weeks, J. (1985) *Sexuality and Its Discontents: Meanings, Myths and Modern Sexualities*, Boston, MA: Routledge.

West, C. (1993) *Race Matters*, Boston, MA: Beacon Press.

Wienir, D. and Berley, M. (eds) (1999) *The Diversity Hoax*, New York: Foundation for Academic Standards and Tradition.

Williams, J. (2005) 'Skill as metaphor: an analysis of terminology used in "success for all" and "21st-century skills"', *Journal of Further and Higher Education* 29(2): 181–190.

Willis, P. (1977) *Learning to Labour*, London: Saxon House.

Wilson, A. (2005) *Improving the Higher Education Application Process*, London: DfES.

Wilson, J. K. (1996) *The Myth of Political Correctness*, Durham, NC: Duke University Press.

Wilson, W. J. (1978) *The Declining Significance of Race: Blacks and Changing American Institutions*, London: University of Chicago Press.

Wilson, W. J. (1987) *The Truly Disadvantaged: The Inner City, the Underclass, and Public Policy*, Chicago, IL: University of Chicago Press.

Wolf, A. (1995) *Competence-based Assessment*, Buckingham: Open University Press.

Young, R. M. (1994) *Mental Space*, London: Process Press.

Zangwill, I. (1909) *The Melting Pot*, New York: Macmillan.

Zimmerman, J. (2002) *Whose America? Culture Wars in the Public Schools*, Cambridge, MA: Harvard University Press.

Zimmerman, J. (2006) *Innocents Abroad*, Cambridge, MA: Harvard University Press.

Zukav, G. (1980) *The Dancing Wu Li Masters*, London: Fontana.

Note on the author

John Lea is a principal lecturer in Education at Canterbury Christ Church University, UK, where he is the programme director for the Post Graduate Certificate in Learning and Teaching (HE). He is a sociologist by background and also teaches on the university's American Studies degree programme. He has worked throughout post-16 education for the past twenty-eight years, and lived in the UK and the US during that period.

Index